Dedication

To my wife Laurie, my parents Pat and Gerry, the talented, fun-loving individuals at Online System Services and to everyone who jumps headfirst into this new communications medium. Enjoy, and happy searching!

Credits

Acquisitions Editor
Deborah Abshier

Product Directors
Mark Cierzniak
Kathie-Jo Arnoff

Production Editor
Mitzi Foster Gianakos

Copy Editors
Danielle Bird
Patrick Kanouse
Heather Urschel
Noelle Gasco

Technical Editors
Jeff Bankston
Lori Leonardo
John McDermott

Figure Specialist
Cari Ohm

Book Designer
Barbara Kordesh

Cover Designer
Dan Armstrong

Operations Coordinator
Patty Brooks

Acquisitions Coordinator
Ruth Slates

Editorial Assistant
Andrea Duvall

Production Team
Steve Adams, Claudia Bell,
Anne Dickerson, Chad Dressler,
Amy Durocher, Karen Gregor-York,
Daryl Kessler, Michael Thomas,
Scott Tullis

Indexers
Virginia Bess
Brad Herriman

Composed in *Stone Serif* and *MCPdigital* by Que Corporation

Net.Search

Written by

William Eager
Larry Donahue
David Forsyth
Kenneth Mitton
Martin Waterhouse

que®

Net.Search

Copyright© 1995 by Que® Corporation

Library of Congress Catalog Number: 95-69234

ISBN: 0-7897-0242-8

97 96 95   3 2 1

Interpretation of the printing code: the rightmost double-digit number is the year of the book's printing; the rightmost single-digit number, the number of the book's printing. For example, a printing code of 95-1 shows that the first printing of the book occurred in 1995.

Publisher and President: Roland Elgey

Associate Publisher: Stacy Hiquet

Publishing Director: Brad R. Koch

Director of Editorial Services: Elizabeth Keaffaber

Managing Editor: Sandy Doell

Director of Marketing: Lynn E. Zingraf

About the Authors

Bill Eager lives in Conifer, Colorado. With more than twelve years of communications technology experience, Bill designs, writes, and speaks about electronic communications. While Manager for the Corporate Communications Department at BASF Corporation, Bill proposed and helped develop a system that distributes hypertext-based multimedia to thousands of employees at sites across the country. Bill has been an editor of several national trade magazines, including *ComSat Technology* and *Communications Technology*, as well as the author of several books, including *The Information Payoff*, by Prentice Hall, which details how companies and businesses use electronic communication to improve productivity, enhance training, and become more competitive; Que's *Information Superhighway Illustrated*, which uses vivid color drawings and photographs to explore cutting-edge technology and applications of the information highway; *Using The World Wide Web*, which provides an in-depth look at the Internet's multimedia information system and reviews more than one thousand Web sites; and *Using The Internet*, which is designed to help new users learn how to use the Internet. Bill is President of the Colorado Chapter of the International Interactive Communications Society (IICS). In addition to computers, Bill enjoys photography, hiking, and skiing. Bill can be reached electronically at AOL: **BILLE2000**, CompuServe: **74010,1511**, and Internet: **bill.eager@ossinc.net**.

Larry S. Donahue, Jr., holds a Bachelors of Science in Electrical Engineering from New Mexico State University and will graduate from Chicago-Kent College of Law with a Juris Doctor of Laws in July 1995. He has developed Internet applications and consulted for over 10 years, working for such organizations as IBM, the U.S. Army, the Physical Sciences Laboratory of New Mexico State University, and Chicago-Kent College of Law.

David S. Forsyth is currently a Research Officer with the Institute for Aerospace Research at the National Research Council of Canada. He started working with computers to write reports in high school using an Apple II3. He has published a number of technical papers on various topics in non-destructive evaluation, and is currently researching AI applications, data organizations, and information for work and pleasure. He can be reached on the National Capital FreeNet in Ottawa, Canada at **bg40@freenet.carleton.ca**.

Ken Mitton is a biochemist and cataract researcher currently with the Biochemistry Department at Virginia Tech in Blacksburg, Virginia, located in the beautiful Blue Ridge Mountains of southwest Virginia. He obtained a B.S. degree in Biochemistry in 1985 from Carleton University in Canada's capital city of Ottawa, Ontario. In 1994, he completed a Ph.D. in cataract biochemistry in the Faculty of Medicine at the University of Western Ontario in London. Laboratory research and publishing have made the use of computers (PCs, Macintosh, and UNIX) a must in his occupation. More recently, he has ventured onto the LensNet: Internet E-mail and WWW Service for Lens and Cataract Researchers used by lens researchers in eight countries. He has also recently set up his department's Web server, which can be linked from the Central Virginia Tech WWW server at **http://www.vt.edu/**, under the directory for Agriculture and Life Sciences.

Virginia Tech is known for its innovative use of computers, networking, and multimedia, both for University education and Out-Reach programs to high schools and communities in Virginia.

Martin Waterhouse currently works for Chevron corporation, a major oil company located in California. He has been involved with computers for over 20 years and started programming ALGOL and FORTRAN at school in 1973 while living in the UK. In 1976, he built his first home computer and progressed through a number of machines until getting his first IBM PC in 1983. He has continued to work in the PC arena specializing in communications, database systems, and object oriented languages and was even an assistant SYSOP on CompuServe for a couple of years. He has co-authored a number of titles since 1987, including the *MS-DOS Power User's Guide Vol. II* and *Introduction to Hard Disk Management and Norton Desktop for DOS*. He is also a contributor of magazine articles and has been invited to speak at numerous computer-related conferences. When not working at Chevron or writing, he loiters on the Internet and CompuServe and likes to play pinball in his garage, where there's a growing collection of tables.

Acknowledgments

I would like to thank the companies and individuals who helped provide complimentary software and accounts for the research involved in this book. This includes John Buckman at InfoMagnet, Zara Haimo at InfoSeek, Chris Cooper at Quote.Com, Jim Leightheiser at Individual, Dow Jones News Retrieval, Lexis-Nexis, and Knight Ridder.

I'd like to acknowledge the wonderful writing as well as the ongoing suggestions and support offered by individuals who contributed to this book including Peter Burke, Larry Donahue, David Forsyth, Ken Mitton, and Martin Waterhouse. Thank you all!

I would also like to acknowledge the great effort of the many individuals at Que who have both the insight and talent to make a practical, hands-on book like this possible. Thanks to Stacy Hiquet, Brad Koch, Mark Cierzniak, Deborah Abshier, Mitzi Foster Gianakos, and the production team!

Trademarks

Foreword

A Handbook for the Internet Mind Meld

by A.M.Rutkowski
Executive Director
Internet Society
Reston, VA USA

From the earliest days of the Internet, it was apparent that the primary value of the technology was the ability to share the knowledge and enhance the collective creativity of people. At first, it was the many diverse researchers supported by the U.S. Department of Defense Advanced Projects Research Agency; then the circles of connectivity enlarged to encompass scientific, academic, and development communities around the world.

The effect reminded many of another kind of media development—the Vulcan Mind Meld of Star Trek fame.

In the final analysis, the Internet is "flat information space." It's a giant global cloud into which almost any kind of computer can be plugged to directly interact with any other information or process on any other connected computer. As of May 1995, there are about 6 million of these computers and new machines continue to plug in at the rate of 10,000 per day.

This massive "bottom-up" infrastructure enables all kinds of things to occur. All of those connected computers, which the Internet community calls *hosts*, allow innumerable webs of information to be constructed on top. It allows users to access information; but equally important, it allows those same users to provide information.

During the 80s, as the Internet grew ever larger, an entire new discipline known as Networked Information Retrieval was born. Perhaps the first distributed discovery tool was the Domain Name System itself. Even with just relative simple structures like anonymous FTP files, as they became more numerous, innovative Internet initiatives began to spring up in research circles.

As the scale of this discipline grew, many of the key practitioners of this new discipline began exchanging ideas on the network, writing code, and meeting under the aegis of the Internet Research and Engineering Task Forces. Luminaries included Michael Schwartz (IRTF, NetFind, and Harvest), Peter Deutsch and Alan Emtage (Archie), Brewster Kahle (WAIS), Tim Berners-Lee (WWW), Mark McCahill (Gopher), together with many others including Kevin Gamiel, Steve Foster, Cliff Neuman, Fred Barrie, Steve Kill, Cliff Lynch, Vint Cerf, Chris Weider, and Jill Foster.

The Internet also allows people to interact with other people on specific questions or subjects. Virtual "collaboratories" can be created in the process. It's frequently said that no two people on earth are further apart than five intermediate links or queries. Similarly, it's also asserted that more than 80 percent of all the scientists who ever lived are accessible via the Internet. The combination of the two places an enormous repository of "people knowledge" in the hands of the world.

The result is a vast new virtual universe that is constantly growing, evolving, and responding every second. Considering that Internet's hosts are nothing more than extensions of many millions of people throughout the world in 180 different countries, it really is a kind of collective human consciousness.

So responsive is the Internet today, that it's not uncommon to see articles in major national newspapers focusing on Net-based information and discussions reflecting late-breaking news developments occurring in near real-time. In some cases, the Internet itself has become an intrinsic part of the current events.

Clearly, for research and strategic analysis purposes in almost any profession or enterprise, the ability to effectively use the Internet is essential. Knowing how to search for resources—both information and people—across the Internet is not only fun and interesting, it is a critical skill of the 90s and beyond. If ever a book was ripe for the times, this is it.

Some notes of caution are in order:

As the Internet continues its exponential growth with ever more hosts with burgeoning amounts of information, still more tools and techniques will become available. The Internet is itself in a constant state of evolution and revolution. With each passing day, gigabytes of new information and software from every imaginable individual and institutional source—public and private—are made available on Internet hosts. Thousands of new discussion groups are formed. New and improved programs are being developed.

Although a vast preponderance of people will use these capabilities wisely and for a common good, some will not. An emerging Internet Code of Conduct combined with provider enforcement should curtail inappropriate behavior. Still, some vigilance by parents and guardians may be in order.

On a positive note, however, consider using the skills imparted by this book to keep up with the constant change that makes the Internet a place of constant discovery and fascination and, if you're so inclined, contribute to the rest of the world out there. It's part of maintaining the Internet culture.

Contents at a Glance

Contents

II Internet Search Tools   41

3 Searching the World Wide Web   43

4 Information Detectives: Gopher, Veronica, and WAIS 79

5 Finding and Retrieving Files from Remote Computers 107

6 Internet Files and Copyright Issues   127

7 Advanced Searching Techniques   143

III Search People Resources 157

Introduction

Imagine that you're in the local library searching for a book, a magazine article, or a video. If you can't find what you're looking for, you turn to the expert—the reference librarian. He or she has the knowledge, experience, and tools to help you locate that hard-to-find resource.

Less than a decade ago, instant access to information and knowledge of the skills required to locate a specific resource was a luxury enjoyed by a select few. This privileged group included librarians, corporate executives, financial analysts, and information brokers. These individuals subscribed to expensive electronic information, news, and financial services.

The Internet (Net for short) has become a great equalizer—an electronic gateway that provides instant access to global news and information. The databases, documents, files, and programs that are "sitting" on Internet computers contain a tremendous amount of information. You can search for and find up-to-the-minute stock market activity, a copy of Shakespeare's *Macbeth*, weather reports, music by The Rolling Stones, toll-free phone numbers for thousands of companies, photos of Jupiter, the recipe for chicken casserole, and even the electronic mail address of a long lost friend.

In fact, it's getting to the point where the Internet has become a repository, a knowledgebase, of all human intelligence. And, unlike the local library, which may add a few new books or magazines to its collection each week, the Internet increases its base of information by thousands of new records every single day. Anyone with a personal computer and an Internet connection can be privy to this information and these vast resources. It's a little like having the world's largest interactive library and information system available at your fingertips.

This book teaches you how to use the Internet to search for and locate the information that you want or need for your personal or professional life. By the time you finish this book, you will be able to quickly identify and use the best Internet search systems and tools to find specific information. You'll also learn how to use a variety of search strategies and techniques that are the foundation of information retrieval. By the time you finish, you'll "graduate" with the knowledge and skills required to be a successful Net searcher.

The book has four sections. Each offers valuable insight into the various Internet systems, sites, and searching strategies that can most effectively get you to the information you're looking for. Here's a brief overview.

Part I: Internet Resources and Searching Techniques

In these first chapters you'll learn about the variety of information resources that are available on the Internet. Also, you'll gain an understanding of the different Internet search systems and search tools and how to determine which ones are your best bets for specific types of searches. You will be introduced to the art of successful information retrieval with an overview of databases and search strategies. There are lots of helpful, hands-on tips and reviews of sites that are terrific starting places for your global information search.

Part II: Internet Search Tools

There are literally millions and millions of files, documents, and software programs on Internet computers all around the world. In fact, if you were to print a copy of every document or book that you have access to, you would more than fill the Grand Canyon with paper! Now imagine that the information you need is somewhere in this massive pile. It sounds like an impossible task to sift through and locate one specific resource, but fortunately you have several different search tools and information systems at your disposal.

Gopher, Veronica, WAIS, FTP, Archie, and Web Crawlers may sound like words in a foreign language, but they are the nicknames and acronyms for some of the Internet systems search tools that you can use to locate exactly what you're looking for. Whether it's the atomic weight of oxygen, a copy of the North American Free Trade Agreement, a photograph of the Eiffel Tower, or a software program to play chess, you'll learn how to use search tools that scour the Internet and keep track of all of the resources that are out there in cyberspace.

Not only will you master these tools, you'll also learn how to transfer and save information, files, and software programs directly to your hard drive. Then, you'll find out how to organize, manage, and even search for information that's stored on your PC.

Part III: Search People Resources

One of the best information resources on the Internet is the 30 million other people who use it. These people all have knowledge, ideas, and experiences that can help you in your quest for information. Indeed, two-way communication can be more productive than the one-way flow of communication that occurs when you simply read, view, or listen to information.

Sometimes an answer to a question raises a new question. Rather than simply retrieving information, dialog with other people can change the way you think about a problem. You begin to discover new ideas, even realize that you need to look for a different type of information. Add a third, fourth, fifth, or even several thousand people to the conversation and the discussion of your topic can open up avenues of thought and information that you never imagined. You upgrade from simple searching to dialog and even brainstorming.

The Internet offers several ways for you to have two-way or multi-way conversations with other Internet users. The chapters in this section offer information about the Internet systems that provide two-way communication: newsgroups, electronic mail, and mailing lists. You'll also learn how to search for and locate the addresses of other people who are on the Net, so you can find a long lost friend or get the name and phone number of a business contact.

Part IV: Search Commercial and Educational Services

In the chapters in this section you'll learn about specific Internet sites—both free and commercial—that can help you locate information.

Libraries have always been ahead of the curve when it comes to using computer technology to assist with the storage and retrieval of information. Now, they are rapidly gaining a significant presence on the Internet. Electronic libraries on the Net offer searchable databases that you can use to locate books and documents and even view and download entire texts. Or, you may want to search the contents of a periodical or book to see if there is relevant information. Does the latest issue of *Time* have an article about computer technology? How many times does the King James version of the Bible mention marriage? You'll also find out about interactive reference tools, such as an Internet site where you can translate words from English to Spanish and vice versa.

Companies known as information providers recognize the potential for great profits as they package information on subjects ranging from agricultural studies to zoology. You can access their information databases through the Internet to locate documents and records that aren't available anywhere else. Some of these services offer free samples of their information.

If you're looking for information about companies, business news, financial information, government reports, or educational training tools and resources, then the Internet can be your one-stop-shopping place. All of these areas have extensive coverage on Internet sites around the world.

Where will all of this electronic information lead to as we approach the 21st century? Will the Internet continue to expand? And, what does the future hold for advanced searching applications? Find out about the development of new software programs that you can program to go out onto the Net and search for information, even deals on buying products, while you're sleeping or out playing golf. Learn about cutting-edge communications technology including the Internet Phone, which is a software program that makes it possible to conduct real conversations—that's right, you actually speak and listen—with people all over the world via the Internet. The latest Internet communications technology will soon allow users to conduct video conferences directly from their desktop PCs.

Now fasten your electronic seatbelt and enjoy Net searching.

Conventions Used in This Book

This book uses various conventions designed to make it easier to use. With most Windows programs, you can use the mouse or keyboard to perform operations. The keyboard procedures for Windows software may include shortcut key combinations or *mnemonic* keys. In this book, key combinations are joined with plus signs (+). For example, Ctrl+X means hold down the Ctrl key, press the X key, and then release both keys. Some menu and dialog box options have underlined or highlighted characters that indicate mnemonic keys. To choose such an option using the mnemonic key, you press the Alt key and then press the indicated mnemonic key. In this book, mnemonic keys are set in bold: for example, **F**ile.

The book uses several other typeface enhancements to indicate special text, as indicated in the following table.

Typeface	Meaning
Bold	Bold indicates text you type and actual addresses for Internet sites, newsgroups, mailing lists, WWW pages, and terms used for the first time.
Computer type	This special type is used to represent text on-screen.

Note

Notes provide additional information that may help you avoid problems or offer advice or general information related to the topic at hand.

Caution

Cautions warn you of hazardous procedures and situations that can lead to unexpected or unpredictable results, including data loss or system damage.

Troubleshooting

Troubleshooting sections anticipate common problems...

...and then provide practical suggestions for solving those problems.

Tip
Tips suggest easier or alternative methods to execute a procedure.

Part I

Internet Resources and Searching Techniques

Jay

The Listserver

Kittens-l

Scuba-l

Joe

Sue

Politics-l

PATHFINDER

FROM TIME WARNER

Week of March 6 - 12, 199

Guided Tour | What's New | Questions | Net Search | Net Directory | News

HOT PAGE | TIME | Money

NEWS & FINANCE

VIBE | People | THE O.J. FILES

the Virtual Garden

Today's News
- Dole: "Cut 4 Cabinet Posts"
- House Passes Tort Reforms
- Fuhrman: "I Didn't Frame O

Hot This Week
- Baseball's Dead End Kids
- Greg Louganis-My Private He
- The Sounds of Science Fiction

TIME WARNER PRODUCTS

ABOUT | BULLETIN BOARD | WRITE BACK | OFFERS | SEARCH | HELP!

Not loading images? Try here.

Netscape: [NLM HyperDOC: World Wide Web (WWW) Server of the U.S. National Lib

File   Edit   View   Go   Bookmarks   Options   Directory   Help

Back | Forward | Home

Location: http://www.nlm.nih.gov/

What's New! | What's Cool! | Handbook | Net Search | Net Directory | Newsgroups

NATIONAL LIBRARY OF MEDICINE

Welcom
A Multi
U.S. Na

Donald A. B. Lindberg, M.D
Director

Pekka@Finland | Chris/USGS | Mobeus@Bellcor

BellCore Com

20 Kbps | 3 fps | 34 Kbps

Back | Forward | Home | Reload | Images | Open | Print | Find | Stop

Location: http://www.umr.edu/~cisapps/MSDS.html

What's New! | What's Cool! | Handbook | Net Search | Net Directory | Newsgroups

Enter a MSDS Search Criteria Below:

• **Chemical Name:** TriNitroTolulene

What's New!

The Listserver

Jay

Tom

Sue

Scuba-l

Joe

Kittens-l

Politics-l

Guided Tour | What's New | Questions | Net Search | Net Directory | New

PATHFINDER

FROM TIME WARNER   Week of March 6 - 12,

HOT PAGE | TIME | Money

NEWS & FINANCE

Today's New

- Dole: "Cut 4 Cabinet Pow
- House Passes Tort Refor
- Fuhrman: "I Didn't Fram

Entertainment | VIBE | People | THE O.J. FILES

REVIEWS
MUSIC, MOVIES
TV, BOOKS &
HOLLYWOOD

the Virtual Garden

SPECIAL INTEREST

Hot This We

- Baseball's Dead End K
- Greg Louganis–My Private
- The Sounds of Science F

Sports Illustrated | TIME WARNER ELECTRONIC PUBLISHING

TIME WARNER PRODUCTS

ABOUT | BULLETIN BOARDS | WRITE BACK | OFFERS | SEARCH | HELP!

Not loading images? Try here.

Netscape - [NLM HyperDOC: World-Wide Web (WWW) Server of the U.S. National Lib

File   Edit   View   Go   Bookmarks   Options   Directory   Help

Back Forward Home   Reload Images Open   Print   Find   Stop

Location: http://www.nlm.nih.gov/

What's New! | What's Cool! | Handbook | Net Search | Net Directory | Newsgroups

NATIONAL LIBRARY OF MEDICINE

Welcome to HyperDOC
A Multimedia/Hypertext Resource of the
U.S. National Library of Medicine (NLM)

Donald A. B. Lindberg, M.D.
Director

Pekka@Finland   Chris/USGS   Mobeus@Bellcor

heloll!   Bellcore C

7.1 fps   34 Kbps   1.2 fps   28 Kbps   3 fps   34 Kb

Back Forward Home   Reload Images Open   Print   Find   Stop

Location: http://www.umr.edu/~cisapps/MSDS.html

What's New! | What's Cool! | Handbook | Net Search | Net Directory | Newsgroups

Enter a MSDS Search Criteria Below:

●**Chemical Name:** TriNitroTolulene

Chapter 1

A Global Warehouse of Information

Have you ever tried to put together one of those 5,000 piece jigsaw puzzles where the picture is something impossibly difficult like a photograph of jelly beans? You think you may go crazy trying to find the next piece. The Internet may seem like a giant puzzle. But, instead of thousands, there are literally millions of different pieces—text-based documents, images, software programs, video and audio files. Where do you begin to find the one piece that you need today, right now?

This chapter provides a foundation that you will be able to use as you learn about the specific Internet tools and systems that are available for Net searching. In this chapter you will learn the following:

- What types of information and resources are available on the Internet

- How searching the Internet for information can save time and money

- About the different information systems and search tools on the Internet and how to choose the best one to begin a search

- That the Internet is alive with more than 30 million people who can help you find information

Information Can Be Valuable

The information that you locate from a search has real value. Information helps us make informed decisions—whether it's about which college to attend or how to save money when traveling abroad. You can also use information to save money and make money. You might want to do a search to find the most competitive price on a product or learn about new investment or employment opportunities.

Businesspeople can find information that can be of value in all aspects of running a company—from product development to marketing. The use of the Internet to gain a competitive edge in the marketplace can have tremendous economic value. Individuals and small companies can use the information resources of the Internet to level the playing field for locating and seizing international business opportunities. Using Internet searching tools, it becomes possible to learn about new trading partners or requests for proposals. An Internet connection in Hong Kong becomes a gateway for doing business with China as you can access a database of more than 1,000 companies locating company contacts, financial data, product information, addresses, and phone numbers (Web address: **http://www.hk.super.net/ ~rlowe/bizhk/bhhome.html**).

Educators and students can use the Internet to find information useful for course curriculum, study programs, and class reports. As a reference source, the Internet provides "just-in-time" information. Log on to the Internet 10 minutes before you have to make a presentation or finish a report and get the information you need.

When you tap into the resources of the Internet, you can search for and retrieve information that will help with decision making, improve productivity, and even enhance your economic situation. There is another, almost hidden, value in using the Internet to locate information. That's in the savings associated with the time and expense that it traditionally takes to find information. No longer do you have to drive to the library or make long-distance phone calls to find information. Now you can search a global warehouse of information by connecting to the Internet from your home or office. In the current "information age," the ability to quickly locate, retrieve, and use information has tremendous value for everyone. And, with its global connections and millions of users, the Internet is the world's biggest electronic library and public gathering place.

What Type of Information Can I Find on the Internet?

Here you are reading the words on this page. Your brain translates the printed characters and words—which you learned back in grade school—into meaningful information. Words clearly are one form of information, but information also comes in several other forms. A symphony by Beethoven, a speech by Winston Churchill, a photograph by Ansel Adams, a movie by Steven Spielberg—all these different forms of media contain information. And, every one of these forms of media can be converted into a digital format and saved as a computer file. Software programs, spreadsheets, and databases are also digital in form, and contain useful applications and information. For the remainder of this book all of these different things will be referred to as "information."

The term **multimedia** has come to define the capability of computer technology—especially CD-ROMs—to offer users a multisensory experience as you quickly move from a picture to sounds to movies. The Internet itself is perhaps the biggest multimedia system ever created. Table 1.1 identifies some of the media types that you'll find on the Internet. All of these forms of digital information can be stored as files on Internet computers, searched for by users like you, then distributed directly to your personal computer as shown in figure 1.1.

Table 1.1   Media Types on the Internet

Types of Media	Examples of Content
Text	Articles, books, reports, periodicals
Images	Photographs, weather maps, digital art
Sound	Voice and music recordings
Movies	Short (10 second—2 minute) videos
Programs and files	Software, spreadsheets, databases

The digital format means that all of this information is accessible via the Internet. The subjects or categories of information that you will find on the Internet are vast. In fact, it would be difficult to think of a subject that you couldn't find on the Internet. What makes the Internet such a comprehensive warehouse of digital information is that you can use the various Internet systems to access computers and information maintained by governments, educational institutions, commercial companies, and non-profit organizations all around the world. Here are a few examples of information and software programs you can access:

- Library catalogs and electronic books from libraries around the world, including the extensive collection at the U.S. Library of Congress (see fig. 1.2).

- Commercial databases on thousands of subjects.

- Business catalogs that describe products and services.

- Information directories such as AT&T's Internet site, which offers a searchable index of companies that have 800-numbers.

- Publications and books. Thousands of quarterly, monthly, weekly, and daily periodicals, electronic versions of newsstand magazines, and the complete text of books.

- Vast repositories of government information. From searchable databases of space flight information offered by NASA to a directory of all of the towns and cities in Canada.

- Software programs and utilities for all computer platforms including financial, word-processing, graphic, educational, and Internet programs.

Fig. 1.1
There are hundreds of thousands of digital images stored on Internet computers including sports heroes, distant planets, and rare coins.

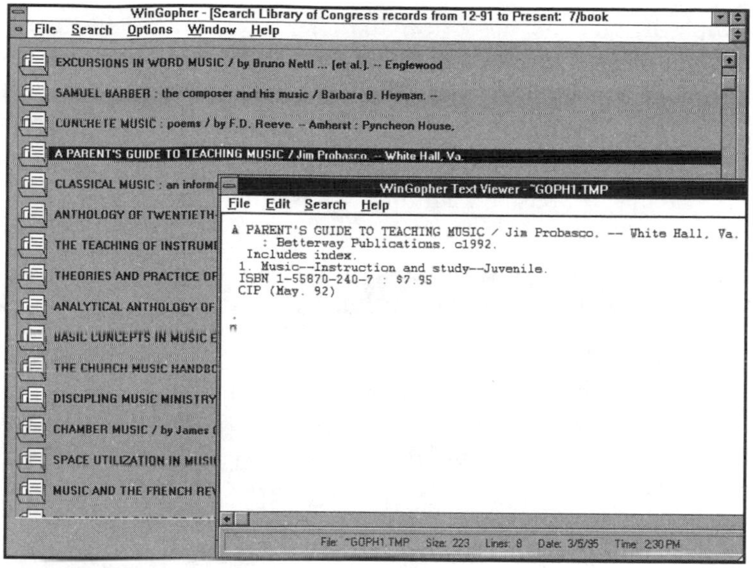

Fig. 1.2
A search of the Library of Congress records for books about "music" retrieves several hundred titles ranging from *Ancient Greek Music* to *The Church Music Handbook*.

Global Information from a Global Network

The overwhelming U.S. participation in the initial development of the Internet has one important ramification for Net searchers. English has become the de facto standard for text-based documents and interfaces to the various Internet systems. When you visit Internet computers in Japan, Germany, or Argentina the odds are that you will either get English language information on your computer screen or you'll will have an option that will take you to an English-based version of the information.

Although a significant portion of the users and computers that are connected to the Internet are in the United States, the Internet is truly a global communications system. More than 80 countries around the world have connected networks to the Internet. For example, Canada has the second largest Internet infrastructure in the world—with well over 1 million users. Other countries that have a significant presence on the Internet include France, Germany, the United Kingdom, Australia, and Japan—each operating more than 1,000 networks that connect to the Internet.

The global nature of the Internet means that it is just as easy to connect with and search through information on a computer in China or Australia as it is to access one that may be located in the United States. As foreign governments, educational institutions, and companies continue to connect to the Internet and allow Net searchers to access their information, it becomes increasingly easy to find information that previously would have been difficult or even impossible to locate.

For example, if you're planning a trip to India, you could visit a site that has a city-by-city menu that leads to descriptions of each town, directions of how to get there, local sightseeing opportunities, and lodging accommodations (Gopher address: **soochak.ncst.ernet.in**). You can even search and find obscure works of literature that you'd never find any place else. A site in Ireland, for example, collects and puts online Irish literature dating from 600 to 1600 A.D.

> ### Note
>
> There are several ways to measure the continual growth of the Internet. One is by the number of people who have access to the Internet. It's estimated that there are 40 million Internet users, and the number of users continues to increase at the rate of approximately 2 million each month. A second measure is in the number of host computers that are connected to the Internet. A **host computer** is a computer that is connected to the Internet on a continual basis, and you may connect to hosts all over the world during a Net search. The number of hosts has grown from 235 in May 1982 to more than 4 million hosts in May 1995. And, because each host can store lots of files, the quantity and variety of information that's available continues to grow at an amazing rate.

From Academic to Business Applications

Although you don't need a history lesson on how to search the Internet, a quick snapshot of the evolution of the Internet will give you some insight into the quantity and types of information that are available.

With more than 25 years of academic involvement, a significant portion of the hosts, information, and users of the Internet revolve around education. Approximately 900,000 educational and research organizations operate Internet hosts—about 25 percent of the total hosts on the Internet. As a result, there are scholarly reports, studies, journals, images, and software programs encompassing every educational and scientific subject you can think of. Figure 1.3 shows the Harvard University Internet Web site and figure 1.4 displays a sample of the financial information that is available on the Internet.

The commercial sector is rapidly getting a large presence on the Internet. The commercial sector now operates more than 800,000 hosts. According to telecommunications giant MCI, 38 percent of all publicly traded companies with sales that exceed $400 million have some type of presence on the Internet.

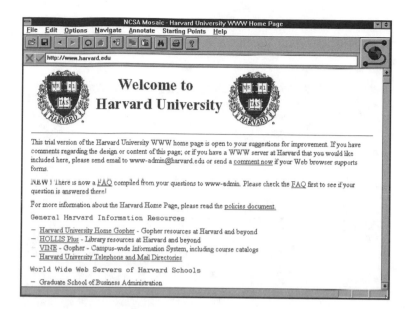

Fig. 1.3
An Internet search for "colleges" provides a list of more than 1,000 different U.S. educational institutions that maintain Internet sites. Here is the main page for Harvard University's World Wide Web site.

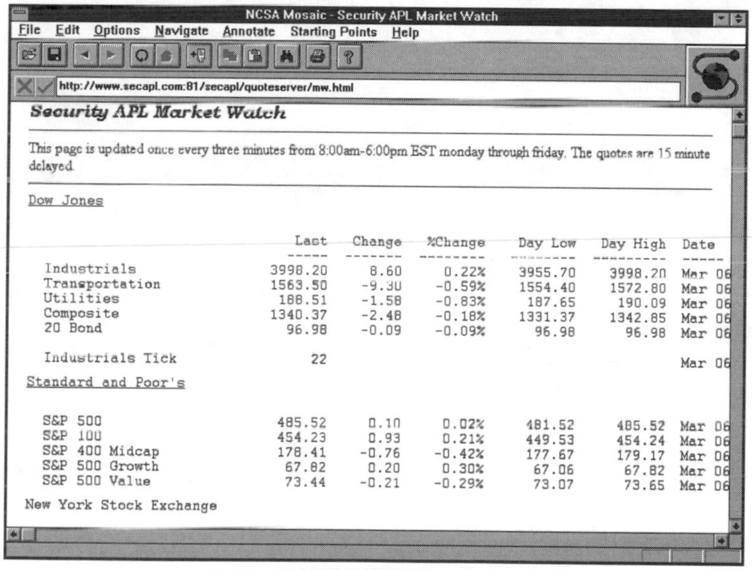

Fig. 1.4
Information on the Internet is extremely current. This Internet site updates stock and security market information every three minutes.

Fortunately, the trend for commercial Internet sites is for companies to offer product information, news, articles, interactive brochures, free software utilities, and even games as opposed to blatant advertising. A good example of this is Time Warner's Internet site, which is shown in figure 1.5 (Web address: **http://www.pathfinder.com/**). Among other things, you'll find the "Virtual Garden," which maintains a collection of horticultural information and articles about gardening from *Sunset* and *Southern Living* magazines.

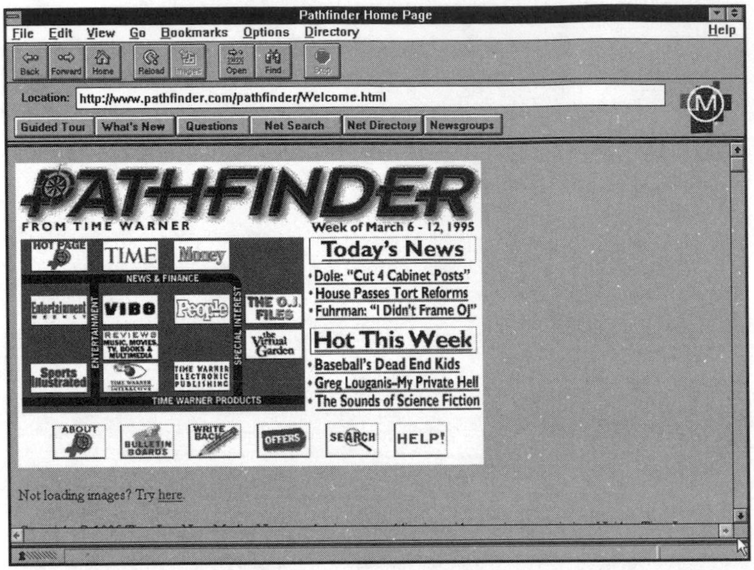

Fig. 1.5
Commercial Internet sites offer a variety of useful information and software programs. The Pathfinder site is a gateway to articles and news from several Time Warner publications.

> **Note**
>
> When a college or company registers its Internet computer it has to pick a unique domain name or address that identifies its site. In the United States, educational sites get an address that ends with .edu. Commercial sites get addresses that end with .com, and government hosts end with .gov. This naming system makes it easy for you to quickly identify what type of site you are visiting—if you don't already know.

Internet Access from America Online and "Friends"

The tremendous publicity and rapid growth of the Internet has not gone unnoticed by commercial companies that provide online services and access to databases. America Online (AOL), CompuServe, Prodigy, and Delphi all offer their users—more than 5 million people—access to the Internet. If you use the Internet, you can send electronic mail and have conversations with all of these people. These commercial online services also have software programs (known as browsers) that enable you to access the Internet World Wide Web system.

Other commercial companies, like Dow Jones and Dialog, specialize in collecting, organizing, and selling access to information databases. These companies now let Internet users subscribe to their services, then use the Internet to access their information and database services.

How Do I Search the Internet?

Looking for information is similar to hunting for buried treasure. You look for clues that may lead to new clues that in turn lead to finding the treasure. So, consider yourself an information explorer. Every good explorer carries a few tools—map, compass, shovel. Your tools are the various Internet systems and search tools. Let's take a brief look at these tools to get an overview of how they can help you uncover the buried information. Each of these are described in much more detail in the next two sections of this book.

For the purpose of searching, it's helpful to categorize the Internet into three areas:

- Navigation and information systems
- Search tools
- Communications applications

Part II of this book provides detailed explanations of the navigation and information systems and search tools. Part III of the book overviews the communications applications.

Navigation and Information Systems

Internet navigation systems encompass computers that store and organize information. There are three different navigation systems that you can use for Internet searching:

- Gopher
- World Wide Web
- FTP (File Transfer Protocol)

Gopher is a system that organizes information into menus (see fig. 1.6). You connect to an Internet Gopher computer, take a look at the menu of information and make a selection. The selection will take you to a new menu with more choices, take you to a new computer with a menu of choices, or, if the selection represents a file, you get the information you're looking for. A large percentage of the information that you'll find on Gopher systems will be text-based documents and files.

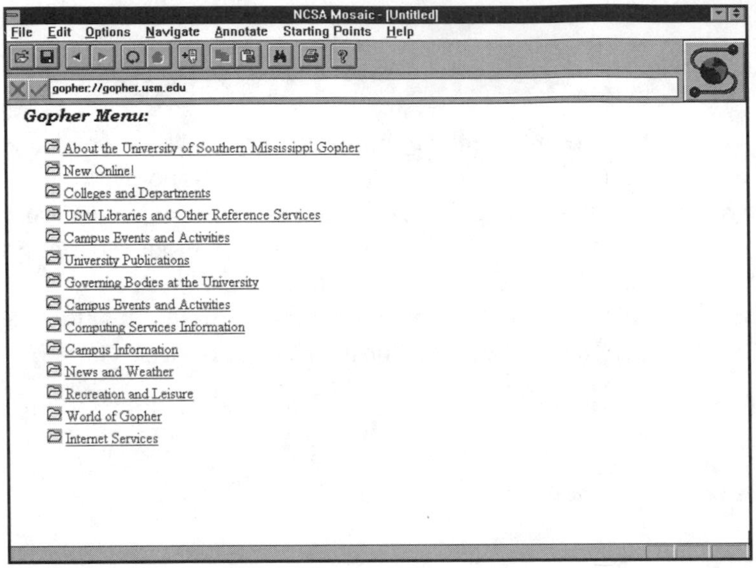

Fig. 1.6
The Gopher system displays information resources with on-screen menus.

The **World Wide Web**, Web for short, is one of the fastest growing systems on the Internet. Why? Because it delivers multimedia information directly to your PC. Like a magazine, you see pictures embedded in documents. And, using your mouse, you can point-and-click to access other types of media—a song by Tom Petty or a video clip from David Letterman's show.

The Web organizes and distributes information in a "non-linear" fashion. What this means is that you might start with a site that has information on Europe, then jump to a site that features wine, then jump again to a document about liquor stores. The way you navigate through information on the Web is similar to having a discussion with a friend—the conversation may jump from subject to subject as you talk. You'll find lots of documents, images, and multimedia-media on Web sites. And you can use the Web and Web software to access both Gopher and FTP sites.

FTP stands for file transfer protocol. This is the Internet protocol that enables you to download or retrieve files from Internet computers. FTP sites maintain huge collections of files. Much like the MS-DOS system, these files are stored in directories or subdirectories. When you navigate through FTP sites, you move from one directory to another to locate the file you're looking for.

Unlike Gopher or the Web, you don't jump from one FTP site to another. You connect to one site then disconnect before you can visit another site. So, to keep with the analogy of conversation, it's similar to calling someone on the phone. You can't start a new conversation or a new call until you finish the one you're having, hang up, and dial again. You'll find many software programs and text files on FTP sites.

There are several Windows- and Macintosh-based software programs designed specifically for each of these Internet systems. For example, you can use WSGopher to visit Gopher sites, Netscape to cruise Web sites, and WSFTP to navigate through FTP sites. These are the software programs that you see in most of the screen captures in this book. We've "standardized" on these programs because they are extremely popular and have excellent features. There are, however, many other free, as well as commercial, programs that you can use to access the information on the Internet information systems.

What Tools Are Available for Searching?

In addition to having several information systems, the Internet also has several different search tools that will help you search for, locate, and retrieve information. In fact, as table 1.2 shows, each of the three Internet information systems also has a specific search tool designed to help you locate information on the system.

Table 1.2 Internet Information System Search Tools

Information System	Search Tool
Gopher	Veronica
World Wide Web	Web Crawlers or Searchers
FTP	Archie

Veronica searches Gopher menus from around the world and delivers a custom-tailored menu that meets your information needs. The Web Crawlers search Web sites for information and, after a search, return a "clickable" list of resources that you can instantly jump to. Archie looks through a comprehensive list of FTP files to locate files that match your search criteria. In the second section of this book, you'll learn how to access and use each of these search tools.

Communication Applications

The 30 million plus people who use the Internet don't sit passively at their keyboards keeping their thoughts to themselves. No, the Internet is very much a living space where two-way communications occurs all of the time. One of the best resources for finding answers to questions or locating information is by communicating with other Internet users.

You'll quickly find that the Internet is one of the fastest and most economical systems around for the exchange of information. You can communicate with people all around the world for the cost of your monthly Internet access fees—literally sending large 200-page documents around the world for pennies. And, time of day becomes a non-issue with the Internet. You can send a proposal or even a question to someone who lives 8,000 miles away. Plus, there's no need to worry about time zones, country, postal ZIP codes, or local delivery systems. There are four major interpersonal communication applications available to Internet users. Table 1.3 offers a brief summary of the Internet communication systems.

Table 1.3 Internet Communication Applications	
Internet Application	**What You'll Find or Can Do**
Electronic mail (e-mail)	Send messages and files to more than 30 million people.
Newsgroups	Ongoing discussions in more than 10,000 different subject areas (see fig. 1.7).
Mailing lists	E-mail messages in specific topic areas, read or send messages to other people who are on a list.
Internet Relay Chat (IRC)	Conduct real-time conversations with other Internet users. Use the Internet Phone™ software to carry on voice conversations with other Internet IRC users via your multimedia PC.

Just as the Internet navigation systems have specific search tools, there are search tools, software programs, and techniques that will help you locate other people, their electronic mail addresses, and relevant newsgroup and mailing list messages (see table 1.4).

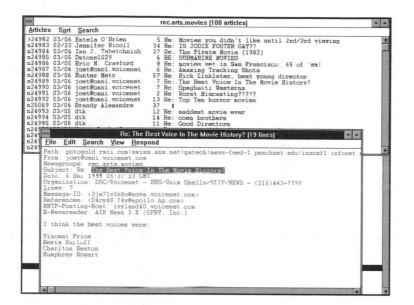

Fig. 1.7
Internet newsgroups offer active and lively discussion on thousands of topics. Connect to the **rec.arts. movies** newsgroup to read reviews of the latest films, or join in on a discussion about which film actor has the best voice.

Table 1.4   Tools for Locating People

Communication System	Searching Tool
Electronic mail	WHOIS, Finger, X.500
Newsgroups	Search through newsgroup software, Web Crawlers, or archives of lists.
Mailing Lists	Search through archives of each list, or use mailing list software such as InfoMagnet.
IRC	Get an online list of current IRC users.

Each of these searching tools is described in detail in upcoming chapters. With the exception of IRC, the other systems examine databases or lists to locate addresses and messages that meet your search criteria. The IRC system provides an on-the-spot list of other people who are currently online.

Where Should I Start My Search?

With all of these different systems and search tools it may seem like just beginning a search is a complex process. Not true. It actually helps to have several different systems because you can start with the one that's most likely to locate the information you're looking for.

If, for example, you're trying to hunt down a copy of Abraham Lincoln's Gettysburg Address, you'd know that Gopher sites often have text documents and that Veronica can search Gopher menus to look for this document. On the other hand, if you wanted to find a copy of the shareware utility PKZIP, which compresses and uncompresses files, you'd first want to try Archie to search FTP sites and then use FTP to download the program. Or, if you wanted to get the e-mail address for a friend who works for the Postal Service, first stop should be one of the e-mail searching tools. Table 1.5 gives you some basic guidelines for choosing the system that is most likely to help you with a Net search.

Table 1.5   Internet Search System Guide

	A software program	A document	An image, movie, or sound file	Communicate with someone	Locate an e-mail address
Gopher	■	■	■		■
Web	■	■	■	■	■
FTP	■	■	■		
Newsgroup		■	■	■	■
E-mail		■		■	
Mailing List	■		■	■	
IRC		■		■	■

What you'll find as you begin to use these different information systems and tools is that a search of one system can bring up different results (and information) than a search of another system. The bottom line is if you don't instantly find what you're looking for, or you need to perform a comprehensive search, you may use several different Internet navigation systems and search tools. Although a Gopher search may quickly find a copy of the Gettysburg Address, a Web search might also find information about the U.S. Civil War and the town of Gettysburg. An FTP search may uncover a digital photo of Lincoln. The good news is that you can easily jump from one system and one software program to another right from your PC.

Summary

Multimedia files, software programs, books, historical records, and up-to-the-minute financial information—the resources of the Internet are vast. No matter what your personal hobbies or professional career, you can locate valuable information on the Internet. The remaining chapters in this book provide step-by-step instructions to help you save time and money by quickly locating what you're looking for during your Net search.

Chapter 2

Strategies for Effective Searching

It seems like an impossible task. The Internet contains millions of files and documents. How do you locate the one that has the information you need right now? Finding the needle in the haystack is both the challenge and the reward of Net searching.

Databases, the computer equivalent of gigantic electronic Rolodexes, store and organize information. This chapter explains how you use keywords to search for and locate information in databases on Internet computers.

The manner in which you organize and conduct your search also has a direct impact on the results you get and how pertinent the results are. Certainly it would be annoying to perform a series of searches and either never get any information, or get information that isn't close to what you're looking for. To be productive you need to follow some relatively simple strategies for information searching and retrieval. This chapter explains the basic procedures that will help you conduct a successful search with any of the Internet or commercial online systems. Specifically you will learn the following:

- How a database and a database index organize and store information

- How keywords can be used to quickly locate relevant information

- How to develop a search strategy based on the type of information you are looking for

- How you can modify a search to improve the results

- How to examine and interpret the results of your search

What Is a Database?

You'll come across the word *database* many times in this book—and many more when you start Net searching. A **database** is a computer-based collection of related information. A database can contain many types of information. There are databases of articles in *Time* magazine, addresses of fishing clubs, names of U.S. senators, photographs of planets, bird songs—you name it. Each entry in a database is known as a **record**. A database of recipes might have separate records for chicken noodle soup, chicken fajitas, and chicken fettuccine.

Databases are created with database programs. If you use Microsoft Windows, you have a very simple database program that comes in the Accessories group called Cardfile. In addition to performing mathematical calculations very quickly, computers are very good at searching through the digital information in a database to locate specific records. Table 2.1 identifies a few other features and advantages of computer databases.

Table 2.1 Attributes and Advantages of Computer Databases	
Database Feature	**Advantage for Net Searcher**
Searchable	You can enter search terms to locate specific records contained in the database.
Speed	Computers can retrieve records very rapidly.
File size	Many records can be stored on a computer hard drive.
Timely	Records can be updated frequently.
Accessible	Many people can simultaneously access one database.

The thousands of databases that are available via the Internet each represent large collections of related information. Most online databases are searchable, although they have to be programmed and configured to enable a search for individual records. Figure 2.1 shows the different database categories that the commercial service Dialog offers. This is one of the services you can subscribe to and access via the Internet.

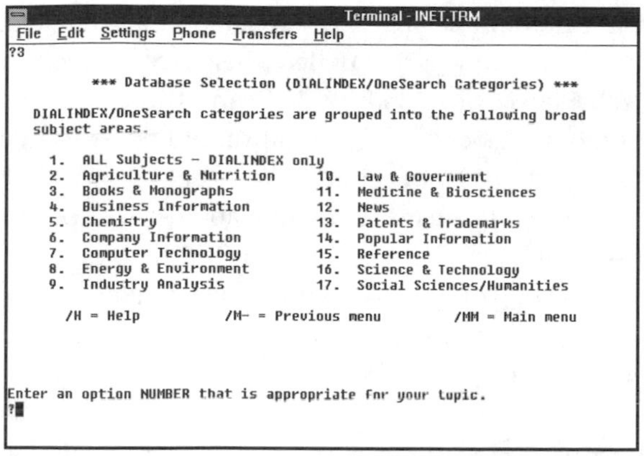

```
┌─────────────────────────────────────────────────────────────────┐
│ ▭                        Terminal - INET.TRM                      │
│ File  Edit  Settings  Phone  Transfers  Help                     │
│ ?3                                                                │
│                                                                   │
│         *** Database Selection (DIALINDEX/OneSearch Categories) ***│
│                                                                   │
│    DIALINDEX/OneSearch categories are grouped into the following broad│
│    subject areas.                                                 │
│                                                                   │
│       1.  ALL Subjects - DIALINDEX only                           │
│       2.  Agriculture & Nutrition    10.  Law & Government         │
│       3.  Books & Monographs         11.  Medicine & Biosciences   │
│       4.  Business Information        12.  News                    │
│       5.  Chemistry                  13.  Patents & Trademarks     │
│       6.  Company Information         14.  Popular Information      │
│       7.  Computer Technology        15.  Reference                │
│       8.  Energy & Environment        16.  Science & Technology     │
│       9.  Industry Analysis          17.  Social Sciences/Humanities│
│                                                                   │
│         /H = Help        /M- = Previous menu        /MM = Main menu│
│                                                                   │
│                                                                   │
│                                                                   │
│  Enter an option NUMBER that is appropriate for your topic.       │
│  ?▮                                                               │
└─────────────────────────────────────────────────────────────────┘
```

Fig. 2.1
You can access Dialog, a commercial service that maintains more than 450 databases, through the Internet. This menu shows the major categories of information.

Resources and Techniques

Linking Databases with the Internet

The reason the Internet has opened a world of information retrieval for Net searchers is that computers containing searchable databases can be connected to the Internet. Some of these databases—like the list of books in print contained at the U.S. Library of Congress—contain millions of records. When you connect to the U.S. Library of Congress Internet site you can search the database to locate a specific record—perhaps an abstract for a particular book, or a list of all books that have information about the Internet.

In addition to all of the wonderful databases on different subjects, there are also databases that contain records of the files and information that's stored on Internet computers. For example, when you use the Archie search tool to locate files on Internet FTP computers you actually search through a database that contains records of these files. Likewise, Web Crawlers maintain databases of information about Web sites and electronic mail search tools maintain databases that have records of e-mail addresses.

The Internet is dynamic and the information that's available on the Internet changes continuously. Every day thousands of new files are added to FTP sites, new Web and Gopher documents are created and put online and new individuals and companies get Internet addresses. The Internet information databases must be updated regularly to provide searchers with timely information.

Some Internet information databases get updated more frequently than others. Newsgroups, for example, often update their records every couple of hours. Some Web Crawlers run updates daily and the Veronica databases are updated once a month. Does this mean you should never use Veronica to search the Gopher system? Not at all. It means that if you're looking for today's top news stories—perhaps something about a United Nations peacekeeping effort—you'll have a better chance of finding it on a newsgroup than on Gopher. If, however, you're looking for a comprehensive report that explains how the United Nations operates and what countries belong to the UN Security Council, Veronica would be just fine.

Keywords and Hits

There are several techniques by which you can search a database. The most common is the **keyword search**. Search words are appropriately called keywords because they are "key" to your ability to locate information. The keyword represents the information that is sought. For example, a keyword might be "fishing," "airplane," or "electricity" as shown in figure 2.2. The database software takes your keyword and compares it to indexes to locate records that match your search criteria.

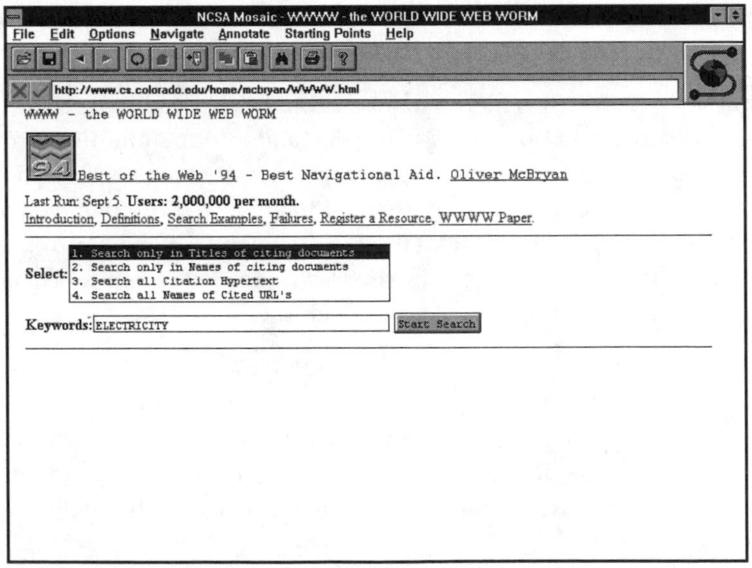

Fig. 2.2
The keyword "electricity" is used here with a Web Crawler to search for Internet sites where information about electricity can be found.

With some of the Internet search tools you can use more than one word to search a database. When you use several words or phrases to perform a search it is known as a **search term**. You could, for example, enter "trout fishing" or "jet and airplane" or "electricity in the home." When the database locates records that match your search term (or keyword) it responds by providing you with a list of those records. These matches are called **hits**. A hit could be a specific article, photograph, or stock quote that you could view on-screen or download to your hard drive. Hits can also be a list of other reference sources, or even other Internet sites that contain information relevant to your search.

Sometimes you'll get a lot of hits from a search. For example, if you were to search a database about gardening and you enter the keyword "flower," you'll get a lot of hits. If you were to search the same database with the keyword "columbine," you might not get any hits.

What Is an Index?

One of the most important elements of a database is an **index** that references each record. The index may be created by the database program, another software program, or by a person. This database index is similar in function to the index at the back of this book. The book index provides an alphabetical listing of topics that are in the book, and you use it to help you quickly find the page that contains information you're looking for. Likewise, when you perform a search on a database the computer will check the index to quickly locate any records that are relevant for your search.

The challenge for the person who indexes a database (or a software program that creates an index) is to anticipate the index terms that you, the Net searcher, will use to retrieve a specific record. For example, say you want to search a cookbook database to find a recipe for chicken noodle soup. A good computer database would have this recipe indexed with both chicken and soup so if you search for either chicken or soup, you'd be able to find the information. If there was a bad index and the recipe was indexed only as "noodle," odds are you'd never find the recipe because you probably wouldn't enter the keyword "noodle."

Tip
Most of the Internet search tools are case insensitive. This means that you'll get the same results if you enter the keyword "COOKING," "Cooking," or "cooking."

Troubleshooting
I'm not getting any hits for my search. Does that mean the database has a bad index?
Not necessarily. It's always possible that the database simply doesn't have any records that match your search term. However, if you think that the database you're using should contain records that relate to your subject, then try a new search. And, start with just one keyword instead of a long search term that may not be part of the database index. If you're still not getting any results, try a different database or Internet search tool.

When Searching Becomes Surfing

Searching is more of a process of exploration than a single act. Normally you don't just enter your keyword, locate one record, and call it quits. Searches usually deliver some unexpected information that relates to your topic. This information can open up new avenues of exploration.

Both Gopher and the World Wide Web allow you to jump from one Internet computer to another just by choosing on-screen selections. As an example, say you enjoy playing the piano and are looking for some new music to perform. A search for the keyword "piano" delivers a variety of intriguing results.

- King's Keyboard House, classical sheet music

- My Favorite Extracts

- Eaken Piano Trio

- Complete Schedule of the San Francisco Symphony

- Musicware, Inc. piano music education system for Windows

- David Cartledge, a piano instructor

Perhaps you'd only been thinking about locating sheet music, which is one of the first hits. You decide to explore the Internet site labeled "My Favorite Extracts" because it sounds intriguing. This turns out to be a site where a fellow Internetter has saved a series of audio file of piano pieces including Rachmaninoffs Piano Concerto No. 1. This is one of your favorites. You download it to see how you measure up. The site also has a link to another Internet site devoted to Mozart's music. You love Mozart's piano music—gotta go there. And so, without intending to do so, your search turns into the classic Internet navigation known as **surfing**. One Internet site leads to another, where a piece of information inspires a new search, and so on. Although searching by surfing can eat up a lot of time, it's also one of the best ways to locate relevant information that you would never have found with the initial keyword search.

Newsgroups and mailing lists invoke a slightly different type of surfing. Because these are interactive communications, you'll find that a question or idea that you or another Internet person contributes quickly leads in new directions as others join in the conversation.

To Begin, Define What You're Looking For

It may sound obvious, but it's important to have a clear idea of what you want to find before you can effectively search. If you were going to take a cross-country trip, you'd probably want to get some good maps, plan out the routes you'd drive on, maybe even the sights you would see and places you'd stay before actually getting in the car. This pre-trip planning makes the entire journey much easier and more enjoyable—and it certainly doesn't preclude sidetrips where, just for the heck of it, you turn off on some road just to see where it goes. In a similar fashion, you'll find that your Internet searching is much more productive and enjoyable if you plan where you're going before you start to cruise. Here are six things that you can do to help make your search more productive before you even begin your search.

Use What You Know

Write down what you already do know. This information can be extremely valuable in helping you define your keywords, search terms, or search criteria. For example, you've heard that the computer trade magazine called *Information Week* might have an Internet site. You might also know that the publisher is CMP Publications. Well, you've already got three good search terms: "Information Week," "CMP Publications," and "computer magazine."

Decide What You Need

Determine the type of information that you need. Is it a specific piece of data (the score of the 1964 World Series), general information (a list of travel destinations in Germany), or do you have a question that would best be answered by another person (Is the Town Council meeting going to be on Wednesday night?). This will help you decide how you want to phrase your search and which Internet system is the best for finding the information.

What Is the Nature of the Information?

Determine the nature of the information. Is it most likely a document, a photograph, a video, a computer program? These different types of information will have different file formats. For example, a photograph will usually be stored as a JPEG or a GIF file. You can use some of the Internet searching tools to locate specific file formats. This can save you a lot of time as it will narrow down the results of a search.

Define the Subject of Your Search

Determine the general subject area for the information that you're looking for. General subject areas include art, business, government, education, science, and so on. Make a list of several possible subject areas. Say, for example, you want to locate information about horse racing. You might make a subject list that includes "sports," "horses," and "gambling." These general subject areas can become your initial keywords for searching. If you run out of ideas, use a dictionary or thesaurus to locate more words.

Select the Best Internet System

Determine which Internet system will be the most likely to find what you need. A comprehensive search might require the use of all of the Internet systems described in this book. However if you find what you're looking for right away, you don't need to look any further. If, for example, you want to locate recipes, you'd first want to use the World Wide Web or the Gopher system—the Web because of its ability to show onscreen images of cuisine and Gopher because of all of the document files that it contains.

Remember What Works

As you begin to search on the Internet you'll quickly realize that there is usually more than one resource or database that has relevant information. Either use your Internet software programs to keep track of and save relevant sites or get in the habit of writing down the Internet address for useful sites. You don't want to spend an extra hour retracing your searching steps to get back to a place you can get to in a matter of seconds if you have the address. Table 2.2 provides a checklist that will help you review the search tips you've just learned.

Table 2.2 Internet Search Checklist			
Identify keywords	1.	2.	3.
Select subjects	1.	2.	3.
Define information	1. General	2. Specific	3. People-oriented
Information format	1. Text or document	2. Image, sound, or video file	3. Computer program
Pick best Internet system	1. Archie & file protocol	2. Gopher transfer	3. World Wide Web
List good sites	1.	2.	3.

Move from General to Specific

Searching is similar to detective work. You begin your investigation with very broad-based assumptions and information, then keep working until you find exactly what you want. As a general rule you will get more results from a search if you start with a general topic keyword or phrase than a very specific one. For example if you're looking for a copy of a new Senate bill, then start with the general subject area "U. S. government." If you're looking for information on vineyards in France, general topic keywords could be "wine" or "France."

From the results or hits of the general topic search you can fine tune your search for specifics. The reason to use this general-to-specific approach goes back to the way database indexes are created. If you search the Internet for the keyword phrase "vineyards in France," you might not find the tremendous amount of information about French vineyards that is indexed by the word "wine."

Specific Topics Require Narrow Searches

There's always a catch. Now that you've been told that starting with a general subject keyword is a good idea, it's time to add a "but if" clause. That is when you go extremely general in your search keyword or phrase you may get so many hits—and numerous irrelevant ones—that you don't know where to go next. For example, using the keyword "science" brings up a list of more than 16,000 Internet sites.

Clearly if you are a scientist, teacher, or student trying to quickly find the atomic weight of the element Boron, you could spend a week searching through these 16,000 sites. In this case you'd be better off trying the keyword "chemistry." Figure 2.3 shows a partial list of results from a search for Internet sites using the keyword "chemistry." The search engine found more than 2,300 possibilities! Finally, a search with the search term "periodic table" returns 337 choices; the first of which is the Periodic Table of the Elements (see fig. 2.4). If you are looking for specific data, then you can always try a very narrow search first. If the search produces no results, then you can broaden your search terms.

Some search systems return multiple hits based on **relevancy**. This means that the first hits on the list are deemed by the program to be more relevant to your search word or phrase than hits that are further down on the list.

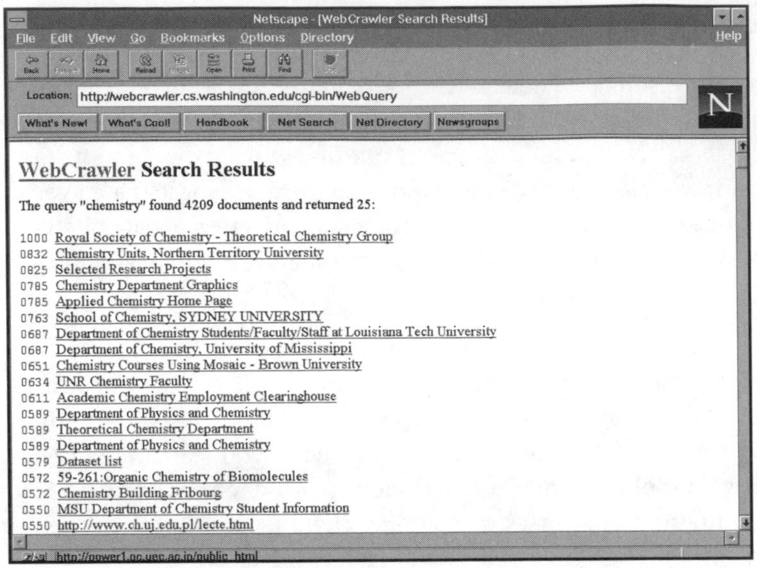

Fig. 2.3

Using the
WebCrawler
search engine, the
general keyword
"chemistry"
locates more than
2,300 Internet
sites.

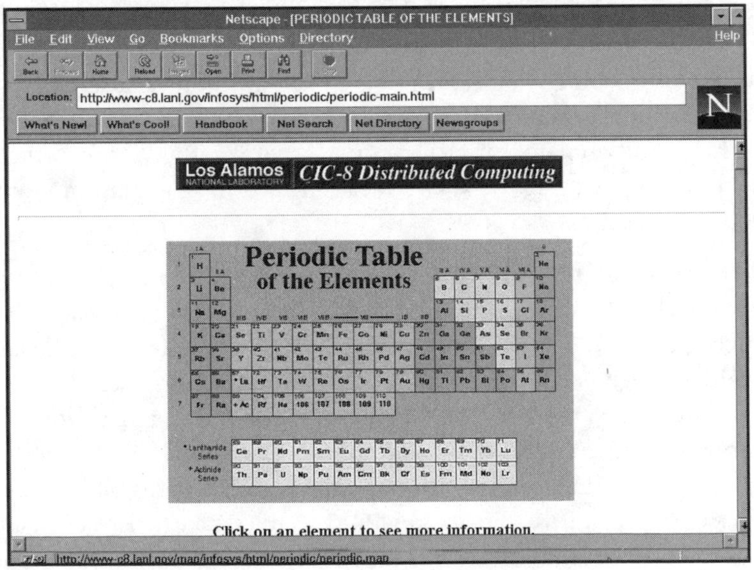

Fig. 2.4

Narrowing the
search term to
just "periodic
table" produces a
list of which the
first site is the
Periodic Table of
the Elements
shown here as a
Web page man-
aged by the Los
Alamos National
Laboratory.

Troubleshooting

What can I do if my search terms aren't producing any results or the results aren't even close to what I'm looking for?

If your search produces no results, then try it one more time and check your spelling. It's possible that you may have misspelled the keywords. If that doesn't work, try broadening your search keyword or phrase. Go from "Australian sheepdog" to "dog", and then, if you need to, try "pet."

If the hits or results of a search seem to be way off target from what you were looking for, then you need to try a new set of search words. If you're looking for information about buying and selling collector's automobiles and the keyword "antiques" brings up information predominately on furniture and jewelry, then try "vintage autos" or "collectable."

Computers Are Literal

Computers are precise in terms of how they process information and respond to search queries. If you were talking to a friend about the current state of baseball, you might ask him what he thinks about the Cardinals. Because you were talking about baseball your friend would instantly know that you were referring to the baseball team that goes by that name. Computers can't do this type of situational inference. And, if you go to one of the Internet Web Search engines and search for "cardinal," you get addresses for the following Internet sites:

- Pascal's Aviation Picturebook has information on the Cessna Cardinal (a plane)

- The Vatican Exhibit (Catholic Cardinals)

- Cardinal Information Systems (a computer company based in Finland)

- Bridgewater College in Pennsylvania (They have a Cardinal—the bird—in the college seal.)

There is another way in which the computer's literal interpretation of your keywords can produce erroneous results. A keyword can be part of another word. As an example, there are several Internet mailing lists that deal with the world of art. Using the keyword "Monet" (the painter) for a search of all of the messages of the list ARTIST-L for an entire month brings up seven related messages. Here is the copy from a portion of one of the messages.

"... I think it is unfair when artists make the assumptions that creating art and making a living are incompatible. Pursuing an "impractical dream" for the love of it and passion of it is admirable and noble. My question is this, can you pursue this dream and seek **monetary** compensation without sacrificing your artistic and personal integrity?"

You can quickly see the problem. The computer did find several references to Monet; however, they were all in fact part of the word monetary.

Start Your Search in a Specific Country

Let's imagine that you're doing a research paper on Egyptian hieroglyphics. If you had tons of money and could fly to any library in the world to get information, you'd probably start with a library in Cairo, Egypt as opposed to one in Calgary, Canada. The reason is obvious. Every country, state, and town in the world offers resources that are specific to that area.

The Internet is similar. The information resources of the Internet are spread out on millions of computers all over the world. True, some of the search tools that you'll use maintain large databases that point to many of these resources. But they will miss some things. If you know that the information that you're looking for might be found in a specific city or region, you may find more useful information by traveling to an Internet computer in that area and then doing a search.

Here's an example. I searched the Gopher system for information that fit the keyword "politics." First, I connected to a computer at the University of Koeln in Germany. It located more than 50 different papers and articles including:

- Politics under socialism

- Culture and society in postwar Italy

- Politics of the Bauhaus

The same keyword search at the Gopher site at the University of Michigan in the United States turned up these articles:

- Race and ethnicity in Chicago politics

- Melville and the politics of identity

- American Indian cultural politics

Each computer located several articles that were unique to the region. In the first case, articles about politics related to Europe and in the second case, articles about politics in the United States.

Just about now you might be wondering, "Where do I get a list of all of the Internet sites around the world?" There are several sites that maintain directories of other Internet sites. Following are a few addresses and suggestions that will come in handy if you want to begin your Internet search by region. Don't worry if you don't know how to connect to these sites right now. Part II of this book provides step-by-step instructions.

Gopher Sites Around the World

First, try the Gopher site at the University of Minnesota. The address is **gopher.tc.umn.edu**. When you connect there will be a selection titled "Other Gopher and Information Servers." Choose this and you'll get several options including "All the gopher servers in the world" and a region by region listing that includes areas such as the Middle East, South America, North America, etc.

If you know the area of the world that you want to visit, you're better off starting with a region. The "All the Gopher servers in the world" selection brings up an enormous (more than 150 kilobytes) alphabetical listing of Gopher sites. While this may seem nice, it is difficult to quickly find any one part of the world. However, if you're looking for an organization, this is great. It starts with the As, such as the American Association of Teachers of French Gopher, and moves through the alphabet with many international sites such as the Chinese University of Hong Kong Library. You can select any of these individual listings to instantly jump to their Internet computer.

If the University of Minnesota is busy, then try the University of Southern Mississippi Gopher site at **gopher://gopher.usm.edu**. Select the "World of Gopher" option, which then offers lists of Gopher sites by region, by subject, and U.S. Government sites.

World Wide Web Sites Around the World

CERN, the Physics Lab in Switzerland where the Web was originally developed maintains a Web site that has a listing of all of the Web servers in the world. The Web address is **http://www.w3.org/hypertext/ DataSources/WWW/Servers.html**.

This lists Web servers in alphabetical order by continent, country, and state.

Tip
The concept of starting at the most logical source also holds true of organizations and companies. If you're looking for information about Microsoft software products, then your first stop should be the Microsoft Internet site. If you don't know whether a company or organization has a site, you can use one of the search tools to keyword search for them.

Resources and Techniques

There are several Web sites that have sensitive maps (see fig. 2.5). These are pages that display maps of a region of the world or country. When you click on a specific area of the map you are transported to Web servers in that region. This is a fun and fast way to do some Internet globe-trotting.

Fig. 2.5
This Web site displays a sensitive map of Europe. When you click on the flag for a specific country you are transported to Web computers located there.

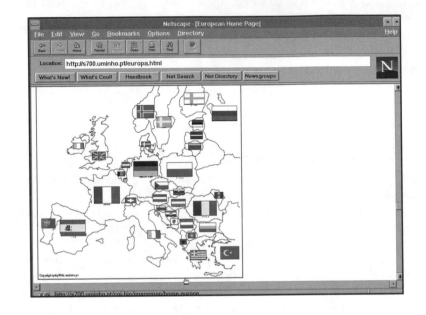

FTP Sites Around the World

You can use file transfer protocol to download a list of all of the FTP sites in the world that allow unregistered users to connect. You login as "anonymous" to these sites. Here are the addresses, directories, and filenames for lists of FTP sites.

FTP site address: **rtfm.mit.edu**
Subdirectory: **/pub/usenet/new.answers/ftp-list/**
Filename: **sitelist**

FTP site address: **garbo.uwasa.fi**
Subdirectory: **/pc/doc-net/**
Filename: **ftp-list.zip**

FTP site address: **oak.oakland.edu**
Subdirectory: **/pub/msdos/info/**
Filename: **ftp-list.zip**

Note that the last two files are .zip files. This means they are compressed with PKZIP and you'll need PKUNZIP to uncompress and use the file.

Summary

The terms, concepts, and advice in this chapter lay a foundation that will help you conduct successful searches on the Internet. After you do a few searches these concepts will start to become second nature, and, just like riding a bicycle, you'll soon hop right on and get going without giving it a second thought.

Resources and Techniques

Part II

Internet Search Tools

The Listserver

Jay

Tom

Sue

Kittens-l

Scuba-l

Joe

Politics-l

PATHFINDER

FROM TIME WARNER

Week of March 6 - 1:

HOT PAGE | TIME | Money

NEWS & FINANCE

Entertainment | VIBE | People | THE O.J. FILES

REVIEWS
MUSIC, MOVIES
TV, BOOKS &
MULTIMEDIA

Sports
Illustrated | TIME WARNER
ELECTRONIC
PUBLISHING | the
Virtual
Garden

TIME WARNER PRODUCTS

ABOUT | BULLETIN BOARDS | WRITE BACK | OFFERS | SEARCH | HELP

Today's Ne

• Dole: "Cut 4 Cabinet
• House Passes Tort Re
• Fuhrman: "I Didn't Fra

Hot This W

• Baseball's Dead End
• Greg Louganis--My Priv
• The Sounds of Science

Not loading images? Try here.

Netscape ~ [NLM HyperDOC: World-Wide Web (WWW) Server of the U.S. National Lib

File   Edit   View   Go   Bookmarks   Options   Directory   Help

Back   Forward   Home   Reload   Images   Open   Print   Find   Stop

Location: http://www.nlm.nih.gov/

What's New!   What's Cool!   Handbook   Net Search   Net Directory   Newsgroups

NATIONAL LIBRARY
OF
MEDICINE

Welcome to HyperDOC
A Multimedia/Hypertext Resource of the
U.S. National Library of Medicine (NLM)

Donald A. B. Lindberg, M.D.
Director

Pekka@Finland | Chris/USGS | Mobeus@Bellco

helo!!!

7.1 fps   34 Kbps   1.2 fps   28 Kbps   .3 fps   34

Back   Forward   Home   Reload   Images   Open   Print   Find   Stop

Location: http://www.umr.edu/~cisapps/MSDS.html

What's New!   What's Cool!   Handbook   Net Search   Net Directory   Newsgroups

Enter a MSDS Search Criteria Below:

• **Chemical Name:** TriNitroTolulene

Chapter 3

Searching the World Wide Web

Although it's the Internet's new kid on the block, the World Wide Web (Web for short) generates cover stories on international magazines like *Time* and *Business Week*, captures the imagination of corporate giants ranging from General Electric to Viacom, and convinces the most computer-shy individuals that they need to be "on the Net."

The Web is nothing short of a new communications medium. And, much as the printing press, telephone, radio, television, and cable have had a significant impact on society, the Web has the potential to completely change the way people around the world communicate ideas and search for and retrieve information. In this chapter you will learn:

- How to search for and locate pictures, audio, and video that are available on the Web

- How to use features of Web software (browsers) to navigate, search, and retrieve information

- What's involved in accessing other Internet systems (Gopher, FTP, Newsgroups) from the Web

- How to connect with and use Web searchers to locate specific resources

- Web catalogs that link you to a variety of subject-based information

Multimedia Is Just a Click Away

One of the reasons the World Wide Web has gained such positive notoriety is because Web sites provide easy access to multimedia—text, images (pictures and graphic artwork), sound, and video. Links embedded in Web pages can deliver these forms of media directly to your PC. And, depending upon how you use your Web software, you can either play or view these images, sound, and video clips or download them for future use. In fact, a majority of Web sites have built-in pictures, known as **inline images**, which display on-screen when you connect with them. Figure 3.1 shows a small inline image that depicts a scene from the American Civil War. If you click on this image, a larger, high-resolution JPEG digital photograph loads to your computer as seen in figure 3.2.

Fig. 3.1

The inline image on this Web page is a link to a JPEG graphic file. Click on it and the digital photograph loads to your PC.

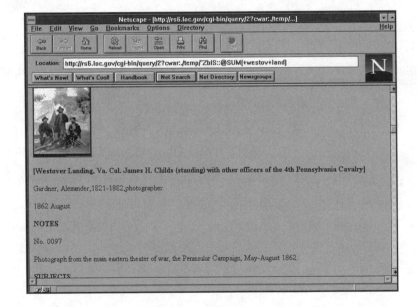

As a Net searcher, when you locate a Web site devoted to a specific subject there's a good chance you'll not only find text files, but also images and perhaps even videos and sound recordings. Also, you can use the Web to search for these forms of multimedia. Here are a few examples of the practical applications of multimedia:

- You'd love to get photographs of the Civil War taken by Mathew Brady in the 1860s for a report on American History. From the Library of Congress Web site you can keyword search through an extensive collection of images and view or download the pictures (**http://lcweb.loc.gov**).

- You're thinking about taking up the sport of hang gliding but you'd like to see someone else do it first. Find hang gliding videos at Stanford University (**http://cougr.stanford.edu:7878/**).

- It's Sunday afternoon and you'd like to sit back and listen to an interesting radio program. Tune into Quirks and Quarks, a weekly radio program broadcast both live and via the Web by the Canadian Broadcasting Corporation (**http://debra.dgbt.doc.ca/cbs/cbc.html**).

Fig. 3.2
Here, the full picture of officers from the 4th Pennsylvania Calvary appears on-screen.

Web Page Fundamentals

Your journey into the Web begins at a home page—the first or opening document for every Web site. Figure 3.3 shows the home page for the Web site called "MasterCook." This home page is a good example of the elements that you'll find on most home pages. Here we're using the Web software program Netscape to load and view the home page.

The title of the page is shown at the top of the screen. The Web address for this site appears just below the Netscape button bar in the location window. The page has a large inline image or graphic, some text, and several hyperlinks—both text and pictures. When you use your mouse and aim and click on a hyperlink you jump to a new Web page, either another page at this site, or a page on another Web site or computer. Notice that the cursor has changed from a standard arrow to a small hand as it points at a hyperlink.

Fig. 3.3
This Web site features information for people who like to cook. Notice the inline image and the links that lead to more information.

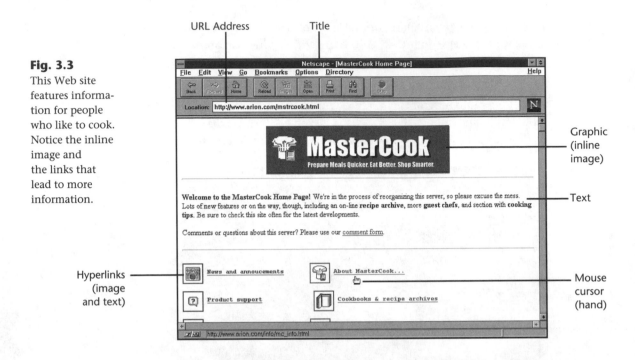

Basic Web Terminology

Browser—The generic name for the Windows and Macintosh-based software programs that you use to connect with the Web.

Home page—The starting point for a specific Web site.

HTML—Acronym for Hypertext Markup Language, the programming language that creates Web pages.

Hypertext—Refers to computer-based documents (like Web pages) where you can jump from one location to another by clicking on highlighted links.

Inline Image—The pictures that appear on Web pages.

Link—A word or image in a Web page that, when you click on it, will jump to another document or resource.

URL—Stands for Uniform Resource Locator. It is the address system that you use to access Web sites and other Internet resources.

Web, WWW, W3—Some of the different terms that can be used to refer to the World Wide Web.

Hypertext and Hyperlinks: The Language of the Web

Hypertext is the glue that holds the Web together. In fact, Hypertext Markup Language, HTML, is the programming language used to create Web pages. HTML enables people who author Web pages to incorporate links in their pages that point to any other Web site, document, or resource on any other Internet computer. The links can be either the inline images or the text on a page. Figure 3.4 shows a Web page that uses both inline images and hypertext as links to other documents and Web sites.

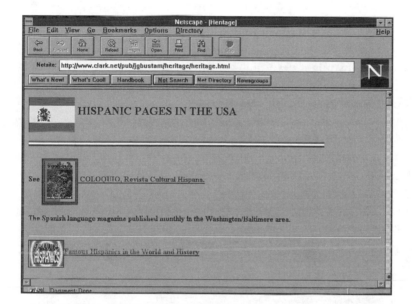

Fig. 3.4
The links in a Web page can be either the inline images or the text itself.

Note

You can easily identify the links on Web pages. Text-based links appear in a different color than the rest of the text on a page. When inline images are links they appear with a thin, colored border surrounding the image. Hypertext and hyperlinks are commonly used in both Windows and Mac-based Help systems.

What does this mean for you? Hypertext presents information in a non-linear fashion. In other words, you click on these links and jump randomly from one Web page to another and may be on a computer that's geographically 5,000 miles away from the first computer. You jump by using your mouse to click on the hypertext links.

II

Search Tools

If you've never tried the Web before, this system may sound like pure chaos. In reality, Web jumping or surfing works well as a way to find information. Web page authors generally incorporate links that bring you to sites that have related information. For example, a site devoted to the environment may have a link to a Sierra Club Web site, which may in turn have a link to the Web home page for the Center for Renewable Energy. This unintentional interconnection of related (and sometimes unrelated) information allows you to move through the Web in a manner that emulates the way people think or brainstorm as one thought leads to another.

You'll find that Web surfing can be a very productive way to locate relevant information about your specific subject area. And, the information you find through surfing might never show up with a keyword search.

URL: The Web Page Address

The Web uses an address system known as **Uniform Resource Locators**, URLs for short. Addresses for Web sites begin with the URL format http://. For example, **http://www.mcp.com** brings you to the Macmillan Computer Publishing Web site, which has terrific information on Macmillan's computer books, shareware programs, and online ordering. (See fig. 3.5.) Most Web browsers have an "Open" button on the toolbar that pops up a dialog box where you can directly enter a URL address.

Fig. 3.5
You access the Macmillan Computer Publishing Web site by using the URL address **http://www. mcp.com**.

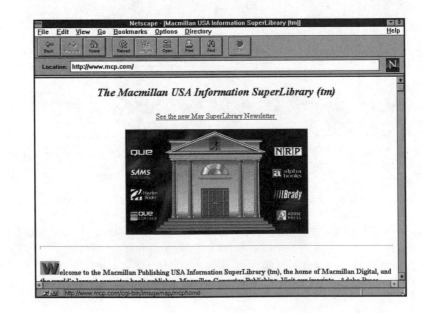

URLs Take You Beyond the Web

The truly great aspect of the Web is that you can also enter URLs to jump to Gopher or FTP sites, read newsgroup messages, or begin a Telnet session. In fact, every Internet system and search mechanism can be accessed via the Web. Here are the various Internet systems and the URL address formats you need to use to get to these other systems and the resources they hold.

Internet System	URL Address Format
Gopher sites	gopher://<gopher site address>
FTP sites	ftp://<ftp site address>
Newsgroups	news:<name of newsgroup>
Web sites	http://<Web site address>
Telnet session	telnet://<telnet address> (You may need a password once you connect to a computer via Telnet.)

URL Address Tips

If you're leaping from one site to another by clicking on links in Web pages, you don't have to worry about entering URL addresses. However, on many occasions you'll read about a Web site in a magazine, or a friend will give you the URL for a site they enjoy. When this happens you need to enter the URL address into your browser.

Nine times out of 10, you'll enter an address and be at your site within seconds. However, there are times when you can't connect. There are a few tips regarding URL addresses that will help prevent or minimize frustration.

■ Always make sure you enter the address exactly as it appears. The number one reason for not connecting to a Web site is incorrectly entering the address. If you get an error message like Error Accessing or Failed DNS lookup, enter the address a second time. You may have accidentally made a typographical error. Even an extra space in an address—for example, **box.ht ml**—can prevent a connection.

■ If an URL address doesn't work, try a root address. Many home pages actually reside in complex subdirectories on a computer. It's possible that the information has moved to another location on the Web computer. For example, the following is the address for an electronic art gallery in New York City:

http://www.egallery.com/egallery/homepage.html

Search Tools

Tip
Web documents and servers do change their addresses. Good ones will leave a forwarding address; bad ones just seem to disappear.

The address tells you that this home page resides on a commercial server (**www.egallery.com**) that has a special area for the gallery. It's possible that the company also lets other New York City vendors operate Web pages on the computer. So, if the full address doesn't work, try again but eliminate the ending:

> **http://www.egallery.com/egallery**

And if that doesn't work, go one more step:

> **http://www.egallery.com**

It's very likely that you will connect with the commercial company's home page and then be able to find links to the art gallery.

Troubleshooting Troublesome Addresses

You're certain that you entered the correct address, but you still can't connect. There are a few other things that can prevent a connection.

■ The host is busy. Wait a few minutes (longer if necessary) and try again.

■ The server is down. The Web server may be literally unplugged. Sometimes computers are pulled off-line to be repaired or upgraded.

■ The server/home page has moved. It's possible for a server to get a new address. If this happens, your old address will no longer work.

■ The server or home page has died. Yes, it is possible for a server to completely vanish. You can be pretty confident that NASA won't pull the plug on their Web site. However, it's possible that commercial companies, information providers, or even college students that host Web home pages may simply stop doing it. If this happens, the server's gone.

Tip
If you're mysteriously not connecting to any of the resources, it's possible that your Internet TCP/IP connection has disconnected. Depending upon your system and software, you may not realize this has happened (unless you hear the phone connection disconnect) and your system may, or may not, automatically try to reestablish the connection.

Just Follow the Links

Let's take a look at one example of Web searching to illustrate how you can rapidly jump from one Web site (or computer) to another that may be thousands of miles away. Remember, you make a "jump" by clicking on a hyperlink. These links actually contain the URL address for the site you're jumping to. The URL address doesn't appear next to the link because it is "hidden" in the HTML programming language. With Netscape you can see the URL address that a link points to as it appears at the bottom of the screen when you position your cursor directly over a link. In this example we are surfing to locate information about South America.

1. We begin with the Hispanic Pages in the USA Web site. This home page has a variety of information about the Hispanic culture and links to related resources. The URL address is **http://www.clark.net/pub/ jgbustam/heritage/heritage.html**. We click on a link that jumps to the Latin American Network Information Center.

2. We are now at the Latin American Network Information Center, a Web site maintained by the University of Texas. It offers a collection of links to documents and reports about Latin America. The URL address is **http://lanic.utexas.edu/**. Because this site has a variety of links that directly relate to the information search, you'll want to return to the site and follow several links. To begin, click on the "World Wide Contacts in Latin America" link.

3. The World Wide Contacts in Latin America Web page is located on a computer in the United Kingdom. It may seem ironic to jump from a computer in Texas to one in the UK for information about Latin America, but that's the nature of the Web. This page offers a detailed listing of bookstores that are in cities in Latin America. The URL address is **http://www.cup.cam.ac.uk/Moreinfo/LAmCaribb.html**.

Browsers Make It Happen

The software programs that enable you to navigate through the Web are called **browsers**. There are about two dozen different Windows- and Macintosh-based browser programs in the marketplace. Certain browsers are free for individuals (such as NCSA Mosaic) and you can download copies from FTP sites. Other browsers (such as Netscape) offer both evaluation and commercial versions. There are also commercial-only browsers (such as Internet-In-A-Box Air Mosaic) that you can purchase at computer stores.

Two of the most popular browser programs are Netscape (created by Netscape Communications) and NCSA Mosaic (created by the National Center for Supercomputing Applications). Figure 3.6 shows the White House home page (**http.//www.whitehouse.gov**) loaded with Netscape.

Key Browser Features

All browser programs incorporate several common navigational functions that help you navigate and locate information and Web sites. We'll take a look at how Netscape handles these, but you should be able to locate similar functions on any Web browser.

II

Search Tools

Fig. 3.6
The Netscape Web browser with the White House site loaded.

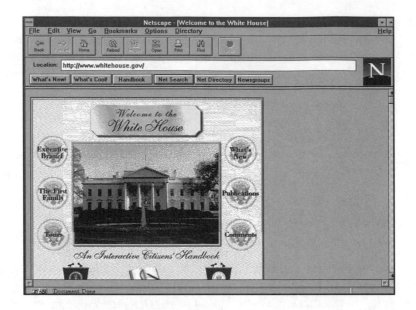

Forward / Backward Toolbar Buttons

Essential for Web navigation, almost every Web browser incorporates the Forward / Backward buttons on the toolbar. After you click on a link on a page you are brought to a new Web page. The backward button takes you back to the previous Web page. After you have gone "backward" you can then use the forward button to jump to the page you just came from.

History

The History function keeps track of the Web sites that you visit during one Web session. You can use History to quickly return to any site that you've visited. History becomes a valuable tool after you surf through several links and want to rapidly jump back to a site you visited perhaps as many as 10 links ago. With Netscape you have two steps for jumping to a site you've already visited:

1. Open the Go pull-down menu.

2. Select one of the sites listed at the bottom of this pull-down menu.

You can also use the View History feature.

1. Open the Go pull-down menu.

2. Select View History. This opens a History information box, which shows both the names and URL addresses for sites you've visited. You can also make a bookmark of any of these sites. Figure 3.7 shows this feature.

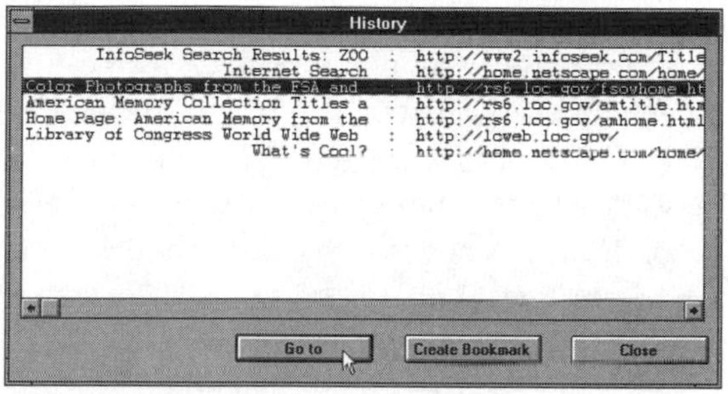

Fig. 3.7

The History feature in Netscape (and most browsers) helps you quickly jump back to a site you've already visited during one Web session. Netscape lets you add sites you've visited to the bookmark list.

Bookmarks

Netscape uses the term bookmarks and NCSA Mosaic calls them hotlist items, but the concept is the same. You find a Web site that's absolutely perfect for your information retrieval needs—perhaps it's one of the Web Searcher home pages. You can add the URL address for this site to a list that the browser saves. Then, during any future Web session, you can quickly jump to this site by selecting the saved URL. Figure 3.8 shows bookmarks that have been saved with Netscape. You can also create subcategories for your bookmarks. For example, an entire collection of bookmarks that fit under the category of "arts."

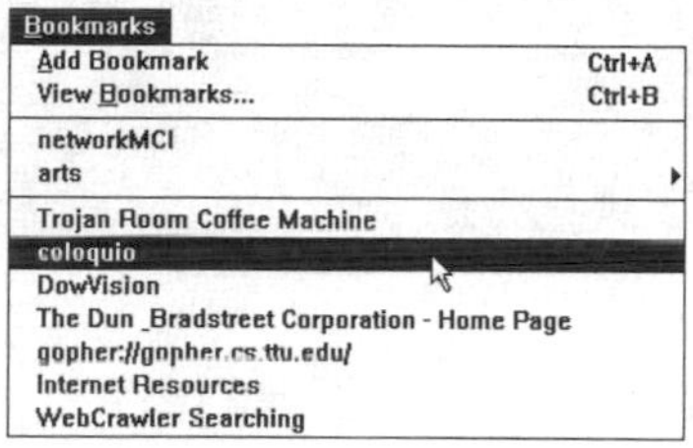

Fig. 3.8

Bookmarks are a convenient way to save the URLs for your favorite Web sites. Then, you can quickly jump to these sites during any session.

Find

Most browsers incorporate a Find feature directly on the toolbar—and many times the icon on the button is appropriately a little pair of binoculars. This button opens a dialog box where you can enter a keyword or phrase. (With Netscape, Ctrl+F also opens this feature.) The browser searches the currently loaded Web page to see if there is a match.

II

Search Tools

When would this be helpful? This feature becomes valuable in two distinct situations. For example, when you reach a Web page that is very long—perhaps it's a Web page that offers links to every known government-based Internet site. You can use the Find feature to quickly see whether there's a site for the Transportation Department by using the keyword "transportation." Another situation would be when you locate and load an electronic document that's huge—the digital version of *Moby Dick*. You can use Find (and Find again) to search for every reference to "Ahab," the main character (in addition to the whale) in *Moby Dick*. Figure 3.9 shows the use of the Find feature using Netscape. Other options let you decide if the "Find" should match case (that is, Culture as opposed to culture) and whether you want to search UP (which means toward the top of the page/document) or DOWN (which means toward the bottom).

Net Search

The Netscape browser has a series of buttons just above the main viewing area. One of these is "Net Search." When you click on this button Netscape loads a Web page that's on the Netscape Communications Web server. The page offers information and links to several Web searching systems. One, InfoSeek (which is detailed later in this chapter), lets you enter a keyword or search term directly from this page and begin a search. Because the Net Search page is on a Web server and not built into the browser, the information will undergo changes and updates on a regular basis. It's a convenient way to have instant access to several Web searching tools. The only downside is that the Netscape server itself may be too busy to allow a connection.

Fig. 3.9
The Web browser Find feature is a convenient way to search through the text of the Web page that is currently loaded.

How To Save Web Pages

It's the end of a long day and you've just found the perfect Web page. It has links to a hundred different sites that all relate to your topic. There's valuable information here. But, you're tired and you want to quit. You could simply save this site on your bookmark or hotlist and begin again tomorrow. However, there's another option that may be even more useful; you can save this Web page on your hard drive. There are four possible reasons you might want to do this:

- You can reference the information on this page without starting another Internet session—simply load the page.

- If you want to explore the links on the page, you're ready to go—no need to worry about whether you can successfully connect to the Web site to begin.

- You can copy and incorporate a portion of the HTML programming code from a Web page into your own HTML documents.

- You can access the text and, if there are no copyright issues, even load it directly into any word-processing program.

To use this option, locate a Web page you want to save. Then, if you are using Netscape, follow these steps:

1. Open the File pull-down menu.

2. Select the Save As option (Ctrl+S).

3. The Save As dialog box appears. (See figure 3.10.)

4. Enter a filename in the File Name dialog box.

5. Select a file type in the Save File as Type option box. You can either save the file (the Web page) as a Source file (*.htm), a Text file (*.txt), or any other type of file.

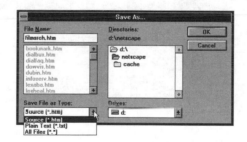

Fig. 3.10
The Netscape Save As feature makes it easy to save Web pages as either HTML documents (*.htm) or as text-based files.

If you choose to save the page as a source file with an .htm extension you are saving it as source HTML code. This will keep all of the HTML programming language, the formatting, and behind-the-scenes links in the page. When you load this file during a future Netscape/Web session the file loads and appears exactly as you saw it when you first connected—except inline images will not appear. That's because when you save the file you save the text and the links,

II

Search Tools

but not the graphics (which load separately). The next time you want to load and use this page with Netscape you:

1. Open the File pull-down menu.

2. Select Open File (Ctrl+O).

3. Locate and double-click on the name of the file that you want to load.

If you save the Web page as a text file (.txt), the page is translated into ASCII text and the HTML formatting codes are stripped away. You can then load this text file in Netscape, or in any word processing program.

Figure 3.11 shows a page from the DowVision Web site that has been saved as an HTML file (.htm) and reloaded. The right half of the screen displays the source code for the top of this page. If this page had been saved as a text file (.txt), then a line like

```
<B>Enter Search Terms: </B><input type="text" name=Search SIZE=24>
```

would only appear as "Enter Search Terms:" because the HTML code would be taken out.

Fig. 3.11
This screen shows a Web page that has been saved as an .htm file and reloaded off-line. The source html code appears in the View Source box.

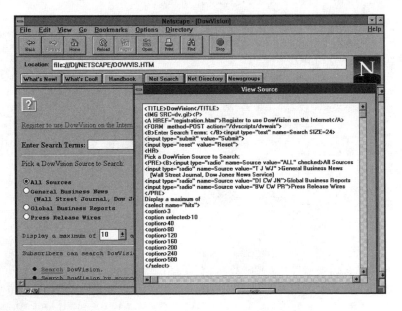

How To Download Files

In addition to saving Web pages, you can save other types of files that you find through your exploration of the Web. For example, you might find an image file (JPEG, GIF, etc.), a sound file (AU or WAV), or even a software program file (EXE)—such as the latest version of your favorite browser—that you want to download to your hard drive. Again, if Netscape is your browser, follow these directions:

1. Using your mouse, point the cursor over the link on the Web page that "points" to the file.

2. Hold down the Shift key on your keyboard and click on the left mouse button.

3. In the Save As dialog box enter the name of the file, making certain that you give it the proper extension for the type of file. So, if it's a JPEG image file, save it as "picture.jpg," or if it's an executable program, call it "picture.exe."

You can then open the file (or run the file if it is an executable).

> **Note**
>
> Netscape has a built-in image viewer and you can save and load most popular graphic file formats directly into the Netscape viewing area.

Web Searchers Scour the Net for You

Web searchers are computer programs that search the Web on a periodic basis (as frequently as every day) and collect information about new Web pages. This information is then compiled into a searchable database. Depending on the searcher, the information collected may contain only the name and address of home pages, or it may also include information about the contents of a page, the words in a text-based document, or information about multimedia files. Some Web searchers don't go out to look for their information, but rather ask people who create home pages to send in details of their page. In either case, the information is stored in a database that resides on the searcher's World Wide Web server.

II

Search Tools

You connect to a Web Searcher just as you do any other Web resource, by entering the URL address for the site into your browser. When the searcher's home page appears, you have an opportunity to enter keywords or search terms to locate the resources that meet your needs. Recent versions of NCSA Mosaic, Netscape, and Spry's Air Mosaic, all support a forms feature. The forms feature enables the browser to present fill-in-the-blank boxes, check buttons, and pull-down menu selections on-screen.

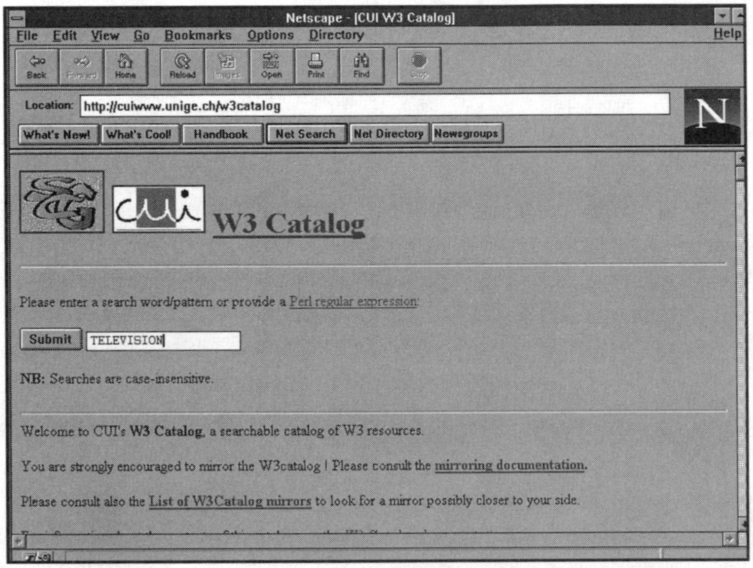

Fig. 3.12
The Netscape browser uses the forms interface in a search using the W3 Catalog search system. Enter search words in the on-screen box.

The result of a search is a list of Web locations that may contain the information you request, along with hyperlinks that take you directly to those sites. Sometimes, the list simply has the name of the home page. Other times it includes a short description of what the site offers and tells you how large the home pages or files are that you can access.

> **Note**
>
> The Web continues to explode. In March of 1994 there were approximately 1,200 Web sites. By March of 1995 the number had skyrocketed to more than 27,000 sites. According to Business Week magazine the number of Web sites doubles every 53 days. All tolled there are more than 2 million Web pages, documents, images, sound, and video files with URL addresses. Even if you clicked on links as fast as you could you'd never be able to reach all of the resources on the Web in your lifetime.

Web Searcher Options Can Refine a Search

Each Web searcher has its own unique search system as well as a unique database of Internet resources and Web sites. Some only ask you to enter a keyword to begin a search. Others give you on-screen options with click-on buttons and pull-down menus that offer refinements to the search. Here is an overview of six of the most common options and their functions.

- **Truncate/complete words.** Select keywords as substrings or complete words. In other words, should it look for truncated matches? So, if your keyword is "paint" the searcher would also locate records related to "painting" and "painters" if you select substring. Complete words or exact matches will only locate records that have identical matches to your search terms.

- **Case sensitive option.** You can determine whether you want the searcher to find records that are exact matches to the case of your word(s). For example, is it okay to find a record that includes "brazil" with a lowercase b if you have entered "Brazil" with an uppercase B?

- **Specify domain.** You may be able to narrow the search down to specific Internet domains, such as .edu for educational sites and .com for commercial sites.

- **What to search.** You may have options to search for matches with Web site titles, URL addresses, descriptions of the Web sites, and keywords that are included on the home page of the site. Usually the searcher default is for all of these.

- **Boolean search options.** You may be able to selectively choose Boolean operators with a default being all of the keywords. This means an automatic "AND" is placed between the keywords and the results will be Internet Web sites that contain all of the keywords—but not necessarily in the exact sequence that you enter. Another choice is a Boolean "OR," which would find records with any one of the keywords.

- **Specify hits.** Choose the number of records or hits that you will get from a search with choices ranging from 25 through an unlimited number.

Now you know what Web Searchers do, and the basics of how to effectively use them. Following are brief reviews of some of the most popular Web Searchers. The reviews provide the URL address of each searcher, a description of how the searcher works, and the types and quantity of records that the searcher can locate.

ALIWEB

URL address: **http://www.cs.indiana.edu/aliweb/form.html**

The ALIWEB searcher is mirrored on several Web servers. This means that the database and the search forms have been copied and are available for access via these other Web sites. For Web users who live in the U.S., the mirror site at Indiana University (at the preceding address) often has faster response time than the original site in the United Kingdom.

People who maintain a Web home page write descriptions of their services in the HTML file format. This file has a link to their home page. They then tell ALIWEB about the file, which ALIWEB retrieves and combines into a searchable database. The results of an ALIWEB search are listed in order of relevance (and are scored) to your search criteria with the resources and links at the top of the page more relevant than those later down the page. Figure 3.13 shows the search input page and figure 3.14 shows the results of a search.

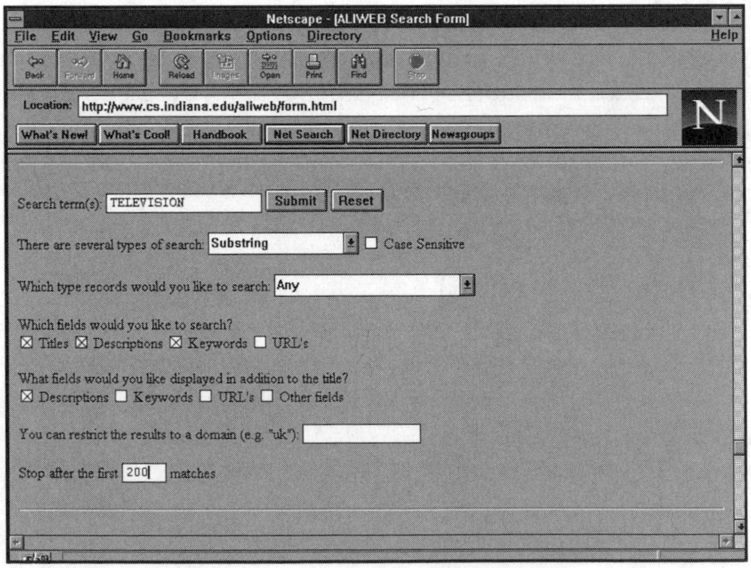

Fig. 3.13
The search input page for ALIWEB gives you a few options to refine your search.

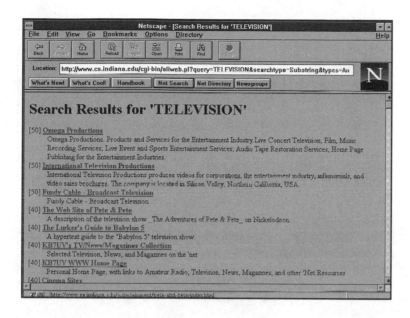

Fig. 3.14
Here are the results
of an ALIWEB
search for the key-
word television.
The search looks for
matching keywords
in the description
of what the site
offers.

CUI Search Catalog

URL address: **http://cuiwww.unige.ch/w3catalog**

W3 Catalog is a searchable catalog of resources that's created from a number
of manually maintained lists available on the Web. The result of a search is a
chronological list of resources that meet your search criteria. Thus, if you do
a search in September, the first entries on the list represent sites that came
online in September and later entries date back to July, January, and so on.
Listings also usually include a short paragraph description of the sites. The
name of the sites (which are underlined) are hyperlinks that take you to that
site if you click on it.

EINet Galaxy—Search the World Wide Web

URL address: **http://galaxy.einet.net/www/www.html**

This searcher maintains an index that points to Web home pages around the
world. When you connect, the home page automatically opens a simple-to-
use search dialog box. The result of a search is a name-only hyperlink list of
possible resources. The list is prioritized in a fashion similar to a WAIS (Wide
Area Information Server) search, with the first entry receiving 1,000 points
and the remaining entries getting fewer points. Each entry also indicates the
size of the document or home page that you will jump to. This is useful because it tells you how long it will take to load that page. Figure 3.15 shows
the search input page and figure 3.16 shows the results of a search.

II

Search Tools

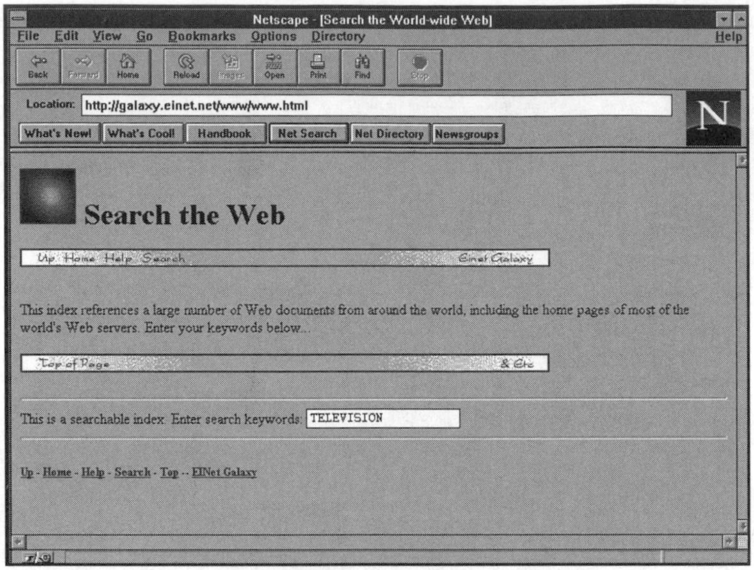

Fig. 3.15
The search input page for EINet's search.

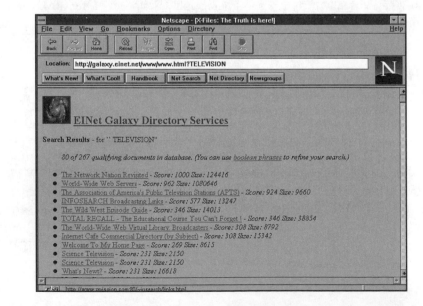

Global Network Academy Meta-Library

URL address: **http://uu-gna.mit.edu:8001/uu-gna/meta-library/ index.html**

GNA is a non-profit corporation incorporated in Texas. Affiliated with the UseNet University project, it has a long-term goal of creating a fully accredited online university. This searcher is one of the information management tools that GNA offers. Figure 3.17 shows the results of a search.

Fig. 3.16
The search results for EINet's search: A succinct list including a priority rating system and size of the documents and files.

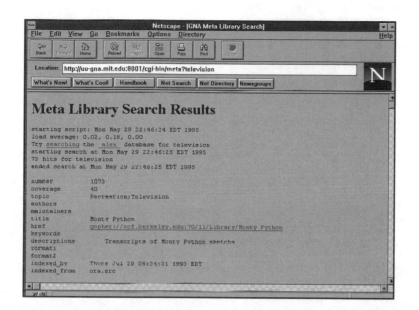

Fig. 3.17
The results of the
search with GNA.

InfoSeek

URL address: **http://www.infoseek.com**

InfoSeek is one of the new breed of commercial Web search systems that are cashing in on the fact that people don't mind paying for information if they can quickly locate what they're looking for. InfoSeek has several "subscription" options ranging from a per-use option where you pay $.20 for each search to a monthly $9.95 fee that gives you 100 queries.

InfoSeek does seem to be more diverse, if not more comprehensive, in its database offerings than other Web searchers. They've indexed 250,000 Web pages, 10,000 newsgroups, and articles from more than 100 computer publications. The newsgroup searching is unique because you can enter a search keyword like "adventure" and you'll get articles from various newsgroups.

Figure 3.18 shows some of the searching options that you have.

InfoSeek allows for natural language search expressions such as "Where can I go scuba diving?" Search results tell you the size of the various home pages—this is useful because you may not want to jump to a home page that's 300,000 bytes in size because of the long load time. Figure 3.19 shows the results of a search. You can try InfoSeek for a limited time at no charge. If you just want more information send e-mail to **info@infoseek.com**.

II

Search Tools

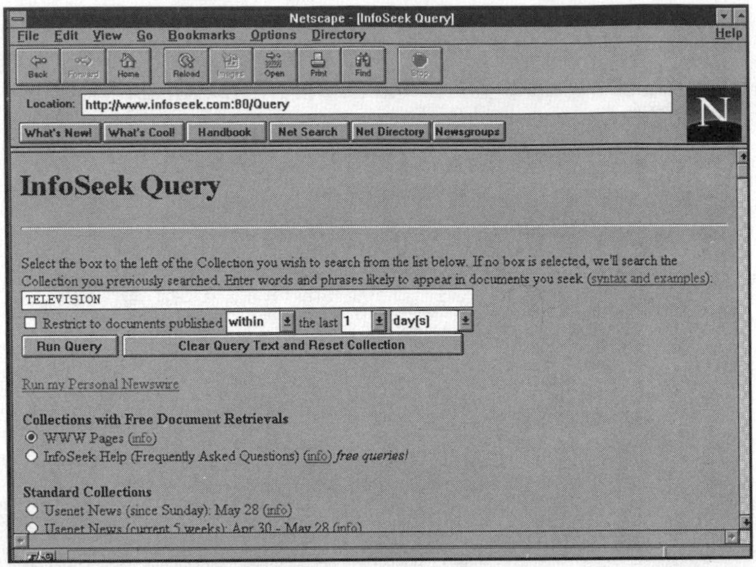

Fig. 3.18
InfoSeek lets you search through a database of 250,000 Web sites and articles from 10,000 newsgroups.

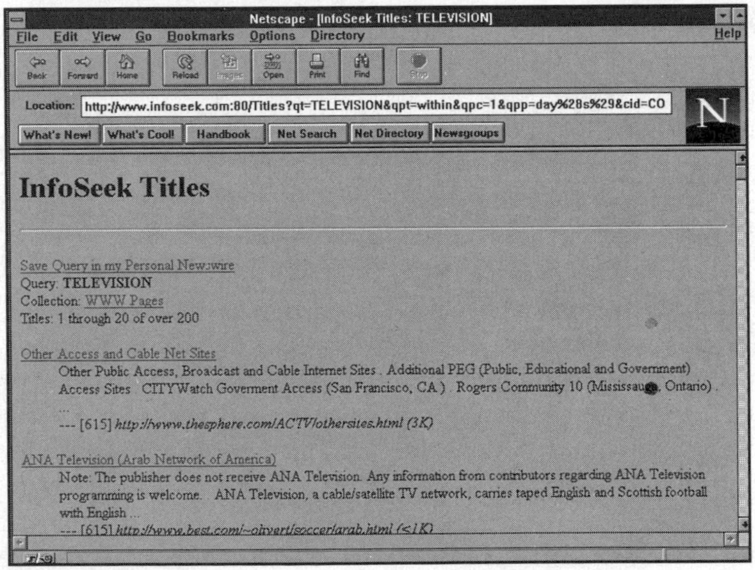

Fig. 3.19
The results from an InfoSeek search provide information about the site or resource.

Lycos

URL address: **http://lycos.cs.cmu.edu/**

Lycos is a research program that focuses on information retrieval and discovery on the Web. Lycos currently does its retrieval based on abstracts of Web documents, and it claims to have a database of more than 4 million unique

URL addresses. There are several computers connected to this searcher and you can pick and choose the one that is currently least busy—which means you'll get your results faster. In all, Lycos runs six different computers: Lycos 2 and 3 are Sparc 2s, Lycos 5 and 6 are Sparc 5s, and Lycos 10 and 11 are Pentium 90s. You might try the URL **http://query1.lycos.cs.cmu.edu/ lycos-form.html** to get a direct connection to one of the searching computers. There are approximately 300,000 users per week, up from an average of 50,000 in November '94. When the load or number of users on the system exceeds a certain limit, access is halted for other users. You can register your Web site with Lycos from the home page. Figure 3.20 shows the search input page and figure 3.21 shows the results of a search.

Nomad Gateway
URL address: **http://www.rns.com/cgi-bin/nomad**

This Web resource searching site represents a joint effort between Rockwell Network Systems and Cal Poly, San Luis Obispo to develop a pool of replicated Web resource locators. The result of your search is a list of single line entries, each of which is a hyperlink to another Web resource. Figure 3.23 shows the search input page.

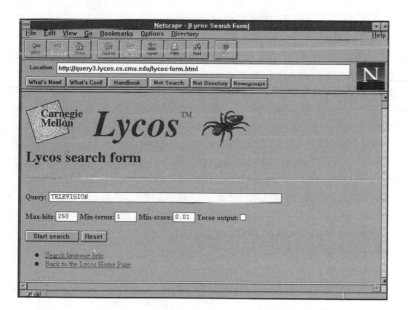

Fig. 3.20
The search input page for Lycos.

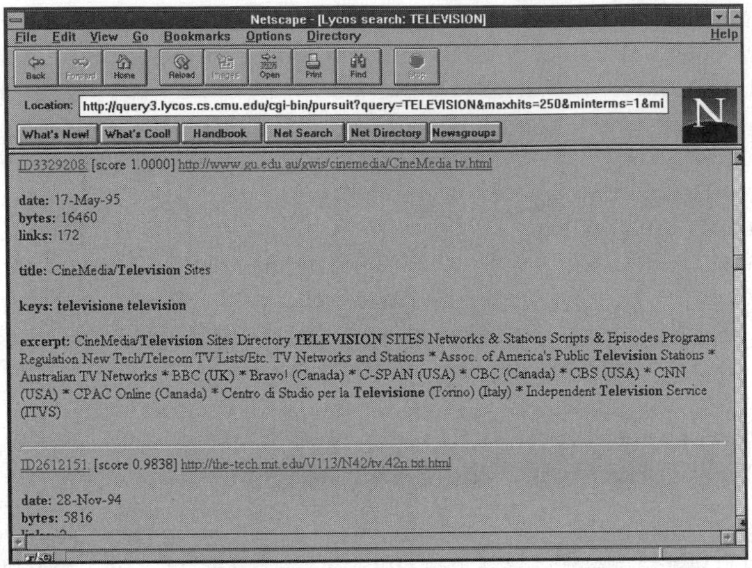

Fig. 3.21
The search results
page for Lycos
includes descrip-
tive text with
the search term
highlighted. The
search for the
keyword "televi-
sion" retrieves
4,300 Web
documents.

WebCrawler Searcher
URL address: **http://webcrawler.cs.washington.edu/WebCrawler/Home.html**

Developed by Brian Pinkerton at the University of Washington, the
WebCrawler program focuses on accumulating information about the specific
documents that reside on Web servers. The WebCrawler database is approximately 100 megabytes with a total record base of 700,000 documents. It creates indexes of the documents it locates on the Web and lets you keyword
search these indexes. It's very easy to do a search with WebCrawler, enter
keyword(s), and begin. The result of a search is a list of sites, home pages, and
documents that match your criteria. The list is prioritized. The first resource
receives a rating of 1,000 and should most closely match your criteria, while
a resource farther down on the list is less likely to match. From the simple
search entry form you have the option to select the number of "hits" that are
returned up to as many as 500. Figure 3.23 shows the search input page and
figure 3.24 shows the results of a search.

W3 Search Engines
URL address: **http://cuiwww.unige.ch/meta-index.html**

This is the same computer system that brings you the CUI catalog. Here, the
home page presents a list of several different Web searchers. Next to the
name of each searcher is a box where you can enter your search phrase and

then submit it directly to the searcher. As an alternative, you can click the name of the searcher and go to its home page. You'll also find forms to conduct FINGER, WAIS, and Jughead searches.

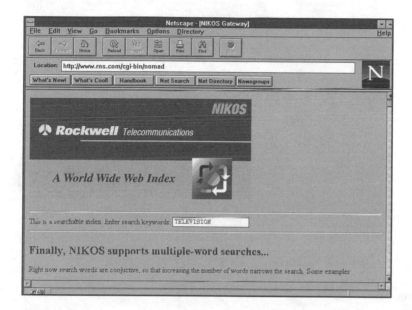

Fig. 3.22
The search input page for Nomad.

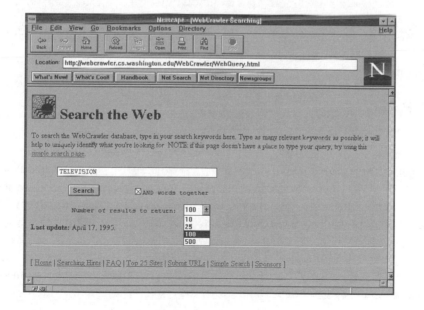

Fig. 3.23
The search input page for the WebCrawler.

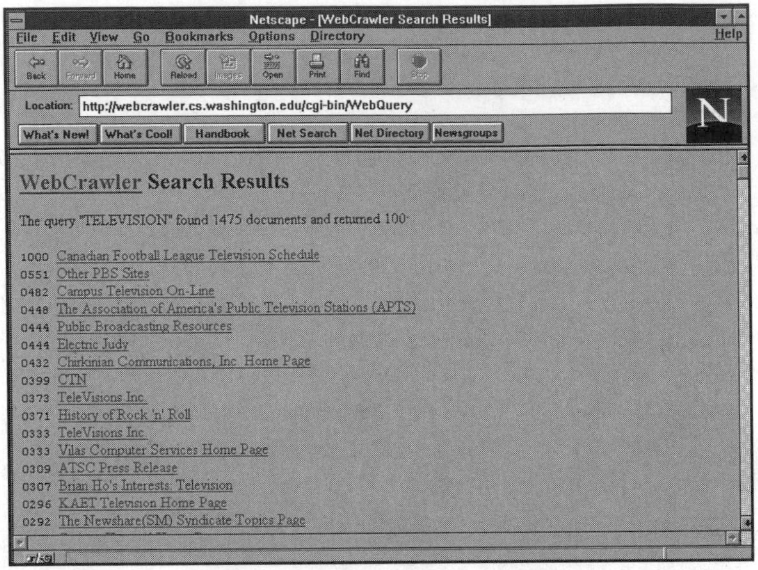

Fig. 3.24
The results of a WebCrawler search provide a priority-based list of hyperlinks to resources.

WWWW—The World Wide Web Worm
URL address: **http://www.cs.colorado.edu/home/mcbryan/ WWWW.html**

This searcher gets used more than 2 million times every month. The home page offers several options for refining a search including Boolean "and" and "or" as well as number of hits and selection of what types of records to search. Figure 3.25 shows the search input page and figure 3.26 shows the results of a search.

Yahoo
URL address: **http://www.yahoo.com/**

A comprehensive database of Web sites and pages. There are more than 50,000 entries that reference different Web resources. The site adds about 100-200 new links each day. Web pages are organized into subject categories such as art, entertainment, and social sciences. You can also search the entire database for specific keyword and search term matches. According to the statistics (which are available via a link on the home page), the site has had more than 2 1/2 million visits. The Yahoo home page also has links to a daily "what's new," other Web Searchers, and directories. Figure 3.27 shows the search input page and figure 3.28 shows the results of a search.

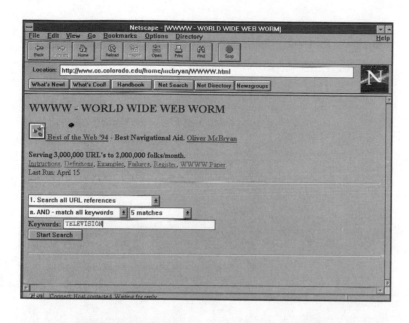

Fig. 3.25
The search input page for the World Wide Web Worm. It offers several types of searches, including a search by home page title and names of URLs.

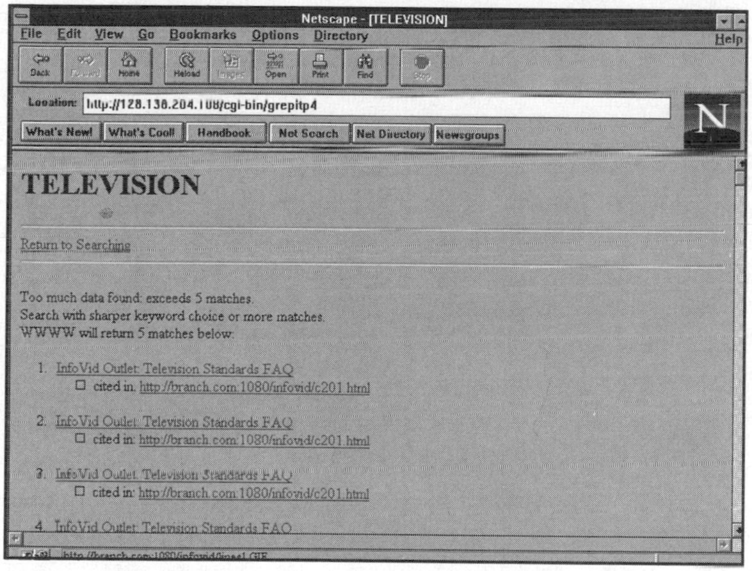

Fig. 3.26
The search results from World Wide Web Worm.

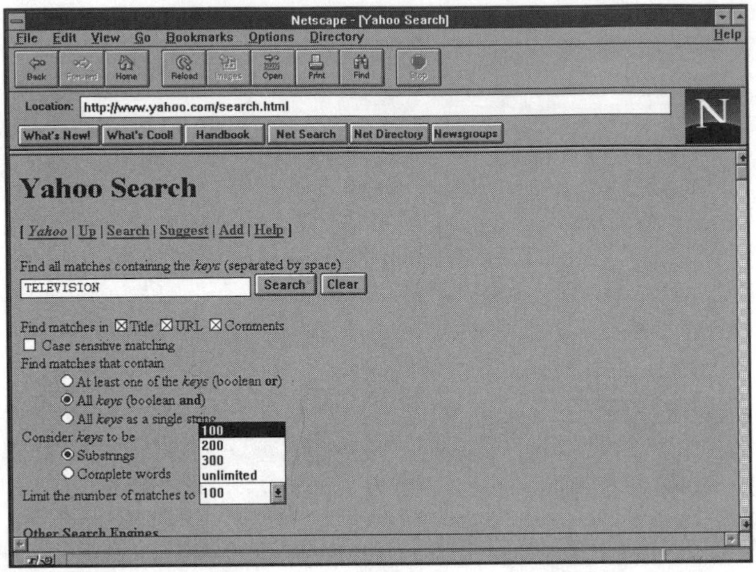

Fig. 3.27
With links to
more than 37,000
entries, Yahoo has
become a very
popular Web
searcher.

Web Searcher Shootout: Which One Is Best?

How do all of these different Web crawlers and searchers stack up against each other? The best way to compare them is with an informal contest. I accessed five of the searchers that I use frequently, Yahoo, Lycos, WebCrawler, World Wide Web Worm, and InfoSeek. To be fair I used the same keywords and search terms and did not adjust any of the default settings on the searchers. These different searchers respond to a very general topic keyword, a very specific topic keyword, and a search term (using several combined keywords). Because I was hungry when I tried this, I chose "food," "pizza," and "art history." (I'm sure there are paintings of food.)

Also, it is easy to access these searchers and they quickly respond to the query. I was able to access all of the searchers the first time I tried and received response to each query in under one minute (6:00 p.m. Denver, Colorado time).

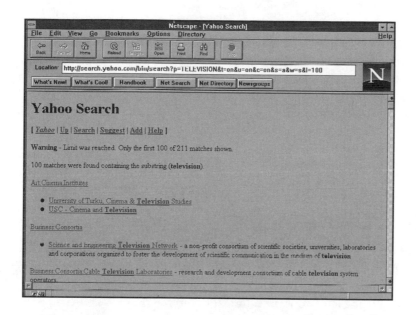

Fig. 3.28
The results of a Yahoo search put links into subject categories.

The following chart shows the results of this searcher "shootout." The number of hits that each searcher found for the three types of searches is noted and the very first record/entry from the results of the queries for food and pizza are listed.

Searcher	General Topic 1 keyword	Specific Topic 1 keyword	Multiple Word Search
	FOOD	**PIZZA**	**ART HISTORY**
Yahoo	141 hits Food supplements	8 hits Backstreet Pizza	18 hits
Lycos	4,718 hits Center for Food Safety	752 hits Pizza Hut	22,641
WebCrawler	1,604 hits Food Labeling	280 hits Important Restaurant Numbers	1,406
World Wide Web Worm	500 hits Chefs King Seafood	242 hits Applewood Pizza	2 hits
InfoSeek	200+ Food Allergies	200+ Junk Food Places	200+

Tip

Here's another great way to conduct a thorough search of one subject area and eliminate the time that it takes to locate and connect with a Web searcher and re-run a search! First, use your favorite Web searcher to perform a search. When the results of the search appear—usually as a long list of hypertext links to other Web sites— save the page as an HTML file (such as results.htm). Then, during this or future sessions, you can simply reload this file from your hard drive and continue your exploration of the links or sites that match your search criteria.

A couple of noteworthy results. Lycos was the big winner in terms of number of hits for each search. This shouldn't be too surprising because Lycos claims to have more than 4 million URLs in its database. More significant is that while each searcher did come up with some duplicate records and results, they all each offered some unique results as well. In fact, each of the first records in the search results was completely different. This means that if you want to do a comprehensive search of Web resources, you need to use several different searchers.

Combine Browser Tools with Web Searcher Results

Using your browser navigation tools in combination with the results from a Web search can be a very powerful searching technique. The Web search creates a page of links that take you to sites related to your search terms. Click on a link, and check out the information on the home page to determine its value for your search. If it looks like a real winner and has lots of valuable information and links, then add it to your bookmark or hotlist.

Then, click on the backward button to go back to the search results list where you then click on the next link in the list. Use this procedure to follow through as many of the search results links as you deem valuable. Once you've saved the URLs for the most valuable sites, go back and more thoroughly examine those sites.

Web Directories: Pick a Subject, Any Subject

Unlike the searchers, the following Web sites offer directories. More like an encyclopedia, you start your search by choosing a subject or even a letter of the alphabet to locate relevant Internet resources. In this sense the Web directories attempt to organize the information that's on the Internet. This type of subject-oriented searching is a good way to find information if you know exactly what you're looking for. One way to broaden the results of a subject search is to use a dictionary or thesaurus to find several words that relate to your subject and look for each of these in the directories.

Clearinghouse for Subject-Oriented Internet Resource Guides

URL address: **http://www.lib.umich.edu/chhome.html**

Maintained by the University of Michigan's University Library and the School of Information and Library Studies, this Web site lets you search through a database of subject-oriented Internet guides. There are three general categories for the guides: Humanities (art, religion, theater, etc.), Social Sciences (business, communication, education, etc.), and Sciences (agriculture, biology, weather, etc.). Each guide is a text-based document that gives you all sorts of information and addresses for Internet sites that relate to that subject. This includes mailing lists, newsgroups, Web, Gopher, and FTP sites. You could do a search for "cable" or "fishing" and the database will locate an appropriate guide for you.

Comprehensive List of Web Sites

URL address: **http://www.netgen.com/cgi/comprehensive**

Matthew Grey at Net.Genesis maintains this interesting site. This search tool fits somewhere between the Web searchers that try to match keywords and search terms and the directories that provide subject-specific searching. Here you search a database for Web sites based on their domain type or domain name (see figure 3.29). For example, you could search for all of the Internet/ Web sites in Belgium that are recognized by the .be domain; or search for all commercial sites that have the .com address. You can even narrow down the search with more specific information. For example, if you submit "mit.edu," the search retrieves a list of all of the computers that MIT has connected to the Internet. In all, the database contains addresses for more than 16,000 host computers.

Global News Network Directory

URL address: **http://nearnet.gnn.com/gnn/GNNhome.html**

A directory of the resources compiled by this commercial service, many links in this directory are to businesses and companies.

Online System Services

URL address: **http://www.ossinc.net/**

The home page has an image of a spaceship traveling through outer space (see figure 3.31). The various parts of the image (like the planets) are links to directories and search tools. Choose from Hot Sites, Amusement and Travel, and Searchers. The Hot Sites link opens up a page with more than 16 subject-oriented categories. Amusement and Travel sites can be found through their respective home page planets and Searchers opens a page that offers links to Web, Archie, Veronica, WAIS, X.500, and Whois search tools.

Fig. 3.31

Pick a planet. This site has several subject-based directories as well as links to Web, Gopher, and FTP search systems and Internet "telephone" directories.

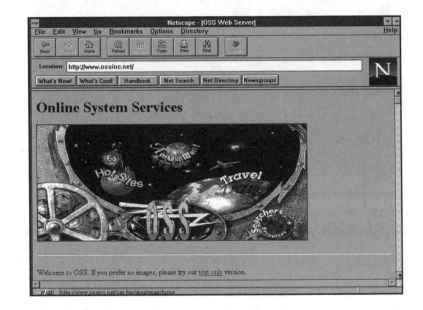

Web of Wonder

URL Address: **http://www.digimark.net/wow**

This is a hierarchical list of more than 6,000 links from all over the world.

World Wide Web Virtual Library

URL address: **http://info.cern.ch/hypertext/DataSources/bySubject/Overview.html**

This is a subject catalog that begins with the subject of Aboriginal Studies and ends with Unidentified Flying Objects—but rest assured, not every category relates to outerspace.

Yanoff Special Internet Connections List
URL address: **http://www.uwm.edu/Mirror/inet.services.html**

This is a very useful resource. It is a hypertext-based listing of Internet/Web sites based on subject categories. There are two pages to this list. The top of the first page lists all of the subject areas. When you click on one you jump to the listings for that subject. Because this entire directory fits on two Web pages, you can save it as an HTML file to your hard drive for future reference and use.

Summary

The Web may actually be better than books, radio, and television. In fact it combines the best of all of these media. And, unlike radio and TV, no network decides what program you can listen to or watch at a predetermined time. You go where you want, when you want. You're in the driver's seat. The Web entertains, teaches, and informs with a dazzling array of multimedia. The Web uses hypertext to enable you to jump effortlessly from one subject (and computer) to another. And the Web can connect you to all of the different Internet systems, such as Gopher, FTP, newsgroups. The Web searchers and directories are designed to help you locate information you want, and often point toward valuable information you never thought you needed. As the Web grows these systems will also expand to offer new services and searching capabilities.

Chapter 4

Information Detectives: Gopher, Veronica, and WAIS

This chapter will introduce you to three very powerful Internet searching systems and tools: Gopher, Veronica, and WAIS.

In this chapter you will learn the following:

- What Gopher is and how it can be used to find items on the Net

- Gopher starting points—Gopher Jewels

- How to refine your search and create menus using Veronica

- How to use WAIS for extensive text searching within files

What Is Gopher and How Does It Work?

Gopher is a system that organizes and presents Internet information and files as a series of on-screen menus (see figure 4.1). The thousands of Gopher servers worldwide are data libraries that hold a massive collection of resources. It is primarily used to locate text-based documents, but it can turn up and present to you the location of the following kinds of file types:

- documents

- graphics

- sound

- binary programs

- archives

- terminal sessions

- database queries

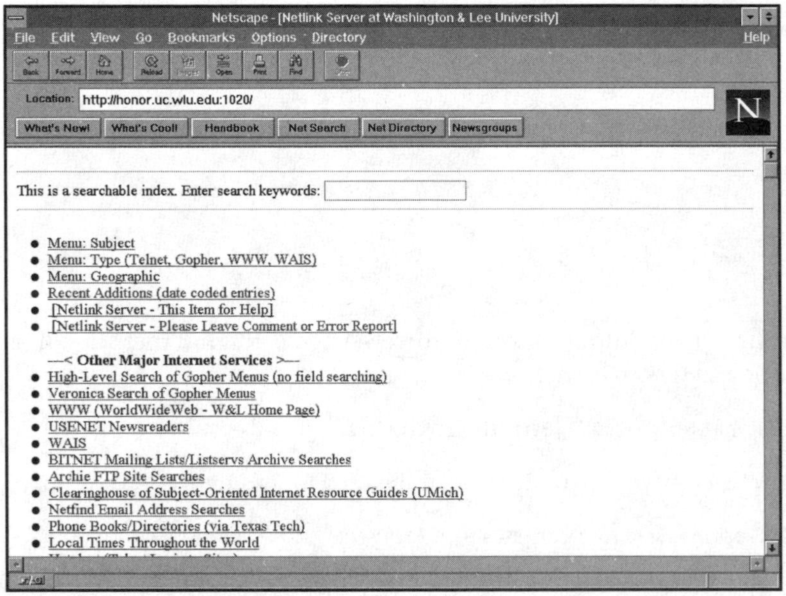

Fig. 4.1
Gopher presents
Internet informa-
tion and files as a
series of on-screen
menus.

Gopher is designed for ease of use. Like an electronic table of contents, Gopher menus help you quickly navigate to the information and resources you
need. Simply double-click on a menu to retrieve a specific item. Sometimes
the item is a text document, a photograph, a communications program, or
another set of menus. Often one menu item points to yet another set of
menus, and so on. Another way to look at Gopher is as a global resource
catalog and delivery service.

> **Note**
>
> Gopher got its name from two sources. The obvious one is from "go-fer," alluding to
> its purpose of fetching things based on what it was asked to look for. The other
> source is from the college mascot (the Golden Gopher) of the University of Minne-
> sota, where Gopher was developed in the Information Technology Laboratory in April
> 1991.

Like other Internet information systems, Gopher is a **client-server** system. There are many Gopher servers all around the world. These computers house the menus and information that you want to access. The Gopher Client is a software program that runs on your PC and becomes your interface for Gopher.

There are many Gopher Clients available for a number of different computer platforms including Windows. Figure 4.2 shows WSGopher, which is a freeware, Windows-based program. Others such as HGopher, Chameleon Gopher, GopherBook, and Gopher for Windows can also be viewed in text mode from a UNIX shell (see figure 4.3) or by a World Wide Web Browser such as Netscape.

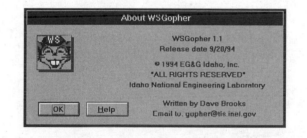

Fig. 4.2
WSGopher Client.

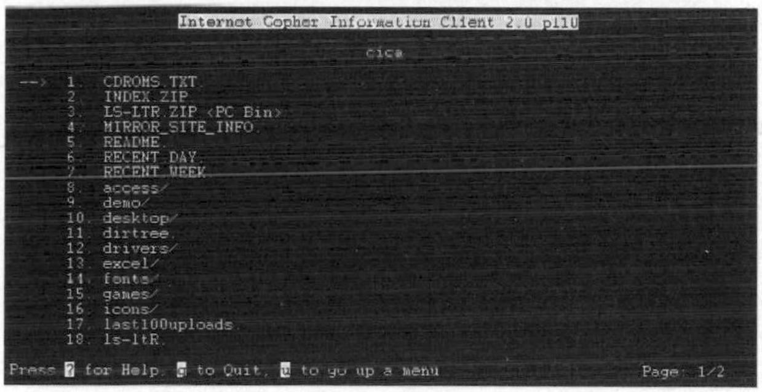

Fig. 4.3
Gopher in Procomm for Windows on a UNIX Shell.

With the popularity of Web Browsers and many of the World Wide Web search tools, Gopher is sometimes overlooked. Gopher is a very powerful search and retrieval system that can locate information not found using conventional Web search tools.

When Gopher presents information, it appears as a series of nested menus. These menus look remarkably similar to the Windows/UNIX/Macintosh file-management style organization of a directory with subdirectories and files. These subdirectories and files could be physically located anywhere on the Internet. From your viewpoint all information items are available from a locally presented menu. In addition to all of the information resouces, you can use Gopher to access other information systems such as Archie, Telnet, and FTP.

Fig. 4.4
Downloading a
binary file (it
could be a
software program)
from Gopher.

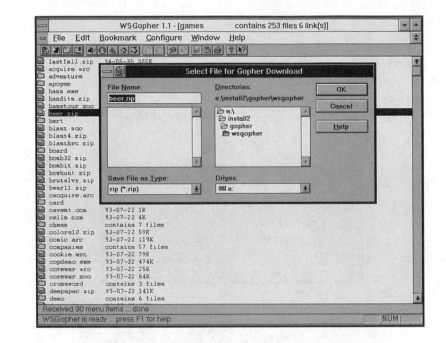

Gopherspace and How It Works

Gopher computers are all interconnected through the menus. This means that you can weave or "tunnel" your way from one Gopher computer/menu to any other Gopher computer. The beauty of this system is that you can access all of the resources and information from any starting point. This interwoven electronic universe has been nicknamed Gopherspace. The total number of Gopher servers is currently estimated to be 5,500, though this number can vary significantly as many of the Gopher computers are on isolated segments of the Internet or may be down. There are more than 2,400 Gopher servers indexed and accessible via Veronica (a search tool covered later in this section). Three years ago, there were less than 300 known servers. Each Gopher server has access to many files and utilities of differing types including text, pictures, video, sound, and executable programs. The following listing is a sample of the places you can visit in Gopherspace.

International Employment Listings

Need a job? Search for international employment by subject areas that include corporate, education, government, science, and social services.

Gopher address: **sun.cc.westga.edu**

Submenus: **coop/JobNet/**

The National Institute of Allergy and Infectious Diseases

Does your nose drive you crazy during hay fever season? Do your eyes water every time you pet a cat? Visit this site and get some advice.

Gopher address: **gopher.niaid.nih.gov**

Oriental Recipes from the University of Minnesota

Recipes for several exotic dishes including barmi-goregn, Chinese spaghetti, potstickers, sagh, sambal-bajak, sambal-lilang, shu-mei, sukiyaki, and tofu-meat.

Gopher address: **spinaltap.micro.umn.edu**

Submenus: **fun/Recipes/Oriental**

U.S. Senate and U.S. House of Representatives

Find out what your elected officials do and learn about current legislative issues and proposals.

Gopher address: **gopher.house.gov:70/1** or **gopher.senate.gov:70/1**

Notice that to retrieve some of these resources you first connect to a Gopher, then go through several submenus.

Where To Start Gopher Exploration

Your first adventure into Gopherspace usually starts wherever your Gopher software program or client (also known as a browser just like the Web programs) decides is "home." Just as you can set up a Web browser to always open one specific Web site when you start it, you can configure most Gopher programs to start at a specific Gopher server, or home. To illustrate using WSGopher, we'll start at the main menu for the University of Illinois Gopher site (the Gopher address is gopher.uiuc.edu). This is shown in figure 4.5.

II

Search Tools

Most Gopher servers present their own local files as folders, utility, and file icons. If you're using WSGopher, the magnifying glass utility icon indicates that you can start a keyword search of the files, folders, and utilities on this particular server.

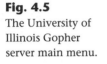

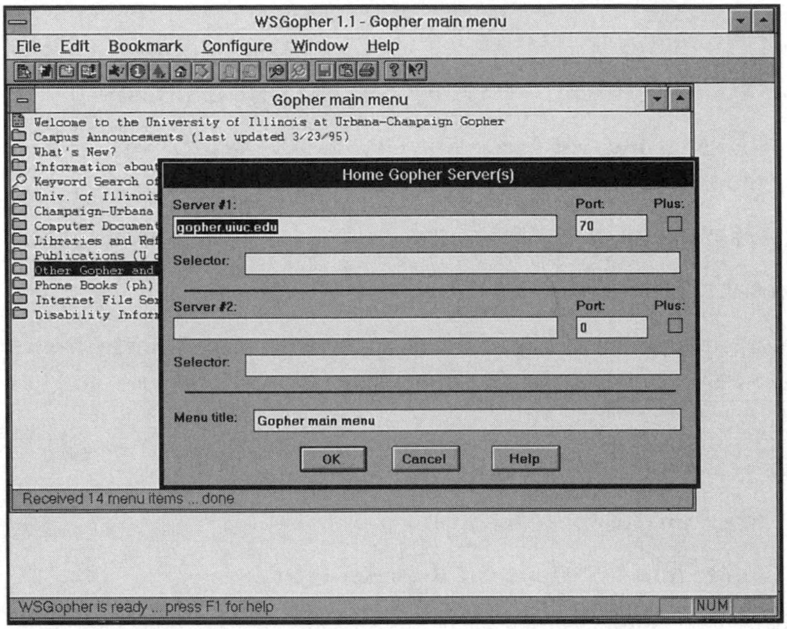

Fig. 4.5
The University of Illinois Gopher server main menu.

Right now, our Gopherspace excursion only includes the files, utilities, and directories at the University of Illinois. We can quickly expand our viewable Gopherspace by clicking on additional folders (menu selections). Figure 4.6 shows just a part of the "All the other Gopher Servers in the World" folder. This folder contains a menu with 2,429 lines, which is the current number of known server locations from this site.

With thousands of Gopher servers all around the world it's nice to have a starting place. Table 4.1 is a list of Gopher sites that have main menus which offer broad selections like libraries, news, phone books, and access to other Gopher sites. You may want to make one of them your home site.

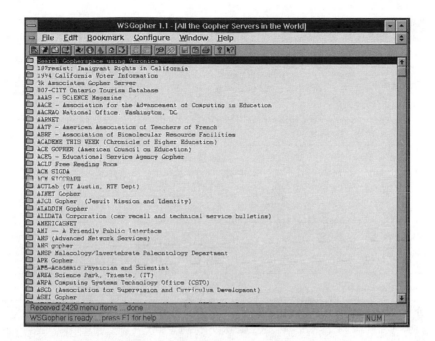

Fig. 4.6
All the Gopher
servers in the
world?

Table 4.1   Popular Gopher Sites

Gopher Address	Location
United States	
scilibx.ucsc.edu	California
panda.uiowa.edu	Iowa
gopher.msu.edu	Michigan
consultant.micro.umn.edu	Minnesota
gopher.unc.edu	North Carolina
sunsite.unc.edu	North Carolina
ecosys.drdr.virginia.edu	Virginia
Foreign	
info.anu.edu.au	Australia
tolten.puc.cl	Chile

(continues)

Table 4.1 Continued	
Gopher Address	**Location**
Foreign	
ecnet.ec	Ecuador
gopher.th-darmstadt.de	Germany
gopher.isnet.is	Iceland
gopher.torun.edu.pl	Poland
gopher.ncc.go.jp	Japan
gopher.uv.es	Spain
gopher.chalmers.se	Sweden
gopher.brad.ac.uk	United Kingdom

Note

One requirement when searching Gopherspace is patience. With the vast growth of Internet usage, the limited resources are often overwhelmed with requests. You may often get an error message or indication that too many resources are already in use and that you should try later. This is basically good advice. Don't give up on a site just because you can't get in the first time you try it. Because of the worldwide nature of the Internet, it is difficult to predict what is an off-peak time. The best method is to log all the times when you successfully connect to a service and see if there is a pattern.

Tip
One of the nice time-saving features of WSGopher is that you can minimize (or switch away from) the current window for the selection being searched and begin an additional search or continue browsing in another window. I had as many as three different searches going on at the same time while browsing in a fourth window.

Gopher Jewels Organizes Gopher Resources

Gopherspace can seem like a huge, unorganized collection of information. One attempt to organize the millions of resources available on Gopher servers around the world is the Gopher Jewels, an electronic catalog of Gopher sites organized by subject categories. In fact, the Gopher Jewels contains more than 2,000 pointers to information and files in Gopherspace. With categories like Education, Government, Health, and Law, it's pretty easy to navigate your way towards the information you need. Each of these menu choices will open new menus with additional information in that subject area.

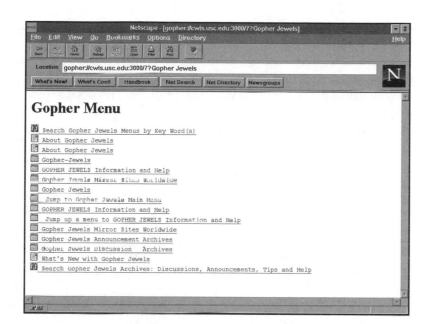

Fig. 4.7
Locating Gopher
Jewels.

The Gopher Jewels catalog is maintained on several Gopher sites. One of the easiest ways to locate Gopher Jewels is to perform a keyword search for the string "jewels" from any Gopher Search option as in figure 4.8. The University of Southern California is one of the original Gopher sites with this catalog. The address is **cwis.usc.edu**. The menu path you need to take to locate the Gopher Jewels at this site is: Other_Gophers_and_Information_Resources/ Gophers_by_Subject/Gopher_Jewels.

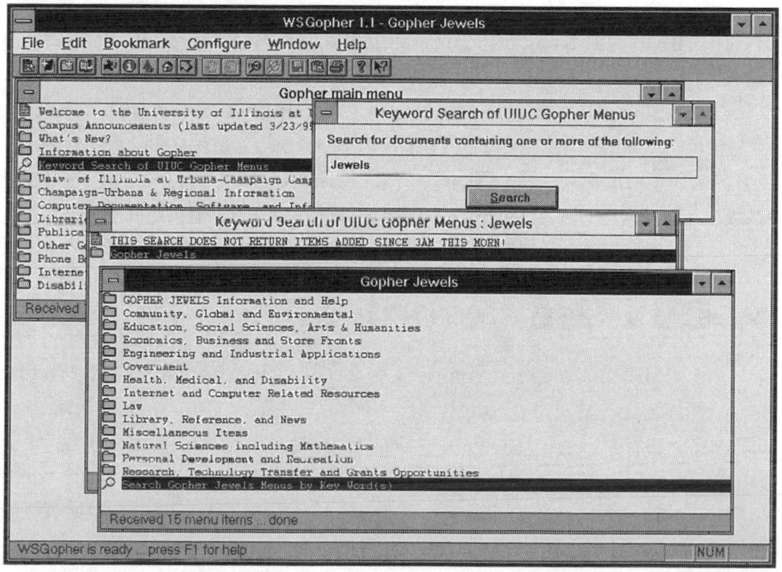

Fig. 4.8
Locating Gopher
Jewels with a
keyword search.

Search Tools

II

As you begin to explore Gopher, the sheer size of Gopherspace will become apparent. Even with the sophistication of search tools such as Veronica, many useful sites are very elusive. One service that can help you keep on top of the ever-expanding resources is the Gopher Jewels List Service, which sends you regular updates via electronic mail. With more than 3,000 subscribers, this is a popular mailing list. Once you've subscribed, you'll receive notices of lists that are available on request containing information on many of the sites considered especially useful by other users.

To subscribe, send e-mail to **gopherjewels@einet.net**. Leave the subject line blank. In the body of the message type **subscribe gopherjewels <your first and last name>**. For example: **subscribe gopherjewels david riggins**.

An acknowledgment and information file will return to you with details about using the list, setting user options, and retrieving Gopher Jewel's archive files.

Use Veronica To Search Gopherspace

Gopher is a success because it reaches around the world and points to millions of documents and files. These attributes also create a problem. As you weave your way through Gopherspace how do you know that the file or information you want resides on the one, or two, or three Gophers you connect to? The answer is: You don't. It's purely a hit-and-miss operation. To perform a comprehensive search for a topic you'd need to connect to all 5,000+ Gophers and examine every menu—you'd never finish.

To solve this problem, two computer scientists at the University of Nevada developed a program called Veronica. Veronica helps you search through all those Gopher menus. Veronica maintains a database of the menu selections on all Gopher servers and updates this database twice a week. As with other Internet utility names, Veronica is a semi-humorous acronym that translates to: Very Easy Rodent-Oriented Net-wide Index to Computerized Archives.

How Do I Use Veronica?

For once you don't have to learn a new system. You access Veronica from a Gopher menu. Most of the publicly accessible Gopher sites have a menu selection that opens Veronica. When you use Veronica you enter a keyword into an on-screen box. Veronica then looks through its database and creates a custom-tailored Gopher menu where every selection contains the word or words you entered.

To give you a better idea of how Veronica operates, the following figures walk through a typical series of search steps using Veronica. Figure 4.9 is our starting point where you can select your desired Veronica search format. For the purpose of this exercise, we will be looking for some information about soccer World Wide Web pages. As you can see, "sports" has been selected as a topic of interest and we will use the simplified search to speed things up.

> **Note**
>
> As a general rule, when you see the word "simplified" with reference to searches, this usually means the search will be limited to an area of each document. Because the search is not that extensive it will be relatively quick. In this case, we are only searching within title strings of the documents. This is very useful for a quick first pass or when searching for a non-specific or vague subject.

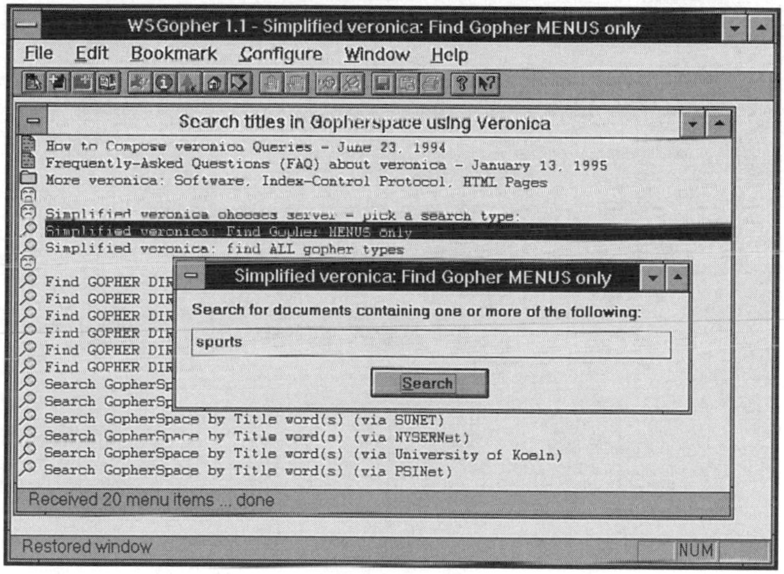

Fig. 4.9
Starting point using a simplified Veronica search.

After locating a collection of locations where sports-related documents have been found, you can "drill down" into an area of more specific interest. In figure 4.10, we have selected "Sports and Hobbies." Figure 4.11 shows the results.

Ultimately, we would want to get to the goal of our search and thus look at any relevant documents that we found. Figure 4.12 shows what we were looking for, in this case a pointer to a Web page relating to a newsgroup—**rec.sports.soccer**.

Fig. 4.10
Drilling down into
a specific area.

Fig. 4.11
Results of the
drill-down.

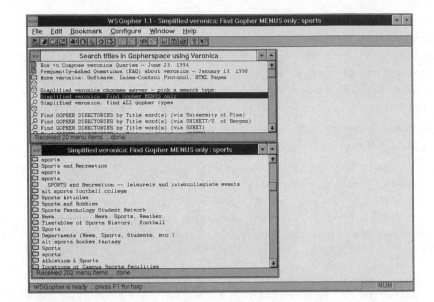

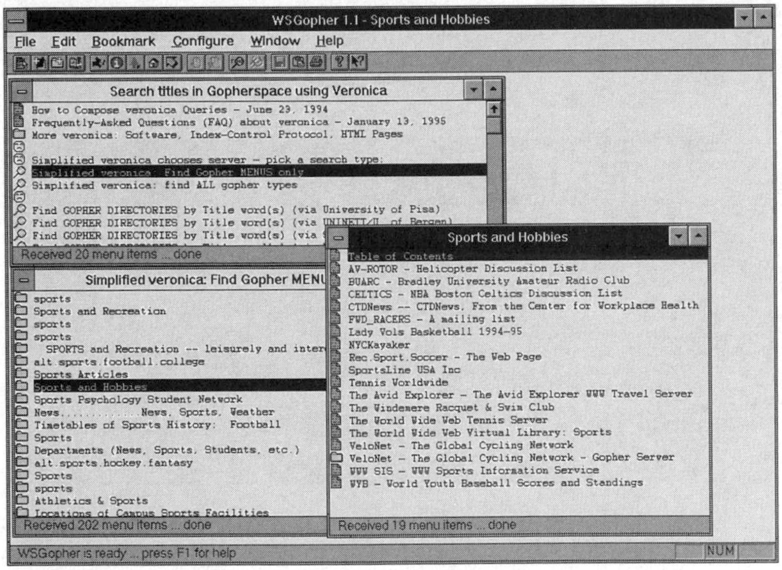

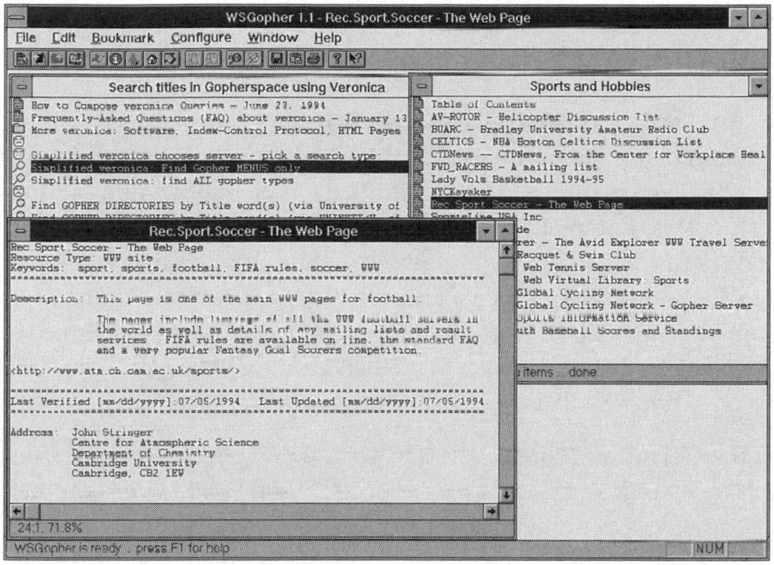

Fig. 4.12
Final result of our search.

The result of a Veronica search is an automatically generated Gopher menu, custom-tailored to your keyword specification. Items on this menu are usually extracted from many other Gopher servers around the world. You need never know which Gopher server is actually involved in filling your request for information. Items that appear particularly interesting can be saved as a bookmark for future reference (shown in figure 4.13).

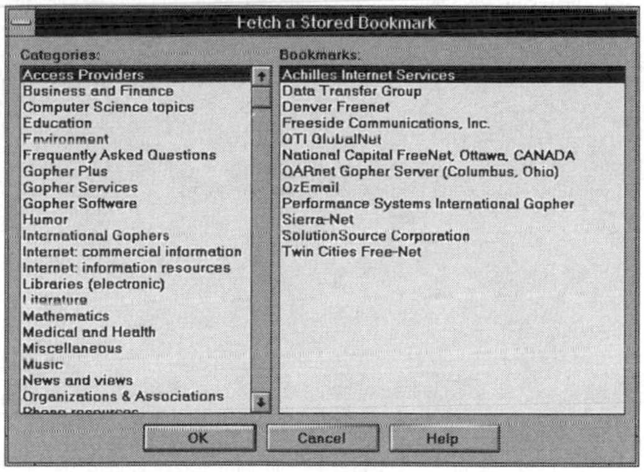

Fig. 4.13
Saving useful discoveries in a bookmark.

An important thing to consider with Veronica searches is that they are only looking at the keywords in the **titles** of items at each site, not the contents of the text within an item. The title in this case is the reference to the resource as it appears on the menu of its home Gopher server. The Veronica index contains about 10 million items from the thousands of Gopher sites.

Each one of those 10 million items could contain the equivalent of one to several hundred pages of text.

How To Start a Veronica Query

To start a Veronica query you must first locate Veronica on a Gopher menu. Usually there is a main menu selection titled Other Gophers and Information Resources. This is normally where you'll find Veronica. Veronica actually runs on specific computers and you'll select the computer that you want to do your Veronica search. When a text-entry box appears (see figure 4.14) you can enter a keyword, search term, or control flags that help refine your search. A **control flag** is a code that tells Veronica what type of information you want to find—an image, a file, a software program, etc.

When the search is finished, the results will be presented as a regular-looking Gopher menu that Veronica has generated for you. You may browse the discovered resources in the generated menu, as you would any other Gopher menu.

Fig. 4.14
Veronica presents a simple keyword entry box.

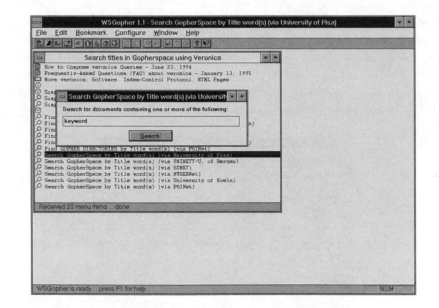

Types of Searches

Most Veronica-access menus offer several types of searches. In addition to the default types, you can compose Veronica queries using a number of special options to limit or expand your search more in line with your requirements. You should use these options when appropriate, as they will make it much easier (and often faster) to locate resources. (See the following sections for pre-defined search types and narrowing the search to find resources of a certain Gopher type.)

Multiple Servers

Many Veronica-access menus offer you a list of various Veronica server sites as in figure 4.15. Here, you select a server site that will perform your Veronica search. In theory it's not supposed to matter which server you use, as all servers will give the same results. In practice, the servers do not all update the index simultaneously, so there may be some minor differences in the results of any search. You will also notice that some servers will offer a better response time than others, depending on the load, capacity of the server, complexity or size of the query, time of day, and network traffic. After awhile you will recognize patterns such as which server is the most responsive and when.

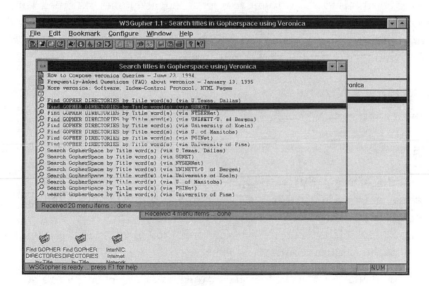

Fig. 4.15
Veronica server
selection.

Once you have selected your Veronica server, you should be offered two pre-defined search types: Search Gopherspace by Keywords in Titles and Search Gopher Directories Only for Keywords in Titles.

Search Gopherspace by Keywords in Titles

This search will find all Gopher resources whose titles contain your specified search words. The resources may be of any Gopher data type such as ASCII text files, Gopher directories, image files, binary files, and so on. This is a useful search if you are not specifically looking for text or a document, but rather a program or picture.

Search Gopher Directories Only for Keywords in Titles

This is a narrower search that locates Gopher directories with titles containing the specified words. This search can be very useful to focus on textual information specific to your query. Once Veronica finds the Gopher directories, you can open any of them to view the contents in more detail. This is especially useful to avoid being overwhelmed by using a common word or phrase.

Searches can be narrowed further by the use of control flags, which will be described in detail later in the chapter. Simply put, a flag is an indicator to the search program to ignore or include certain results of a search. Flags are normally added along with the text of the search itself.

Why flags? The main reason is usually to speed up the response time for the search; another is to avoid having to wade through volumes of entries. The downside of using flags is that they usually complicate the search. The flag format itself (that is, -t0) comes from UNIX roots and is typically how control information is passed to any UNIX program.

Entering a Query

When you select a query type, your Gopher client will present a very simple one-line dialog box. Enter your query words and and click on the search button—that's all there is to it. The search is not case-sensitive.

Default Query Type

You may get more accurate results by entering a multi-word query rather than a single word, especially if they are common words such as "the," "red," or "text." Multiple word queries will find only those items with titles containing *all* of the specified words.

You should also consider the logical construction of a Gopher site and how the documents might be titled so you can select the right level of granularity. You may be looking for information on "pistons" and "bearings," but simply putting a query in for those in document titles might not turn up all the available information. A better bet would be to place "engines" or "engine components" in the title.

There is no particular order in a multiple word query, so "components engine" is just as valid as "engine components."

Use Boolean Operators To Narrow a Veronica Search

Veronica query searches can use Boolean operators such as AND, NOT, and OR. The interpretation of the query string starts from the right end. Parentheses can be used to group the operators in case there's any question as to the order of operation. The only anomaly found so far is the Veronica server at University of Koeln, which interprets the query logic from left to right.

If you use a simple multiple-word query, the default is an implied AND between each word.

AND can be used successfully to create a tightly-focused query, however too many ANDs will frequently end up with zero hits. The converse of this is the use of the OR operator; indiscriminate use will merely result in a bucketload of hits. A good compromise is to use OR in conjunction with AND. Take the following string, for example:

```
engine AND fuel AND (regular OR unleaded OR sup*).
```

An asterisk (*) at the trailing end of a query word will match with any word beginning with the letters to the left of the asterisk. This is really only a limited form of wildcard search and cannot be used anywhere else in a string, only the end. The search will fail if an * is placed on its own, within a word, or at the beginning of a word. In the preceding example, the sup* will pick up "super" or "supreme."

Search words must be at least two characters long. Shorter words such as "a" will be ignored.

Narrow Your Veronica Search with Control Flags

There are additional Veronica control flags that can help you refine and narrow your search. You enter these "flags" just after your keyword or search term. There are three top-level flag codes that are then followed by a specific number or letter that further narrows the search.

The top-level flags include:

- The -t command limits the search to items of specified data types. The -t is followed by one or more letters or numbers indicating specific document types you are interested in. The default is all document types. If your first search turned up thousands of documents of many differing types, you might consider setting a flag to limit the search to those that you are interested in. If you only wanted text files, you would enter the following search string:

```
sports -t0
```

This tells Veronica to search for anything that included the string "sports" and to reject any document that was not a text file. If you decided that you also needed GIF files and any other image, you would enter the following string:

```
sports -t0gI
```

Tip
If you suspect that you are going to get a large number of hits on your search but are unsure if the Veronica search string you are using is exactly what you want, you can greatly speed up the search by limiting the number of items to be returned.

- The -l command creates a file of links for the discovered resources. This is rarely used in normal searches.

Most Veronica servers will, by default, provide only the first 200 items that match your query.

- You can request a specific number of returned items by including the -m command flag in your query. The -m command on its own will return all matching items if a number is added after your keyword, such as "sports -m." Limiting the number of items is a good way to speed up the search and reduce network traffic.

For example, the simple query **engine** would provide the default 200 items (or whatever the server default is). However, the following query would provide 20 items:

```
engine -m20
```

And the following query would provide all available matching items:

```
engine -m
```

Finding Resources of a Certain Type: The -t Flag

You can use the -t control flag to refine a search to locate specific types of information and data. You specify the types you are interested in by adding a specific -t option to the end of your query. For example, "government -t0" limits the results of a search to only text files, and "engine -ts" will search for and locate sound files that have the keyword "engine."

The -t flag may appear at the beginning or end of a query string. For example:

```
engine -ts
```

```
-ts engine
```

will both result in lists of engine sounds.

Note

There must NOT be any spaces in between the -t and the type specifier; the same goes for any numbers associated with the -m option.

You may specify more than one type in the query, but you should not use separate -t options to do this. Simply string all the desired types together (with no spaces in between, of course) after the -t. For example:

```
-tgs1 engine
```

returns a menu of directories, gif images, or sounds that have the word "engine" in their title.

The -t gopher resource type list is shown in table 4.2.

Table 4.2   The Official Gopher Document Types as Specified by the Gopher Protocol Document

0	Text File
1	Directory
2	CSO name server
4	Mac HQX file
5	PC binary
7	Full Text Index (Gopher menu)
8	Telnet Session
9	Binary File (program or archive)
s	Sound
e	Event (not in 2.06)
I	Image (other than GIF)
M	MIME multipart/mixed message
T	TN3270 Session
c	Calendar (not in 2.06)
g	GIF image
h	HTML, HyperText Markup Language, (Web Page)

The -l option is not supported by all Veronica sites; a link information file will be displayed as the first item on the Veronica results menu. You can then retrieve that file and include the links in menus that you may be building.

Here are some examples that should help make the process clearer:

```
engine NOT steam -m1000
```

In this example, I am interested in only petroleum-based engines, not steam. This will return up to 1,000 entries. To be more precise, I could use the string:

```
engine AND (gas OR petrol) -m1000
```

This is more specific, but assumes that the title contains the words "gas" or "petrol," which it might not, so I may inadvertently exclude things I'm interested in. In the following example, I deliberately removed entries I suspected might clutter up my query by enlarging the string:

```
engine NOT steam NOT siege NOT fire -m1000
```

Another example to find engine, engines, and engineering we would use the wildcard *. This time, we expect there will be more than 1,000 hits, so -m is used on its own:

```
engine* NOT steam NOT siege NOT fire -m
```

Using all of these control flags to refine Veronica queries takes a little getting used to. Odds are that most of your queries can be achieved without using operators or modifiers. However, with the continuing explosive growth of the Internet, these are handy cards to keep up your sleeve.

Use Jughead To Search Keywords and Filenames

Jughead is a tool for getting menu information from various Gopher servers, and acting as a search engine in a specified part of Gopherspace. In your quest for information, Veronica is a wide-ranging search tool that gets you to a general area. Jughead is a deeper burrowing tool that lets you rapidly zero in on specific information of interest. It is an acronym for Jonzy's Universal Gopher Hierarchy Excavation And Display. Jonzy is the nickname for Jughead's developer, Rhett "Jonzy" Jones at the University of Utah. Figure 4.16 shows a selection of Jughead Servers obtained by a Veronica search, including University of Utah.

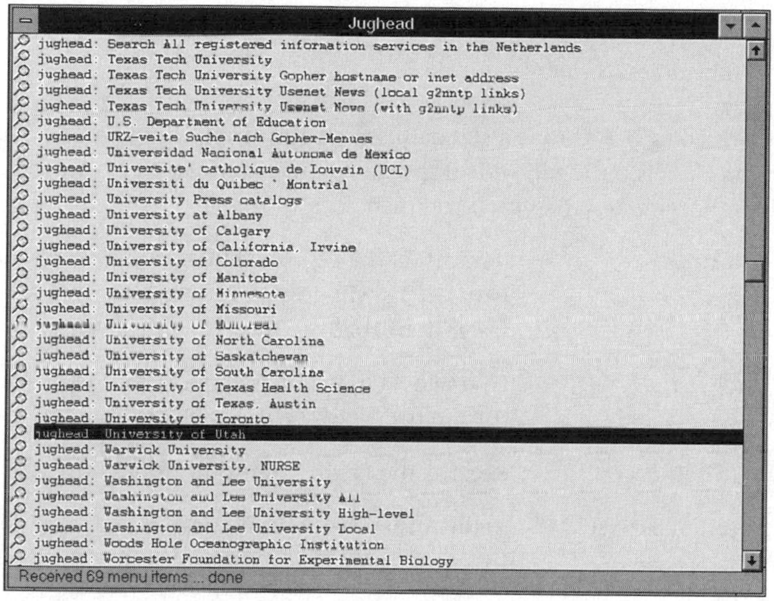

Fig. 4.16
Jughead servers
found by a
Veronica search.

One of the best places to find Jughead is at its home in the University of
Utah (**gopher.utah.edu**). Using WSGopher, you can first go to a Veronica
site, and then perform a Veronica query that will look something like the
following:

```
jughead -m100
```

If you want to limit the hits another way, you can try the following:

```
jughead AND Utah
```

Once you have attached a Jughead engine, you can perform searches almost
identical to those performed by Veronica. The main difference is that Jughead
usually offers some more control over a smaller area of Gopherspace to be
searched. A site featuring Jughead will also offer predefined information
tables that are not available through a normal Veronica search of that site.

In addition to supporting the same Boolean (AND, OR, NOT) and wildcard (*)
commands as Veronica, Jughead supports some special features in which each
special command must be preceded by a question mark '?', and *string* is a
variable changeable by the user. The following are special commands:

?all *string*

?help [*string*]

?limit=n *string*

?version [*string*]

?range=n1-n2 *string*

In the preceding list *string* is a standard search string, anything enclosed in square brackets is optional, and all special commands must be preceded with '?'. The following describes each command:

?all *string*	Returns all the hits on whatever '*string*' is set to. Note: items will only be returned if there are fewer than 1024.
?help [*string*]	Gives you a help document and any optional hits on '*string*'.
?limit=n *string*	Returns the first 'n' items on '*string*'.
?version [*string*]	Returns the version of jughead and any optional hits on '*string*'.
?range=n1-n2 *string*	Returns the matches beginning with n1 up to n2.

Use WAIS To Look into Files

You might think that Veronica is the perfect Internet search tool. Not quite. It's true that Veronica searches the world to find directories and files that match your search terms. What Veronica *doesn't* do is examine the actual *contents* of files—what's inside.

If you have the world's biggest sweet tooth and you want to find information about desserts, you might try the obvious keywords "dessert," "candy," "chocolate," and "sweets." These may bring good results, but they'd miss documents and menus with names like "delicious ice cream sundae" or "fudge galore," which certainly any sugar-loving individual would want to find.

WAIS, which stands for Wide Area Information Server and is pronounced "ways," comes to the rescue. While Archie, Gopher, and Veronica search menus, directories, and files, WAIS looks for information inside individual documents. The people who run WAIS sites index individual files with all of the words in the file. If you search for "dessert" WAIS will find "delicious ice cream sundae" and "fudge galore" if the documents contain the word "dessert." WAIS was originally developed as a project of Thinking Machines, Apple Computer, Dow Jones, and KPMG Peat Marwick. The work has blossomed considerably since then.

What Is WAIS?

WAIS is another client-server based application where the server creates and presents (or serves) lists of relevant information and resources based on your search parameters. WAIS is like Jughead in that it searches documents and resources specifically at a single site—of course, this time it's a WAIS server. Where WAIS differs from Jughead is that the WAIS client can concatenate the search across many servers and come up with an eclectic search result.

Consider what WAIS is trying to achieve from an information retrieval standpoint. This scenario is familiar to anyone who has ever visited a reference desk at a public or corporate library. The client approaches a librarian with a description of needed information. The librarian might ask a few background questions, and then draw from appropriate sources to provide an initial selection of articles, reports, and references. The client then sorts through this selection to find the most pertinent documents. With feedback from these trials, the researcher can refine the materials and even continue to supply the user with a flow of information as it becomes available. Continually monitoring which articles were useful is tedious but can help keep the researcher on track.

WAIS offers a parallel analogy to the traditional information research scenario. The WAIS system is an attempt at automating this interaction: the user states a question in English, and a set of document descriptions come back from selected sources. The user can examine any of the items, be they text, picture, video, sound, or whatever. If the initial response is incomplete or somehow insufficient, the user can refine the question by stating it differently.

How To Retrieve Information with a WAIS Server

First, you need a WAIS client or software program for your PC. The next section tells you where you can find these programs.

Once you start up the WAIS client, you specify what's called a source to search upon. In WAIS terminology, a **source** specifies a specific WAIS server. Some WAIS software programs (such as WinWAIS) have a pre-loaded selection of WAIS server sites. Unfortunately, pre-loading a large amount of sites has its drawbacks in that many of these sites are now unreachable or defunct, but it's a start. Figure 4.17 shows the WinWAIS client's pre-loaded sources sites.

Search Tools

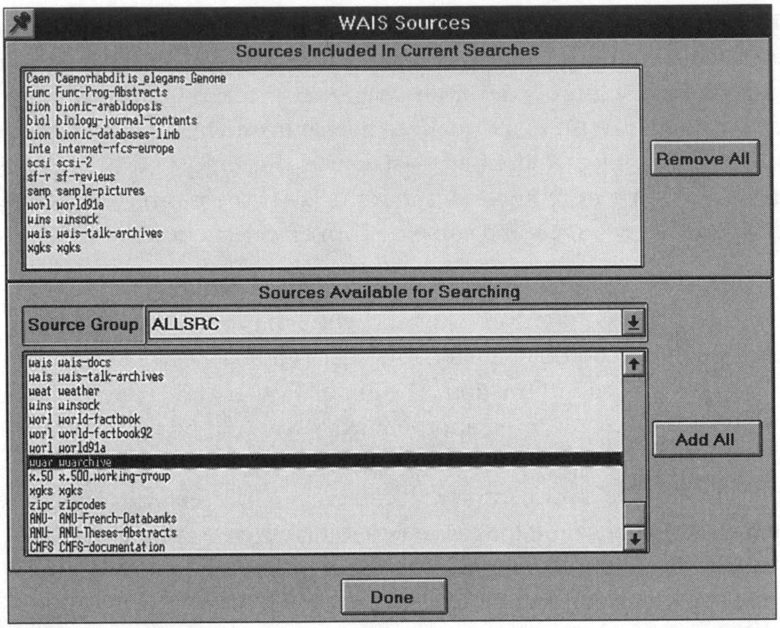

Fig. 4.17
WinWAIS pre-
loaded sources.

You can request that one keyword search (or phrase) be applied across multiple WAIS servers simultaneously. The phrase is basically considered to be a set of keywords to search for, based on weights/percentages of each word in specific documents and files.

All of the selected WAIS source servers search a full text index for the documents and return a list of documents that contain the keyword. Your WAIS software program may then request for the server to send a copy of any of the documents found. These could be text files, binaries, sounds, graphics, and so on.

A WAIS Search Scores the Results

Like an Olympic judge, WAIS judges and gives points to the directories and files it locates. It puts files that most closely match your search at the top of the list and gives them high scores. Files that it considers to be less appropriate get lower scores and appear further down on the list. The highest possible score a file can get is 1000. For example, if your keyword is "trout" the first WAIS document (with the score of 1000) might contain the word "trout" 250 times, the next document might only have 50 occurrences, and so on.

How To Get DOS and Windows-Based WAIS Software

The following FTP sites can be accessed to obtain the latest versions of each of these WAIS client programs. Newer versions of the programs may not have exactly the same filename that you see here.

PCWAIS

PCWAIS is an MS-DOS software program that provides a WAIS interface.

FTP site: **sunsite.unc.edu**

Directory: **/pub/packages/infosystems/wais/clients/ms-dos/**

Filename: **pcdist.zip**

WinWAIS

The USGS WAIS program WinWAIS uses a picture of the globe, which can translate into latitude and longitude coordinates to allow you to perform a search based on physical coordinates as seen in figure 4.18. Here, the area bounded by the lines over the map of the U.S. are translated by the WAIS client into actual limits for searching. The actual work that is going on behind the scenes of the client program is unknown to the user. WinWAIS includes support for SLIP, ODI, and CRYNWR packet drivers.

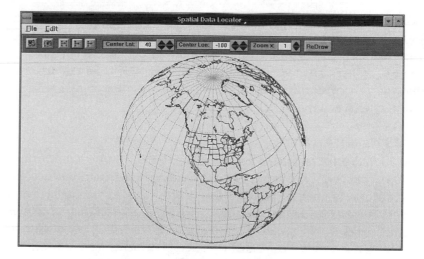

Fig. 4.18
USGS WinWAIS World map used to define physical searches.

FTP site: **ftp://ridgisd.er.usgs.gov**

Directory: **/software/wais/**

Filename: **wwais24.exe**

Search Tools

MCC WinWAIS

A self-extracting archive file of EINet Shareware winWAIS from MCC (Micro-electronics and Computer Technology Corp). Requires Windows 3.1 and Windows Sockets 1.1, which must be obtained separately.

FTP site: **ftp://ftp.einet.net**

Directory: **/einet/PC/**

Filename: **EWAIS204.EXE** (EWAIS204.ZIP—Archive)

So What's Out There?

There are many hundreds of WAIS database servers currently running. Topics range from recipes and movies to bibliographies, technical documents, and newsgroup archives.

The easiest way to get started if you don't have TCP/IP or PPP access is to try WAIS using a simple client running at another site on a dial-up shell account. To do this you must use Telnet to connect to either **sunsite.unc.edu** or **wais.wais.com** and enter the username **wais** at the "login:" prompt. This will permit you to use SWAIS (Screen WAIS). SWAIS is a cursor-based inter-face, so if you have problems, it may be due to your terminal setup. If you are unsure of the commands, try using a question mark (?) at the prompt.

Luckily, one of the main features of WAIS is its ease of use. It was initially designed from the ground up as a business or non-techie researcher tool. When writing papers in your favorite word processor, you can cut out a phrase or sentence and apply it to the WAIS search field as an example of what you are looking for. All of the WAIS servers will then apply a template of your interest and try to get the closest matches.

WAIS as an Agent

In addition to providing interactive access to a vast quantity of information, the WAIS system can also be used to create a rudimentary personal newspa-per. A virtually unlimited number of queries can be saved and updated at periodic intervals. To do this, your PC is directed to contact each WAIS server at certain times. When a source of information is contacted, any questions referencing that source are updated with new documents. You can then browse through the results the next morning.

The WAIS system employs a number of features that will be found in the personal newspaper of the future:

- Clear displays of which questions have new documents.

- Searches performed at night to hide communications delays.

- Documents stored on disk for future reference.

- Tools provided to quickly view stored documents.

Summary

With the majority of the Internet users focusing on the wonders of the World Wide Web and navigating through the maze of home pages, it is easy to forget that there is a vast amount of information not stored on a home page somewhere. Instead it is buried deep inside a gopher site or can be viewed globally using WAIS or located using some of the other powerful search tools discussed in this chapter. If there's one thing to remember it's that these Information Detectives are a valid and significant source of material that you may need to tap into.

Chapter 5

Finding and Retrieving Files from Remote Computers

An early application of the Internet was **file transfer protocol (FTP)**. This is a standard method of sending files from one computer to another, which does not depend on what type of computer you are using. **FTP sites** are computers that allow other people to retrieve files from the site. FTP sites may restrict access to members of an organization or to selected users. There are also a number of anonymous FTP sites, which are open for anyone to retrieve and sometimes post files.

As the number of files available from FTP sites has grown, a method of searching these sites for particular files was developed. This is called **Archie**. An Archie server is a computer that searches through a database of files available from FTP sites. Like FTP sites, Archie servers allow anyone to use them to search the Archie database.

FTP sites contain information, computer programs, pictures, sounds, and anything else that can be stored as a computer file. Many computer hardware manufacturers will store drivers and driver updates on FTP sites. Archives of newsgroups are stored on FTP sites. FTP sites are used by many authors to distribute freeware and shareware programs, such as WSArchie and WS_FTP, which are used in this chapter. We will also use the World Wide Web browser Netscape to access Archie and FTP. For more on this subject, see chapter 8, "Newsgroups."

In this chapter, you will learn how to:

- Find the files you want using Archie
- Transfer files using FTP
- Use the programs WSArchie and WS_FTP
- Run Archie and FTP using Web

Types of Files You'll Find on the Internet

"All files are not created equally"; this could be the motto for the Internet. You'll find literally hundreds of different types of files during your Internet searching. There are files for documents, images, video, sound, software programs, and so on. To make matters even more confusing, there are a variety of file formats for these different categories. For example, there are at least a dozen different still image file formats. Each file format is recognized by a specific extension to the filename. For example, **cat.gif** would indicate a picture of a cat using the GIF file format and **dog.au** would suggest that the file is a sound file of a dog. Don't be alarmed by all of these file formats. The good news is that less than a dozen different file formats are used 90 percent of the time. Table 5.1 provides an overview of the various files you may come across in your Net searching.

Tip

Knowledge of file extensions can come in handy when you're searching for a specific type of information. For example, if you want to search for JPEG image files on the Internet, you can tell the Archie and Veronica search tools to look for only those files that have JPG extensions.

Table 5.1   An Overview of Files on the Net

Software File Format

File Extension	File Format	General Description
EXE	program	Executable software

Document File Formats

File Extension	File Format	General Description
ASC	text	Standard ASCII text document
HTM	text	ASCII text file for Web documents

Document File Formats

File Extension	File Format	General Description
TXT	text	Standard ASCII text document
WRI	Write	Microsoft Windows Write format

Still Image File Formats

File Extension	File Format	General Description
BMP	Windows	Bitmap Windows graphic image
GIF	GIF	CompuServe Graphics Interchange Format
JPG	JPEG	Compressed still image standard by Joint Photographic Experts Group
PCX	Zsoft IMage	Designed for PC Paintbrush
PS	PostScript	An Adobe printer language. Delivers documents with formatting, layout, font, and diagrams via the Internet
TIFF	Tagged Image File Format	A common Macintosh graphics format
XBM	X Window	Image bitmap for X Windows Bitmap

Sound File Formats

File Extension	File Format	General Description
AU	Audio	UNIX audio file format
SBI	Sound Blaster	Microsoft Sound Blaster file format
WAV	Waveform	Windows sound format

(continues)

II

Search Tools

Table 5.1 Continued

Video File Formats

File Extension	File Format	General Description
AVI	Audio Video	Microsoft format for video for Interleaved Windows
MOV	QuickTime	Apple format for video with sound (There is a Windows version.)
MPG	MPEG	Full motion compressed video standard by Motion Picture Experts Group

Looking for a File? Use Archie

The number of files contained on FTP sites is enormous. They are organized like your hard drive (because they are stored on hard drives!), in directories. Because there are so many sites with so many files, it is almost impossible to browse through them and find what you want. That's why there is Archie!

Archie is the name for a database of files available on anonymous FTP servers. Multiple sites have computers that are Archie servers. That means that they let you, the client, search the database using their computing power. Archie is a client-server application, as is the FTP protocol itself. The Archie database is generally the same at each site, but you may notice variations between sites in different countries. Like most Internet applications, the contents of Archie are compiled on a volunteer basis, from anonymous FTP sites that have agreed to participate. These FTP sites have sent Archie a list of the files on their system.

If you know the name of a file, or a subject name that may appear in the name of a file, you can use Archie with a reasonable chance of success. Many files are stored at multiple sites. A site that has copies of files from another site is called a **mirror site** or a mirror. If you can't log on to one FTP server, use Archie to find a mirror site.

Note

There are hundreds of thousands of files available on thousands of anonymous FTP servers around the world. Anyone with an Internet connection can use their computer as an FTP server! A couple of excellent (but busy) sites in the United States are the Center for Innovative Computing Applications (CICA) at **ftp.cica.indiana.edu**, and the Washington University at St. Louis at **wuarchive.wustl.edu**. Both of these sites have thousands of files including many Internet software programs.

Accessing an Archie Server

There are a few different ways to access Archie servers. You can run an Archie software (client) program such as WSArchie for Windows, you can use Telnet to start a session with an Archie server, you can use a Web browser to go to an Archie gateway, and you can even send your information to an Archie server through e-mail.

The best way to use Archie depends on your individual situation. If you don't have a full Internet connection, Telnet or e-mail may be the only way for you to use Archie. Most Internet connections will allow you to use Web browsers or Archie clients that run with Windows. These are generally easier to use than e-mail or Telnet. Details of all these methods are given in this chapter.

Archie Through Winsock

If you are connecting to the Internet from within Windows, you are using a program called winsock.dll (automatically called by your Internet applications). This means you can use WSArchie, a well designed and freeware Windows Archie client. Figure 5.1 shows the opening window for WSArchie.

Note

WinSock is a specification from Microsoft that defines how Windows programs communicate with networks. Different software manufacturers have written different Winsock programs which use this specification. Your service provider should set this up for you, or provide instructions on how to do it when you first sign up.

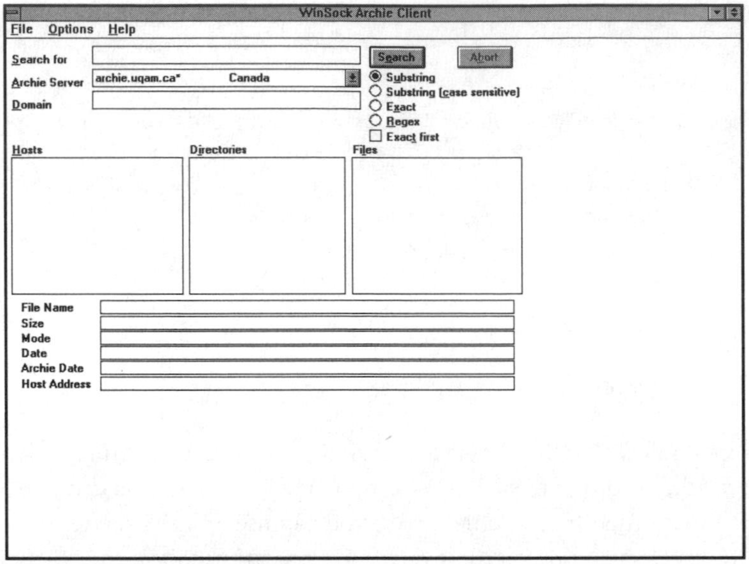

Fig. 5.1
This is WSArchie as it appears immediately after startup. All you have to do is type in your keyword and press the Search button.

> **Note**
>
> WSArchie is a freeware program that you can obtain using FTP. It is made up of a zipped file WSARCHIE.ZIP, which can be found at **ftp.cica.indiana.edu**, in the directory /pub/pc/win3/winsock.
>
> WS_FTP is also a freeware program, and it is available as WS_FTP.ZIP at the same place as WSArchie.

Archie Through the World Wide Web

If you are using a World Wide Web browser such as Netscape, you can go to Web sites that interface between you and an Archie server. This is an easy way to use Archie, although sometimes not as flexible as using a dedicated Archie client such as WSArchie, as the Web sites don't always allow all the options you can get from a dedicated Archie program. A list of Web pages that interface to Archie servers is located at the URL **http://web.nexor. co.uk/archie.html**. Figure 5.2 shows the Archie gateway at **http:// www.csi.nb.ca/archgate.html**. More options than are shown in figure 5.2 are available by scrolling down. The Web browser shown in figure 5.2 is Netscape version 1.1. For more on Web browsers, see chapter 3, "Searching the World Wide Web."

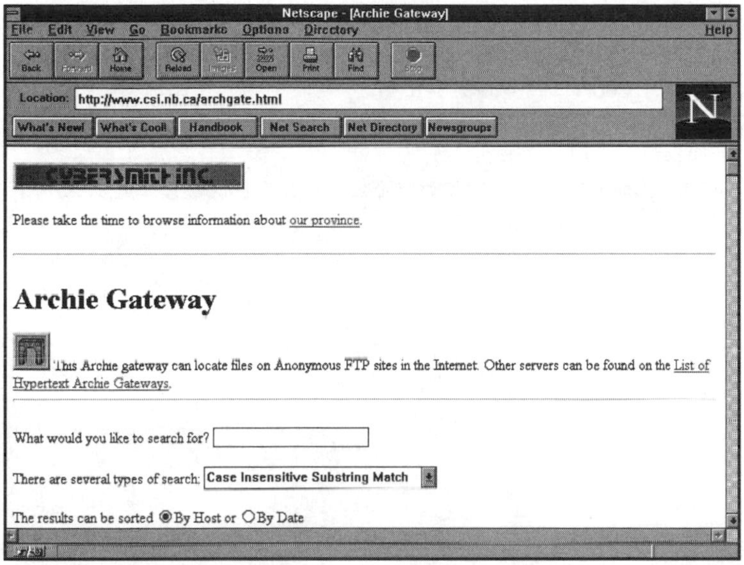

Fig. 5.2
This is the
Cybersmith Inc.
Archie gateway, a
typical Web Archie
gateway.

Archie Through Telnet

If you do not have an Archie client such as WSArchie, or a Web browser that supports forms, you can use a protocol called Telnet to connect to an Archie server. Because WSArchie and Web browsers are available as freeware, you will be better served in the long run to get a copy of one of these programs. The presentation of these programs is generally more user friendly than running Archie over Telnet, which will give you a text interface.

To use Archie through a Telnet interface, Telnet to the Archie server and login as **archie**. Anonymous login does not work. From here what you get will vary from server to server, if you have problems, type **help** to see what commands you can use. See figure 5.3.

Archie Through E-mail

If the only access you have to the Internet is via e-mail, you can still use Archie servers to search for files. It just takes a little longer. Detailed instructions on how to do this can be obtained by sending an e-mail to **archie@archie.internic.net** with the word "help" in the message body. In return, a few days later, you will receive a large e-mail with detailed information on how to use Archie by e-mail.

What you will end up doing is sending e-mail to the Archie server with appropriate messages in the subject or message body to direct the Archie search.

A simple search is performed by sending an e-mail with the text find "FOOBAR.TXT," if you are looking for a file called FOOBAR.TXT. The Archie server will then reply by e-mail. This may save you connect time charges, but it may also take days to get your results!

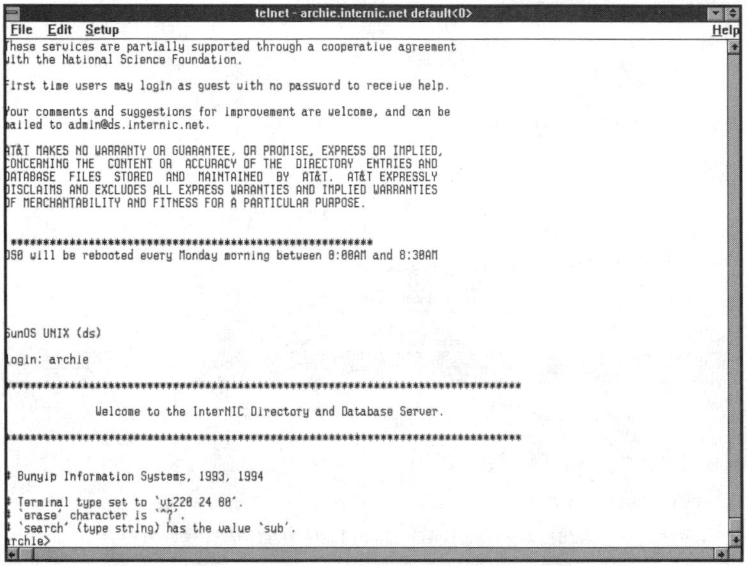

Fig. 5.3
This is the logon screen at the Archie server **archie.internic. net**.

> **Note**
>
> In case you are wondering what this FOO.TXT file is that is mentioned so often in examples from the Internet, FOO and FOOBAR come from a military acronym that can't be expanded in a family book! It's just another tradition, instead of saying "EXAMPLE.TXT" people will say "FOO.TXT" or "FOOBAR.TXT."

Search For and Locate Files with Archie

Searching for files on an Archie database is keyword type searching that is familiar to anyone who uses a word processor. It is *not* a subject search. You must know a name or part of a name (a substring) that is in the file or directory name that you want. Archie searches can also use a more powerful regular expression search, in WSArchie this is done by selecting the Regex radio button. This search type is described in more detail in the following section.

Once you have picked your search, you should choose a server. It is generally wise to choose one geographically close, especially in the same country. In business hours you may not be able to connect and you may want to try something on another continent. Generally, it is very slow to use European servers from North America. Some Archie and FTP servers restrict users to people from the same country, which they can find out from your IP address. The WSArchie program conveniently indicates the location of the servers in its list. If you are familiar with Internet addressing, you should be able to figure out where a server is located.

> **Note**
>
> Archie servers have names that are like any Internet address. The last section indicates where the server is geographically. If the ending is edu, gov, mil, com, or net, it is most likely in the United States and is an educational, government, military, commercial, or large private network site.
>
> If it has a two letter ending, those two letters stand for a country. The letters ca denote a Canadian site, uk for United Kingdom, de for German, and so on. A detailed listing of the abbreviations can be found at **nic.merit.edu**, in the internet/connectivity directory. Look at the text files there for some interesting Internet statistics as well as the definitions of all the abbreviations. You can access this site by gopher or by FTP.

Deciding What To Search: An Example

To help describe the use of Archie and FTP, we will have some fun. Assuming you have a lot of free time, you might want to play a computer game. Tetris is a classic game, which I would enjoy if I had time to play it of course. If you have heard the name of a file but don't know where to find it, this is the kind of search Archie is well suited for: You know, or have been told, that a file exists, and you have a good idea what the file is called. We will use Archie to locate Tetris, and FTP to retrieve it.

Choosing a Search Command

The type of Archie search you perform can affect the speed and accuracy of the response. Different search options are appropriate in different situations. The search options available when using WSArchie are as follows:

- **Substring.** The Archie server looks for directories or filenames that contain the text you specified, as the whole name or part of the name.

- **Substring (case sensitive).** Same as Substring, except the filename or piece of the filename, must match the case of your entry.

■ **Exact.** The filename or directory exactly matches what you enter, including the case.

■ **Regex.** A regular expression search, you can enter wildcards and special codes, described in more detail in the section "Working with Advanced Commands."

■ **Exact first.** You can choose to start with an exact search and move to another type by checking this box and selecting the secondary type. If no matches are found, then the secondary method you selected using the radio buttons will be used.

WSArchie has a help section which describes these options in some detail. To look at the WSArchie help on search commands, select Help->Index and click on the text item Search Type.

The fastest search is the Exact search, but this is obviously useful only when you know the exact name. Substring searching is the most general, will return the most responses, and be the slowest.

Beginning Your Search

The simplest search to perform (using our Tetris example) is to type the text **tetris** in the Search for box in the WSArchie main window (see figure 5.4 for the main window of WSArchie). The default search is a substring search that is not case sensitive. The results should look something like figure 5.4. The Hosts box contains a number of FTP site names. I have selected the **syr.edu** site, which is maintained by Syracuse University. There is no special reason I chose this site, but be warned that there are also UNIX, Mac, and DOS versions of Tetris. We will retrieve a Windows version.

In figure 5.4 I have selected a directory called software/msdos/windows3/ games. This is because I want to use my PC to play Tetris in Windows. This looks pretty promising! All you need to do now is download the file via FTP, which is described in the following sections of this chapter.

Working with Advanced Commands

With our Tetris search, we found many files in many directories on many servers! This included files with different suffixes, and different names like cooltetris, and tetriss. Using some more sophisticated options, you can narrow the results of your search.

An exact or a case-sensitive search aren't appropriate unless you know exactly what you are looking for. You can assume that names will be lowercase if you have to. I didn't know anything about the case of the filenames, so I wouldn't use that in this example. If we had known that there is a windows version of Tetris, called tetriss, we could have searched for tetriss.exe or tetriss.zip.

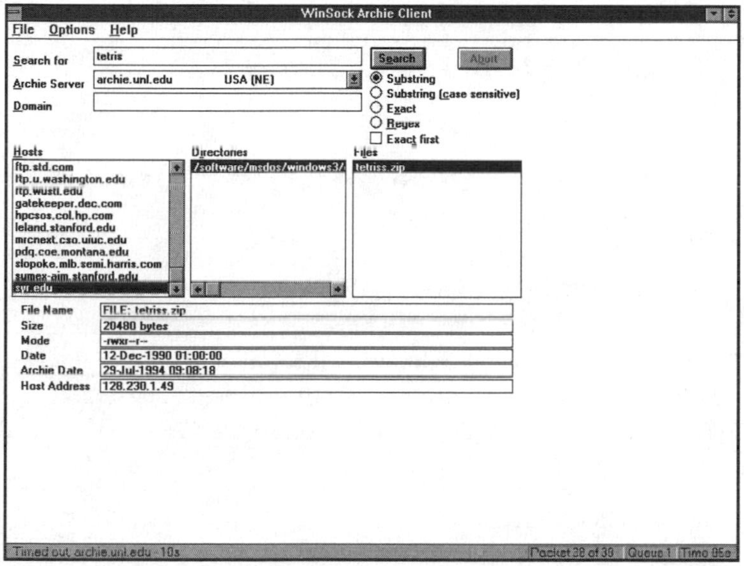

Fig. 5.4
WSArchie results of a substring search on meteor are shown in this figure. I have selected the **syr.edu** server from the list of hosts, and the matches on this host are shown.

In this example, the Regex or regular expression search could have narrowed the results and still found the files we wanted. A regular expression search can include wildcards, can include sets of characters, and can exclude sets of characters. Square brackets [] are used to enclose a range or set of characters of interest. WSArchie describes this well in the Help file.

A Regex search is also a substring type search, that is, if you searched for "tetris" using a Regex search, you would get the same results as with the substring search. You can force it to begin and end using ^ and *, respectively: To look for a file with a ".zip" on the end, and beginning with the word tetris in the name, you would enter **^tetris.*\.zip$**.

The characters .* indicate any number of any characters can be here, like the DOS wildcard *. The backslash \ indicates that Archie should treat the following character as a character, not a wildcard. This search still finds tetriss.zip but doesn't come up with any files ending with the suffix "tar," which are UNIX files.

For more discussion of the Regex search option of WSArchie, read the help file in WSArchie.

> **Note**
>
> Wildcards are symbols that can be replaced by any character. The name comes from card games, where the wildcard can stand for any card. In DOS, the wildcard * can be replaced by a set of any length of any characters, while the wildcard ? can be replaced by any one character. For Archie searching, .* is equivalent to the DOS *. single character.

Now That You've Found It, Use FTP To Get It

While you can use WSArchie to browse through the directories you are interested in, it can be very slow. Once you have found something interesting, if it is a file, you can download it right away. If it is a directory, or if you may be interested in a number of files together in a directory, it is faster to browse using FTP, which gives you a direct connection to the FTP server. Archie is only a database of the server contents.

You can retrieve files from an FTP server using FTP programs like WS_FTP, or using most Web browsers.

> **Troubleshooting**
>
> *When I try to connect to an FTP site, I get the reply "connection refused" (or something similar).*
>
> You may find that FTP server sites are too busy and won't let you log in. This will be stated in a message the server sends back to you, or if the server is really busy, you may get no reply at all. The only remedy is to try again. The best times to get Internet work done seem to be early in the morning or late at night when everyone but the computers are doing something else! Some sites may be restricted and may not allow anonymous access or users from other countries. In this case you should look for a mirror site, which is another site with the same files.

Using WS_FTP to Download Files

WS_FTP is a Windows-based freeware FTP program that allows you to run the file transfer protocol under Windows. It comes configured with the Internet addresses of a number of FTP servers, and allows you to add new servers to a list. The WS_FTP Session Profile dialog box is shown in figure 5.5. Here I have selected the location of the tetriss.zip file we found in our search.

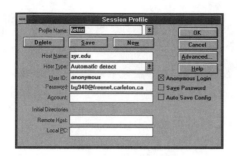

Fig. 5.5
This is the Session
Profile dialog box
of WS_FTP. From
here you can select
an FTP site that is
already set up, or
enter a new one.

You place the IP address or the name of the server in the Host Name: edit box. If you select a saved profile from the Profile Name drop-down list box, the information will be filled in for you. Anonymous login is selected in this example, and I have configured the WS_FTP program with my e-mail address to use as the anonymous login password. You can choose initial directories at both the FTP server and your computer, I usually make a TEMP directory to download the files into to keep them separate from my other work. You should not mix the FTP files with your other work until you have checked them for viruses!

Note

Most FTP work you will do will be to public "anonymous" FTP sites. These are computers that will let anyone retrieve files from them. The standard practice is to log in to the FTP server with the user name "anonymous" and to give your e-mail address as the password. It is not necessary to give your e-mail address, but I have never received any junk mail back yet.

Using Web Browsers To Download Files

Netscape and most other Web browsers also have FTP capabilities. You go to an FTP site by placing the URL in the Location edit box. For an FTP server, use the text ftp:// in front of the name or IP address of the server. Figure 5.6 shows what was returned by the FTP server at **syr.edu**, displayed by Netscape. Netscape interprets the FTP information and allows you to click on directory names to move between directories, and click on files to retrieve them.

Web browsers will handle the login procedures for you but do not have the simple graphical interface of the Windows type FTP programs, which generally look like the Windows File Manager program.

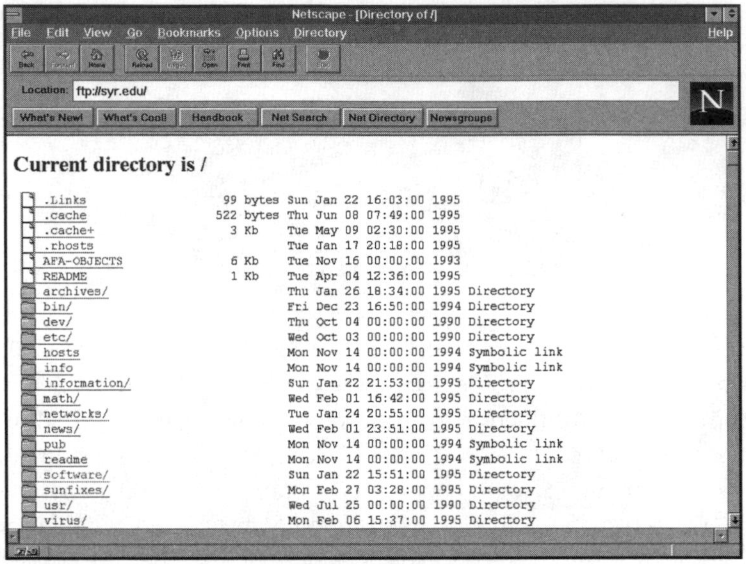

Fig. 5.6
Netscape 1.1 is
shown at the
syr.edu FTP site.
The FTP site
directories are
listed.

How To Navigate Through FTP Directories

Many anonymous FTP servers are university sites that run on UNIX type
operating systems. These systems, and newer ones like Windows NT, allow
file and directory names longer than the eight dot three characters of DOS.
The backslash used to separate directory names may now be a forward slash.
The names are also case sensitive. Some directories may be open for public
access, while others may not be. Often publicly accessible files will be under
a /pub directory.

If you are looking for freeware or shareware programs, they may be organized
in directories according to your type of machine, for example pcdos, mac,
UNIX directories. Just remember that these files are all stored on disk somewhere, and are organized in whatever fashion seemed appropriate to the
organizer.

To move through directories using WS_FTP, select the change directory button or click on the directory names in the window. The listing ".." refers to
the higher level, for example to move from c:\root\pub\ to c:\root\, you
could click on the ".." item. Figure 5.7 shows the /software directory on the
syr.edu FTP server. There are a number of files and directories available to
choose.

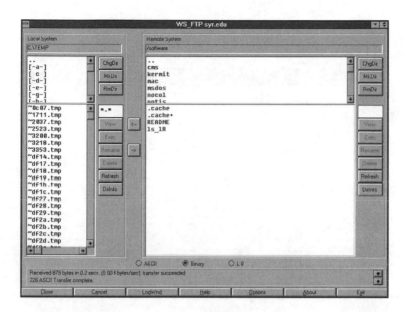

Fig. 5.7
WSArchie at the /software directory of the **syr.edu** FTP site. Subdirectories of /software are shown in the first box under the label Remote System. Files in /software are shown in the second box under the Remote System heading.

You can also use Netscape to navigate through the directories at a FTP site. Netscape shows you the current directory at the top of the page, and lists subdirectories and files underneath as hot links. The ".." listing is replaced with a hot link "Up to higher level directory," which takes you back one level. Clicking on a directory will take you to that directory. Directories are indicated by a folder type icon to the left of the list, files are indicated by an icon that looks like a piece of paper with the corner folded over. Figure 5.8 shows how Netscape presents the same /software directory of **syr.edu** that is shown in figure 5.7 using WS_FTP.

Note

Any decently maintained FTP site will have a file in each directory called README (or some variation) or INDEX. These text-based files describe the contents of files in the directory. Of course, there are exceptions to this rule. Before you download a file, take a look at the readme/index file, using the View button of WS_FTP or by clicking on the file in Netscape. This may tell you more information about the file you want, if it's freeware or shareware, how to use it, who created it, or maybe nothing at all. But take a look first before you proceed.

II

Search Tools

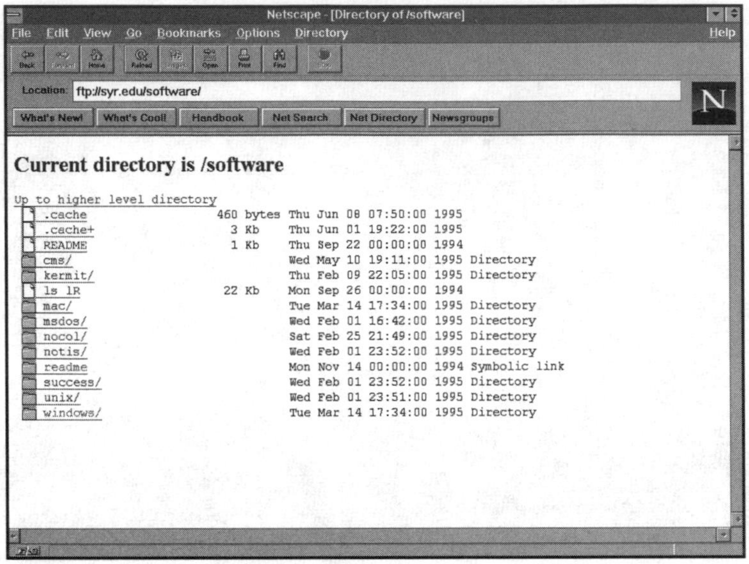

Fig. 5.8
Netscape 1.1 shown at the /software directory of the FTP site **syr.edu**, the same as shown in figure 5.7.

How To Download Files from FTP Sites

Finally we are ready to download the files we want. Before you do any downloading, get yourself a virus checking program! This is very important!

> **Caution**
>
> You must consider any file you get from an FTP site, or any file or disk that you get from anyone other than a software manufacturer, as being potentially infected with a virus. *Get an anti-virus program now!* MS-DOS versions 6.00 and above have an anti-virus program, and numerous shareware programs are available, the most common being the McAfee's Virus Scan, available for DOS or Windows (FTP to **mcafee.com**).
>
> You can only get a virus by running a file (such as an .EXE, .COM, or .BAT) *not* by reading an e-mail or viewing a graphic. But beware and take precautions! The small amount of effort it takes to check for viruses is minuscule compared to the time it will take to replace all the work on your hard drive!

Now that you have the anti-virus program ready, we can continue with our example. I am starting at the /software/msdos/windows3/games directory of the **syr.edu** site. From our Archie search, we know there is a file tetriss.zip in this directory.

Figure 5.9 shows what WS_FTP looks like at this point. I have selected the required file, which is greyed. All you have to do is push the arrow button which points from the FTP site towards your hard drive. If you are paying attention, you will note that I am using a TEMP directory like I suggested! It makes it much easier to keep track of your work by using consistent directories to hold files before using them.

Figure 5.10 shows Netscape at the same point. To save a file in Netscape, hold the shift key on your keyboard and click on the hot link. You can just click on the hot link, and if you have not defined a viewer application in Netscape for the file type, Netscape will ask you if you want to save it.

Now what to do? Read chapter 6, especially "What Do You Do When You Get A File That's Compressed." And don't forget to check your new files for viruses before you run any included executable files.

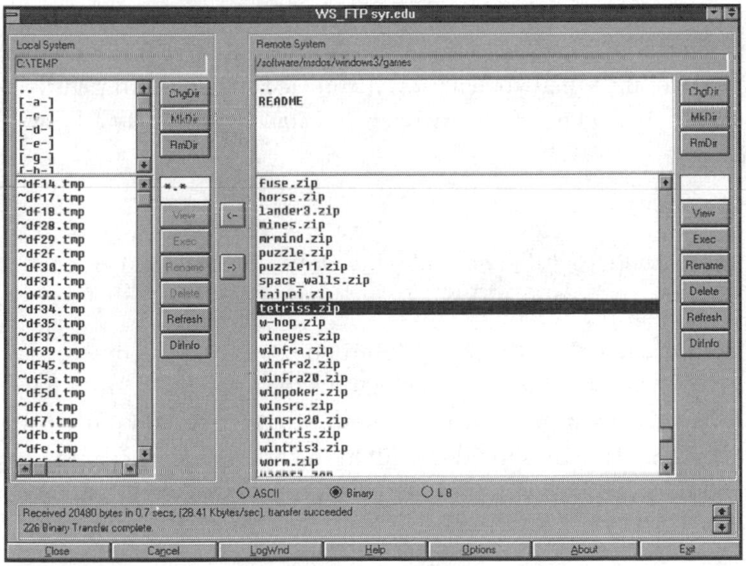

Fig. 5.9
WS_FTP is shown with the file we want to download, tetriss.zip, greyed.

II

Search Tools

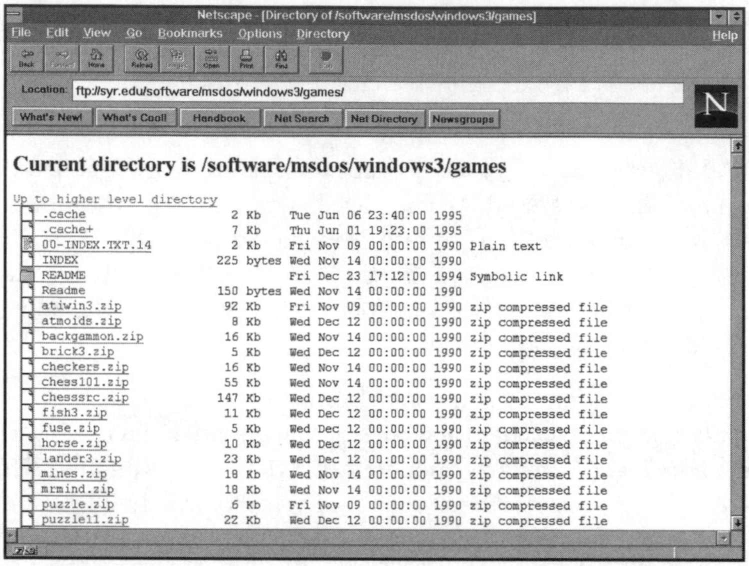

Fig. 5.10
Netscape 1.1 is
shown at the
directory with
desired files, hold
the Shift key and
click on them to
download.

Combining WSArchie & WS_FTP

A convenient way to use Archie and FTP together is provided with the WSArchie program. You can set up WSArchie to "tell" WS_FTP to download files automatically when you click on them. First you must configure WSArchie so that it knows how to open and start WS_FTP. Here's how you do this:

1. Open WSArchie.

2. Select the FTP Setup item under the Options menu, and enter the full path and name of your WS_FTP program.

   Do not delete the "%h:%d/%f" stuff on the end of the line, this is where WSArchie sticks the name of the file to be downloaded. If you do delete it, copy it from the last sentence in this text and put it back in after WS_FTP. You should also fill in the user name with anonymous, and the password with your e-mail address as you would for any anonymous FTP work.

3. Now you are ready to perform your search. If you do our search for "tetris," you can select the server **syr.edu**, and double click on the file listing tetriss.zip. A window will appear asking for you to OK the FTP command. Click on the OK button, and WS_FTP will open in the background and get the file. You're done!

WS_FTP and WSArchie work together, any other combination is not guaranteed! The authors of WS_FTP note that the 32 bit version will not always work with WSArchie properly. This is a problem with the programs, and it may change with new releases.

Summary

Now you are able to find files that you are looking for, it might be a good idea to examine how to find the names of the files you want! Good places to find the names of useful files are newsgroups, mailing lists, and Web sites. Other chapters of this book describe how to use these tools.

Chapter 6

Internet Files and Copyright Issues

Now that you know how to find programs and data on the Internet, it's time to learn how to put them to use. Programs are available on the Internet as shareware or freeware that will enable you to add full multimedia capability to your computer. However, you will also notice that these programs are downloaded as compressed files that are useless if you don't know how to decompress them. **Compression** is the process of converting a file with various programs to save disk space. Different operating systems have spawned many different types of compression. Only a few of these are popular on the Internet, such as .zip, .sit, and .tar. You will also need to get software for viewing image files, sound files, or movies on your particular platform.

Finally, you need to know about copyright, the public domain, and how this applies to the software and information now at your fingertips. When must you pay to use a program or file and when is it free? Can you copy this text for a newsletter or send a copy of this program to your friends?

This chapter answers these questions and introduces you to the following:

- Understanding and recognizing compression versus encoding

- Uncompressing files from PC, Macintosh, and UNIX systems

- Software you can find on the Internet for viewing graphics files or listening to audio files

- Copyright basics and the public domain

Understanding Encoding

When you send or receive any file that is not a simple text file using e-mail or newsgroup client software, you are using encoding. Because your software may handle these files automatically, without your knowledge, you may not know that encoding and decoding is occurring at all. What exactly is encoding?

E-mail and newsgroups use ASCII format files. In other words, files must be composed of ASCII characters only (essentially A-Z, 0-9, and some control characters). A program file or even a document file created by your word processor contains many characters that are not part of the ASCII character set. Such a file is often called a **binary file**. **Encoding** is the process of coding a binary file into a new file that uses only the ASCII characters. Once this is accomplished, the file can be transmitted by e-mail/news protocols to its destination and decoded into the original binary file by the recipient. **File Transfer Protocol** (FTP) was developed to transmit binary files without the need of encoding. Files at FTP sites will often be encoded anyway so that clients can access the files even if they only have e-mail service. You can recognize files that have been encoded and/or compressed by their file extensions (see table 6.1). Encoding a file will actually make it larger than the original. Do not confuse encoding with **compression,** which is used to compress a file into a form that requires less allocated memory.

Tip
Some e-mail software (like Eudora) automatically decodes incoming encoded files and can prompt the user where the decoded file is to be placed. Eudora is available from QUALCOMM Incorporated (**ftp. qualcomm.com**) as freeware versions: 1.1.5 for System 7 and 1.4.4 for Windows.

Table 6.1   File Extensions of Compressed and Encoded Files

	Compression	Encoding
File type	binary	ASCII
Common file extensions	.arc, .exe .zip, .pkg .sea, .sit .z, .tar	.uue, .hqx

UUEncode and **UUDecode** were developed under UNIX, but they are now used on the PC and the Macintosh. Another popular encoding system for Macintosh users is **BinHex**. BinHex files are encoded into a format that uses only printable ASCII characters arranged in lines of reasonable length. Hexadecimal digits, which use 0-9 and A-F (ASCII characters), are used to encode. Files available at FTP sites are often compressed and encoded. Program files are always compressed first and then encoded last. The original file is obtained in reverse: decode first to obtain "file.sit" and uncompress last to obtain "file."

Using UUEncoded Files

To decode a file that has been encoded in UUEncode format, named
"goodbook.uue" for example, do the following:

1. Add the directory of the UUDecode program to your PATH statement in
   your autoexec.bat file.

2. Change to the directory containing the file to be decoded and at the
   DOS prompt enter **UUDecode goodbook.uue**.

Using BinHex Files

To decode a file that has been encoded in BinHex format, named
"goodbook.hqx" for example, using the program STUFFIT-EXPANDER:

System 6 users should do the following:

1. Double-click the STUFFIT-EXPANDER icon.

2. Open the File menu and choose Expand.

3. Choose the file you want to expand.

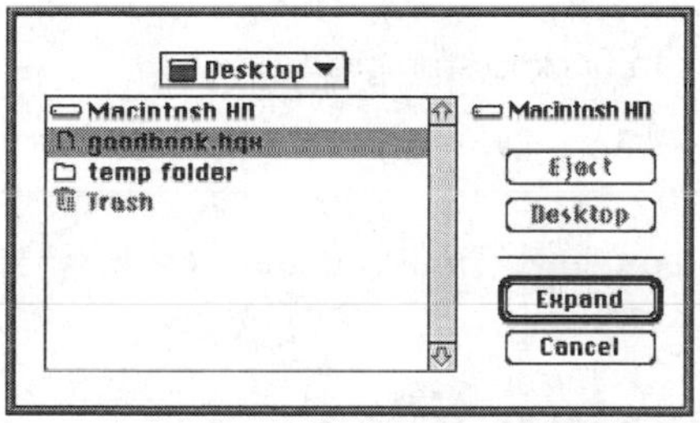

Fig. 6.1
Decoding a BinHex
file with STUFFIT-
EXPANDER.

4. Click the Expand button.

   Decoding progress is reported by a dialog box, and the decoded file is
   placed into the folder of your choice.

5. Return to the Expand option to decode more files or select Quit from
   the File menu to exit STUFFIT-EXPANDER.

System 7 users can follow the System 6 directions or use the drag-and-drop
interface:

1. Click and hold to select the icons of the files to be decoded.

2. Drag the icons over the STUFFIT-EXPANDER icon and they will become
   highlighted.

3. Release the mouse button and watch the progress dialog box.

4. STUFFIT-EXPANDER quits automatically when it's finished.

Working with Compressed Files

If you have seen files with extensions such as .zip, .tar, .sit, or .sea, you have seen compressed files. A **compressed file** is an archive of the original file that takes less space on your disk, but it is not a file you can use directly. Files are compressed using various algorithms that analyze to find ways of storing the characters in a smaller space. How can this be? For example, an algorithm can replace long strings of repeated characters with a shorter code that would mean "repeat character 14 times." You may already be familiar with .arc, the original PC/DOS archived file format developed for backup of hard drives. If you maintain floppy or tape backups of your hard drive, the backup files are in .arc or a different archive format.

Compressed files have three benefits:

- They take up less space on your disks.

- They save space in backup storage.

- They are faster to download and transmit.

If you get a compressed file, you must uncompress it.

Uncompressing Files

Luckily, you can anticipate the decompression method required before you download a file by noticing its filename extension. For instance, compressed files for IBM-PC and compatibles are compressed with the ZIP format and will have the file extension ".zip". Macintosh files are compressed using the STUFFIT format and will have the file extension ".sit". This section will show you how to uncompress files you download from the Internet for your particular platform. You will learn how PKUNZIP is used on the PC, how to use STUFFIT-EXPANDER on the Macintosh, and the basic commands to decompress files at the UNIX command line.

PC Files: PKUNZIP

ZIP files are compressed files created by the program PKZIP, which was written by Phil Katz. PKZIP is a shareware program that can run on all IBM-PCs and compatibles from the DOS command line. PKZIP compresses one or many files into a single ZIP file and adds the .zip extension. If you get a ZIP file, you can unpack the archive with the program PKUNZIP. PKZIP can also compress files into self-extracting archives that are given the .exe extension because they are executable like any other executable file. Self-extracting files unpack themselves when they are run.

To unpack a ZIP file, named goodbook.zip for example, follow these steps:

1. Add the directory of the PKUNZIP program to your PATH statement in your autoexec.bat file.

2. Change to the directory containing the file to be unzipped and enter **pkunzip -d goodbook.zip**.

   (The "-d" switch allows for the creation of any directories that may be part of the archive.)

3. To check the unpacked files, enter **dir /w**.

Macintosh Files: STUFFIT-EXPANDER

SIT files are compressed files created by the STUFFIT group of programs, which were developed by Raymond Lau. STUFFIT Lite™ is a shareware utility for the Mac and STUFFIT Deluxe is a more powerful commercial package. STUFFIT compresses one or many files into a single SIT file and adds the .sit extension. If you get a SIT file, you can unpack it with the freeware program STUFFIT-EXPANDER. STUFFIT can also compress files into self-extracting archives that are given the .sea extension. They are executable Macintosh files and unpack themselves even if the user does not have the UNSTUFFIT or STUFFIT-EXPANDER programs. STUFFIT ".sea" files have a characteristic diamond-shaped icon. See figure 6.2.

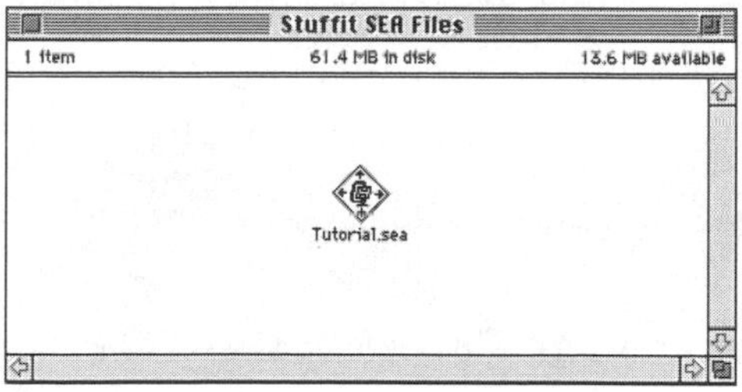

Fig. 6.2
A self-extracting file created by the STUFFIT program.

To unpack a SIT file, use the program STUFFIT-EXPANDER. System 6 users should:

1. Double-click the STUFFIT-EXPANDER icon.

2. Open the File menu and select Expand.

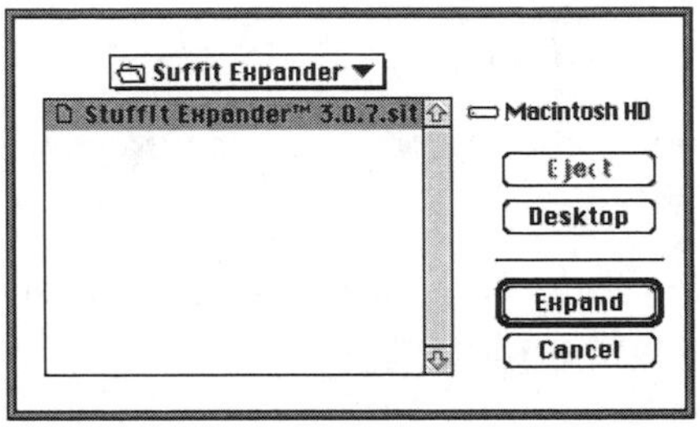

Fig. 6.3
The STUFFIT-EXPANDER Expand dialog box.

Tip
Holding down the shift key until a dialog box appears causes the program to prompt you for an alternative destination for the unstuffed file. Holding down the option key until the progress window appears makes STUFFIT-EXPANDER delete the original archive after expansion is complete.

3. Choose the file you want to expand.

4. Click the Expand button.

   Expansion progress is reported by a dialog box, and the archive is expanded into a new folder in the same folder as the archive. (Single file archives are not placed into a new folder.)

5. To exit STUFFIT-EXPANDER, return to the Expand option to unpack more archives or open the File menu and choose Quit.

System 7 users can follow the System 6 directions or use the drag-and-drop interface:

1. Click and hold to select the icons of the files you want to expand (even the icon of a folder or disk).

2. Drag the icons over the STUFFIT-EXPANDER icon and they will become highlighted.

3. Release the mouse button and watch the progress dialog box.

4. STUFFIT-EXPANDER quits automatically when it's finished.

Internet Sources for Compression/Decompression Software

Table 6.2 is a selection of some software for the PC and the Macintosh to help you unzip or unpack various compressed or encoded files. Sites and their contents change from time to time, so you should also use Archie to search for these same filenames at other anonymous-FTP sites. See chapter 5, "Finding and Retrieving Files from Remote Computers."

Table 6.2   Available Decompression Software

Program Directory	Filename	Computer	Internet Address
PKUNZIP	pkz110.exe, pkz204g.exe	PC	ftp.ncsa.uiuc.edu/PC/contrib
FILEBUDDY	fb315.exe	PC	ftp.mcp.com http://www.ncsa.uiuc.edu
BINHEX	binhex.macbinary	Macintosh Binhex (.hqx) decoding	ftp.ncsa.uiuc.edu (Mac/utilities) http://www.mcp.com/
STUFFIT-EXPANDER	stuffit-expander-352.hqx stuffit-expander-352.bin	Macintosh	ftp.ncsa.uiuc.edu (Mac/utilities) http://www.ncsa.uiuc.edu
EXPANDER-ENHANCER	drop-stuff-with-ee-352.hqx	Macintosh Use with expander to handle: .zip, .arc, .pkg, .gz, .z, .uu	ftp.ncsa.uiuc.edu (Mac/utilities)

Viewing Pictures and Listening to Audio

The Internet is now a vast source of information for education, research, employment communication, and entertainment. Like books, magazines, and television, the providers of information on the Internet make use of visual and even audio information as well as text. You cannot appreciate the benefit of this exciting resource if you are limited to text-only interaction. Time also becomes less relevant on the Internet when you can access this kind of information "now." Who could have guessed, even five years ago, that you would be pointing your Netscape Web Browser at the official Rolling Stones Web Site and viewing video of a recent live show in Australia?

This section provides a basic introduction to using graphics, video, and audio files that you will encounter on the Internet. To this end, the most practical information is the location of programs that will allow you to view and listen to such files. The most fluid manner of accessing this media is by using Netscape, so you will learn how to configure your browser to use helper applications for viewing and listening to files that are not handled directly by Netscape.

Tip
Macintosh users might consider obtaining the commercial STUFFIT Deluxe package (Aladin Systems Inc.). In addition to handling STUFFIT files, the package provides extensions for the conversion of most file compression and encoding formats that you will encounter on the Internet.

Search Tools

II

Experiencing Audio-Visual on Your PC

Most PCs sold today have VGA (Video Graphics Array) or super VGA cards and compatible monitors that are adequate for multimedia use.

> **Note**
>
> VGA supports all previous graphics modes for the PC (MDA, CGA, EGA and MCGA) and in addition displays the red-green-blue components of any pixel in 64 levels of intensity. This provides 262,144 possible color combinations (64x64x64)! This does not mean you can view 262,144 colors; your VGA card can display only 256 of these colors at any one time.

Many image files that you can find on the Internet contain more than 256 colors, but you cannot view them all. Graphics programs, such as Graphic WorkShop, prepare the image for viewing by taking a range of image colors and assigning them to one of the 256 available for display on your monitor. This means you can view the files without any painstaking effort on your part, but you will need lots of RAM or hard disk space for this manipulation of the file. VGA cards have extra sockets for adding Video RAM (VRAM), which is used by your video system to process and display images. By adding 5 Mb of VRAM you can enjoy such benefits as:

- The ability to display larger images with the full 256 color display capacity

- Faster scrolling of large images

- Faster image processing (manipulation)

- Quicker display times

- Less demand on computer RAM

Most software developers provide device drivers that access your particular video system automatically. In Windows or OS/2 WARP, all graphics are run by device drivers, and graphics programs for Windows will run on your current video system.

Listening to audio is best accomplished using a stereo sound card, such as a Sound Blaster card, or a Windows compatible sound card. If you only have the basic PC speaker and Windows 3.1, you can find some audio support provided by Microsoft in the form of a freeware speaker driver for users of Windows 3.X. Try some of the shareware and freeware available on the

Internet and experiment with the limitations of your system. Table 6.3 lists some popular graphics, audio, and video software you can find on the Internet for PC/DOS and Windows.

Table 6.3 Software for Using Video and Audio Files on the PC		
Program and Filename	**File Types Handled**	**Internet Location and Directory**
Graphic Workshop (gwswinll.exe)	Displays most image files and Kodak PCD files Shareware	uunorth.north.net (/pub/alchemy)
Lview & Lview Pro (lview31.zip) (lviewp1a.zip)	Displays JPEG, GIF TIFF,PCX,BMP files Shareware	ftp.ncsa.uiuc.edu (/web/mosaic /windows/viewers)
MPEGPlay (mpegw32h.zip)	MPEG movie player (.mpg files) Shareware	ftp.ncsa.uiuc.edu (/web/mosaic /windows/viewers)
Quicktime (qtw11.zip)	Quicktime movie player (.mpg files)	ftp.ncsa.uiuc.edu (/web/mosaic/ windows/viewers)
WHAM (wham131.zip)	Windows audio files (.au, aiff files)	ftp.ncsa.uiuc.edu (/web/mosaic /windows/viewers)
WPlany (wplny.zip)	Various sound files via Windows 3.1 Wave Out device Some PC speaker support Freeware	ftp.ncsa.uiuc.edu (/web/mosaic /windows/viewers)
Speak (speaker.exe)	Audio files via PC speaker for Windows 3.1 users Freeware	ftp.ncsa.uiuc.edu (/web/mosaic /windows/viewers)

Note

The Rolling Stones Web Server at URL **http://www.stones.com/** has examples of movie files in various formats (.avi, .mpeg). Before you download these concert movies, you should note that 20 minutes of video requires over 40 Mb of hard disk space!

Discovering Audio-Visual on Your Macintosh

If you use any Macintosh model from the LC line on up, with a color monitor, you already have a multimedia computer. Most Macintosh color users have monitors that display at least 256 colors, similar to VGA on the PC. The same principles for viewing images apply, with more memory extending your capabilities. More than 4-5 Mb of RAM is a must for handling movie files. Again, a Power-PC is a good model to have, but an intermediate processor is fine. For example, a Macintosh IIsi with a 68030 microprocessor, a math co-processor, 5 Mb RAM and using 10 Mb of virtual memory (on hard drive) will let you Web browse, play/record audio, and word process at the same time. Table 6.4 lists some software you can find on the Internet for multimedia on the Macintosh.

Table 6.4 Software for Using Video and Audio Files on the Macintosh

Program and Filename	File Types Handled	Internet Location and Directory
JPEG View (jpeg-view-331.hqx)	Viewer for JPEG PICT, GIF, TIFF BMP, MacPaint files Post-card-ware	ftp.ncsa.uiuc.edu (/Web/mosaic/ mac/helpers)
GIF-Converter (gif-converter-273.hqx)	Views and converts PICT, GIF, TIFF JPEG, MacPaint files & more Shareware	ftp.ncsa.uiuc.edu (/Web/mosaic/ mac/helpers)
Fast-Player (fast-player-110.hqx)	Quicktime movie player and converter Freeware	ftp.ncsa.uiuc.edu (/Web/mosaic/ mac/helpers)
Sparkle (sparkle-231.hqx)	Movie player & converter: MPEG, QT, PICT Multiple files	ftp.ncsa.uiuc.edu (/Web/mosaic/ mac/helpers)
Sound Machine (sound-machine-21.hqx)	Audio player and recorder .snd, .au files and more Freeware	ftp.ncsa.uiuc.edu (/Web/mosaic/ mac/helpers)

Using Audiovisual Helpers with Netscape

Searching the Internet with a World Wide Web browser such as Netscape gives you the advantage of an all-in-one interface. Netscape is a powerful tool to access information as shown in chapter 3, "Searching the World Wide Web."

Netscape is capable of displaying GIF and XBM image files without the help of external helper applications. Netscape can pass various file types to other applications, causing the application to launch and handle the file. Most files at Web sites are assigned a **MIME (Multipurpose Internet Mail Extension) type** that designates the type of file you have accessed. MIME types that are handled by Netscape are: text/plain (ASCII text), text/html (HTML files), and image/gif (GIF image files). When Netscape encounters a MIME type that cannot be handled, you are presented with these choices:

- Cancel the file transfer

- Save the file to disk

- Send the file to an application of your choice

You can also predefine MIME type/application pairs so files are automatically passed to an appropriate program (such as a viewer or audio player listed in tables 6.3 and 6.4).

For example, to predefine an application for use with Netscape for Windows, open the Options menu, select Preferences, and then select Helper Applications. Figure 6.4 illustrates the use of the Helper Applications dialog box to configure Netscape to use the helper application LViewPro for the display of JPEG graphic files.

1. To the Mime Type: box enter **image**.

2. To the Mime Subtype: box add **jpeg**.

3. To the Extensions: box add **jpeg, jpe, jpg**.

4. Under the Action group, select the "Launch Application:" button.

5. To the application box add the path of the application by finding it with the Browse button or typing the path directly into the box. For this example, using the LViewPro program, enter **c:\eudora \viewers\lviewpro\lviewp.exe**.

II

Search Tools

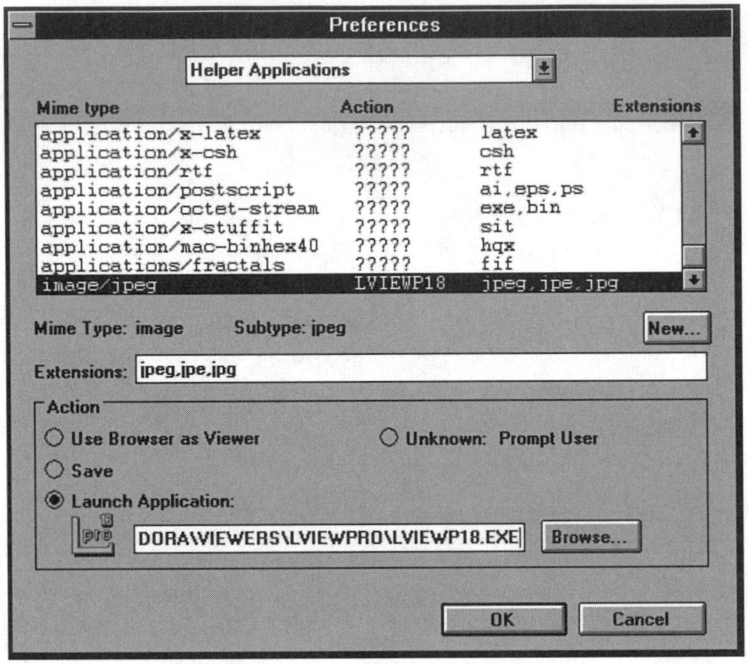

Fig. 6.4

Using the Helper Applications dialog box in Netscape for Windows.

When you encounter a JPEG file, Netscape will launch LViewPro and pass the file to the viewer for display.

To predefine an application for use with Netscape for the Macintosh, open the Options menu, select Preferences, and then select Helper Applications and enter the appropriate MIME type/application associations in the dialog box. Figure 6.5 shows how to associate audio files with the Sound Machine application:

1. To the Mime type box add **audio**.

2. Under Subtype enter **basic**.

3. To the Extensions field add **au,snd**.

4. Choose the Action button "Launch Application."

5. Click the Browse button to obtain a Finder dialog box and select the Sound Machine program by clicking Open.

6. If the application handles more than one type of file, the File Type menu will list the types handled. (In this case only "text" is available.)

7. Close the Preferences Window by clicking the OK button.

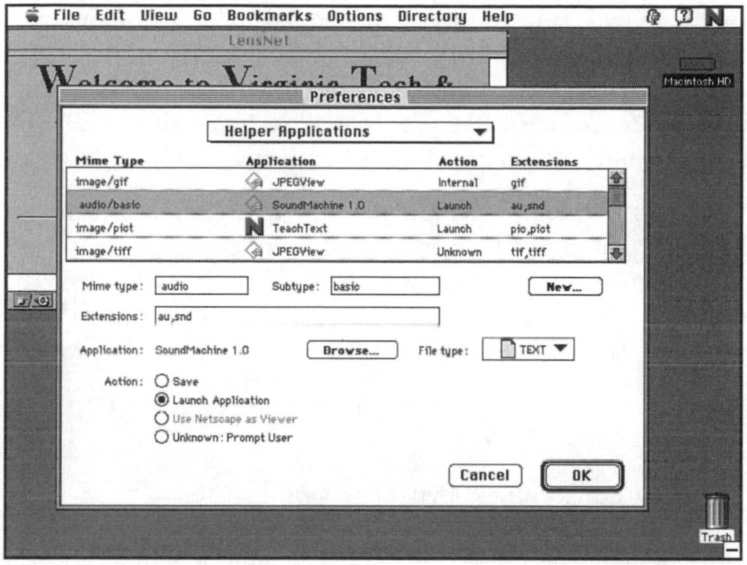

Fig. 6.5
Using the Helper Applications dialog box in Netscape for Macintosh.

Understanding Copyright and the Public Domain

Copyright laws protect an author's ownership of and compensation for the reproduction of original work. Copyright places restrictions on the right to reproduce books, articles, computer software and illustrations. This section shows how copyright and software licenses apply to information and programs you can get off the Internet.

Copyright Law

Books and articles commonly have a copyright notice of the form:

> Copyright 1995 John Doe

In the United States a work is registered with the copyright office or deposited in the Library of Congress. Similar procedures are in place in many other countries (in Canada, you can deposit in the National Library, Ottawa). Computer software does not have to be registered or deposited anywhere to be protected by copyright law. Copyright protects the act of expressing information but does not protect the information itself. Copyright does not apply to inventions or processes—that is the purpose of Patent law.

An original work can be placed into the public domain by the holder of the copyright. When this occurs there are no limitations on the reproduction of the work. Nothing is automatically in the public domain. Placing a file, picture or program on a public FTP server does not mean the work is now in the public domain. The holder of the copyright can place a program into the public domain by explicitly stating so in writing. If you do not see such a notice, then assume the work is protected by copyright.

This decade has seen some redefinition of copyright, in that a work is protected by copyright even if there is no explicit notice of copyright. (The copyright notice is still a good idea for anything you author.) International agreements are continuously establishing this in more and more signatory countries. Copyright is easier to keep straight by remembering two things:

■ The copyright holder has sole authority concerning the reproduction of the work in any fashion.

■ An author can give the copyright to another party.

If we are not the holders of the copyright, we cannot reproduce the work without first obtaining explicit permission to do so (software included). In most industrialized nations, including the United States, copyright law does allow for the limited copying of some materials such as magazine articles and parts of books for educational purposes and personal use. Computer programs can only be copied to provide a personal backup copy. Computer programs and packages are also protected by a software license.

Software License

Special agreements between the publisher of a computer program and the person who buys a copy of the program are called **software licenses**. Software licenses often stipulate that we don't actually own the program copy but just the right to use it in some defined way. Licenses usually allow us to make a working copy (one).

Site licenses are special licenses that allow a set of users to use more than one copy of the same program on more than one computer. Copying the program is legal for use anywhere at the "site." While site licenses are more expensive than a single software license, the site option is cheaper than purchasing an equivalent number of single program copies.

It seems the best advice regarding software is read the license and decide if the program is one you need. If it is, follow the license regulations. Do not make numerous copies without permission or you are in violation of copyright law.

Understanding the Meaning of Shareware and Freeware

Shareware can be distributed free of charge but it is still protected by copyright. (Remember, even without a copyright notice.) This is not free software, although it is usually described incorrectly as free software. Shareware is often licensed for a limited evaluation period, after which the user should pay the author the specified fee for continued legal use of the program. Cost of shareware is quite reasonable and some very sophisticated programs can be obtained by this route. Shareware authors are most likely not getting rich and simply like to write programs. Paying customers can find extra support from the author including program updates, complete manuals of extra unadvertised features, and more powerful versions of the program.

Freeware (free software) are programs for which no money is required for use of the software. Freeware comes in one of two forms:

- Public domain software that is not covered by any form of copyright.

- Copyrighted software that is distributed for free use with explicit permission of the author.

If you are not certain about the status of any file on the Internet, assume it is protected by some form of copyright. The action of placing a work on the Internet does not place it into the public domain. The author must state literally "I place this work into the public domain" or something similar to make this true.

Tip

Look for shareware that has more than one updated version. This is an indication that the author has made some attempt to support and improve the initial release. Some track record is better than none at all.

II

Search Tools

Summary

Programs are available from Internet sites that allow you to use graphics, sound, and video files on your PC or Macintosh computer. The integration of graphics and sound has become especially important on the World Wide Web where audio-visual information is used to both educate and entertain. Shareware and freeware are both available on the Internet, but files on the Internet are not automatically in the public domain. They can be copied and used only under specific conditions.

Chapter 7

Advanced Searching Techniques

If you've ever participated in an Easter egg hunt, you know there are two kinds of eggs—the ones that are right out in the open and you find easily, and the ones that are squirreled behind a piece of furniture and you'd never find without some additional help. There are some similarities between this annual hunt for goodies and an Internet search for information. Sometimes you can enter one keyword, perform a search, and find exactly what you need in a few minutes. On other occasions you have to dig a little deeper to find relevant information. Advanced searching techniques will help you locate those hard-to-find resources. In this chapter you will learn:

- About search engines that perform comprehensive examinations of single or multiple databases

- How knowing the difference between data, information, and knowledge can help you perform a better search

- How to use a Boolean search to refine the results you get

- About search engines that let you ask a computer questions, just like you might ask another person

The Role of the Database Search Engine

Databases are organized collections of data—records and information. Most database software programs enable you to quickly find records in the database. The program—or part of the program—that actually does the searching is called a **search engine**. Even word processing programs have very limited search engines. For example, with Microsoft Word or WordPerfect you can search for specific words or phrases in your documents.

Several different search engines could be used to search one database, or similar databases. As an analogy, consider panning for gold. You find the perfect spot in a creek that contains some gold dust. In this case the database is the dirt in the creek bed and you're searching for records that are pieces of gold dust. Now you could use a gold panning pan, a chefs colander, a coffee cup, or even just your hands—all different types of search engines to start sifting for the gold. Clearly, the gold pan offers the best bet for finding what you want. In a similar manner, some search engines are better than others.

Search engine programs can be quite elaborate, allowing you to enter entire phrases or fine-tune your search by setting up certain parameters that the search engine uses to locate specific information. Advanced features enable you to further define the method by which the search engine examines the database. Search engines can also be tailored for specific databases and types of information. For example, you might connect to a database that contains five years worth of magazine articles. You could have options that would let you select and search this database by any of the following means:

Subject

Title of articles

Text within articles

Date of publication

Name of the author(s)

Some search engines are connected to and can search multiple databases. Dialog is a commercial service that provides access to more than 450 databases that encompass business, government, and research information. A search for the term "information retrieval" returns a set of 10 different databases in which the search term was found anywhere from two to more than 22,000 times as shown in the following table.

Database	Results	Format	Source Type
1 ABI/INFORM	4306	abstract	journals
2 Biobusiness	167	reference	journals
3 Books in Print	1332	reference	books

Database	Results	Format	Source Type
4 Management Contents	172	abstract	journals
5 McGraw-Hill Publications	2	full text	magazines
6 National Newspaper Index	608	reference	newspapers
7 Newsearch	24	reference	multiple sources
8 PTS PROMT	1824	abstract	multiple sources
9 Trade & Industry ASAP	12553	full text	multiple sources
10 Trade & Industry Index	22894	reference	journals

Search Engines That Use Menus

You'll also use search engines that help you search for information by navigating you toward information with a series of on-screen menus, which is similar to the way that Gopher menus take you from one place to another. For example, you might come across a database that offers newspaper articles about many subjects. You first start with a menu that offers a broad selection of subject categories. Perhaps as follows:

1 ART

2 BUSINESS

3 COMPUTERS

4 EDUCATION

You select #2, BUSINESS. Then you get a new menu that offers another series of options that relate to the broad topic of business.

1 Accounting

2 Banking & Finance

3 Companies

4 Economics

5 Industries

6 Insurance

Search Tools

II

7 Management

8 Marketing

9 Real Estate

10 Taxation

Now this menu selection could either go one step further, defining all of these categories, or it could begin a search of the database when you return a selection here. Figure 7.1 shows several menus that help you navigate the resources available from the Colorado Alliance of Research Libraries.

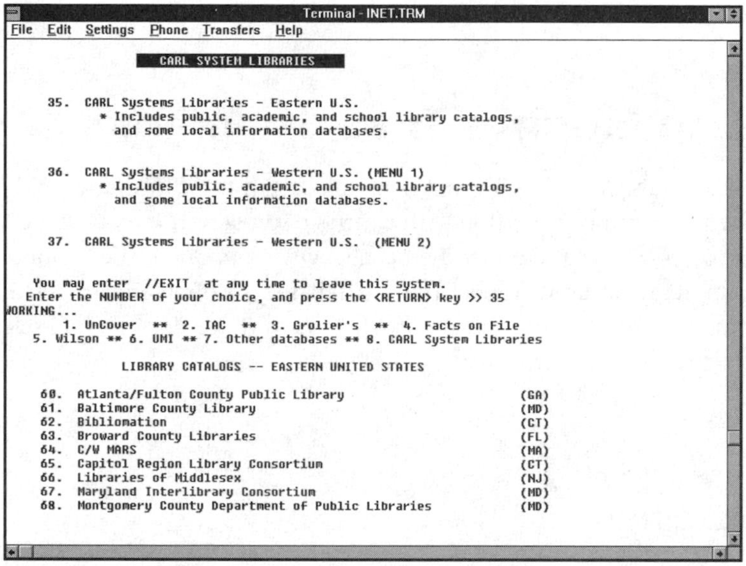

Fig. 7.1

The Colorado Alliance of Research Libraries uses a menu system to help you find and access library catalogs across the U.S.

In addition to searching a database, a search engine can help you search the contents of a specific record or file that has been indexed. The University of Pennsylvania has an Internet site that maintains the full text of the King James version of the Bible. You can use the search engine at this site to look for words or phrases that occur in the Bible. If, for example, you search for the keyword "marriage," you get a list of more than 25 different references and you can quickly retrieve the full text of these references (see fig. 7.2).

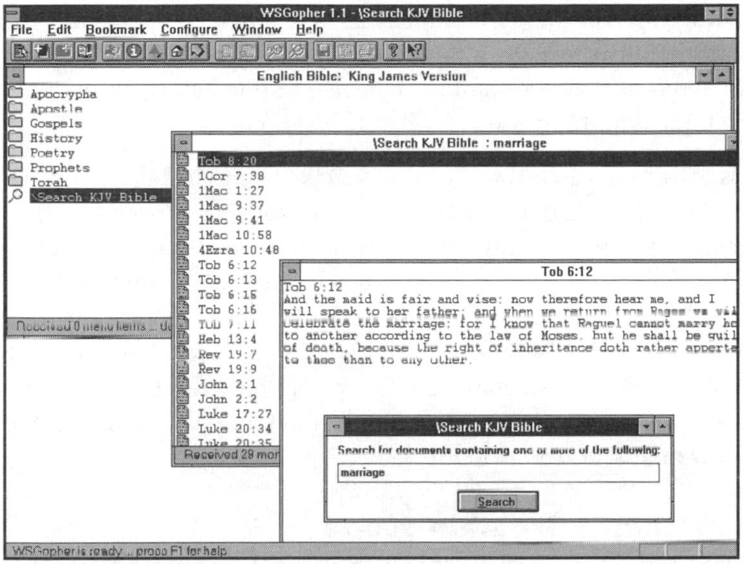

Fig. 7.2
The University of Pennsylvania maintains a site that contains a searchable version of The Bible. Perform a search for the word "marriage" and you'll get a list of specific passages.

Data, Information, and Knowledge

It may seem like an issue of semantics, or even splitting hairs, but there are important distinctions between data, information, and knowledge. By understanding the distinctions you can determine how to best begin and conduct your Internet search. In the next few sections we'll take a look at these three categories and conduct a search for each of these. Each of these example searches is conducted on the World Wide Web using the Yahoo Web Searcher (**http://www.yahoo.com**). You could just as easily use another Web Searcher or search Gopher or FTP sites for similar information.

Data Is Very Specific

Data is the plural of the Latin word datum, which means an item of information. If you are looking for data, you are looking for a very specific piece of information. As an example, if you get audited by the IRS, you may need to locate the amount of money you wrote off to charitable contributions four years ago. Or, you want to find out who the Democratic candidate was in the 1948 U.S. Presidential election for a report on American history; the annual amount of sunlight that falls in Phoenix, Arizona for the design of a solar house; the current stock price for Time Warner; or the date that the North American Free Trade Agreement (NAFTA) was signed. In each case, you are looking for a specific piece of information, and when you perform a search you want to find an exact match for your query. A data search is deterministic, which means that you want the database to find exactly what you're looking for and nothing else.

The goal of a data search is to find one specific thing that answers a question or provides a solution to a problem. You want to use a narrow search term. For example, you want to find the Spanish word for "restaurant." Here, you want to start your search with a very narrow search term. First, we locate a Web search engine (I used Yahoo) and enter the term "Spanish dictionary." This search phrase locates an English-to-Spanish dictionary where you type in the English word "restaurant" and the computer sends back the Spanish equivalent "restaurante." The URL address is **http://www.willamette.edu /~tjones/forms/spanish.html**.

Information Is Broad in Scope

When you search for information you are looking for multiple hits or matches to your search. For example, you're planning your first trip to Australia and you want to find out everything you can about the attractions and accommodations. Or, you're studying Alfred Hitchcock and you want screenplays for his films; you plan to invest in General Electric and need details on all of the divisions and products; you want to understand the potential impact NAFTA has on your business or industry and so you need a complete copy of the NAFTA agreement and business magazine articles on the subject. General information retrieval is probabilistic, which means that you want the database to look for and locate records that have a high probability of matching your needs. You have a general idea of what you want to find but are looking for some help from the database.

The goal of an information search is to locate several pieces of data that are useful for a specific application. You need to start with a broad keyword search. For this example you're planning a trip to Mexico. You want ideas about where to go and what to see. Start with a broad, yet obvious keyword like "Mexico" or "travel." Results from this search turn up several Internet sites that meet your needs. There's a site that offers tour packages, a site that focuses on scuba diving, a site that describes different cities, and one called Mexico Net (URL address: **http://www.udg.mx/cultfolk/mexico.html**) that has information on hotels, travel destinations, and maps. These are all worth exploring.

Knowledge Involves Comprehensive Understanding

Knowledge refers to the ability to use data and information for practical applications. Knowledge generally implies a comprehensive understanding of one specific subject. You gain knowledge through a combination of finding lots of data and information and personal experience. For example, sheet music for a Mozart sonata provides data and information—the individual notes represent data, the pages of sheet music provide information about where to place your fingers on a piano keyboard. Knowledge begins when you sit down and enthusiastically play the music.

The ultimate goal of a knowledge search is to use this broad-based information in a variety of real-world, practical applications. Start with broad keyword searching and combine it with surfing. In this searching example you're planning to spend a few months living in Mexico and you don't want to arrive as a tourista. To gain knowledge about the culture, the history, current news, and language you need to visit several Internet sites. Start with broad keywords on several fronts: "Mexico," "Spanish," and "history." Also, try some search terms like "news in Mexico," "Mayan ruins," and "Mexican cooking." Finally, use the sites that a search delivers as jumping off points for surfing to further sites. Table 7.1 identifies the major differences among data, information, and knowledge searches.

Table 7.1 Comparison of the Main Features and Searching Techniques for Data, Information, and Knowledge

DATA

- Narrow search using specific search terms.
- Locate one relevant database.
- Locate one specific record.
- Answer a question, solve a problem.

INFORMATION

- General search using several broad keywords.
- Locate several relevant sites.
- Locate a variety of documents and media resources.
- Gain data that's useful for specific applications.

(continues)

Table 7.1   Continued
KNOWLEDGE
■ Several broad keyword searches that may lead to new searches using specific keywords or search terms.
■ Locate several relevant sites and then "surf" to other sites.
■ Locate a variety of documents on the subject area.
■ Gain information and data that will help in many, often unexpected applications.

What Is Boolean Searching?

In the mid-nineteenth century, the English mathematician George Boole developed what is known in the computer world as Boolean logic. A Boolean search enables searchers to incorporate several descriptive words into a search phrase. The rules of Boolean searching use a set of logic parameters referred to as operators—the common words AND, OR, and NOT. In a Boolean search you use these operators to narrow the results from a search. A keyword search for "cardinal" locates several different types of information including:

- Pascal's Aviation Picturebook with information on the Cessna Cardinal (a plane)

- The Vatican Exhibit (Catholic Cardinals)

- Cardinal Information Systems (a computer company based in Finland)

- Bridgewater College in Pennsylvania (They have a Cardinal—the bird—in the college seal.)

This is great, but if you're looking for information about the Saint Louis Cardinals, you're out of luck. When the search for "cardinal" is modified to incorporate a Boolean search, as in "baseball and cardinal," the same search engine quickly locates and places at the top of the hit list the Saint Louis Home Page—which contains information about the Saint Louis Cardinals.

How To Use Boolean Operators

You can see by the previous example that Boolean logic can help you narrow down a search. Let's take a closer look at how this works. You've located a database of books about gardening. Tomatoes and cucumbers—that's what you want to grow. You can conduct one of four possible Boolean searches:

- tomato OR cucumber

- tomato AND cucumber

- tomato NOT cucumber

- cucumber NOT tomato

This particular database contains 20 books that are only about tomatoes, 10 books that are only about cucumbers, and 5 books that have information about both tomatoes and cucumbers. In total there are 35 different books that have information about the two subjects. Figure 7.3 shows that if you conduct a search with "Tomato OR Cucumber" you receive a list of *all* of the books—35 records. If you really want lots of information, you should use the OR operator.

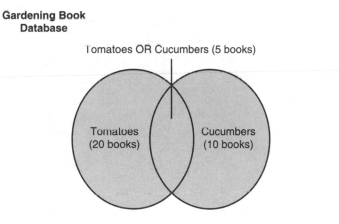

**Gardening Book
Database**

Tomatoes OR Cucumbers (5 books)

Tomatoes
(20 books)

Cucumbers
(10 books)

Fig. 7.3
The Boolean operator OR produces the largest number of results for a search.

Search Tools

Figure 7.4 shows that the AND parameter delivers the least amount of books—only five. However, these five books have exactly what you want, information about tomatoes AND cucumbers. That isn't to say that one of the other books might not have better information, simply that these are the only books that cover both subjects.

Fig. 7.4
The Boolean operator AND produces fewer results, but the results are more targeted to fit your needs.

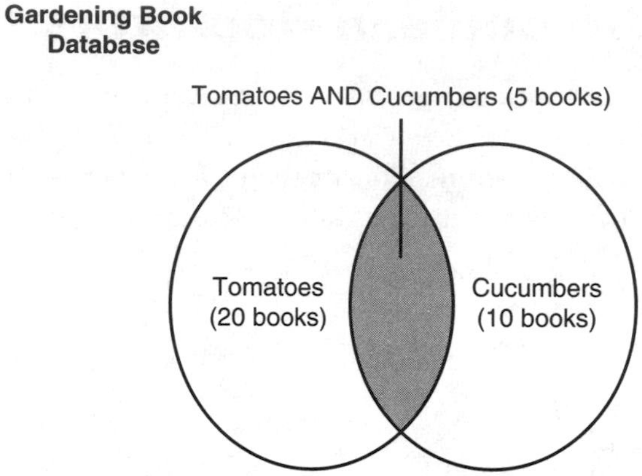

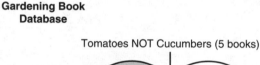

Gardening Book Database

Tomatoes AND Cucumbers (5 books)

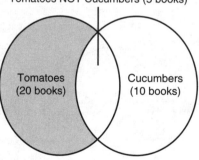

Tomatoes
(20 books)

Cucumbers
(10 books)

Figure 7.5 then shows the results of a "Tomato NOT Cucumber" search—20 records. You could also do a "Cucumber NOT Tomato" search. You might want to use one of these NOT searches if you suddenly decide that you really hate either tomatoes or cucumbers. Otherwise your best bets are to use the OR and AND operators.

Fig. 7.5
The Boolean operator NOT eliminates certain records (or subjects) from being found.

Gardening Book Database

Tomatoes NOT Cucumbers (5 books)

Tomatoes
(20 books)

Cucumbers
(10 books)

Many Gopher and Web search engines let you use Boolean search operators to refine a search. Figure 7.6 shows the search options that are available with the Yahoo Web search engine (**http://www.yahoo.com**). First you enter keywords (here called keys) in the search entry box. With Yahoo, you can selectively choose Boolean operators with a default being all of the keywords. This means an automatic AND is placed between the keywords and the results will be Internet Web sites that contain all of the keywords—but not necessarily in the exact sequence that you enter. Other choices are a Boolean

OR, which would find records with any one of the keywords, and a third option is "all keys as a single string," which means it searches for sites where the keyword string is matched perfectly.

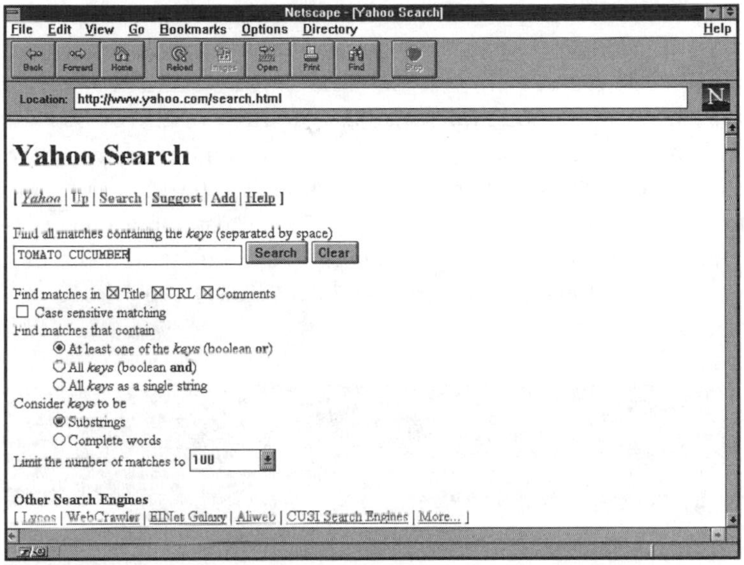

Fig. 7.6
The Yahoo Web search engine lets you refine a search with Boolean operators.

Advanced Boolean Searching

High-school mathematical formulas often use parentheses to indicate which mathematical calculation must be done first. For example:

A. (5 x 2) + 10

B. 5 x (2 + 10)

What's important is that the results *are* different. The result of example A is 20 and the result of example B is 60. You can use parentheses to further define a search and the same rules apply with Boolean searches—the operations within the parentheses are completed first. To continue with our gardening example you might do the following searches:

A. (tomato AND cucumber) OR lettuce

B. tomato AND (cucumber OR lettuce)

As with the mathematical equations, the search results from these two Boolean searches would be very different. Example B would produce many more records than example A.

Natural Language Searching

So far we've examined searches that use keywords, search terms, Boolean expressions, and on-screen menu options. The latest generation of search engines use what is referred to as **natural language searching**. What this means is that you can type a question and submit it to the search engine. The question could be phrased in "plain English." It could be identical to a question that you'd ask a person rather than a computer. So, instead of trying to carefully phrase a Boolean search like "books and children" you can type in: "A list of books for children." The search engine then translates and analyzes your question and returns results (see figure 7.7). Today, only a few of the search engines perform well with natural language searches. The best in my experience is the Infoseek Web Searcher (URL address: **http://www.infoseek.com**).

Fig. 7.7

Natural language queries let you phrase a search in "plain English." Here the query, "A list of books for children" finds several different sources of children's literature.

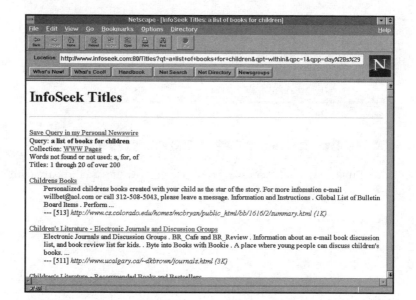

This type of computer "thinking" is the essence of the science of **artificial intelligence (AI)**. AI focuses on creating software and hardware that provides computers with human-like reasoning and thinking capabilities. Speech recognition technology that today allows simple commands to be understood will, within a decade, allow us to talk to personal computers, bank machines, and even our cars. Expert systems, a branch of artificial intelligence, stores the knowledge of human experts in computer programs that analyze and solve problems. An expert system could, for example, guide you through a series of questions and answers to evaluate simple medical problems.

The natural language search engines on the Internet are definitely the early stage of more advanced applications. For example, they are smart enough to eliminate certain words in your question that would produce irrelevant information or simply too many records. The InfoSeek Web search engine (**http://www.infoseek.com**) that looks for "A list of books for children," automatically eliminates the words "of" and "for" because they are not relevant to the search. Likewise the WebCrawler search engine (**http:// webcrawler.cs.washington.edu/WebCrawler/Home.html**) automatically eliminates terms like "WWW" and "Web" from its searches because it knows (actually has been programmed) that these terms are so common in Web site names that you'd get thousands of records that don't relate to your subject.

Additional Tips for Successful Searching

Here are a few suggestions that will help you create successful keywords and search terms, then apply them to the Internet search systems.

- **Use a thesaurus to find additional keywords.** If you're having trouble coming up with keywords or search terms, buy a thesaurus and look up one word that describes the information you're looking for. This will give you a few synonyms and related topics. Likewise, if you have a word processing program that has a built-in thesaurus, you can use it to find other keywords.

- **Truncate keywords to increase the results from a search.** You'll get more hits or results from a search if you truncate keywords. This simply means that you use the root of a word—money instead of monetary, or finance instead of financial. For example, the keyword auto will locate information, records, and Internet sites that relate to auto, automobile, and automotive whereas the keyword automobile will only locate automobile records.

- **Repeat the search using several databases.** As the numerous Internet search engines and databases contain different information and records you should use the same keywords or search terms in several different searches. Some search engines—notably the commercial services—let you save a search and use it to query several different databases.

■ **Let the results of a search lead you in new directions.** Take a look at the results of an initial or first search. If you begin with a broad keyword or Boolean search, the results should provide a list of new subjects, topics, and Internet sites—many that offer potential keywords or search terms that you haven't yet tried.

Summary

In this chapter you've learned the important role that the Internet search engines play in finding the information that you want. Also, you've learned how to refine your search by first determining exactly what you're looking for (data, information, or knowledge), then using Boolean operators to narrow down the results of a search. These techniques can be applied to any type of online search—whether you are using Gopher, Web, or FTP systems on the Internet, or searching through a database on a commercial online system such as America Online or CompuServe.

Part III

Jay

The Listserver

Kittens-l

Scuba-l

Joe

Sue

Politics-l

PATHFINDER
FROM TIME WARNER

Week of March 6 - 12, 1995

HOT PAGE | TIME | Money
NEWS & FINANCE
Entertainment | VIBE | People | THE O.J. FILES
REVIEWS OF MUSIC, MOVIES, TV, BOOKS & MULTIMEDIA
Sports Illustrated | TIME WARNER ELECTRONIC PUBLISHING | the Virtual Garden
SPECIAL INTEREST
TIME WARNER PRODUCTS

ABOUT | BULLETIN BOARDS | WRITE BACK | OFFERS | SEARCH | HELP!

Today's News
· Dole: "Cut 4 Cabinet Posts"
· House Passes Tort Reforms
· Fuhrman: "I Didn't Frame OJ"

Hot This Week
· Baseball's Dead End Kids
· Greg Louganis—My Private Hell
· The Sounds of Science Fiction

Not loading image? Try here.

Search People
Resources

Netscape - [NLM HyperDOC: World-Wide Web (WWW) Server of the U.S. National Lib]

File   Edit   View   Go   Bookmarks   Options   Directory   Help

Back   Forward   Home   Reload   Images   Open   Print   Find   Stop

Location: http://www.nlm.nih.gov/

What's New!   What's Cool!   Handbook   Net Search   Net Directory   Newsgroups

Welcom...
A Multimedia/Hypertext Resource of the
U.S. National Library of Medicine (NLM)

Donald A. B. Lindberg, M.D.
Director

Back   Forward   Home   Reload   Images   Open   Print   Find   Stop

Location: http://www.umr.edu/~cisapps/MSDS.html

What's New!   What's Cool!   Handbook   Net Search   Net Directory   Newsgroups

Enter a MSDS Search Criteria Below:

● **Chemical Name:** TriNitroTolulene

Guided Tour | What's New | Questions | Net Search | Net Directory |

PATHFINDER

FROM TIME WARNER

Week of March 6 - 1

HOT PAGE | TIME | Money

NEWS & FINANCE

Today's Ne

• Dole: "Cut 4 Cabinet
• House Passes Tort Re
• Fuhrman: "I Didn't Fra

Entertainment | VIB8 | People | THE O.J. FILES

REVIEWS
MUSIC, MOVIES,
TV, BOOKS &
MULTIMEDIA

The Virtual Garden

Hot This W

• Baseball's Dead End
• Greg Louganis–My Priv
• The Sounds of Science

Sports Illustrated | TIME WARNER
ELECTRONIC
PUBLISHING

TIME WARNER PRODUCTS

ABOUT | BULLETIN BOARDS | WRITE BA | OFFERS | SEARCH | HELP

Not loading images? Try here.

The Listserver

Jay

Tom

Sue

Scuba-l

Joe

Kittens-l

Politics-l

Netscape - [NLM HyperDOC: World-Wide Web [WWW] Server of the U.S. National Lib

File Edit View Go Bookmarks Options Directory   Help

Back Forward Home Reload Images Open Print Find Stop

Location: http://www.nlm.nih.gov/

What's New! What's Cool! Handbook Net Search Net Directory Newsgroups

NATIONAL LIBRARY
OF
MEDICINE

Welcome to HyperDOC
A Multimedia/Hypertext Resource of the
U.S. National Library of Medicine (NLM)

Donald A. B. Lindberg, M.D.
Director

Pekka@Finland   Chris/USGS   Mobeus@Bellcor

help!!!   Bellcore Co

7.1 fps 34 Kbps   1.2 fps 28 Kbps   .3 fps 34 Kbp

Back Forward Home Reload Images Open Print Find Stop

Location: http://www.umr.edu/~cisapps/MSDS.html

What's New! What's Cool! Handbook Net Search Net Directory Newsgroups

Enter a MSDS Search Criteria Below:

● **Chemical Name:** TriNitroTolulene

What's New!

Chapter 8

Newsgroups

One of the great strengths of the Internet as a research tool is the ability to reach thousands of other people. The Internet is a tool for communication of information, and people are great repositories of information. Newsgroups were one of the first applications developed for the Internet. The concept is simple: Get together with people interested in the same topic, and discuss! Like many Internet facilities, the use of newsgroups began on university campuses. Newsgroups were originally used as a conferencing facility, but soon broadened to encompass entertainment, coffee-house style discussion, and user groups of many kinds.

The newsgroup format is analogous to a bulletin board in that you place a message or an article on a board dedicated to the subject of interest. Other people who are interested in the subject drop by, and if they find your article intriguing, they may post an article in reply. The language of newsgroups has its roots in this metaphor, what you write for the newsgroup is called an **article**, and you **post** the article for all to read.

In this chapter you will learn:

- What UseNet and newsgroups are
- How to search for newsgroups
- How to search for articles in newsgroups
- How to get information using newsgroups

The freeware newsreader program, WinVN, will be used for examples in this chapter. The actions in WinVN are similar to a number of other Windows and Windows NT newsreaders. We will also look at the Netscape version 1.1 World Wide Web (WWW) browser, which provides newsreader capabilities. More information on WWW browsing can be found in chapter 3, "Searching the World Wide Web."

Troubleshooting

Where do I get the WinVN newsreader?

WinVN programmers are constantly adding new features to this Windows-based software. The overview and screen captures in this chapter feature version 0.93.14. If you want to download the most recent release, ftp to **ftp.ksc.nasa.gov**, go to the subdirectory pub/winvn/win3 and download (in binary) a more recent release.

What Are UseNet Newsgroups and Why Would I Want To Use Them?

The cooperative body that distributes newsgroups is called **UseNet** (User's Network). UseNet is not the Internet, but it communicates over the Internet. It has a separate organization, and a separate culture. Like the Internet, the organization only really exists electronically. For the UseNet definition of what UseNet is, look at the articles in the newsgroup **news.announce.newusers**.

A **newsgroup** is like a bulletin board area, to continue our analogy, that is separated from other newsgroups by its subject. Here, people can post articles about that subject. These articles may be providing information, asking for information, rebuttals of other articles, or anything the format can handle.

Under UseNet, participating sites (that is, people with computers) store newsgroups and exchange new articles to keep each site current. Any site may carry all or any fraction of the available newsgroups, and individual sites may have newsgroups of their own, related to local issues. Most Internet service providers will include access to some or all newsgroups with their service. Newsgroups can be accessed or read using programs called **newsreaders**, as well as some of the WWW clients such as Netscape and NCSA Mosaic.

What newsgroups can provide to your search for information is access to people who are interested in the same things—such as using the same computer software/hardware or working on the same subject—as you are. If you want to find the best introductory text on metallurgy, a post to the **sci.engr.metallurgy** (general subject science, more specifically engineering, even more specifically metallurgy) newsgroup will likely get you a number of suggestions from people who have studied metallurgy themselves, and possibly even a few authors! These people who reply to your queries may be at the computer next to you or on another continent.

An important role for newsgroups is the support of computer software or hardware that may not be available anywhere else. (Remember the Amiga?) If your toll-free support expired, or never existed, there is a huge selection of newsgroups devoted to computer user issues. Somebody else has likely had the same problem, and may even know the solution!

Emoticons

Emoticons, or smileys, can convey different emotions, the rotated smiling face :) or :-) is obviously different than :(or :-(. Emoticons can indicate a satirical remark, ;-); or surprise, :-0; which can entirely change the interpretation of the preceding sentence! There are lists of many emoticons, but if you go much beyond these few shown here, they become more cryptic. Use them sparingly.

Abbreviations

The following table deciphers some common abbreviations used.

Abbreviation	Meaning
BTW	By The Way
IMO, IMHO	In My Opinion, In My Humble Opinion
FYI	For Your Information
WRT	With Respect To
RTFM	Read The #?*! Manual (not considered as impolite here as It Is verbally)
<g>	Grin
ROTFL	Rolling On The Floor Laughing
OTOH	On The Other Hand

What Topics and Subjects Do Newsgroups Cover?

Newsgroups cover a broad range of topics. The number of newsgroups is constantly growing as enough people interested in a subject organize and poll for the creation of a new group. This is done within the newsgroups themselves. Newsgroup subjects will also break into specialized branches as the number of posts requires. It becomes hard to keep up with the thousands of articles posted daily to the 10,000+ newsgroups!

Newsgroup organization is reflected in the naming of the groups. Group naming is done in a hierarchical format similar to e-mail addresses except that the newsgroups hierarchy moves from general to specific. For example, **rec.collecting.sport.hockey** is a *rec* (for recreational) newsgroup devoted to the discussion of *collecting*, specifically relating to the *sport* of *hockey*. The subject headers are broken up with the use of periods, again in the fashion of e-mail addresses.

Newsgroups have expanded beyond the original UseNet organization to accommodate more people with more diverse interests. The traditional UseNet hierarchy consists of the following seven main subjects.

Main UseNet Subjects	Topics
comp	Computer related
misc	Miscellaneous
news	Not news, but about newsgroups and UseNet
rec	Recreational activities, hobbies, art
sci	Science related
soc	Social issues and socializing
talk	Lots of talk!

Some categories that have evolved inside particular organizations or among particular groups have become as common as the traditional UseNet groups. There is no difference to the user whether the groups are in the traditional categories or not. The following includes some other common categories.

UseNet Subjects	Topics
alt	Alternative subjects, often political or entertainment
bionet	Research in biology and derived fields
biz	Anything commercial or business related
ieee	Groups organized by the Institute of Electrical and Electronics Engineers professional society (but open to all)
gnu	About the GNU project of the Free Software Foundation

These groups are available worldwide. There are groups that are locally maintained; for example, a university may have a newsgroups discussing campus politics. Employment opportunities are often posted to geographically specific groups like **can.jobs** (for jobs of interest to Canadian readers).

Corporations that provide newsgroup access to their employees may not provide all of these categories. It may be hard to justify why you need to keep up with the conversations on **rec.radio.amateur.homebrew** even if you do know what it means!

Caution

When complaints arise about offensive content on the Internet, they often refer to newsgroups. A group or article within an alt group is almost always the culprit, which is why many organizations will not carry some or all of the alt groups. So if the newsgroup title suggests content that you may consider offensive, avoid reading the articles.

Use the Newsgroup Hierarchy To Identify Useful Newsgroups

The hierarchical format of newsgroup naming should save you from a lot of searching. If you are interested in scientific topics, you should probably go to the sci newsgroups or the bionet newsgroups. If computers are causing you grief, start with the comp newsgroups. Think of the more general ways you would classify your subject of interest, and start from there. Move to the most specific group available. The searching strategies outlined earlier in this book are applicable here. To refresh your memory, see chapter 2, "Strategies for Effective Searching."

Of course, people don't necessarily think to classify things the same way you would, so be flexible. Some of the rec groups have pretty close counterparts in the alt groups. You may have to read the FAQ, or at least a few articles to decide if you are in the right place. If you are interested in beer, you may want to look at **alt.beer** or its child groups as well as **rec.food.drink.beer**.

The huge amount of traffic that can occur will sometimes overwhelm people and convince them to create a sub-grouping or new group altogether. This is why you will find **sci.physics** and **sci.physics.research**. Using the WinVN newsreader, you can list all the available newsgroups from your service provider in alphabetical order. The more general grouping will appear first, followed by more specific derivatives. Figure 8.1 shows the WinVN main window when you have connected to your service provider.

Fig. 8.1

The main window of WinVN with newsgroups loaded. The title bar shows the number of groups available, and the number sub-scribed to.

In the window under the menu bar, the available newsgroups are listed. The ones in black at the top are the ones I was subscribed to. Following these, all other groups are listed in alphabetical order. To avoid paging through the list, use the Find command under the Group menu to find a keyword.

Other items to note from figure 8.1 are the numbers in the title bar. Here the name of the program, WinVN, is followed by the text 2227 groups; 3 subscribed, which means just what it says: I had 2227 groups available from that provider, and I had subscribed to three of them. These three groups appear at the top of the list.

How To Sort and Search Through Newsgroup Messages

The easiest way to organize articles is by subject or, in UseNet language, **thread**. Related articles are grouped together, which makes it easy to follow a discussion.

> **Note**
>
> In each newsgroup, there may be a number of unrelated discussions going on, which are called **threads**. These should be easily identifiable by common subject headings. Replies to previous postings often have subject headings that begin with Re:. This style is common to many e-mail programs. Because the newsgroup server computers only hold a few days of discussion, depending on the server, you may find replies to messages that don't exist anymore! If you are really interested in the original message, you can search archives of newsgroups (see "Finding Newsgroup FAQ Files" later in this chapter).

Many newsreaders will allow you to search for words in the subject headings or even the body of the articles. This is generally done in the same way you search for a word in a word processor document. The WinVN newsreader has a simple Find menu item in each of its windows. In the main window, the find function is under the Group menu title; in the newsgroup and article windows the find function is under the Search menu title.

Using WinVN, if you select a group from the main window by double clicking on it, you will open the newsgroup window. The newsgroup window for **sci.engr.semiconductors** at one point in time looked like figure 8.2.

The newsgroup window in figure 8.2 shows the articles sorted according to thread/subject. You can change the sort method by selecting different options under the Sort menu of the newsgroup window. Using the thread/subject sort in WinVN, if an article is in response to a previous article, it will appear below the original and its subject will be blanked out and replaced by a small, filled box. These boxes are tabbed in to indicate responses to responses, the collection of these under one subject is a thread. In some groups, this can go on for a long time!

WinVN gives you the ability to sort the articles by any of the characteristics of the article shown in the window. As I have mentioned, the thread/subject method is the most useful, unless you want to find out who is posting the longest articles, or read all the articles that you posted!

Netscape 1.1 also has newsreader capabilities. To use Netscape as a newsreader, you must tell it some information so it can find your newsgroup provider. Select the main menu item Options and then the item Preferences. A dialog box appears with a list box at the top, under the text Set Preferences On. Select the item Mail and News. To get newsgroups from Netscape, you must fill in the IP address of the service provider's news or NNTP (fancy name for news server) server. Figure 8.3 shows the Preferences dialog box.

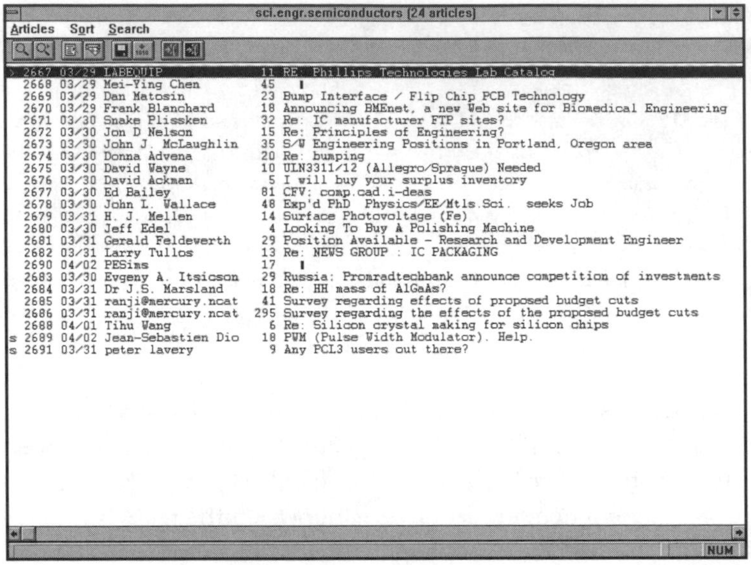

Fig. 8.2

The newsgroup window in WinVN, showing the detailed article information.

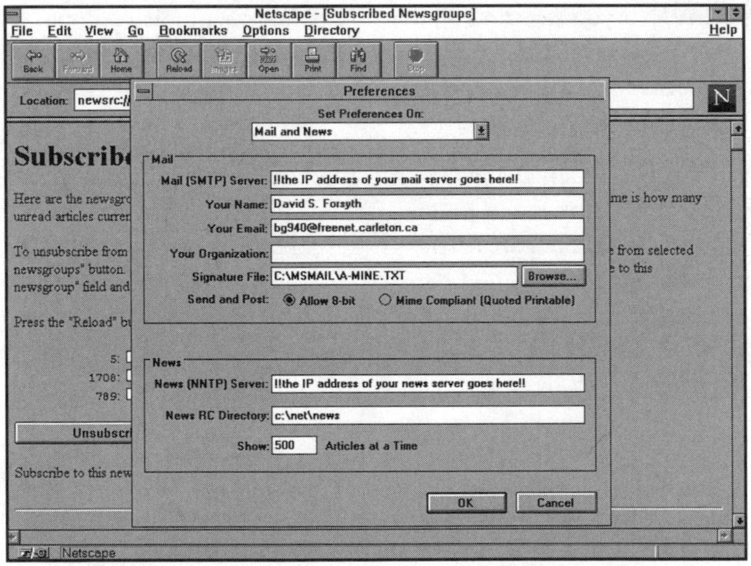

Fig. 8.3

The Mail and News options in the Preferences dialog box for Netscape 1.1.

When you connect for the first time to your service provider, it will show three news newsgroups that you should examine as a first time user. Netscape 1.1 gives you a box to add a group name to subscribe to. If you don't know any newsgroup names, this doesn't appear very helpful! However, you can use the * as a wildcard, or you can press the View all newsgroups button to show all the newsgroups available to you from your provider.

If you place a * in the Subscribe to box, Netscape will add a line with * under the Subscribed Groups heading. If you click on this *, Netscape will then load all the groups that you have available. You can use the * wildcard to narrow your search, for example, to load only the comp.* newsgroups. The first time you run Netscape 1.1, the news window will look something like figure 8.4.

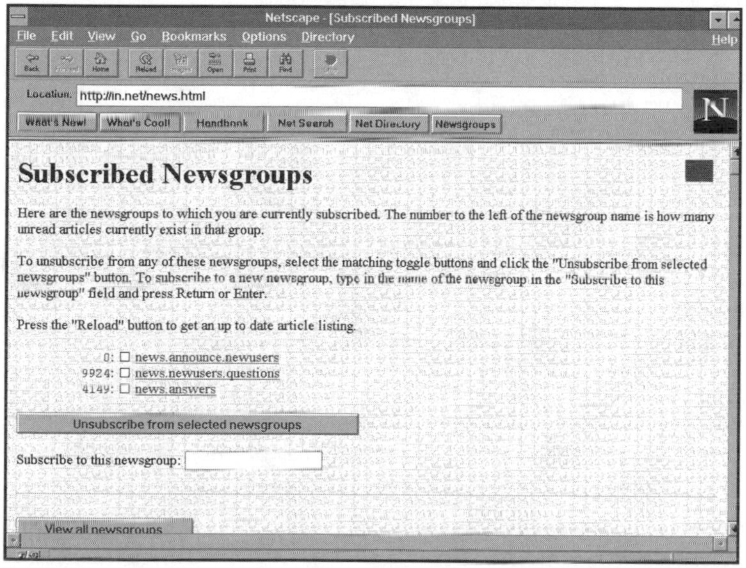

Fig. 8.4
The news window in Netscape (version 1.1), showing some subscribed newsgroups and the Subscribe to box.

How To Read Newsgroup Messages

Using WinVN as our newsreader, you can read an article by double-clicking on the line with its description in the newsgroup window. The letter s will appear at the left side of the article in the newsgroup window. This indicates that you have seen the article. The article window will now open with the text of the selected article. Figure 8.5 shows an article window in WinVN.

Some additional information about the article will appear in the article header, which is very much like an e-mail header. The Path: line gives you an idea of how articles are shared among the UseNet servers. This one has a convoluted path that stretches off the screen! The From: line tells you the e-mail address and a name or alias of the article author. These headings are pretty self-explanatory.

III

People Resources

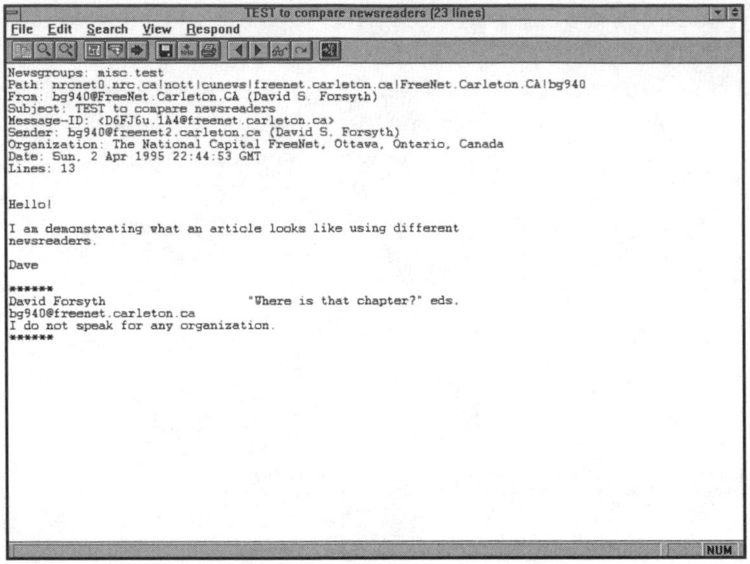

Fig. 8.5

The article window in WinVN, showing article information followed by the article text and signature or SIG.

To read articles in a newsgroup using Netscape, click on the newsgroup. This will bring up a window showing the articles in that newsgroup that you haven't read, organized by subject. You can search these subjects for keywords using the Find command under the Edit menu item. When you have found a subject you find interesting, click on that line to see the message text. The article shown in figure 8.5 looks like figure 8.6 in Netscape.

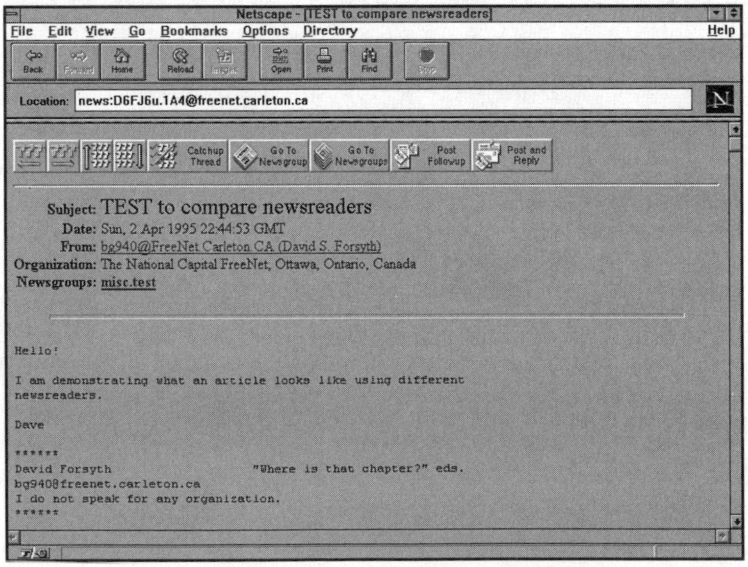

Fig. 8.6

The article window in Netscape, showing the same article as figure 8.5. Article information, message text, and signature block are shown.

> **Note**
>
> If the message looks normal except that the words are meaningless, random letters, the message may have been rot13 encoded, that is, letter changed by rotating through the alphabet 13 places. This is used to avoid revealing joke punch lines, the ending to movies, or possibly objectionable material. You have the choice to view the message using the ROT13 command under the View menu of WinVN.

Another aspect to reading newsgroup messages is the kill file. This is a way to screen out postings from certain people from appearing when you load your newsgroups. This practice is usually only found in the more political discussion groups, which can get very nasty. These shouldn't be necessary, and are not implemented in WinVN. You can sort articles by author to find one person's post, or you could just not read them!

More Tips on Locating Newsgroups That Meet Your Needs

There is a list of all the newsgroups available on the **news.list** group. This is a rather large file (or two), so it is probably most cost efficient to save it as a text file and peruse it using a word processor to avoid paying connect charges. Here you will have available the keyword searching that most word processors provide. To make it easier to remember the groups you want, copy them to another file and keep it handy for the next time you connect your newsreader.

One way to find a newsgroup is to post an article on a newsgroup. If you can't find something you feel addresses your topic, look for a more general topic. If you didn't catch on that **rec.music.gdead** is about the Grateful Dead, a post to **rec.music** would probably get you the information.

An obtuse but often effective way to search for newsgroups is to use other search techniques such as Gopher, Archie, or World Wide Web searching on the topic you want to find in a newsgroup. Often one kind of Internet resource will have references to other related resources.

III

People Resources

Troubleshooting

*There is a newsgroup referred to in the **news.list** group, and I can't find it using WinVN.*

Your service provider may not allow you to access all newsgroups, or may not store all of them. If you get Internet access through your organization, talk to your network manager. If you are paying an external service provider, phone them.

Newsgroups do occasionally get deleted if there is no traffic on them, but this is an irregular process.

Get Answers to Your Questions: Tips on Posting to Newsgroups

Before you post to a newsgroup, there are a few things you should consider. Are you posting to the correct group? Did you read the FAQ, if there was one? Have you been reading the articles, or at least the subjects, for a few days to get a feeling for how messages are written?

In WinVN you can post articles from any window. You will likely be using the newsgroup or the article window. If you wish to reply to an article you are reading, select the Respond menu item. Here you have three options. You can post an article to the newsgroup in the current thread, the Followup Article option. You can send an e-mail to the article author by selecting the Followup Mail option. Finally, you can forward the article through e-mail to someone else using the Forward Article option.

If you are using the Netscape browser, buttons for posting an article will appear at the top and bottom of the window in the newsgroup view or the article view windows. If you are reading an article and wish to reply to that article, select Post Followup from the window with the original article text. If you wish to introduce a new thread, post from the newsgroup by selecting Post Article.

Article Format

Without trying to be a grammar textbook, some discussion of article format can help you be more effective in your communications. As shown in the article of figures 8.5 and 8.6, there is a lot more to an article than the message text.

Like an e-mail message, an article posted to a newsgroup will have a subject written by the person who posted the article. This is an excellent, but often overlooked, way to target your message to your desired audience. The subject should be brief and describe the topic of your message. For example, if you want information on corrosion in 2024 series aluminum alloys, an appropriate subject would be "corrosion 2024 Al: need information." This saves other users from reading the article if they don't feel they have anything to add.

Writing an article with the subject "hello everyone!" is a good way to be ignored. You are competing with hundreds of other messages for attention, use the subject to help your case.

Newsgroup articles do not need a formal salutation or closing. Remember that UseNet began with people using old UNIX systems or even command line terminals on VAX systems. Anything extraneous is considered extraneous. State your case quickly and in only as much detail as is required to get an answer. The subject of your message should have primed the reader for the content. Point form is fine. An example of a well written post, IMHO, is shown in figure 8.7.

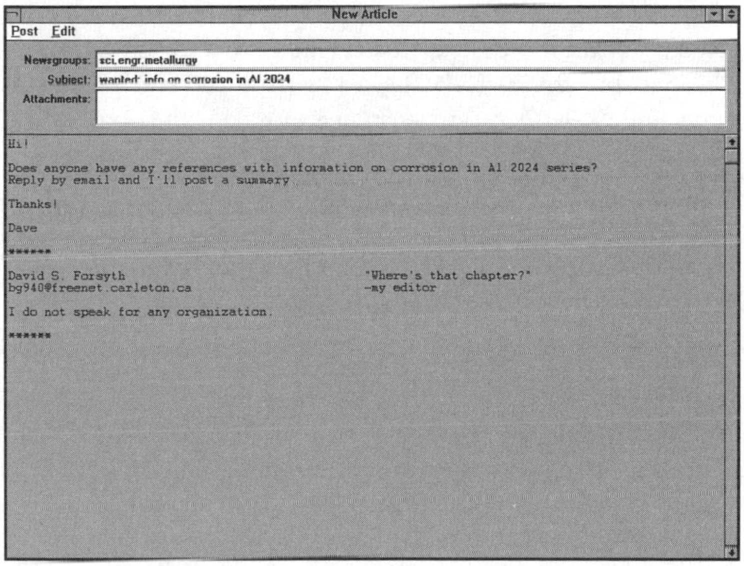

Tip

Keep your subject simple and clear! Avoid multiple RE:s in front if you are replying to someone else. Use keywords to catch other people who are searching through the article subjects.

Fig. 8.7

An article being written in WinVN for posting to a newsgroup. Note the use of the subject to convey the content of the article.

Note

Avoid the use of capital letters when you post an article, except where the normal rules of grammar dictate. THEY MAKE YOU LOOK LIKE YOU ARE SHOUTING! This may get you many replies, but none that you will like! Typing only in lowercase doesn't look very good either. Try to write as if you are writing a letter or memo, as this will look better and be more readable.

Signatures

You should include your name and an e-mail address as a minimum at the bottom of your post. This is often called a **SIG**, which is short for signature. Like the article text, the rule is short and to the point. Most people add some personalization in the form of a quotation. You will also often see disclaimers when people are posting from a corporate site. This is a good way to prevent your article from being read as a corporate policy. WinVN, along with many newsreaders allows you to create an ASCII or text file to use as your signature, and will automatically append it to any posting you make. There was an example SIG in figure 8.7 (the text between lines with ******). If you have an automatic SIG, you shouldn't write one in your article text.

Newsgroup Culture and Netiquette

Newsgroups have existed on the Internet for years, and have developed culture, traditions, and a vocabulary. Many people will forgive you for minor breaches, but some can become extremely rude and aggressive. If they feel you have done something wrong, they will let you and everyone else know in no uncertain terms. The newsgroup language for this is a **flame** or **flaming**.

You can avoid getting flamed by checking out the landscape before you jump in. Newsgroups contain lists of **articles** (also called **postings** or **posts**) that are posted by people. Newsgroups are sometimes **moderated**, that is, a volunteer moderates the discussions to keep them within the newsgroup subject and within some bounds of civility. Note that they are volunteers! This means that they are not responsible to you, except in their responsibility to the newsgroup community.

Tip

Be a lurker! A **lurker** is someone who reads the articles but never posts. Before you post an article, lurk in that newsgroup for a few days. Get to know the acceptable tone and subject matter before you post.

Many newsgroups will periodically post what is know as a **FAQ**, which stands for frequently asked questions. These articles can be many pages long and full of excellent information. If there is a FAQ, read it! If there isn't, ask for one. Finally, if you are flamed, don't take it too seriously. Some people become much more rude over the Internet than they would ever be in person, and responding to flames doesn't help.

In an effort to convey some of the meaning that tone of voice and facial expression add to our verbal conversation, the use of abbreviations and emoticons (sometimes called smileys) have been added to the Internet vocabulary. These will go in and out of fashion. Generally you should keep the use of these to a minimum. Don't show off your newsgroup panache by making your message incomprehensible! "FYI, I'm ROTFL ;)", which translates to "For your information, I'm rolling on the floor laughing (with a wink)" doesn't communicate very well.

Cross-Posting

Cross-posting is the practice of posting your one article to many newsgroups. In a word, don't! It is considered rude and a waste of time and bandwidth (Internet space). Only in rare cases is an article appropriate to more than one group. An employment offer than is available to residents of Canada and the U.S. could be posted in **can.jobs** and **biz.jobs.offered** without offending anyone. Posting to groups and derived subgroups, for example **sci.physics** and **sci.physics.research**, is bad practice. You may have to move to a more general group if a post doesn't get a response after a few days, just don't post to both general and specific groups at the same time.

Distribution

In some cases, it may not be appropriate to send your article around the world. For example, if you are looking for a local supplier of some service related to metallurgy, you may wish to post to **sci.engr.metallurgy** but limit distribution of the article. The default setting for distribution is "world."

Using WinVN, you can change the distribution. In the New Article window where you are writing your post, select Post->Preferences->Composition, and in the dialog box that appears, check the Show distribution header (post only) check box. This dialog box is shown in figure 8.8. Now in the New Article window, you will see another line under the subject line for distribution. Some valid entries may be:

- local (local to this service provider)
- usa (everywhere in the USA)
- can (everywhere in Canada)
- na (everywhere in North America)
- world (everywhere on UseNet in the world)

The distributions that you can use will depend on your service provider, but these five are very common and will work in most cases.

Fig. 8.8

The Composition Options dialog box in WinVN.

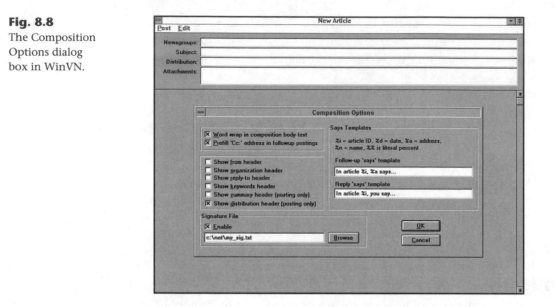

A Trial Run

You can see that the article shown in figures 8.5 and 8.6 is addressed to the newsgroup **misc.test**. This is a good place to post your first article. Make sure you include the word "test" in the subject. Here you can check what everyone will see when you post an article. You may want to check how your name appears in the header, and how your SIG file appears at the bottom. If you do not include the word "ignore" in the subject heading, you will get a number of e-mails from UseNet computer sites around the world notifying you that your test has indeed succeeded.

When To Use E-mail Instead of Posting

On occasion it is appropriate to send e-mail instead of posting an article. This applies to replying to a previous posting. You should not start a new conversation with someone through e-mail unless that person has advertised services or offered to give advice through e-mail.

In a case where someone has asked for specific information that may not be of interest to the entire newsgroup, that person may ask for reply by e-mail. This is appropriate if the person has asked for company information, and you are sending information that could be considered advertising. If someone has asked for replies by e-mail, it is considered good practice to collect the e-mail replies and summarize them in a posting to the entire newsgroup, if the topic is of interest to the group. If not, why would you post it there in the first place?

The practice of replying by personal e-mail seems to be more common in mailing lists (see chapter 10, "E-mail"). This is an effective way of reducing the traffic to the newsgroup, and should be encouraged. Ask for e-mail answers to your questions, and post an article summarizing the answers in a few days. Give credit where credit is due! One of the reasons this practice of replying by personal e-mail may not be common is that people like seeing their names in the newsgroups. So in your summary, note where you got the information.

Caution

Do not post advertisements for your company or consulting services in newsgroups, except for biz groups or groups dedicated to marketing services! If in doubt, read the FAQ of the group. This is considered in exceedingly bad taste, and may result with your network being submerged by automatic mailer replies, multiple public flamings, and your name being added to everyone's kill files. If you are replying directly to one person with an offer of services, do it through e-mail. You can create a positive impression by providing answers to people's questions and including your company's contact point in the SIG at the bottom of your posts. If you are using an educational provider, again you should not advertise any commercial services. There are often local "for sale" groups where you could advertise that you are selling personal items like your old computer.

Finding Newsgroup FAQ Files

Because of the huge volume of information contained in newsgroups, most computers that act as servers will only hold a few days' worth of articles. It may be possible to find archives of postings to the newsgroups, but like most Internet resources, it's done voluntarily by whoever thinks it is worthwhile. You may want to look at the "Answers to Frequently Asked Questions about UseNet" article in the **news.announce.newusers** or **news.answers** newsgroups for a summary of this topic.

FAQs can be an excellent source of information about the subject of a newsgroup. They contain accumulated knowledge about the newsgroup topic, hopefully without a lot of the "noise." FAQs do not exist for all newsgroups. When they do exist, they are generally posted repeatedly to be available most of the time. If you don't know if a group has a FAQ, lurk for a couple of days. If you don't see the FAQ, post an article asking if one exists.

> **Note**
>
> A Gopher, Archie, or Web search can also find you newsgroup FAQs. Figure 8.9 shows the results of a particular Gopher search on the University of Illinois at Urbana-Champaign Gopher (**gopher.uiuc.edu**) with the keyword "usenet." You can perform Archie and Web searches for the keywords FAQ or usenet to get similar results.

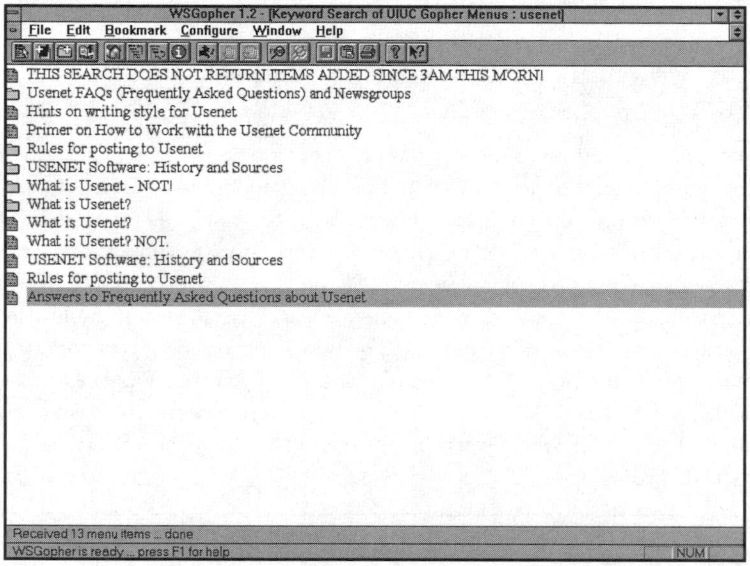

Fig. 8.9
Results of a gopher search on the University of Illinois at Urbana-Champaign (**gopher.uiuc.edu**) using the keyword "usenet." FAQ and achive locations are available from this search.

Search Newsgroups Via the Web

Not only newsgroup FAQs are available on the Web. Web search engines such as Yahoo and WebCrawler will return pointers to newsgroups and newsgroup FAQs where appropriate. Some Web sites devoted to particular topics will archive newsgroups that are related. An example of this is the Career Mosaic site at **http://www.careermosaic.com/cm/usenet.html**, which archives available job postings from many newsgroups. A commercial service at **http://www.infoseek.com** will search through the last four weeks of newgroups articles. So if you are having trouble searching in the newsgroups, Web searching might be another way to try and find what you are looking for.

Summary

We have shown how to use newsreader programs to search and ask for information contained in newsgroups. You should now be comfortable with posting to newsgroups, and able to decipher articles with emoticons and abbreviations. From here you may want to review the chapters on search techniques to most effectively apply what has been learned in this chapter.

III

People Resources

Chapter 9

Mailing Lists

It is said the Internet's most powerful and useful resource is people. To tap into the Internet's collective knowledge base is to tap into the minds of approximately 40 million people from all walks of life, religious and political backgrounds, and nationalities. This **Internet collective** can help you reach your ultimate goal: the information you seek.

Mailing lists are one way to reach the Internet collective, and are in many ways more powerful than UseNet. Every **netizen**, or Internet user, has e-mail access. Not every netizen has UseNet access. Therefore, mailing lists tend to have more participants than UseNet newsgroups.

Even if you have full Internet access, including UseNet access, you will still find mailing lists an important tool in your search. Mailing lists tend to be highly specialized, focused, and dynamic. If you can find the right mailing list, the chances are great that you will find someone with exactly your same interests or needs. In short, finding and participating in the right mailing list could be one of the most important apects of your travels on the Internet.

Like UseNet newsgroups, mailing lists also focus on various topics or subjects. The trick is knowing where to find mailing lists that have subjects pertaining to the information you seek, and knowing how to participate in mailing list discussions.

In this chapter, you learn:

- What a mailing list is and why they are important to your search
- About the various informational resources offered through mailing lists
- How to subscribe and participate in mailing lists
- How to find the right mailing lists for your informational needs
- How to search mailing list archives

What Is a Mailing List and Why Would I Want To Use One?

As just mentioned, mailing lists are an integral part of searching for information on the Internet. Not only can you meet people who may be able to refer you to additional resources, but the people on the mailing lists you may visit will be sources of information themselves. The trick is in finding a mailing list in the area of your interests.

Fortunately, finding a mailing list of interest to you is easier than you think. There are as many mailing lists as there are interests. While no one has an accurate count of the number of mailing lists in existence on the Internet, a figure of 10,000 different mailing lists isn't extreme. The range of topics or specializations for mailing lists is endless: From art history to financial planning to politics to late night TV to horseback riding, and everything in between. Somewhere on the Internet, there is a mailing list that discusses your area of interest.

As a potential mailing list participant, you should know a few simple definitions:

- **Subscriber**. A person who belongs to a mailing list. Typically, a subscriber is interested in following or participating in the discussion activities of a mailing list. Synonymous terms include *list member, participant*, or *lurker* (if you are subscribed but never actively participate).

- **List**. A list is short for a *mailing list*, which facilitates discussions among a group of subscribers. Synonymous terms include *discussion list* and *group*. A list is not to be confused with a *listserver* or *mailing list software*.

- **Listserver**. The mechanism or mailing list software that actually maintains one or more mailing lists. As will be further discussed in a moment, there are many listservers on the Internet. Three listservers, in particular, are the most popular: *LISTSERV, Listproc,* and *Majordomo*.

Figure 9.1 shows how the listserver, mailing lists, and subscribers relate to one another. In a nutshell, a listserver maintains one or more mailing lists at the same location. Each mailing list, in turn, maintains a list of subscribers that are members of the mailing list. In figure 9.1, you see that our fictitious listserver has three lists: Kittens-l, Politics-l, and Scuba-l. Each list has a number of subscribers.

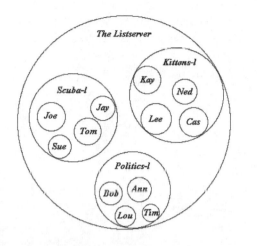

Fig. 9.1
An example of the relationship between the listserver, mailing lists, and subscribers.

Mailing lists are popular because they allow you to communicate with a group of people without having to individually e-mail everyone in the group. A mailing list facilitates discussions among a group of people by remembering all the members within that group and acting as a focal point for group discussions.

In figure 9.2, Joe sent a message to Scuba-l, a mailing list for people interested in scuba diving. Luckily, Joe does not have to remember Jay's, Tom's, or Sue's e-mail address; the mailing list takes care of remembering e-mail addresses. Additionally, should someone unsubscribe (or a new person subscribe) to Scuba-l, Joe would not have to update any mailing list. The listserver takes care of remembering who is interested in Scuba-l.

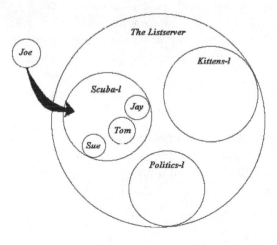

Fig. 9.2
When a subscriber wants to participate, that subscriber sends e-mail to the mailing list.

When Scuba-l receives the message from Joe, the list checks its list of sub-scribers and forwards a copy of Joe's message to everyone subscribed, as shown in figure 9.3. Joe's one message to Scuba-l turns into three separate messages: one for Jay, Tom, and Sue.

Fig. 9.3
When a mailing list receives a message, it forwards that message to all the subscribers in the mailing list.

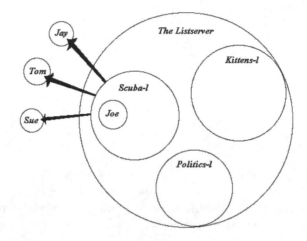

To summarize, when one member of a mailing list, called a **subscriber**, wants to send e-mail to the entire group (or list), that member simply sends one e-mail message to the mailing list. When the mailing list receives an e-mail message, the mailing list immediately forwards the message to all its subscribers.

Tip
Because many mailing lists have hundreds, if not thousands, of subscribers, you might want to carefully edit and review anything you might send to the mailing list.

Mailing lists are important because they can put you in contact with other people who are interested in similar topics. Because mailing lists are usually structured around different topics, once you find the topic you are interested in, you can communicate with people who can help you along your search. In many instances, however, such mailing lists are the object of your search. That is, you may simply wish to communicate and meet others with interests similar to your own. If this is the case, carefully read the "How To Find Current Lists of Mailing Lists" section later in this chapter.

As noted previously, there are many different types of listservers. There are three popular ones, however, and they will probably be the only ones you encounter. Thankfully, they are all similar in nature; therefore, their commands are also similar.

- **LISTSERV**. The original listserver software developed for BITNET. This software is mainframe-based, and has the largest selection of mailing lists. All LISTSERV listservers communicate with each other, which helps with finding particular mailing lists and addressing administrative issues.

- **Listproc**. This is UNIX-based listserver software that is based closely on LISTSERV.

- **Majordomo**. UNIX-based, just as Listproc, but not yet as powerful as Listproc.

What Information Resources Do Mailing Lists Offer?

Mailing lists are extremely informative. Remember that they are discussion areas for people with similar interests. What do people talk about? For starters, they may talk about locations for related or similar information. Additionally, mailing lists provide a direct channel to the experts—those who have been using the Internet and requesting information longer than you.

In particular, mailing lists can provide important information for your search, such as:

- **References to the information you seek**. If you knew Apple Computer Corporation had a Web site, but didn't know where to find it, you could place a question on a mailing list that focused on Macintosh or Apple Computers to find out that Apple Computers is located at **http:/ /www.apple.com/**.

- **Announcements for various sources of information**. Once you find a mailing list pertaining to your interest area, others on that mailing list will routinely send announcements and messages concerning related information and new services.

- **References to related information**. Sometimes, you may not find a mailing list directly related to your interest area. When that occurs, you may find a similarly related mailing list. For example, if you couldn't find a mailing list on Jiu Jitsu, you might find a mailing list on karate or martial arts. You could then use that list to help you find information pertaining to Jiu Jitsu.

III

People Resources

- **Ideas on how to continue, refine, or re-focus your search**. Don't be afraid to ask for help in refining or re-focusing your search. Many times, other subscribers may be looking for similar information and can help you in your search.

- **Discussions of experts in the field you are interested in**. Because educational institutions are a big part of the Internet, it's not unusual to find experts in the field you are interested in as subscribers to the same mailing list as you.

- **E-mail access to experts**. Once you participate in mailing list discussions, you will eventually learn about the experts in your field. Many times, you may actually be able to strike up communications with these experts and find mailing lists invaluable in contacting such experts.

These mailing lists, over time, develop what are called **archives** of mailing list messages. These archives are usually accessible via e-mail or other Internet service, such as Gopher, the Web, and FTP, and can be searched for keywords.

Therefore, a mailing list can provide a wealth of information to help you seek and identify other resources. Additionally, for many people, the ultimate goal in their search is the mailing list, because the mailing list puts people in contact with their peers and people with similar interests.

How Do I Subscribe To and Participate In a Mailing List?

Now that you understand what a mailing list is, and how it could be important to your search, you are probably asking yourself how you can participate in mailing list discussions.

Participating in mailing list discussions provides you with many of the benefits discussed previously. But how do you participate? You participate through e-mail by sending and receiving messages to and from a mailing list. Before you can expect to participate, you must inform the listserver you wish to become a subscriber and that the mailing list should start sending messages to you as it does for other subscribers of the list.

This process of notifying the listserver of your intentions is simply called **subscribing**. Therefore, you must learn how to subscribe to mailing lists before you can expound your words of wisdom to others, or alternatively, learn about some hidden resources you might find particularly interesting or useful!

> ### Note
>
> Que of Macmillan Publishing has an outstanding book, *Special Edition Using Internet E-Mail*, that discusses everything from the basics to the most advanced features of Internet e-mail and mailing lists. In particular, chapter 3, "Using Internet Mailing Lists," and chapter 4, "Getting the Most Out of Mailing Lists," should appeal to you if you are interested in learning more about mailing lists.

Subscribing To a Mailing List

Subscribing to a mailing list is easier than you think, but it does require you to learn a few basics. Just as there are many different Internet services or resources, there are many different listservers. Therefore, there are different commands you will need to know to effectively find and subscribe to mailing lists.

Fortunately, many of the commands and e-mail addresses are standardized. With a few basic concepts in hand, you should be able to subscribe to any mailing list you may encounter, without too much difficulty.

Before You Subscribe

Before you can subscribe to a mailing list, you must find the subscription address of the listserver itself to submit a subscription request. A potential subscriber must contact the listserver to tell it what mailing list a subscriber wants to join, as well as inform the listserver that you are interested in becoming a subscriber. The trick is to find the proper address to send your subscription request to and to know what commands you can send to the listserver.

III

People Resources

> **Note**
>
> There are two important e-mail addresses for mailing lists: the **listserver address** and the **mailing list address**. The mailing list e-mail address is used to participate in discussions occurring on the mailing list. The listserver address is the **command address** that you use to subscribe, unsubscribe, and obtain archives for the mailing list.
>
> When subscribing or unsubscribing from a mailing list, you need to send your request to the listserver e-mail address, not the mailing list itself.
>
> Because a mailing list only forwards messages to everyone subscribed to that mailing list, you want to avoid sending subscribe or unsubscribe commands to the mailing list. Otherwise, your command will be uselessly forwarded to every subscriber on the mailing list.

Finding the proper address to send your subscription request or listserver command usually isn't a problem. Most information concerning mailing lists includes subscription information such as the listserver address and command necessary to subscribe to the mailing list.

Tip

Remember to save the subscription information of a mailing list when you subscribe. That way, you can easily refer to that information when you wish to unsubscribe.

As part of the process of subscribing to a mailing list, you must send a command to the listserver. To send a command to a listserver, you must place your message in the body of your mail sent to the listserver. That is, you don't need to place anything in the subject line of your e-mail. The message body is the place where listservers look for commands, such as subscription requests.

So, what commands do you send to a listserver? Well, that depends on the type of listserver being used. Thankfully, most listservers accept the commands "help" and "lists". Figure 9.4 shows you what happens when you send the command "help" to **LISTPROC@chicagokent.kentlaw.edu**, while figure 9.5 shows you what happens when you send the command "lists" to the same e-mail address.

What you cannot see in figure 9.5 is the five pages following with detailed explanations on how to subscribe, unsubscribe, and use various other commands. As you can see, however, help is available if you know where to look.

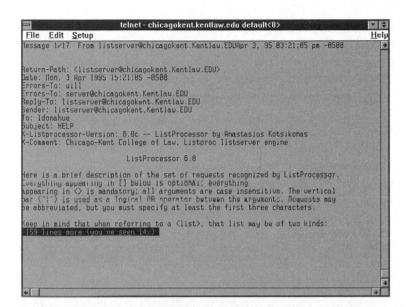

Fig. 9.4
The "help" command provides help from a listserver.

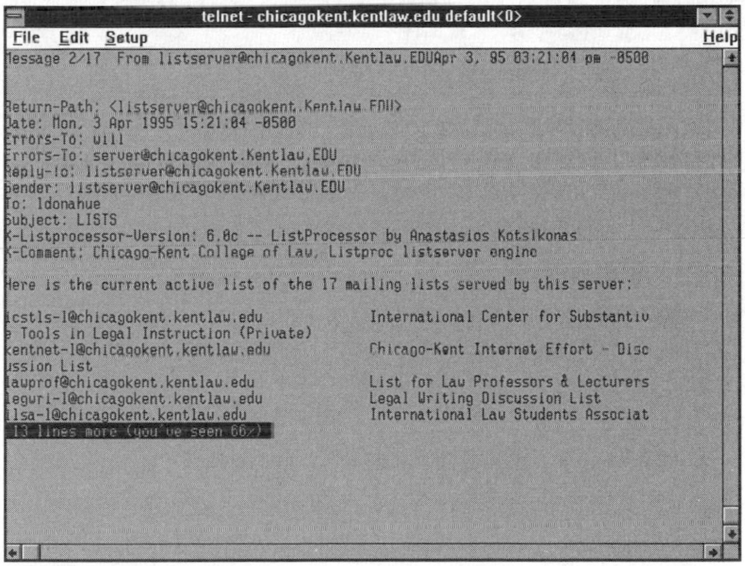

Fig. 9.5
The "lists" command provides an index of mailing lists maintained by a listserver.

In figure 9.5, you can see an index of mailing lists, with a brief description of each mailing list on the right. You can use this index, in conjunction with the help file displayed in figure 9.4, to figure out what to do next. You can usually subscribe or obtain more information about a particular mailing list. If you want to find out more information about ILSA-L, for example, send **info ILSA-L** in the main body of your e-mail message to **LISTPROC@chicagokent.kentlaw.edu**.

Steps To Subscribe

Once you have figured out where to send your subscription request, the process to subscribe is quite simple. The easiest way to learn how to subscribe is to follow an example.

The Chicago-Kent College of Law sponsors a mailing list called ILSA-L, for the International Law Students Association, and is located at **ILSA-L@chicagokent.kentlaw.edu**.

Tip

Every mailing list and listserver are different. Therefore, make sure you write down any instructions to subscribe when you learn of a new mailing list.

Before you can even think of participating in ILSA-L directly, you must first subscribe by sending a subscription request to the listserver located at **LISTPROC@chicagokent.kentlaw.edu**. This listserv address is the location of Chicago-Kent College of Law's listserver.

To subscribe to ILSA-L, send **subscribe ILSA-L Your Name** in the main body of your e-mail message to **LISTPROC@chicagokent.kentlaw.edu**. Note that *Your Name* is your full name, not your e-mail address.

Tip

Remember that some lists are busier than others. Don't be alarmed if you do not receive list e-mail right after you subscribe.

If you send this command to Chicago-Kent's listserver, you will receive a welcome message from ILSA-L within a short amount of time. Most lists will send you such a welcome message, which usually contains important information on how to unsubscribe, what rules (if any) exist for the mailing list, and how to find more information about particular topics.

Once you successfully subscribe to a mailing list, you will automatically start receiving posts to the list by other subscribers. How soon you start receiving e-mail depends on how long it takes for the listserver to subscribe you to the list and how busy the list is. Some mailing lists are extremely busy and you will receive messages immediately. Others are very slow and it could be weeks before you receive your first message.

Hot Mailing Lists You Can Subscribe To

There are thousands of mailing lists and you'll soon find the perfect mailing list for your personal or professional interests. Here are a few that may get you started. A lot of the mailing lists here are listservs, which means you don't have to put any Subject: heading in your e-mail—only a message to subscribe in the body of your letter. If there is a person in charge of a mailing list, his name and possibly e-mail address appears after the address for the mailing list.

Art and Music

Art News

If you want to find out what's what in the world of art, museums, and collections, subscribe to this mailing list. It offers coverage from various print sources about the world of art.

To subscribe: Send e-mail to **artnews-request@arttrak.metronet.com** with the body of message simply **Subscribe**.

Chinese Music

This list offers reviews of new Chinese music (on CDs).

To subscribe: Send e-mail to **newwave@rahul.net** with the body of the message **subscribe whatsnew**.

Classical Music

Classical music encompasses several hundred years of compositions—many of which are still being performed and recorded. This moderated mailing list is for the discussion of the music, musicians, composers, instruments, history, and so on. Contact address: **music@pulse.com** (Dave Lampson).

NetJam

NetJam provides a mechanism for musicians to collaborate on musical compositions using electronic communications—specifically by sending files such as Musical Instrument Digital Interface (MIDI) via e-mail.

To subscribe: Send e-mail to **netjam-request@xcf.berkeley.edu** with the subject **Line request for info**.

(continues)

III

People Resources

(continued)

Business & Finance

Futures Market

A mailing list for discussion of futures and commodity trading.

To subscribe: Send e-mail to **sub.futures@stoicbbs.com** with the body of the message **Subscribe Futures <your e-mail address> <your full name>**. You'll receive acknowledgement of subscription and information about how to participate.

International Trade

Business is a global topic. This mailing list posts messages that discuss international trade, overviews of global companies, and tips on successful investing. Contact address: **info-request@tradent.wimsey.bc.ca**.

Stock Market

A daily mail message that provides a review of activity on the stock market. Also, the moderators answer questions on topics related to financial investment. Contact address: **smi-request@world.std.com**.

Computers

Info MIME

MIME (Multipurpose Internet Mail Extensions) is the Internet's multimedia electronic mail standard that allows a variety of information to be included in a mail message.

To subscribe: Send e-mail to **info-mime-request@cs.utk.edu**.

Net Happenings

This mailing list is a service of InterNIC Information Services and Gleason Sackman of North Dakota's SENDIT Network (he moderates). You'll receive about 15—20 messages per day which include calls for papers, publications, newsletters, and network resources. The messages are archived daily.

To subscribe: Send e-mail to **majordomo@is.internic.net** and type **subscribe net-happenings** in the body of the message.

New Mailing Lists

Subscribe to get announcements of new mailing lists. Contact address: **info@vm1.nodak.edu** (Marty Hoag).

The Scout Report

This is a distribution-only mailing list provided by the InterNIC Information Services.

Distributed weekly, The Scout Report highlights new resources and Internet news.

To subscribe: Send an e-mail message to **majordomo@is.internic.net** with the message **subscribe scout-report**. You can also access via Gopher at **is.internic.net/Information Services** or the World Wide Web URL address **http://rs.internic.net/scout_report-index.html**. If you have a Web browser, you can receive the HTML version via electronic mail by sending the message **subscribe scout-report-html**.

Education

A.Word.A.Day

Need to increase that vocabulary to impress friends or English teachers? This is a "wordserver" that sends you one English vocabulary word and its definition every day. Contact address: **anu@viper.elp.cwru.edu** (Anu Garg).

To subscribe: Send an e-mail message to **wordsmith@viper.cwru.edu** and type **subscribe <your full name>** in the subject line (leaving the body of the message blank).

The Learning List

The focus of conversation on this mailing list is learning and development for children. To be eligible to receive mail, members must agree with the charter of the list. A copy of the charter is available at **Learning-Request@sea.east.sun.com** (Rowan Hawthorne).

Health

Americans with Disabilities Act

Discussion of the Americans with Disabilities Act (ADA) and disability-related legislation around the world. Contact address: **wtm@bunker.afd.olivetti.com**.

To subscribe: Send an e-mail message **Subscribe ADA Law <your name>** to **listserv@vm1.nodak.edu** or send e-mail to **wtm@bunker.afd.olivetti.com**.

Quit Smoking—Smoke Free

This mailing list serves as a support function for people on the road to recovery from addiction to cigarettes. Contact address: **maynor@ra.msstate.edu**.

To subscribe: Send e-mail to **listserv@ra.msstate.edu** with the message **subscribe smoke-free <Your Full Name>**.

(continues)

III

People Resources

(continued)

International

Africa

This mailing list will keep you informed on the issues and events in Africa. Contact address: **frabbani@epas.utoronto.ca** (Faraz Rabbani).

To subscribe: Send e-mail to **LISTSERV@utoronto.bitnet** with the message **SUBSCRIBE AFRICA-N <Your Full Name>**.

Croatia

A mailing list that offers news about Croatia.

To subscribe: Send an e-mail message with your name, your e-mail address, state, and country to **Croatian-News-Request@Andrew.CMU.Edu.** Put the state/country information in the subject line. If you'd like to receive the news in Croatian, indicate that in your message.

Middle East Peace

Discuss the ongoing peace process between the PLO and Israel and Jordan and Israel.

To subscribe: Send e-mail to **LISTSERV@AIS.NET** with the message **Subscribe MIDEAST-PEACE <Your Full Name>**. Questions about the list should be addressed to **Hanania@USG.ORG** or **Rayhanania@Delphi.Com**.

Uruguay

Discusses news and events related to Uruguay.

To subscribe: Send your name, e-mail address, topics of interest, address, and phone number to **uruguay-request@db.toronto.edu** (Mariano Consens). Note: Most messages are in Spanish.

Sports & Recreation

American Hockey League

Discussion about the American Hockey League. Contact address: **ahl-news-request@andrew.cmu.edu**.

Celtics

Put in your two cents about the players, the season, draft prospects, and anything else that relates to the Boston Celtics basketball team.

To subscribe: Send e-mail to **celtics-admin@hillel.com** with the message **SUBSCRIBE CELTICS <Your Full Name>**.

Gymnastics

For those with the inclination and ability to participate in the sport of gymnastics, this mailing list will provide advice, tips, routines, warm-ups, and lots more. People of all levels of ability join. Contact address: **owner-gymn@mit.edu** (Robyn Kozierok).

Martial Arts

Martial arts are great for self-defense as well as self-discipline. Share training tips, equipment, routines, and philosopical discussions for several different forms. Contact address: **martial-arts-request@dragon.cso.uiuc.edu** (Steven Miller).

Participating In a Mailing List

Once you have subscribed to a mailing list, participation is almost automatic. At the very least, the mailing list will begin to forward messages to you as they are sent to the mailing list. You can read these messages at your leisure in e-mail, and respond to them either directly or through the mailing list (so others can read your response).

If you want to send a message to other subscribers in a mailing list, all you need to do is send an e-mail message to the mailing list's e-mail address (after you have subscribed). For example, if you want to send a note to the ILSA-L mailing list, send your message to **ILSA-L@chicagokent.kentlaw.edu**.

It's that easy. Don't be alarmed if you don't receive a copy of your message from the mailing list. Some lists don't send copies of messages to the originators. That is (in most cases), all subscribers will receive messages sent to a mailing list, except the one who originally sent the message.

Tip

When responding to a mailing list message, ask yourself whether you want everyone in the list reading your response. If not, make sure your response is only addressed to the original sender of the message and not being forwarded to the mailing list.

Troubleshooting

Every time I try to send a command to a listserver, I receive an e-mail message that indicated my message failed with an "unknown host" message.

It's likely you don't have the right hostname for the listserver. Double-check the e-mail address for the hostname. If you have a copy of Que's *Special Edition, Using Internet E-Mail,* look at chapter 1, "Understanding Internet E-Mail Addresses," and chapter 21, "Introduction to Internet Addressing." Also, make sure you do not have any spaces in the e-mail address.

(continues)

III

People Resources

(continued)

Every time I try to send a command to a listserver, I receive an e-mail message that indicated my message failed with an "unknown user ..." message.

It's possible you might have to try a different e-mail address for LISTSERVER. If LISTSERVER doesn't work, try LISTSERV, LISTPROC, LISTKEEPER, and MAJORDOMO. If none of these addresses work, double-check the overall mailing list address you have.

Alternatively, you may be attempting to access a mailing list maintained by a human being rather than a listserver. Such lists are rare, but if all of the listserver names fail with an "unknown user" message, you may need to add a hyphen followed by the word "request" after the username portion of the mailing list address. For example, if you were interested in KARATE-L, but couldn't reach the listserver with any of the usernames listed previously, try using KARATE-L-REQUEST as the username portion of the e-mail address of the mailing list.

When I send the "info <listname>" command to the listserver, I receive an empty file or nothing at all.

Contact the owner of the mailing list, and kindly ask for the location of the mailing list FAQ (which stands for *Frequently Asked Questions*), or ask where you might obtain further information about the list.

If you don't know who the owner of the mailing list is offhand, there are several places you can go. The most obvious place is the 'welcome' message that you receive when subscribing to a mailing list. If you haven't yet subscribed, do so, following the steps above. When you receive the welcome message for subscribing to the list, the message will usually indicate who the mailing list owner is. If the welcome message doesn't directly indicate who the mailing list owner is, look for an Errors-To: line near the top of the welcome message. The e-mail address indicated on the Errors-To: line is usually the mailing list owner or manager. Alternatively, you can simply send a message to the mailing list, inquiring about a FAQ or the e-mail address of the mailing list owner.

How To Access Message Archives

Mailing list archives represent an important source of information. Archives give you the ability to review mailing list discussions before asking questions on that mailing list. Not only do some people get upset rehashing old information, some of the knowledgeable people will simply not respond because they have already done so in the past. Additionally, what you seek may already be in an archive, which means you can avoid subscribing to a particular mailing list if you are not interested in participating.

Regardless of whether you actually subscribe to a mailing list or not, once you identify the location of a mailing list and its listserver, you can usually obtain access to the mailing list's archives.

When considering how to access particular archives, it's important to understand that archives can be maintained in many ways. If the archives are maintained by the listserver, you can usually send commands to the listserver to obtain copies of archives and their indexes. If the archives are maintained in some other way, you will quickly find that listserver commands are not effective in accessing the archives. You can, when confronted by such a situation, either send a help command to the listserver for more information concerning the archives or subscribe to the mailing list and ask someone by posting a question to the mailing list.

The first thing to do is send the help command to the listserver to determine what commands are available to help you obtain archives. Another command to consider is the info command. When used in conjunction with the mailing list name, the listserver will usually send you a helpful message concerning the mailing list. Sometimes, this info message contains instructions on how to obtain access to the archives. For example, you could send **info ILSA-L** to **LISTPROC@chicagokent.kentlaw.edu** to obtain information about ILSA-L and any information concerning ILSA-L archives.

Finally, the index command used in conjunction with the mailing list name usually gives you a list of archives available through the listserver. Since many listservers vary in the way they deal with archives, other commands may be necessary. Be sure to check the help file issued from the listserver. To obtain a list of archives for the ILSA-L mailing list, send **index ILSA-L** to **LISTPROC@chicagokent.kentlaw.edu**.

How To Find Current Lists of Mailing Lists

It won't take long before you find out that actually finding a particular mailing list is the hardest part in trying to participate in them. Without knowing what exists and where, it's impossible to participate in a particular mailing list.

There are several ways to find various mailing lists. First of all, there are comprehensive lists of lists. Of course, these lists are never 100% accurate or complete, but they help in getting started. Second, there are specialized lists of mailing lists focusing on a particular topic, such as law, education, music, hobbies, or sports. Third, you can use UseNet groups or mailing lists you are aware of to look for other mailing lists.

Comprehensive Lists of Lists

There are several places to go to obtain comprehensive lists of mailing lists. Comprehensive lists attempt to index all discussion lists, of any conceivable topic. The problem is, the author doesn't necessarily have expertise in all subject areas, and therefore may not be aware of all possible mailing lists in a given area. Additionally, such authors usually rely on the managers of new mailing lists to contact them for inclusion of their mailing list into the comprehensive index. The problem is, the manager of a new mailing list may either not be aware of the comprehensive index or not want to advertise the new list to keep subscriptions down to a few experts (or invited guests) within a particular subject area.

Comprehensive lists, or indexes, may have the mailing list you're looking for or act as a springboard to more specialized mailing list indexes.

The LISTSERV Web Site

The first comprehensive list of mailing lists is The LISTSERV Home Page, shown in figure 9.6. This list is located at **http://www.clark.net/pub/ listserv/listserv.html**.

This Web site currently only references those mailing lists located on LISTSERVs, not Majordomo or Listproc. What the LISTSERV Home Page does have is a rather extensive listing of LISTSERV mailing lists by category. Figure 9.7 shows a portion of the mailing lists by category screen, which is ultimately composed of over 30 topics ranging from Art to Technology and UNIX. What you will find are references to appropriate LISTSERV mailing lists, as well as explanations on how to subscribe and participate in interesting mailing lists.

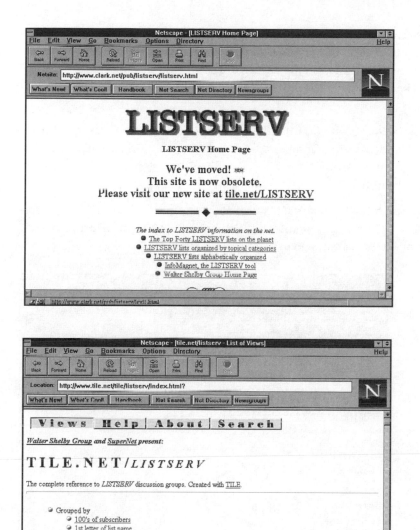

Fig. 9.6
The LISTSERV
Home Page
references almost
all LISTSERV
mailing lists.

Fig. 9.7
The LISTSERV
Home Page has
mailing lists by
category index.

People Resources

E-Mail Discussion Groups Web Site

Another resource worth looking into is Nova Southeastern University's E-Mail Discussion Groups home page. Nova Southeastern is located in Ft. Lauderdale, Florida, and has created a nice interface to help you search for mailing lists.

Figure 9.8 shows you what the Web page for Nova Southeastern University's E-Mail Discussion Groups home page looks like. This page interfaces into the Dartmouth List-of-Lists reference and has some good documentation explaining what mailing lists are and how to use them.

To reach the Web page for Nova Southeastern University's E-Mail Discussion Groups home page, point your Web browser to **http://alpha.acast. nova.edu/listserv.html**.

Fig. 9.8
Nova Southeastern University is a nice stop to help you search for mailing lists.

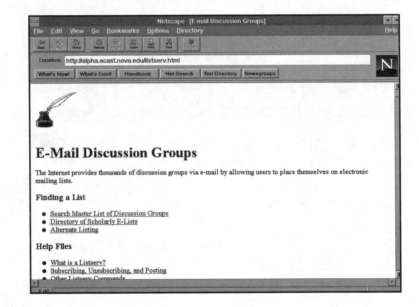

The Dartmouth List-of-Lists

Dartmouth maintains an extensive collection of mailing lists, which includes LISTSERV mailing lists as well as many Listproc and Majordomo lists. Unfortunately, this service is very busy and therefore very slow. Fortunately, you can download the list-of-lists database and run programs available from Dartmouth, as shown in figure 9.9.

To reach the Dartmouth list-of-lists, you can use FTP or Gopher. The Web URLs for these resources are **ftp://dartcms1.dartmouth.edu/siglists/ internet.lists** and **gopher://dartcms1.dartmouth.edu/11/siglists**.

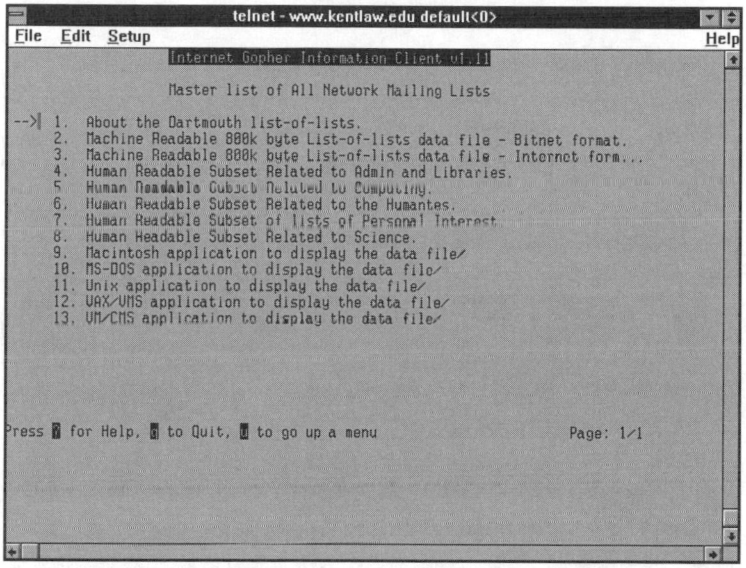

Fig. 9.9
The Dartmouth List-of-Lists is one of the most comprehensive databases of mailing lists on the Internet.

Publicly Accessible Mailing Lists

The Publicly Accessible Mailing Lists is a copyrighted compilation by Stephanie da Silva that represents her significant efforts to map out currently existing mailing lists. She publishes her list in UseNet, under the group of **news.answers** and **news.announce.newusers**, and as a consequence, it is one of the easiest comprehensive lists available on the Internet today.

The UseNet post of Publicly Accessible Mailing Lists is done in 14 parts. For access to the actual UseNet post, you can use the URL **http://www.cis. ohio-state.edu/text/faq/usenet/mail/mailing-lists/top.html**.

Figure 9.10 shows the Web home page of this wonderful reference to search for mailing lists. As with all other list-of-lists, Publicly Accessible Mailing Lists isn't necessarily complete. But, it does have a wealth of information that is sure to come close to the topics that interest you. This list is located at **http:/ /www.neosoft.com/internet/paml/**.

Figure 9.11 shows a partial listing of Publicly Accessible Mailing Lists' index by subject listing. This is one of the more complete subject listings available.

Fig. 9.10
Publicly Accessible
Mailing Lists is a
very nice Web
interface to use for
finding specific
mailing lists.

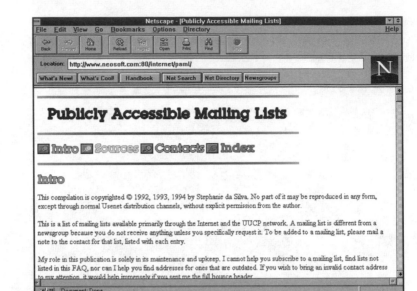

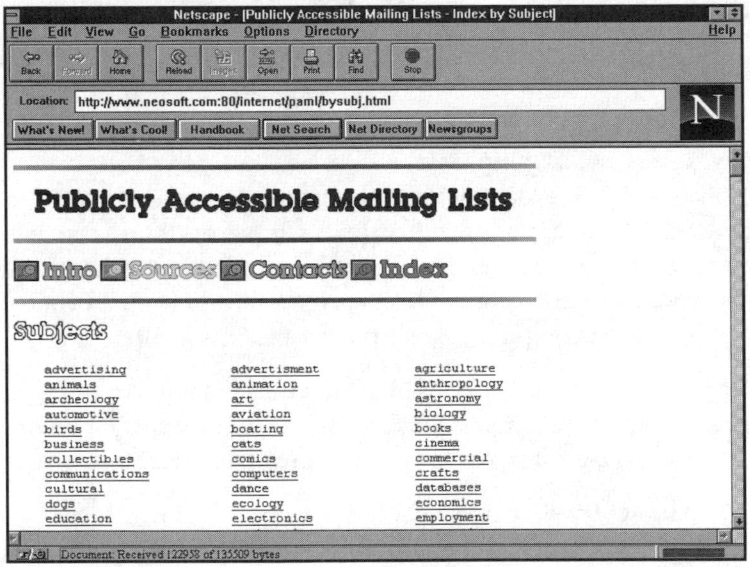

Fig. 9.11
Publicly Accessible
Mailing Lists also
has a very
comprehensive
index by subject
list.

> **Note**
>
> Before you head off to the more specialized lists that focus on certain mailing list topics, you might want to do a comprehensive search on Yahoo, located at **http://www.yahoo.com/**, the popular WWW index tool.
>
> Yahoo, believe it or not, is a comprehensive list of mailing lists. The trick is to narrow your search so it encompasses only mailing lists. To narrow your search in this manner, search for "list and <topic>", where "<topic>" is related to your area of interest (for example, try searching for "list and law").

Selected Examples of Specific Specialized Lists

Because there are more topics than could possibly be covered in this book, we'll show you three specific examples of specialized lists. These examples are accessible from any of the general resource guides. Remember to look over chapter 4, "Information Detectives: Gopher, Veronica, and WAIS," because many good references are indicated that could function as highly specialized lists.

For those interested in law, there are two services we would like to call to your attention. The first is called The Legal Domain Network, which was created and designed by Larry Donahue and maintained by the Chicago-Kent College of Law. It is pictured in figure 9.12 and contains the actual archives of over 60 substantive law-related discussion lists. It is located via the Web at **http://www.kentlaw.edu/lawnet/lawnet.html** or Gopher at **gopher://gopher.kentlaw.edu/11/Internet%20Services/News/lawnet**.

The Legal Domain Network is powerful, since it provides a single place to review many mailing lists of specific interest in law. I know of no other place on the Internet that actually has archives of mailing lists like the Legal Domain Network, since most other sites only give you information about the list (not actual access to archives).

III

People Resources

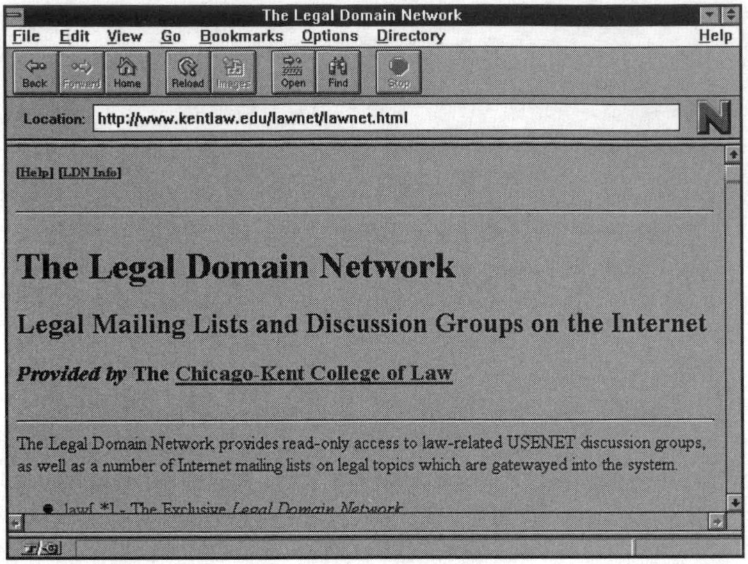

Fig. 9.12

The Legal Domain Network allows you to read the archives of over 60 law-related discussion lists.

Another valuable resource for law mailing lists is Law Lists, maintained by Lyonette Louis-Jacques at the University of Chicago. To obtain the latest copy of Law Lists, use the URL **gopher://lawnext.uchicago.edu/00/ .internetfiles/lawlists**.

Also check out the University of Chicago's Law-Related Discussion Lists on the Internet at **gopher://lawnet.uchicago.edu/hh/.web/lists.html**.

If your interest is sports, you might be interested in the Sports Pointers Web home page shown in figure 9.13. This Web page has quite a few references to other sports information, which can help you reach the mailing list of interest to you. It is located at **http://www.cs.cmu.edu/afs/cs.cmu.edu/ user/clamen/misc/Sports/README.html**.

While we can go on forever pointing out specific resource guides and how they help you identify specific mailing lists, you have enough background using some of the sources indicated (or listed in chapter 5) to help you find just the right information resource or mailing list you are seeking. Remember to start as general as possible until you can narrow your focus to find the right resources.

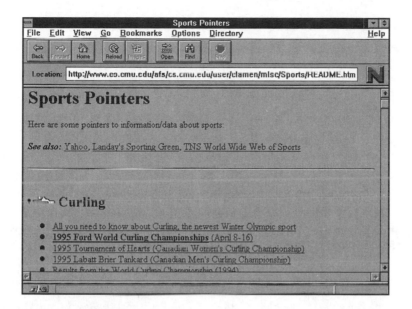

Fig. 9.13
Sports Pointers
Web home page
can help you find
your sports
resource.

Using Known Mailing Lists To Find New Mailing Lists

Lastly, you can use mailing lists you are aware of to find new mailing lists. First, look over the archives for mention of new and related mailing lists or references. If you can find references to more or related information, review that information for mention of new mailing lists.

If the archives are not revealing, post a message to the mailing list asking for advice or suggestions on how to find more information or a mailing list that is more related to the information you seek. Of course, when posting, consider whether the list is tangentially related to your area of interest. If there is no relation whatsoever between the mailing list you are considering posting a question to and your area of interest, you might want to think twice before posting your message. Not only is it likely no one will be able to help you, you might actually upset a few people on the list!

How To Search a Listserver Archive Via E-mail

You can search most mailing lists via e-mail, right from the comfort of your own office or home. Searching mailing lists depends, however, on the type of mailing list software being used. Therefore, this section is broken up into the three major listserver software groups, to help you use just the right commands and syntax to get the most out of your search.

III

People Resources

Searching LISTSERV Mailing List Archives

LISTSERV software is very advanced, and therefore quite complicated. If you can, I recommend pursuing InfoMagnet, described in the next section. Otherwise, you can make use of the e-mail searching facilities of LISTSERV software.

The first thing I recommend is obtain help from a LISTSERV. You can send the commands **info refcard** and **help** to obtain good documentation on basic LISTSERV commands. You might also consider sending the command **info database** to receive an approximately 30-page document on how to conduct good searches using the LISTSERV software. Remember to send your commands to a valid LISTSERV listserver where you may be considering obtaining archives. If you are simply interested in these help files, you can send the preceding commands to **listserver@wuvmd.wustl.edu**.

Before you can conduct a search, you have to know what databases (or archives) are available for searching. For starters, you must have a mailing list to search. Once you have identified a mailing list, send the command **database list** to the listserver to see what archives are available. You can also send the command **lists** to see what mailing lists are maintained by the listserver, but understand that many listservers do not maintain archives for all the mailing lists they serve.

Once you know a particular database or archive exists, you can perform searches and retrieve particular archive messages. To conduct a search on a LISTSERV listserver, you must issue a series of commands to perform your search. Since the series of commands is complicated, make use of a **command template** to help you perform your search. A command template is a series of pre-defined statements you can use as a base, when constructing your search command to LISTSERV.

When attempting a LISTSERV search, use the following template:

```
//      JOB Echo=No
Database Search DD=Rules
//Rules DD *
command 1
command 2
...
/*
```

As an example of this template in action, please refer to figure 9.14. This figure shows an example of using the template to search for the word "friend" in the VETINFO LISTSERV mailing list. That is, we have two commands: The first command is **search friend in VETINFO** and the second command is **index** to print an index of the articles meeting our search requirements.

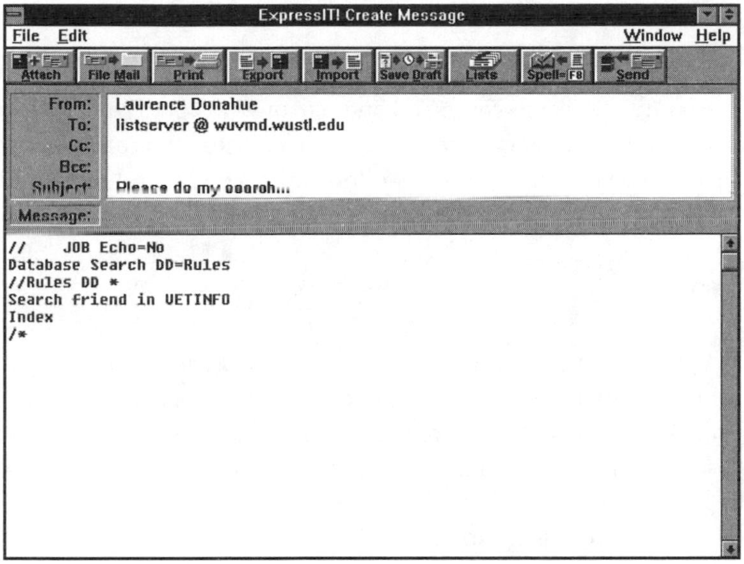

Fig. 9.14
An example of how to use the LISTSERV listserver command template to perform a search.

The template will be modified by you, in the command 1, command 2, and ... lines when performing your search. When performing your search, you will have to indicate a <pattern>, which indicates the search pattern LISTSERV is to use in searching its archive. <pattern> can be quite complex for LISTSERV. It can be a whole sentence, with "and" and "or" and "not" syntax to narrow your search. Additionally, you can place quotes to perform literal searches. You can also use parentheses to perform nested searches.

In particular, the command syntax for searching is:

```
Search <pattern> in DATABASE

Index
```

This command sequence will search for <pattern> in the archives specified by DATABASE. The Index command will display an index for you once the search is completed, which you can use in a print command to obtain matching archives.

You might be interested to know that LISTSERV supports field and scope searching, as well as using multiple archives in its search. All of these topics are beyond the scope of this book, but are fully documented in the document you receive with the **info database** command.

> **Caution**
>
> Do not issue the **print** command until you are reasonably sure that you do not have too many hits. Otherwise, you will receive very large amounts of output from the listserver.

You can re-issue the search command and narrow the <pattern> until you have a list that is reasonably short and contains documents that seem interesting to you. You can then send the following as a command (remember to place the following command in the command template):

```
Search <pattern> in DATABASE
Index
Print
```

Figure 9.15 shows a sample output after performing a search, indexing that search, then issuing the print command, as shown in the example. While you cannot see the actual articles (since they are beyond the screen in this figure), you can see a portion of the index. All articles in the index are sent to you with the print command. Therefore, be sure you don't have too many articles in the index, or your print command will yield a *very* large e-mail message being sent to you.

To summarize searching on LISTSERV:

1. **Obtain help**. Send the commands info database, info refcard, and help to obtain more information.

2. **Figure out what archives you wish to search**. Typically, the archives you will want to search are the mailing lists you are interested in.

3. **Obtain more help**. Do this by sending the command **database <list>**, where <list> is the actual name of the mailing list you are interested in searching.

4. **Conduct an initial search**. Once you have a good idea of the mailing list you wish to search, use the template above to construct a search command sequence that you e-mail to the LISTSERV listserver. Make sure that you *do not* send a print command at this time. Only the search and index commands should be sent.

5. **Narrow your search if necessary**. If the results of your previous search have listed too many articles (more than 100) matching your search pattern, you should try narrowing your search. Repeat steps 4 and 5 as necessary.

6. **Issue the print command**. Once you have a respectable number of articles matching your search pattern, you can add the print command to your command sequence for a search. LISTSERV will then send you articles matching your search.

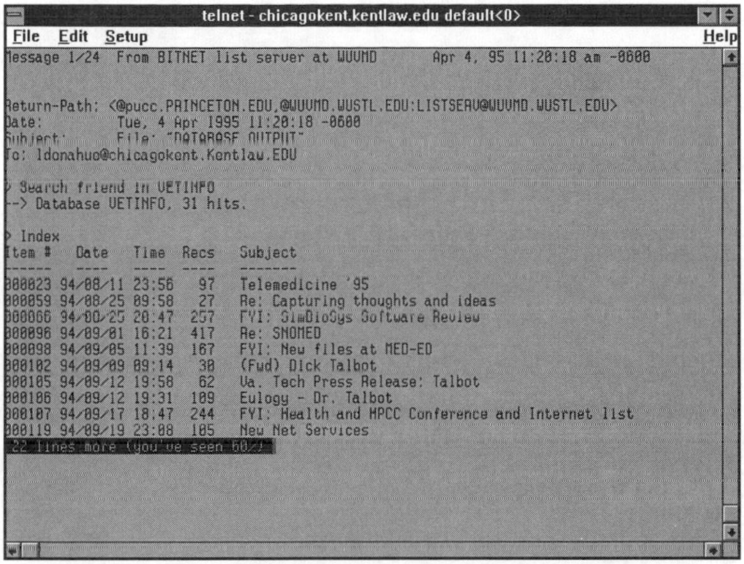

Fig. 9.15
An example of the output from a LISTSERV listserver after performing a search.

Searching Listproc Mailing List Archives

Listproc is actually quite powerful, and has good searching features for archived mailing lists. As mentioned previously, the e-mail address to contact is the Listproc software itself, not the actual discussion list you are interested in. For Listproc, LISTSERV, LISTSERVER, or LISTPROC may be used as the e-mail address for the Listproc software, such as **LISTPROC@chicagokent. kentlaw.edu** used in previous examples.

Just like the help, info, or index command, you can send other commands to the Listproc listserver. Listproc supports a search command, as does LISTSERV, but uses it somewhat differently. Like LISTSERV, Listproc utilizes a <pattern> to help indicate the search parameters you are interested in.

In particular, <pattern> can be one or more words, with control and Boolean information. "&" means AND, "|" means OR, and "~" reverses the meaning of your <pattern>.

For example, if <pattern> was "oranges", it would search for all instances of "oranges", without being case sensitive. If <pattern> was "~oranges", it means anything that doesn't contain "oranges". If searching for "oranges|apples", you are searching for "oranges" OR "apples". If searching for "oranges&apples", you are searching for "oranges" AND "apples". Finally, "oranges&~apples" will find all hits matching "oranges" AND NOT "apples".

You should be familiar with three commands when interested in searching or browsing Listproc archives:

- **index listname**. Gives you a list of archives for a mailing list. For example, the command **index ilsa-l** sent to **LISTPROC@chicagokent.kentlaw.edu** will give you a list of archives available for the International Law Students Association. See figure 9.16.

Fig. 9.16
Listproc listserver software allows you to obtain an index of mailing list archives.

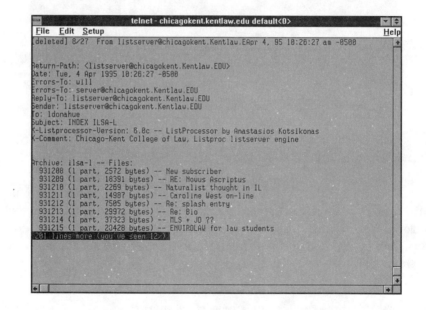

- **get listname file**. This command will get a particular archive, or file, from the given mailing list. For example, **get ilsa-l 931212** will give you the ILSA-L archives for December 12, 1993, starting with "Re: splash entry" in figure 9.16.

■ **search listname <pattern>**. This command performs searches on the mailing list specified by *listname*. The <pattern> indicates the search parameters and can be as simple as one word, or as complex as a UNIX regrep expression. For example, the command **search ilsa-l foreign** produced the results in figure 9.17.

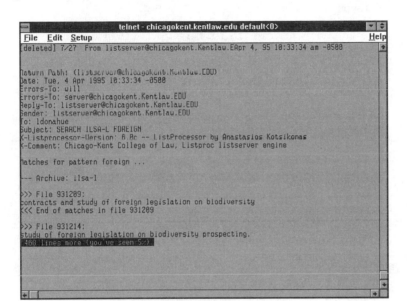

Fig. 9.17
Listproc listservers can also be searched, returning output similar to what is shown.

Now, when searching archives of known mailing lists for Listproc listservers, I recommend following a series of steps:

1. Issue the index listname command first. Use this command to determine if archives for the given mailing list in *listname* even exist. If they do, you will be presented with a nice list of archive entries, sorted by date. You can use this list to get archives directly, or to give you an idea of what is available.

For example, send the command **index ILSA-L** to **LISTPROC@ chicagokent.kentlaw.edu**.

2. Issue the get listname file command if you found an interesting archive with the index listname command, as shown in figure 9.16. The index listname command has files listed in the left-hand column that can be used in the get listname file command.

For example, try sending the command **get ILSA-L 931212** to **LISTPROC@chicagokent.kentlaw.edu**.

3. Issue the search listname <pattern> command for more information if you are not satisfied with the index listname command. You will get back a list of archives that match your search. What's nice about this software is you will obtain a list of matching lines, so you can read those lines that match your search to determine if the archive is exactly what you are looking for.

   For example, try **search ILSA-L foreign** at **LISTPROC@ chicagokent.kentlaw.edu**.

4. Finally, issue the get listname file command for any archives you find that match your search, as shown in figure 9.17. Again, the output of the search listname <pattern> command gives you a file you can use in your get listname file command.

   For example, again try the command **get ILSA-L 931212** to **LISTPROC@chicagokent.kentlaw.edu**.

For more information about the searching facility for Listproc listservers, send the command help search to a Listproc listserver.

This command will send you a two-page document on how to conduct searches in Listproc. While you are at it, you might consider sending the commands help get and help index for more information on those commands as well.

Searching Majordomo Mailing List Archives

Currently, many Majordomo listservers do not support direct searching via e-mail. However, this may change in the very near future, as the developers of majordomo are very active in maintaining their software.

Majordomo does support the index listname command, however, as the other listservers do. Therefore, you can send the index listname command to obtain a list of contents for the archives maintained by Majordomo. Additionally, you can contact the manager of the list, usually by sending e-mail to **listname-manager**, where *listname* is the name of the list. For example, if ILSA-L were maintained on a Majordomo listserver, you could send a note to **ilsa-l-manager@chicagokent.kentlaw.edu**, where your message would be routed to the person who is in charge of managing ILSA-L. You can ask such a person how you might search their archives.

InfoMagnet Searches Mailing Lists and Messages

There is a very powerful software package called InfoMagnet, which can be used to help you search many mailing lists. This software currently costs $99, but is available in a demonstration version. It was developed by John Buckman of the Walter Shelby Group, Ltd., and can be reached via e-mail at **info@shelby.com**.

There are many advantages to using InfoMagnet over regular e-mail. First, you do not have to find the e-mail addresses of mailing lists you are interested in. Second, InfoMagnet gives you firsthand information as to what mailing lists exist, so you don't have to hunt around for new mailing lists. Third, it gives you the ability to search many mailing lists at the same time.

The third advantage is probably the most important. InfoMagnet is capable of acting as a central control mechanism for many discussion lists. While it currently only handles LISTSERV mailing lists, the author promises InfoMagnet will handle Listproc and Majordomo mailing lists soon. This is not a great problem, however, as there are over 5,000 LISTSERV mailing lists available for searching and participation.

All LISTSERV mailing lists are available to you via InfoMagnet, which controls your subscriptions as well as gives you a nice interface to search all the lists for information. Everything is contained in a local database, while it has the intelligence to update its database from the Internet. Without a doubt, this package can be all you need to navigate around mailing lists on the Internet.

Figures 9.18 through 9.21 illustrate the specific features and functions of InfoMagnet and the process by which you can search for mailing lists.

The InfoMagnet Discussion Group List box gives you the ability to either select from a general subject category or search for keywords within an index of mailing lists. Figure 9.18 demonstrates the use of the Discussion Group List box by entering the keyword **internet**. Figure 9.19 shows the results of that search: A list of all of the mailing lists that focus on your subject. This list also has a very brief description of the main topics that are covered in the mailing lists found. You have three button-bar choices: You can Peek at more details on a specific mailing list, Search a mailing list for specific messages, and Join a mailing list.

III

People Resources

Fig. 9.18
The InfoMagnet
Discussion Group
List Box allows
you to search for
specific mailing
lists.

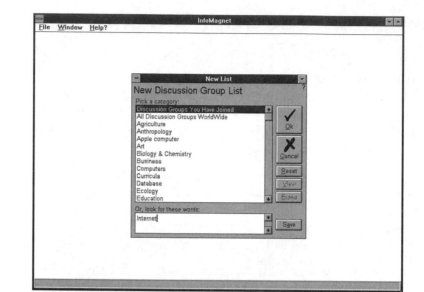

Fig. 9.19
A search of
mailing lists
within InfoMagnet
produces a
description of
matching mailing
lists.

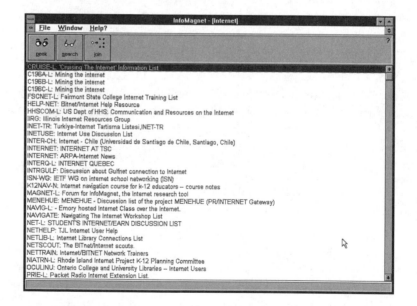

If you decide to Search a mailing list, you will be confronted with a dialog
box as shown in figure 9.20. In addition to entering keywords and search
terms to locate specific messages, you can also determine how far back in
time you want to search—up to a full year. The advanced settings have
InfoMagnet continue the search in the future. (It will check the mailing list
every seven days or so.)

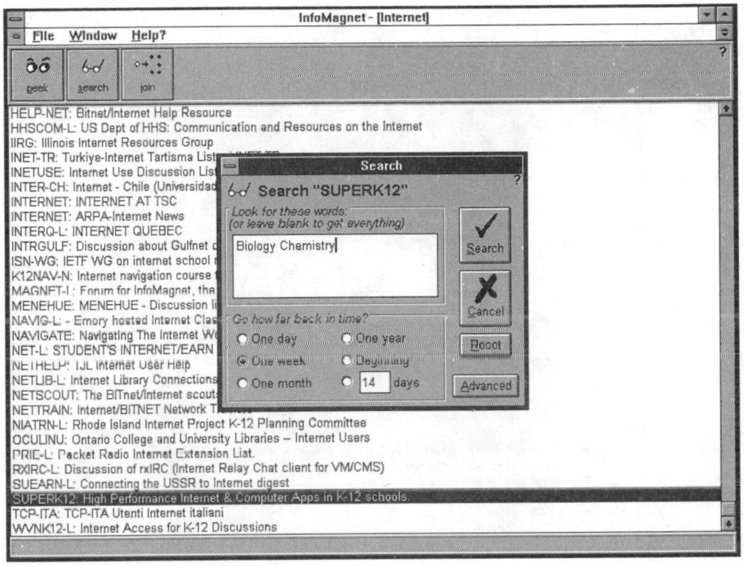

Fig. 9.20
InfoMagnet is powerful enough to search mailing list archives within specified dates.

If you decide to Peek a mailing list, you will be confronted with a dialog box as shown in figure 9.21. This dialog box shows detailed information about a mailing list, including the number of members, who is eligible to join, a more detailed description of the subjects, the country and site where the mailing list originates and the mailing addresses for the computer and human administrators as well as an address that sends mail to the entire group. You can also click on a topics button to have a list of message topics sent to you via e-mail.

> **Note**
>
> For more information concerning InfoMagnet, you can point your Web browser to:
>
> **http://www.clark.net/pub/shelby/imag.html**
>
> If you are interested in downloading a demonstration of InfoMagic, you can use ftp to obtain a copy at:
>
> **ftp://ftp.clark.net/pub/wsg/magnet**

As you can see, InfoMagnet represents a superior way in which to deal and access a large number of mailing lists. With InfoMagnet, you don't have to deal with some of the arcane commands described above, since the software handles everything for you automatically. If you are interested in accessing a large number of mailing lists, or their archives, simultaneously, InfoMagnet may be your best choice to help you with your search.

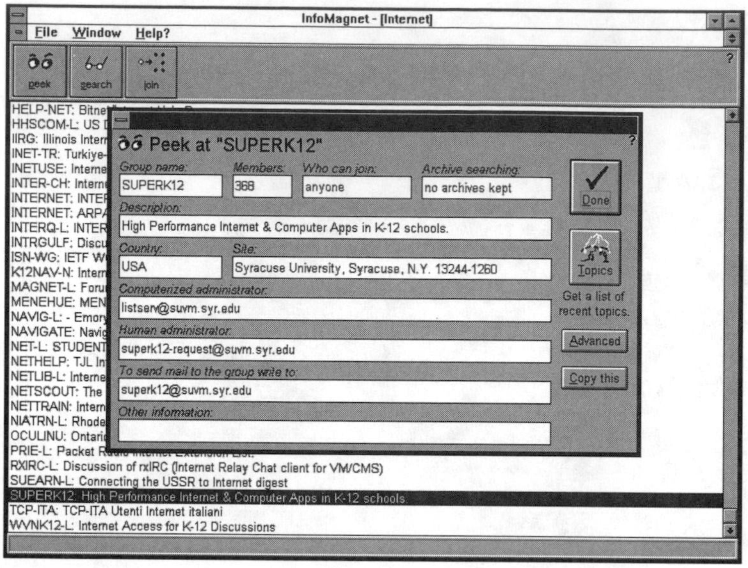

Fig. 9.21

The Peek option in InfoMagnet gives you advanced information about a mailing list.

Summary

In this chapter, you have learned the basics of mailing lists and where to find them. They can provide powerful means to find information and resources on the Internet, by tapping into the collective knowledge of others.

Mailing lists are a powerful tool to help identify the informational resources that you seek. They are also sources of information themselves, by opening up communications channels to peers as well as allowing you to search and browse archives of past discussions.

Any decent search of Internet resources should include obtaining advice and suggestions from those who have more experience on the Internet than you. In particular, you would benefit by finding people who (1) share your interests and (2) have more Internet experience than you. Mailing lists help you contact these people, who in turn will make valuable contributions towards your search of particular information on the Internet.

Now that you understand the basics of mailing lists, you have the ability to participate in some very interesting discussions. These lists may, by themselves, provide you with the actual information you seek or help you to reach your final destination.

Chapter 10

E-mail

Electronic mail—better known as e-mail—is one of the best two-way communication applications available on the Internet. You can use e-mail to carry on an electronic discussion, ask questions, share information, and send and receive computer files with one person or hundreds of people. In addition to being faster and less expensive than ordinary postal delivery (known as snail mail on the Net), you can quickly search through, sort, and save e-mail messages.

You can also use electronic mail to perform a variety of Internet information searches. In fact, if you don't have full Internet access or you use a commercial online service, you can do a lot of Internet searching via e-mail. You can use e-mail to perform an Archie file search, locate addresses of other Internet users, and search for and retrieve the full text of articles from magazines and newspapers. In this chapter, you learn:

- What features make e-mail an effective tool for information retrieval and electronic conversation

- How to write e-mail messages that ensure rapid and appropriate responses

- Techniques to help you sort e-mail messages and locate specific information that's in a message

- How several commercial services can deliver personalized news reports and articles to your e-mail address

Electronic Mail: Fast and Global

According to *Electronic Mail & Messaging Systems,* the number of electronic mailboxes in the United States alone reached an incredible 40 million by the end of 1994, and approximately 56 percent of these had connectivity to the Internet. Table 10.1 shows the growth of electronic mailboxes. If the current growth pattern for e-mail continues, by the turn of the century it'll be as common for people to have an e-mail address as a telephone number.

Table 10.1   Number of U.S. E-mail Boxes

Installed Base in Thousands   (Source: EMMS)

Year	Total Mailboxes
1980	430
1981	470
1982	540
1983	670
1984	1,000
1985	1,675
1986	4,100
1987	5,250
1988	6,960
1989	8,675
1990	12,750
1991	19,000
1992	25,000
1994	40,000

The time it takes for an e-mail message to travel from your computer to another person's PC varies between a matter of seconds to perhaps as long as several hours. The largest time variable is the speed of the telecommunication lines. And, of course, you don't have much control over the time of day that the recipient actually checks their mailbox. In any case, it's pretty much a sure thing that an electronic mail message will travel from your PC to its destination—anywhere in the world—in less than a day.

The speed and global connectivity of e-mail makes it an effective communications tool. Say, for example, you live in San Francisco, California, and are embarking on a hobby of growing Bonsai trees. You've got (or found) a friend who lives in Tokyo, Japan, who's an expert at this gardening art form. Send him or her an e-mail message with your question—send it at midnight your time and, because of the time difference, when you wake up the next morning the answer can be waiting in your mailbox. What's even better is that the cost of sending a message around the world is the same as sending it across the street. Typically a 200-page document can be sent via e-mail for less than 25 cents!

The E-mail Program

There are dozens of different electronic mail software programs. Some of these programs are designed to be installed on individual personal computers. Others are designed for local and wide area networks where hundreds or thousands of employees of a company or university use the same program. Commercial online services like CompuServe have their own e-mail programs, too.

Although the specific features, toolbars, and commands for e-mail programs vary, there are some common functions and e-mail etiquette that will help you effectively use this communications tool. Just as a letter you send through the post office has an address, a return address, and a stamp, e-mail messages must include certain elements to successfully move from your computer to someone else's. Figure 10.1 shows an e-mail message composed with the Windows-based program Eudora. The message contains the following six elements.

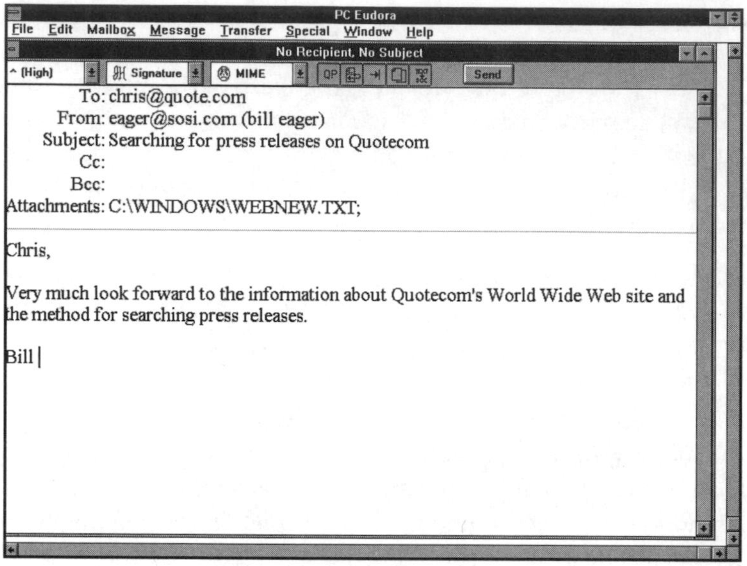

Fig. 10.1
With pull-down menus and point-and-click options, Eudora is a popular Windows e-mail program.

- **TO:** This is the e-mail address of the recipient—the person that you are sending the message to. If you send e-mail to someone who is not directly on the Internet (perhaps they subscribe to America Online), you must enter information that will route the message to their mailbox. Every e-mail message *must* include a From: and a To: line.

- **FROM:** This is your electronic mail address. It is an important field because it helps the person receiving your message identify the sender and makes it easy for them to respond.

- **SUBJECT:** This is a short description of the content of the message that gives your recipient(s) a sense of what your message or question is about. Just as when you leave a message on someone's answering machine or voice mailbox, your e-mail subject should be concise, specific, and meaningful. In many ways it should resemble the headline of a newspaper article. Say, for example, you've got a friend who's good at auto repair. You need advice on replacing the timing belts in your '88 Honda. Instead of a subject that reads, "My old car needs repair, please help," try "How much $ to replace Honda timing belts?" Some e-mail systems will limit the length of your Subject: line to 43 characters—even more reason to get right to the point.

- **CC & BCC:** Short for carbon copy and blind carbon copy, you can send one message to several people simultaneously. You don't have to fill in this line if you're not sending a copy.

- **ATTACHMENTS:** Attachments are files that are created in separate programs and then "attached" to the message.

- **MESSAGE:** This is the body of the e-mail message or letter.

Note

You may want to get a copy of the Eudora e-mail program. There are freeware and commercial versions for both the PC Windows environment and for Macintosh. To find out more or download the freeware version you can visit the Qualcomm Web site (URL address: **http://www.qualcomm.com/**), or you can use FTP to acquire the program. Here is the information for locating the Windows-based version from the FTP site. Simply navigate to the mac directory to get the Mac version.

FTP site: **ftp.qualcomm.com**

Directory: **quest/windows/eudora/1.4**

File: **eudor144.exe (294 K)**

Use An Address Book To Save Time

Most Windows and Macintosh-based e-mail programs offer some type of electronic address book—a place where you can keep the names and e-mail addresses of people you send messages to frequently. Address books can be real time-savers. If, for example, you are the president of a local computer users group, or the manager of a multi-regional sales force, you can use the address book to store all the e-mail addresses of the people you communicate with. Then, when you have a message that needs to go out to the entire group—perhaps announcing the time, place, and topic for next week's meeting—you can simultaneously send one message to all the people in the group. Figure 10.2 illustrates the use of an address book. In addition to speeding up the process of sending e-mail, the address book provides these other helpful functions:

- Prevents you from losing e-mail addresses of important contacts

- Helps you quickly locate someone's e-mail address

- Ensures that you don't accidentally mistype an e-mail address

Tip
Some e-mail programs allow you to keep the subject line on a message that someone sends to you when you reply back to them. Even though it's very easy to simply keep this subject line and send it back with your reply, avoid doing so. What tends to happen in an on-going e-mail conversation is that soon you don't know whether you're actually getting a new message or simply recycling old messages.

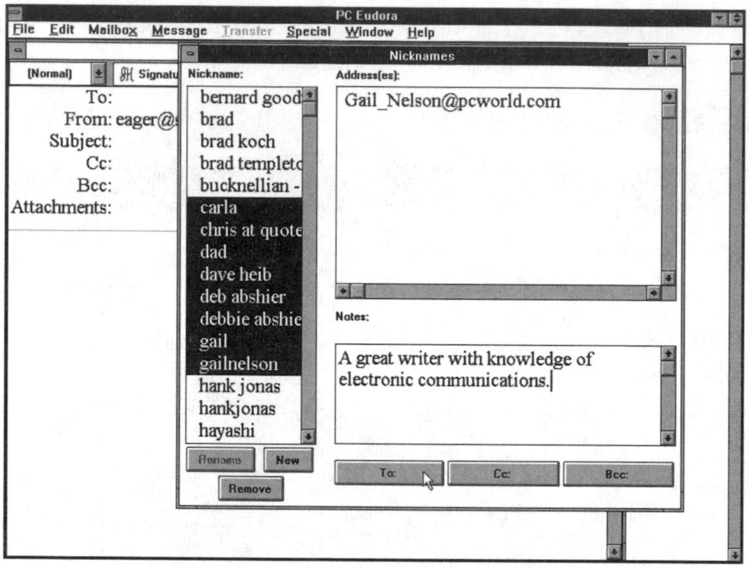

Fig. 10.2

If you have an electronic address book, you can save e-mail addresses, and then quickly send a message to one person or a group of people.

Tips for the Eudora Address Book

Here are a few useful tips for using the Eudora e-mail address book.

- If you receive e-mail from someone, you can quickly add their name and address to the address book. First, either highlight the message from the In Mailbox, or open the message. Then, open the Special pull-down menu and select Make Nickname or press Ctrl+K to add the name and address.

- If you want to send one message simultaneously to several people in your address book, start a new message by opening the Message pull-down menu and selecting New Message, or press Ctrl+N. Next, open the address book by opening the Window pull-down menu and selecting Nicknames, or press Ctrl+N. Then hold down the Control key while you highlight specific names by clicking the left mouse button. Or, click one name and drag the mouse up or down to highlight multiple names. Finally, click the To: button to send the message to all the people you have selected.

- You may want to print out the list of your address book. Use your word processing program and go to the directory where Eudora resides. Locate and open the file nndbase.txt. This file contains the names and addresses of everyone in the address book. Another file, nndbase.toc, is the file that Eudora uses to maintain the directory of addresses. At some point you may want to copy this to a floppy disk as a backup measure.

What Good Are Attachments?

Attachments can really enhance the utility of e-mail. An **attachment** is a file that you attach to your message. The file can be a word processing document, a digital image, an audio or video message, a spreadsheet, or a software program. How might this be helpful? Maybe you're doing a report for the management in your company on the economic impact of the North American Free Trade Agreement (NAFTA). You call up your stock broker to see if she's seen any studies on this. Yes, it turns out she's got a 20-page government report and several graphic images that predict future economic trends. She can e-mail you both the report and the graphics.

You can take this information and incorporate what you need into your own report, including graphics—you find the information you need, save a lot of time, and look like a real hero. As chapter 6 explains, there are certain issues with respect to copyright when it comes to distributing, copying, and printing information. As a rule-of-thumb, if you want to distribute something you've found on the Internet and you're not sure whether there are any copyright issues, you should probably locate the source of the information and ask permission.

Troubleshooting

Someone sent me a file as an attachment but I can't seem to read it. Why?

When you ask someone to send you a file (or you send one to someone else), make sure they have a software program that can load the file. For example, if you send a Word for Windows 6.0 file to someone who uses WordPerfect for Windows 5.2, they may not be able to open the file. Likewise, a Mac graphic PICT file can't be viewed by PC users. To get around this obstacle, you can see whether your software program will save the file in another format. For text-based documents, ASCII text is a universal file format that can be opened by all types of word processors and on all computer platforms.

Tip
You'll save both time and money if you compress your files before you attach and mail them.

How To Handle E-mail Overload

If you're like most people, there are days when you open your real mailbox and find that it's full of junk mail—solicitations to subscribe to magazines, sell your house, buy a waterbed. E-mail is becoming such a popular application that you can receive junk e-mail. Or, even worse, get e-mail overload where you have to sort through and read 50 messages every day. This can be

III

People Resources

time-consuming, frustrating, and very unproductive. Sophisticated e-mail programs offer solutions to this modern-day dilemma. Filters in the program help you sort your messages, and many sorts are possible. Figure 10.3 shows how you can quickly sort messages with the Eudora mail program. Here are a few possible sorts:

Sort Type	What It Does
Date	The date they are received—oldest go to the top of the list.
Status	Tells you if the message has been read.
Priority	Sorts by level of urgency.
Sender	Sorts by last name of sender.
Subject	Sorts alphabetically by the first letter in the subject line.

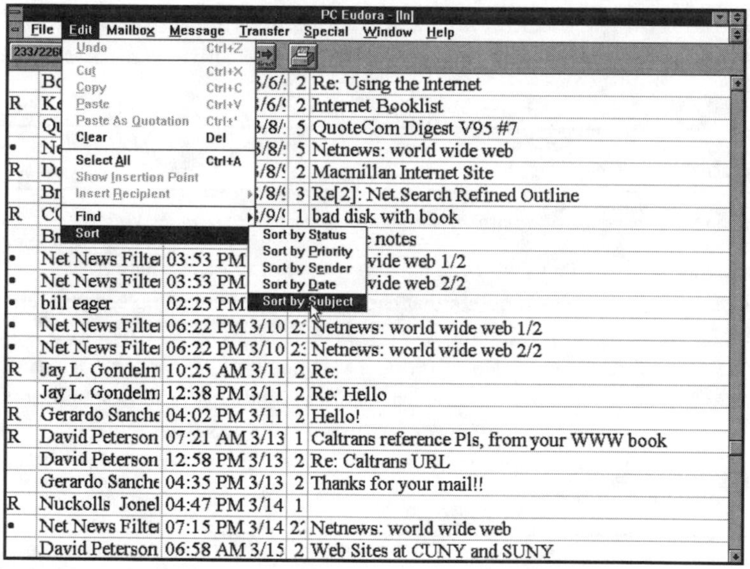

Fig. 10.3

With Eudora, you can quickly sort your e-mail messages before or after you read them. This becomes increasingly important as your mailbox begins to fill up.

Some e-mail programs can automatically store messages in specific electronic folders. You can have folders for special news items or mail from your boss. This provides another convenient way to get through the clutter of e-mail messages.

With **rules-based messaging** programs, individual users or network administrators can define criteria for automatically routing and acting on e-mail.

Banyon's Beyond Mail program is one example of this type of software. For example, you could "tell" the e-mail program that you are going to be out of the office for a week. Further, during the week the program will automatically reply to all normal messages with a note that tells people you're on vacation. And it will automatically transmit urgent messages or messages from your boss to the fax machine at the hotel where you're staying. Essentially, the program becomes your message agent, accomplishing tasks that would normally require human interaction.

How To Manage E-mail If You Have Several Mailboxes

If you're an online junkie, you may subscribe to several different services and have more than one e-mail address. Just checking and responding to your e-mail every day on one service can take 15 minutes or longer. Add the time it takes to log into several services and it can be a real time-killer. In fact, if you start to favor one account over the others, you may one day log on to a lesser used online service to find 30 messages that were left for you a month ago!

There's a software program designed specifically to help out prolific e-mail users. E-Mail Connection by California-based Connect Soft will actually connect with your Internet, CompuServe, Prodigy, and MCI Mail accounts, check your mail, and deliver all messages via one program—you don't even have to be present while it happens. Basically you check one mailbox as opposed to several. In addition, you can take advantage of a feature known as Messaging Application Programming Interface (MAPI) that allows you to send mail directly from non-mail applications. For example, from Microsoft Word or Excel you can send a letter or a spreadsheet without ever leaving the program. To find out more:

> ConnectSoft
> 11130 NE 33rd Place
> Suite 250
> Bellevue, WA 98004
> (800) 234-9497
> **techsupp@adonis.com**

People Resources

Search the Content of E-mail Messages

Just as you can search through a database to find records that match keywords, you can also search or scan through e-mail messages to look for specific content. Clearly if you've got a message that's only a few lines long, you can read it faster than you could search through it. On other occasions, though, searching e-mail messages becomes a true time saver.

Here's an example of how this works. Later in this chapter there is an overview of NetNews, a service that searches through thousands of Internet newsgroup postings to locate messages that meet your search terms. The messages are sent back to you via e-mail. Other services, such as Dow Jones News Retrieval, will search through publications and send you relevant articles via e-mail. In writing books about the Internet, I've submitted the keywords "Internet" and "web" to several services. This generates as many as 30 e-mail messages every day. Some of these messages are more than 20 pages long.

Now, if I want to quickly sort through this pile of information to quickly locate new addresses for World Wide Web sites, I rely on my Eudora e-mail program to help. Figure 10.4 shows the Find dialog box in Eudora. I know that all Web site URL addresses begin with http, so I enter this into the search box. The search will look through the message to find and highlight any references to http. If it doesn't find any, or it gets to the end of a message, I can then go on to search the next message.

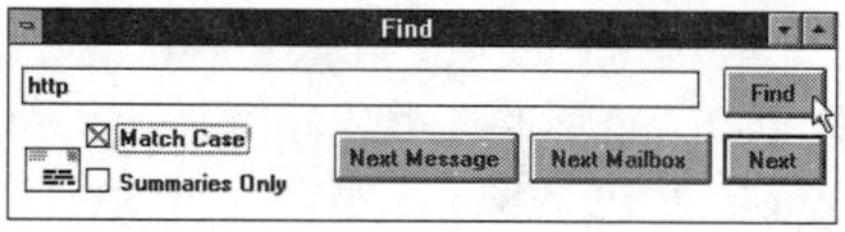

Fig. 10.4
With Eudora you can search through the contents of e-mail messages to locate specific topics or information.

It Doesn't Hurt To Save That Mail

Can you imagine saving every piece of mail that the postman delivers for the period of one year? You'd be swamped! And, you might ask, why would you want to?

With e-mail it's a little different. Sure, you'll get junk mail or short thank you notes—go ahead and trash them. You'll also get a lot of messages from friends, business colleagues, and new electronic acquaintances. There are a couple of good reasons to save a large percentage of these messages. First, if you save the messages, you'll have instant access to both the information and the e-mail addresses of all the people who have contacted you. In either case this could prove to be valuable later on. Maybe someone sends you information about a project you're working on, or a short letter that includes details about their flight information—the date isn't for several months. True, you can print all this information on your laser printer. But, keeping the message ensures that you really save the information. There's another reason to save e-mail messages—legal proof. E-mail messages are increasingly becoming acceptable as legal proof of business transactions or correspondence— especially when they use true electronic signatures and date stamps.

> **Note**
>
> There are two types of **electronic signatures**. With one kind you can simply type in your name and address and save that as a "signature," which you can attach to your e-mail. A more sophisticated approach involves attaching a digital copy of your signature to an e-mail message. **Date stamping** refers to the automatic attachment by the electronic mail program and Internet mail systems that shows the exact time and date that a message is sent and the route it takes as it moves from sender to receiver.

Now if you think saving all these messages sounds way too difficult, or that you don't have enough space on your hard drive, consider these facts. First, with almost every e-mail program you can save a message to your hard drive as an ASCII text file. With Windows-based programs it's as simple as one, two, three.

1. Select the File pull-down menu.

2. Choose the Save As option.

3. Enter the location on your drive where you want to save the message, making sure you give the message a .txt extension.

And, this doesn't really take all that much space. An average size message may have about 272 words and represents around 1,670 bytes. It would take 862 of these messages before you reached 1.44 MB—the amount of space available on one formatted floppy disk. In fact, if you're concerned about clogging up the hard drive, save messages directly to a floppy. You could save around 8,620 e-mail messages on a pack of 10 floppy disks, which costs less than $10. So, unless you're absolutely positive you never need to see the information in an e-mail message again, or really don't need the e-mail address of the person who sent it to you, then save it!

III

People Resources

Use E-mail To Receive Personalized News and Articles

There are a couple of Internet services that you can use to search for and receive personalized news, information, and magazine articles via e-mail. The concept and technology of personalized news has really opened up new avenues of information retrieval for Internet users. A few years ago only corporate communication departments could afford the high-cost services that deliver custom-tailored news information directly to electronic mailboxes.

The benefits can be enormous. Say, for example, you work in the automotive industry. You send the news service several keywords that identify the type of stories you have an interest in; perhaps "Japanese automakers," "auto regulatory affairs," "auto business," and "electric cars." Then, on a daily basis, articles that fit these parameters are electronically clipped from newspapers, magazines, and wire services around the world and delivered to you via e-mail. You get timely information about your competitors, industry trends, and government regulation. Today, you can subscribe to one of several personalized news services that send custom-tailored information to your Internet e-mail (or online service) address. These services range widely in price from a low of $0 to as much as $400 per year.

Tip

Sometimes when you sign up with a personalized news service, you want to send in many different search terms and use very broad terms. What can happen is that your e-mail box can be flooded with messages. You're better off starting with one or two specific terms, and then waiting a day or two to see how many e-mail articles you get. You can always add more requests or change your search criteria if you don't get what you want.

Netnews Filtering Service from Stanford University

While there may not be such a thing as a free lunch, there is a free news filtering service on the Internet. Stanford University maintains two distinct information searching and retrieval services as part of an electronic library. Overall the project is known as the Stanford Information Filtering Tool, SIFT for short. If you have access to the World Wide Web, you can visit the SIFT Web site at **http://sift.stanford.edu/**.

One information service is the Computer Science Technical Report filtering service. This service is valuable if your overall subject of interest relates to computers and computer science. You send keywords or search terms to the service, which then searches through technical reports and sends you, via e-mail, a list of relevant articles, the name of the author, the institute where the study was completed, and other relevant information.

If your information needs are more general in nature, you're more likely to appreciate the SIFT Netnews Filtering Service (NFS) shown in figure 10.5. Initially developed with funding from the Pentagon, the Netnews Filtering Service takes your keywords and search terms and scours through a daily listing of UseNet newsgroup postings to find articles that match your search criteria. These articles—which are actually messages from people who contribute to newsgroups—are then sent to you via e-mail. The articles arrive in alphabetical order by newsgroup (that is, the alt. newsgroup messages are first).

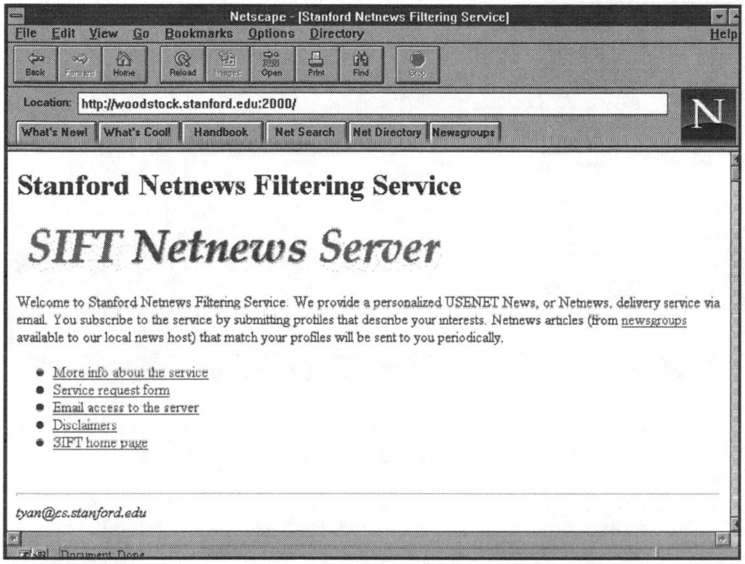

Fig. 10.5
The Stanford Netnews Filtering Service site is your gateway to a free personal news service.

There are two ways you can subscribe to NFS. First, you can subscribe via e-mail. Address your message to **netnews@db.stanford.edu**. Leave the subject line blank and in the body of the message, place a subscription request followed by your search terms. Here's an example:

subscribe internet educational applications

This subscription would search for messages that contain the words "internet educational applications." On a daily basis you will be mailed a list of relevant messages with the first 20 lines of text in each message. If you want to do a different search, you need to send in a second subscription request.

It is slightly more user-friendly to use the NFS Web site to subscribe. The URL address is **http://woodstock.stanford.edu:2000/**. Figure 10.6 shows the forms page that you use to subscribe.

III

People Resources

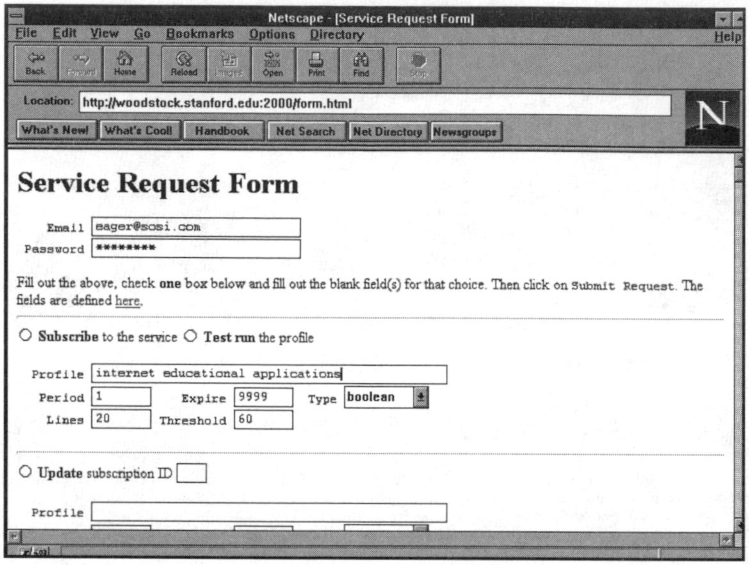

Fig. 10.6
From the Netnews Filtering Service Web site you can enter a search profile and choose several options that define the search and determine how often you will get articles.

Here's a brief description of the function of the various fields.

- **Email:** Enter your e-mail address.

- **Password:** Enter a secret password.

- **Subscribe or Test run the profile:** Click Subscribe if you are satisfied with your search profile. Click Test if you want to test your profile.

- **Profile:** Enter one keyword or a search term.

- **Period:** The period determines how frequently you receive the articles. The default is 1, which means you'll get something every day.

- **Expire:** Expire determines the number of days that your subscription will continue for. The default is 9999, which means your subscription is good for 28 years!

- **Type:** You can select Boolean or weighted. A **Boolean search** automatically puts the word AND between your words. **Weighted searches** give scores to each news article based on the number of occurrences of your profile words. The best score an article can get is 100. Articles that score higher than a preset threshold are returned and others are not.

- **Lines:** This is the number of lines from each newsgroup article that you will actually receive. The default is 20 lines. If you then want to receive the entire article, you can send back a request for it.

- **Threshold:** This is the minimum score that you want an article to have for it to be returned to you. The default is 60. If you set it higher—say at 90—only extremely relevant articles would be returned.

Figure 10.7 shows one of several articles that NFS sent back via e-mail. The profile for this search was the term "world wide web." This profile returns approximately 20 articles every day.

```
PC Eudora - [Net News Filter, 11:10 AM 3/26/95, Netnews: world wide web 2/2]
File  Edit  Mailbox  Message  Transfer  Special  Window  Help

[Normal]      Subject: Netnews: world wide web 2/2

Article: alt.online-service.compuserve.3012
Message-ID: <3l32j0$7u7@toolbox.rutgers.edu>
From: matthew@toolbox.rutgers.edu (Matthew Bernardini)
Subject: Internet and WWW survey and census needs your help !
Score: 100
First 20 lines:
=======================================================
World Wide Web and Internet Census is underway !!!
Stand up and be counted.  If you use the World Wide Web and the Internet
then we need you to fill out a brief survey.
How do you fill it out ?  The Web of course, you need a form capable browser.
The URL is http://bohica.rutgers.edu/research/
The survey is sponsored by a group of graduate students at Rutgers
University in New Brunswick, NJ.  The data will be used in Statistics,
Marketing and MIS classes.  A copy of the findings will be made
available to anyone who requests it in the form of an academic paper.
Please pass the message onto as many people as possible.  Even better,
post it to as many of your favorite newsgroups, forums, irc channels,
and mailing lists as possible.  For this project to succeed it needs
broad exposure.
Thanks in advance for your help.
```

Fig. 10.7
This article comes from the alt.online-service.compuserve newsgroup and it received a NetNews score of 100. The search profile was "world wide web."

The Individual HeadsUp News Service

Based in Burlington, Massachusetts, Individual, Inc. offers several electronic news services. They use a search engine called SMART (System for Manipulation And Retrieval of Text), which was developed at Cornell University. The SMART system "reads" through more than 20,000 articles delivered from some 500 news sources every day. It ranks them in order of priority for each subscriber and then determines which articles are interesting enough to be sent to your e-mail address. SMART even decides when an article should be delivered in full-text, an abstract, or only a headline.

You can choose one of three services from Individual. One called First! allows you to enter natural language queries such as, "News on commercial real estate trends in upstate New York." It then searches and delivers full-text articles to your e-mail address. A second service, HeadsUp, lets you choose specific industry categories, such as "Business Litigation," "Drug Manufacturing," or "International Travel & Tourism." It then sends headlines and brief descriptions of the articles, as shown in figure 10.8. If you want to see the full-text of a story, simply send back a request for it. At the time of this writing, HeadsUp offers a free trial of the service.

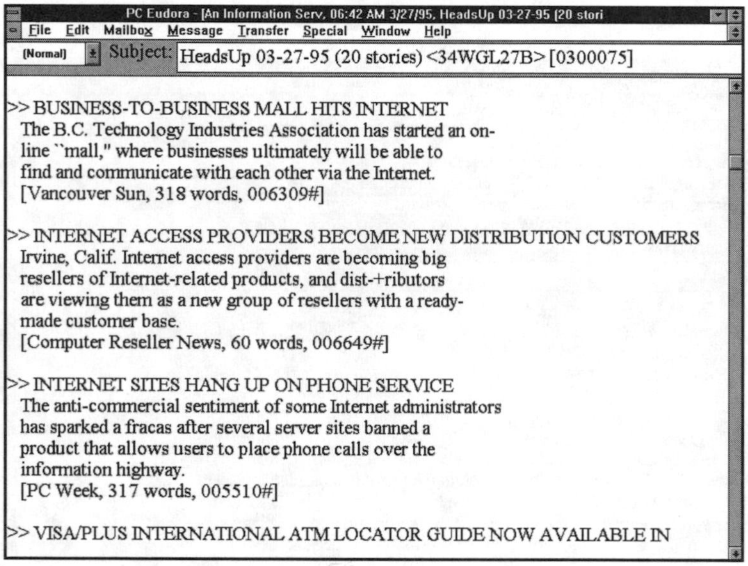
PC Eudora - [An Information Serv, 06:42 AM 3/27/95, HeadsUp 03-27-95 (20 stori

File Edit Mailbox Message Transfer Special Window Help

(Normal) Subject: HeadsUp 03-27-95 (20 stories) <34WGL27B> [0300075]

>> BUSINESS-TO-BUSINESS MALL HITS INTERNET
The B.C. Technology Industries Association has started an on-line "mall," where businesses ultimately will be able to find and communicate with each other via the Internet.
[Vancouver Sun, 318 words, 006309#]

>> INTERNET ACCESS PROVIDERS BECOME NEW DISTRIBUTION CUSTOMERS
Irvine, Calif. Internet access providers are becoming big resellers of Internet-related products, and dist-+ributors are viewing them as a new group of resellers with a ready-made customer base.
[Computer Reseller News, 60 words, 006649#]

>> INTERNET SITES HANG UP ON PHONE SERVICE
The anti-commercial sentiment of some Internet administrators has sparked a fracas after several server sites banned a product that allows users to place phone calls over the information highway.
[PC Week, 317 words, 005510#]

>> VISA/PLUS INTERNATIONAL ATM LOCATOR GUIDE NOW AVAILABLE IN

Fig. 10.8
Forget the newspaper. The HeadsUp news service delivers custom-tailored headlines and articles from national and international newspapers and magazines directly to your e-mailbox. In this example the category for searching was "Internet."

Last but not least, Individual has a news service called NewsPage which it delivers via the Web. The URL is **http://www.newspage.com/**. The site tells us: "It's designed to provide World Wide Web users like yourself with current, presorted news across a broad array of topics and industries."

In fact, NewsPage has more than 25,000 pages which are updated daily. Figure 10.9 shows the home page. As you can see, you start by selecting a topic category. From here you weave your way to the information and story that fits your needs. As an example, from the home page I selected the category Energy. From the next page Electric Power Industry, then U.S. Electric Power, at this point I received 17 summaries of stories of the day. Here's an example of one summary:

"The Federal Energy Regulatory Commission last week said all members of the Pennsylvania-New Jersey-Maryland Power Pool must provide comparable transmission service to Duquesne Light Co. [Oil Daily, 416 words]"

The summary not only describes what's in the article, but also tells what publication ran the article and how many words it contains. Figure 10.10 shows how the article displays in Netscape.

For more information:

HeadsUp
84 Sherman Street
Cambridge, MA 02140
(800) 414-1000 (800) 766-4224

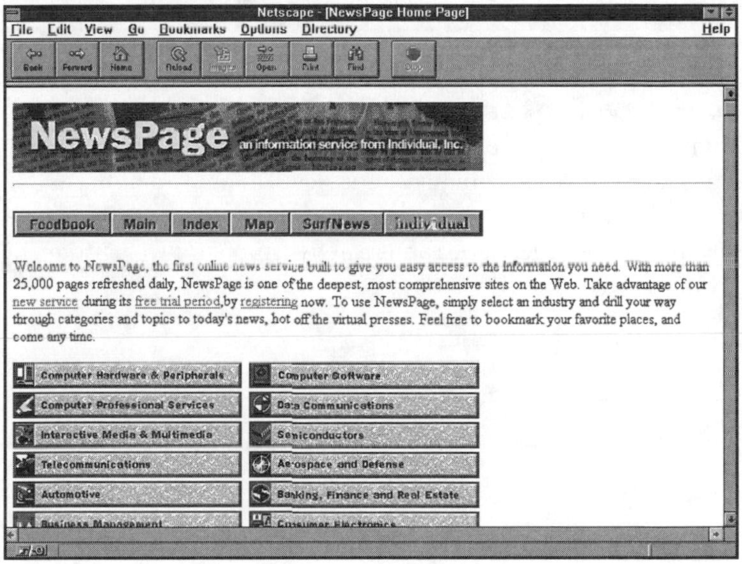

Fig. 10.9
This is the Web home page for the NewsPage news service. You begin your exploration by choosing a news category.

III

People Resources

Fig. 10.10
This screen shows
an article from the
NewsPage service.

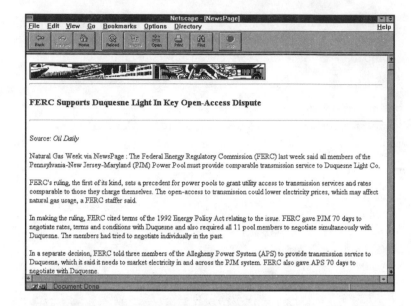

The Mercury Center NewsHound

NewsHound is another personalized news service that delivers the goods to your e-mail address. What's unique about NewsHound is that it can deliver both articles and advertisements that match your search criteria. NewsHound checks for new stories every hour and searches through several different news and information databases, including:

- Associated Press

- *Chicago Tribune*

- *Detroit Free Press*

- *Miami Herald*

- *Philadelphia Inquirer*

- PR Newswire

- *San Jose Mercury News*

You send your search terms to NewsHound via e-mail and each set of search terms becomes a profile. So, you could have one profile that looks for articles about The Rolling Stones, a separate one for the aerospace industry, a third for football quarterbacks, and so on. For $9.95 per month, you can enter five separate search profiles and there is no limit to the number of stories that you receive. Check out the NewsHound Web site. For more information:

NewsHound
Web URL Address: **http://www.sjmercury.com/hound.htm**
750 Ridder Park Drive
San Jose, CA 95190
(800) 818-NEWS (408) 297-8495
newshound-support@sjmercury.com

Other E-mail Searching Capabilities

You can also use e-mail to send in searches to locate files stored on FTP servers or find e-mail addresses of other Internet users. Chapter 5, "Finding and Retrieving Files from Remote Computers," provides an overview of how to use e-mail to send in an Archie search. The names of files and the FTP site addresses are sent back via e-mail. Chapter 11, "People, Companies, and Places," describes how you can perform a search for information about other Internet users via e-mail. E-mail is one of the most versatile Internet applications, and one that you'll probably use on a daily basis. You can use e-mail to communicate with other people around the world, sort through messages, or conduct information searches.

Summary

Electronic mail will always remain one of the most practical and powerful applications of the Internet. You can use e-mail to quickly and inexpensively send and receive messages and files with people all around the world. Add to this the ability to sort and search through messages and even get custom-tailored news reports and you have an unbeatable information system that will help you locate what you're looking for and save valuable time.

Chapter 11

People, Companies, and Places

The classic advertising motto for The Yellow Pages sums it up beautifully, "Let your fingers do the walking." Why drive 25 miles to a store only to find out that it doesn't have what you want? In this age where nobody has enough free time, directories, phone books, and almanacs help us quickly locate information about companies, organizations, and people.

With 3 million host computers and 30 million plus users, the Internet certainly has a lot of addresses. The average telephone book contains about 280 names and numbers on one page, so a comprehensive Internet directory would be around 107,142 pages. Similar to owning a collection of telephone books for every city in the world, this would fill several bookshelves. Fortunately, you can use some of the Internet's electronic directory systems to search for and locate the addresses and telephone numbers of people and companies that are on the Net.

The applications are numerous. Maybe you're in charge of planning your high school class reunion and can't find Sally Jones. Perhaps a new business contact wants you to send your credentials and you want to go high-tech, sending the information via e-mail. Or, you've lost contact with a good friend who moved overseas and you remember that he was into computers.

You can also use the Internet as a reference source for locating information about postal mailing codes and telephone area codes around the world.

In this chapter, you learn:

- How to locate e-mail addresses using electronic directories

- How to find the address and phone number of employees and students at companies and educational institutions

- How to find addresses of people who post messages to newsgroups

- What Internet sites offer directories of telephone and postal codes

Where To Begin

First, you need to define whether you are looking for information about a person, company, organization, or geographic location. Use the following checklist as a starting point for your search. All of these systems and tools are described in detail in this chapter.

Checklist for Finding People on the Internet

I. People

- **Finger.** Use this to identify the real name of an Internet user from his e-mail address.

- **Four 11 E-mail Searcher.** Use this Web site to both register your own name and e-mail address and locate addresses for other people.

- **Netfind.** Search this directory to locate a user's e-mail address.

- **X.500Search.** Access this global white-pages directory for information about individuals who work for specific organizations.

- **Whois.** Use this to look up information about people, including their e-mail and real-world mailing address and phone number.

II. Organizations, Institutions, and Companies

- **Phone Books (Nameservers).** Access phone books to search organizational directories for companies, government departments, and educational institutions.

- **Whois.** Use this to look up information about organizations or companies, including their Internet address, real-world mailing address, phone number, and a contact name.

III. Geographic Locations

- **World Country and Telephone Area Codes.** Connect with this comprehensive, searchable directory to locate phone codes for countries and cities around the world.

- **U.S. Geographical Information by City and ZIP.** Use this searchable directory to find information about towns and cities in the United States. Includes ZIP code, population, elevation, longitude, and latitude.

Four Ways To Find an E-mail Address

You can use the telephone system to look up addresses and phone numbers. If you know that Thomas Franklin lives in Chicago, Illinois, you can call up local information (312-555-1212) and ask for a listing. Odds are, however, the operator won't have access to Tom's electronic mail address. Clearly, before you can send electronic mail to anyone, you need that person's e-mail address. Not so obvious are the methods by which you can search for and locate e-mail addresses. Here are some options:

- The number one method for getting someone's e-mail address is the same method you use to get telephone numbers—you ask him. E-mail is becoming so prevalent that many people now include their e-mail address on their business cards.

- A second technique involves checking a directory of e-mail addresses. Bookstores now carry both white- and yellow-page directories of e-mail addresses. These are lists of addresses for people and companies all over the world. Organizations that publish directories often add e-mail addresses of members. If you work for a company that belongs to the Electronic Messaging Association (EMA), you can get a copy of its membership directory. Call 703-524-5550 to find out more about the EMA.

- The minute you receive e-mail from someone, you automatically have a copy of his address. Unlike a real letter, where people occasionally forget to write their return address, electronic mail always has a return address. Simply check out the From line in the header of the message and write down the e-mail address or add it to your electronic address book for future use. In a similar fashion, messages in mailing lists and newsgroups contain the e-mail address of the person who created the message.

III

People Resources

■ Last, but not least, you can search for someone's e-mail address. There are several sites on the Internet that maintain searchable databases of e-mail addresses. This chapter explores these options.

Use the World Wide Web To Find People

With its point-and-click interface and fill-in-the-blank forms, the Web is perhaps the easiest Internet system to use for locating people. The first thing you should know is that there are several different Internet directories of people. Second, there is not one all-encompassing list. This means you may need to search several places, and there is no guarantee that the person or company for which you're looking is actually in any directory.

> **Note**
>
> All Internet directories rely on individuals to submit or register their information to be placed in the system. So, unless you actively participate in getting your name and address into a directory, you remain unlisted.

Four 11 E-mail Web Searcher
Internet URL address: **http://www.Four11.com/**

Make this Web site your first stop in your search for someone's e-mail address. Not only is it easy to use, you can add your name and address to the database and search for other users, all at no charge. SLED Corporation from Palo Alto, California offers the service. The home page tells readers that the main goal is:

> "...helping Internet users find the most important resources around— each other. The Four 11 Online User Directory provides the Internet community with a much needed service: a free and easy-to-use directory of online users and their e-mail addresses."

With more than 500,000 listings, the Four 11 database is comprehensive. Many of the addresses are for people who have e-mail addresses on non-Internet systems—such as the commercial online systems. One of the nice features of the site is that you have to register your name and e-mail address before you can start to search. This ensures that the database of information will continue to expand. For a $20 annual fee you can upgrade to an account that lets you add a link to your own Web page, enhance your listing, and enter names that the system keeps on file and continues to search for even after you disconnect.

Figure 11.1 shows the forms page where you can enter a person's first and last name, city, state, country, or old e-mail address to begin your search. The group search tries to find people based on groups that they either currently or previously belonged to. A group could be the company they work for, the name of the college they go to, or the high school they attended.

To begin, try a search with only a name. For example, the name Steve Adams brings up a list of people, as shown in figure 11.2. If the names are high-lighted, they are links to more information—presumably these are people who have registered with Four 11. Figure 11.3 shows the type of information that you can retrieve.

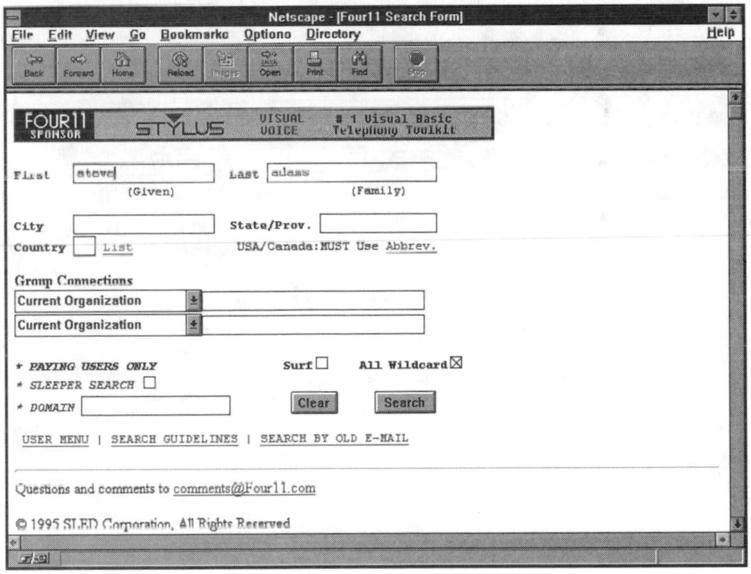

Fig. 11.1

At the Four 11 Web site, you start your search for a person by entering any information you already know about him—from a last name only to information about where he lives.

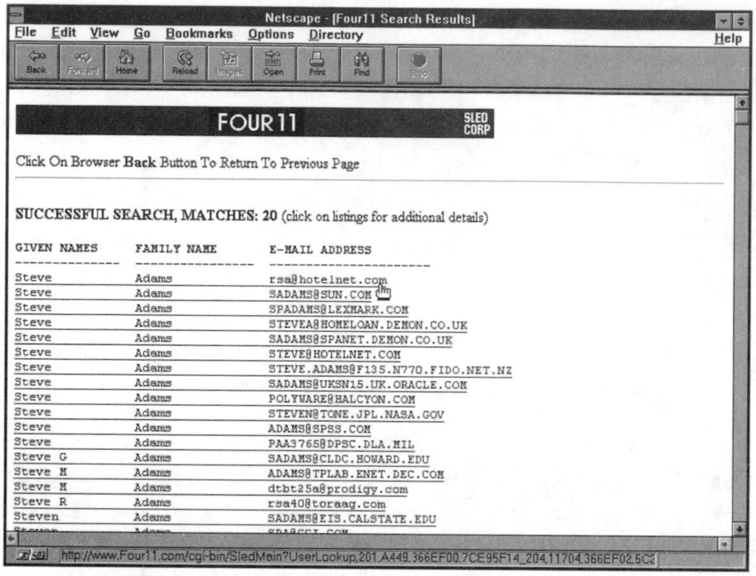

Fig. 11.2
Your search results provide a list of people who meet your search criteria.

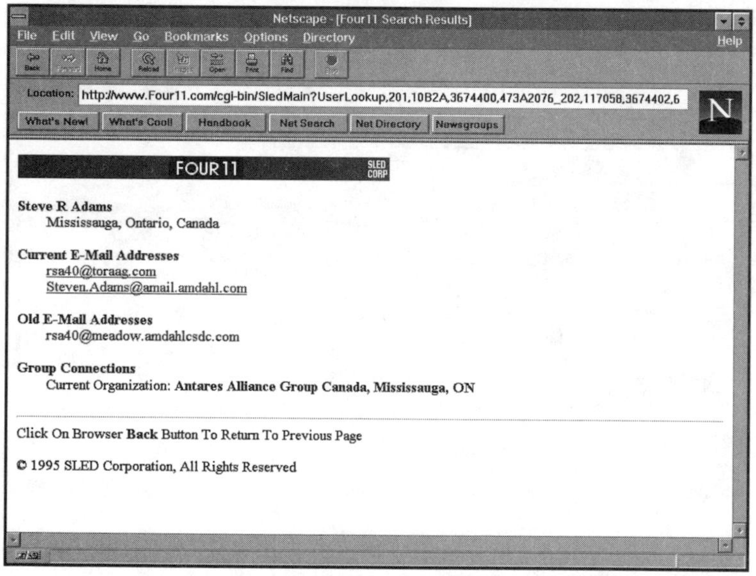

Fig. 11.3
Individual records often provide several e-mail addresses.

Here are some tips for searching the Four 11 database:

- Start with simple search criteria, such as a first and last name. You can use the asterisk key to designate **wild card** searches. With a wild card search, the computer will look for several records with different endings. This is helpful when you're not certain of the exact spelling of someone's name. For example, Cole* will locate Cole, Coleman, Colen, Coleson, Coley, and so on.

- Although all search fields are optional, if your search matches too many entries, you'll be asked to narrow the search.

- Searches are not case sensitive, so Bill, bill, and BILL will all get the same results.

- The search criteria are combined as a Boolean AND rather than an OR search. As a result, for a record to match, it must meet all search criteria.

- If you're looking for classmates from your high school, you could try group connection = Lewisburg Area High School. If this produces too many hits, you can narrow the search by adding state criteria, such as PA. Other possibilities for the group field include a company where a person works or the name of an association he belongs to.

Tip

If you don't have access to the Web or a Web browser, you can send and receive information about Four 11 by sending e-mail to **info@Four11 .com**. No message is necessary.

Troubleshooting

How do I find someone if he gets a new e-mail address?

That's when you want to use the Four 11 search field Old E-mail Address. It's a convenient way to track a person who either has more than one e-mail address or changes his address. In fact, if you ever send e-mail to someone and it gets returned, you can try this service to see whether it can find the new address.

The InterNIC Directory and Database

Established in 1993 by the National Science Foundation, the Internet Network Information Center, known as simply InterNIC, offers many resources for people and companies that use the Internet. The InterNIC is a collaborative effort of two organizations—AT&T and Network Solutions—that work together to offer Internet users a variety of information and support.

There are several ways you can access the InterNIC site. You can visit the Web site, the Gopher site, or Telnet. The Web address for the InterNIC Directory and Database Service (DS) is **http://www.internic.net**. Figure 11.4 shows the first screen that appears.

Before you enter this site, you should know that it offers so much information that it's a bit like traveling through a complex maze. Hopefully, these instructions help prevent you from getting lost. For the purpose of locating e-mail addresses—as well as several databases that'll help you locate other

Internet sites—you want to click AT&T's Directory and Database Services. This opens the screen shown in figure 11.5.

Fig. 11.4
Begin your
journey into
various online
directories at the
InterNIC home
page.

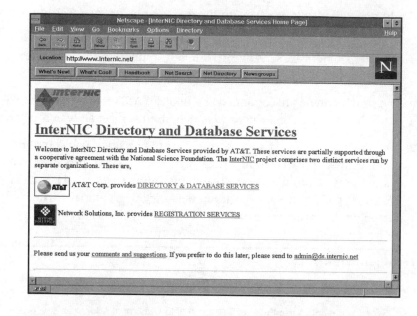

Fig. 11.5
AT&T maintains
several databases
designed to help
you locate people
and companies.

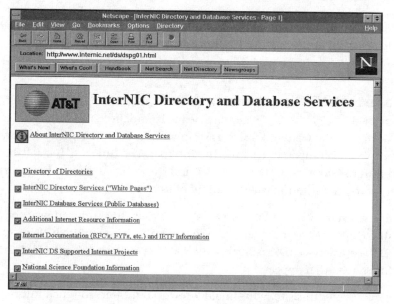

Now you confront several links that each contain a wealth of information. Here's a quick overview of links that will help you locate information about Internet sites, locate e-mail addresses, and learn about the Internet:

- **Directory of Directories.** This is a searchable database of Internet sites where the records provide a description of the site and, frequently, a phone number and address so you can get in touch with people at the sites. You can either browse by categories (like arts) or enter a keyword search. Many of the database entries are hypertext links to other Web sites

- **InterNIC Directory Services ("White Pages").** This is the service that will help you find e-mail addresses.

- **InterNIC Database Services (Public Databases).** There are three categories of information. First, material contributed by the National Science Foundation provides an introduction or tutorial about the Internet. Second, there are communication documents that relate to the NSFNET. Third, there is information supplied by individuals, schools, or institutions that could be valuable to groups of users on the Internet. A fee is charged for the maintenance of these databases.

- **Additional Internet Resource Information.** This link opens two more Gopher-site choices. One is a listing of the policies and procedures of Internet Service Providers across the U.S. The second is the NNSC (NSF Network Service Center) Internet Resource guide, which offers information about Internet sites and phone directories. Most of these are government-related and the listings seem to be somewhat out of date (the most current I found was 1992).

Note

You can Gopher or Telnet to connect with InterNIC by using the address **ds.internic.net**. You can also send a query for instructions on searching for people. Send e-mail to **mailserv@ds.internic.net**, and place the word **help** in the body of your message. Get a copy of a user-tutorial by downloading a file with the name **guest.tutorial**, which is in the subdirectory **ftp/internic.info**.

The InterNIC "White Pages"

Internet URL address: **http://www.internic.net/ds/dspgwp.html**

Figure 11.6 shows the InterNIC Directory Services "White Pages" screen. This service and Web page offer three distinct search systems to help you locate information about other Internet users, companies, and organizations. These include:

- WHOIS

- Netfind

- World Wide X.500 Directory

The following three sections in this chapter provide details about each system. Many of the services listed in the White Pages are actually run on Gopher servers, not Web servers. This, however, doesn't affect your ability to use the Web and a Web browser to access them.

Fig. 11.6
From the "White Pages" page you still have three choices to begin your search for information about people and companies.

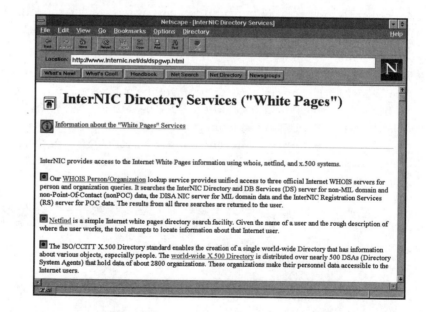

Find People with WHOIS

Internet URL address: **gopher://ds.internic.net:4320/7whois**

Pronounced *who is*, this is a combination computer server/database/utility program that stores the names and electronic addresses of Internet users, as well as information about companies that have Internet addresses. WHOIS databases were started in the 1970s as a means of registering host computers and the network administrators at different sites.

Today, they also include names and addresses of Internet users. There are many WHOIS servers and databases. The InterNIC WHOIS system provides simultaneous access to three separate WHOIS computer servers for searches for individuals and organizations. These three servers are:

- **DISA NIC** (**nic.ddn.mil**) contains information about individuals who work in the armed services.

- **InterNIC Registration Services** (**rs.internic.net**) contains information supplied when companies register with InterNIC.

- **InterNIC Directory and Database Services** (**ds.internic.net**) contains information about individuals that doesn't fit into either of the other two categories.

The InterNIC computer sends your query to all three WHOIS servers, and then provides you with the results from all three at once. (Nice one-stop shopping.) When you click the WHOIS link, you again have choices:

- Query search instructions

- Perform a query

The search instructions provide details on ways in which you can refine your search. If you'd rather jump right in, select Perform a Query. Figure 11.7 shows the query screen.

Using the Netscape browser, the query entry box appears on-screen. In this example, the name Kennedy is entered. Figure 11.8 shows the results of the query—the WHOIS servers have found 125 people and organizations that match this keyword. Common sense tells us there are probably more than 125 Kennedys who have e-mail addresses—but this is a start. By clicking an individual entry, you get the record details. In this example, the individual's name, company, mailing address, phone number, and e-mail address are all available (see fig. 11.9).

Note

If you click the first item—which is always Raw Search Results—you'll get a text file with information about everyone on the list.

Fig. 11.7
Simply enter a
name in the
WHOIS query
form to begin your
search. Here the
search looks for
people with the
name Kennedy.

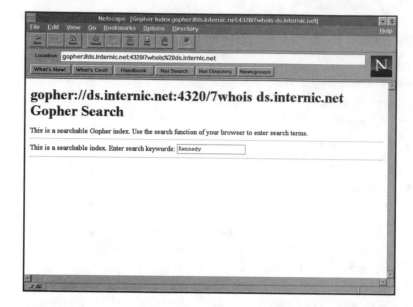

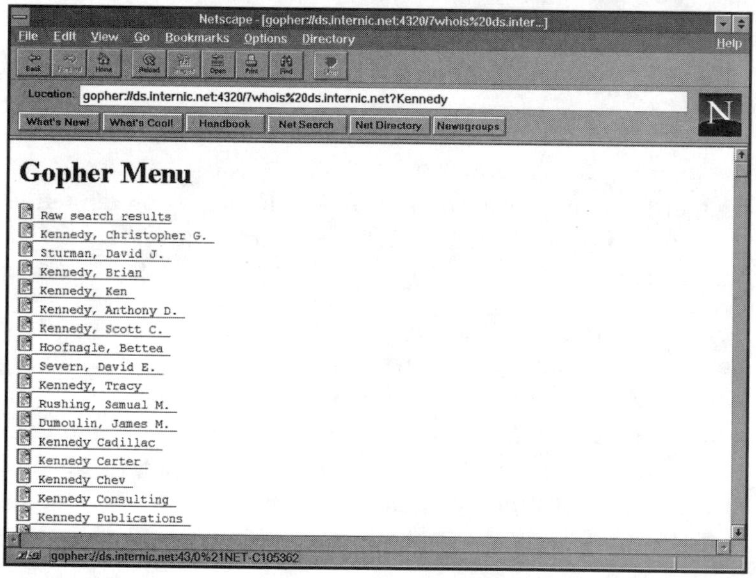

Fig. 11.8
With common
names, such as
Kennedy and
Smith, you'll get
lots of choices.
Narrow your
search by using
a first and last
name.

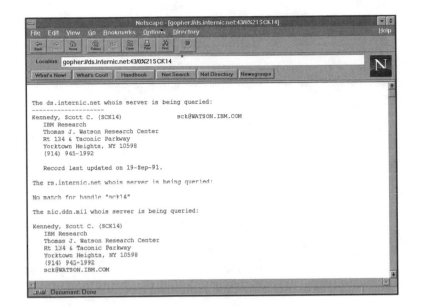

Fig. 11.9
Individual records can be quite detailed, offering mailing addresses, e-mail addresses, and phone numbers.

Troubleshooting

My search returns too many names. How do I narrow it down?

If you search for all of the people and companies in the WHOIS database with the keyword Smith, you'll get a very long list indeed. Try to narrow down a search by entering the first and last name of an individual (like Mary Ann Smith) or the entire name of a company (Smith Floorwaxing) and you will get more valuable results.

Use WHOIS To Find Out About a Company

You can also use a separate WHOIS system to search for information about organizations and companies. From the InterNIC home page (URL address: **http://www.internic.net/**), select the link to Network Solutions Inc. Registration Services. At the next Web page, select whois searches. You may have to scroll down the page to find this link.

In the search query field, enter a company or organizational Internet domain name. This is the last two parts of the e-mail address, such as **kodak.com** for Eastman Kodak. If the company or organization has a registered Internet address (which is likely), you'll get information about its mailing address, Internet address, a contact person, and phone number. Figure 11.10 shows a record for Eastman Kodak that comes from the previous search.

Tip
While the official WHOIS servers at InterNIC provide a great deal of information, there are also organization-specific WHOIS servers accessible via the Internet. You can get a list of them by ftping to **ftp sipb.mit.edu**. Login as anonymous, go to the pub/whois directory, and download the file whois-servers.list.

III

People Resources

Fig. 11.10

A search for KODAK.COM retrieves a record that gives the company's registered domain name, mailing address, and contact name.

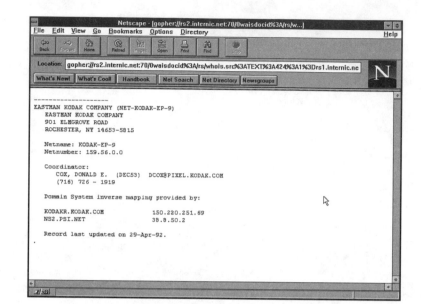

Tip

To start a company or organization WHOIS search a little faster, go directly to the URL address **gopher:// rs2.internic. net:70/11/rs**.

> **Note**
>
> If you're planning to register an Internet domain name for your company, you can use this process to find out whether anyone already has staked a claim to a name that you might want. Please note that even if you don't find a company with the name you want (like ACME.COM), it's possible that someone may have started the registration process for the domain name. This process can take several weeks.

NETFIND

Internet URL address: **gopher://ds.internic.net:4320** (select the Netfind link)

The instructions at Netfind explain:

> "This Gopher gateway performs Netfind searches. It uses the go4gw software. To use this gateway, supply keywords for a Netfind search. A list of matching domains will be returned as documents. Choose from one of the domains to retrieve the results from a Netfind search for that domain. Due to the strict query format for Netfind, keywords must be in the format: name key..."

For example, to find information about Darren Hardy at the University of Colorado in Boulder, use the keywords "hardy boulder colorado" or "hardy boulder colorado computer science."

To test this system, I entered a slight variation in the keywords "kennedy boulder colorado education" to see what would happen. This search turned up a list of two addresses for the University of Colorado in Boulder, shown in the following table. If I hadn't specified "computer science" in the search term, the search would have delivered a much bigger list, including companies.

Organization	What It Is
cs.colorado.edu	computer science department, University of Colorado
wox.colorado.edu	Wozniak scholarship recipients

After clicking the first choice (cs.colorado.edu), I received a list of addresses (e-mail and postal) and phone numbers of people with the last name Kennedy involved with the computer science department at the University of Colorado—both students and faculty. This is shown in figure 11.11.

> **Note**
>
> The only downside to Netfind is that you can waste a lot of time searching through and locating organizations that don't actually have the last name you're looking for or don't seem to offer their information base to the search system. Netfind is best if you already know both a person's name AND where he lives and works.

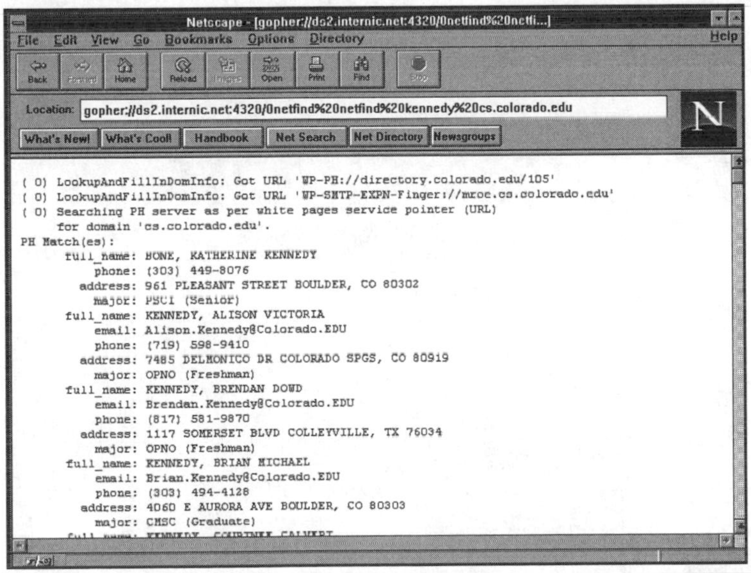

Fig. 11.11
If you know where someone lives or works, the Netfind directory may locate him.

III

People Resources

World Wide X.500 Directory

Internet URL address: **http://www.internic.net/ds/dspgx500.html**

Although it sounds like a nickname for a sports car, X.500 is actually an international standard for electronic mail. The X.500 standards and system creates a series of white-page directories that contain information that's similar to what you might find in a phone book—the names of people with their e-mail addresses, real addresses, and phone numbers. Organizations, companies, networks, and countries create their own electronic white page directories, and Internet X.500 computers (like InterNIC) maintain collections of these phone books.

> **Note**
>
> The InterNIC X.500 Directory is the closest thing you'll find to a global listing of Internet users. Currently, more than 2,800 organizations around the world connect their white pages of personnel data to this system.

In order to begin a search using the X.500 Directory, select the flag of the country you want to search. Figure 11.12 shows one of these country-by-country screens. Say you know that your second cousin Gary Kennedy works at Queen's University in Belfast. You haven't spoken in years, but you're planning a trip to the UK soon. First, click Great Britain. Figure 11.13 shows the long list of organizations (both companies and universities) that have information about people in this region. Scroll down to the entry for Queen's University, click it, and do a search for Kennedy. You get Gary's address and phone number.

Fig. 11.12
Begin a search of the X.500 directory system by choosing a country.

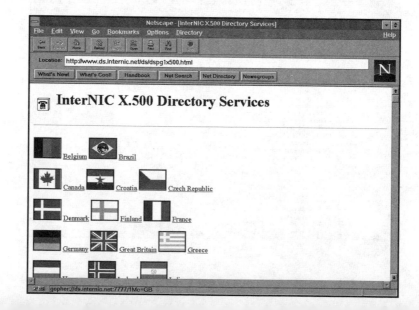

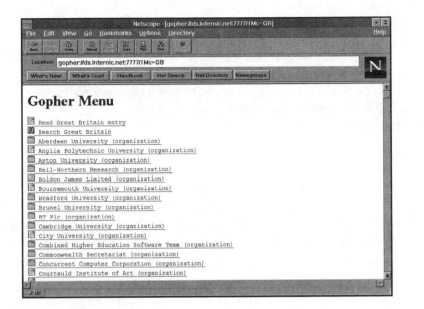

Fig. 11.13
Once in a country, you can search through the database of names for specific organizations and companies.

Troubleshooting

How do I get my company or my name into the X.500 Directory?

AT&T has a request form that you can fill out and send in (even electronically) for your organization and individuals in an organization. You can get the form either from the InterNIC Web site or by anonymous FTP from host **ds.internic.net**. (You need to go to the subdirectory **internic.info**. The file name is **x500.org.request**.)

This request form can also be retrieved using the AT&T mailserver. Send e-mail to **mailserv@ds.internic.net** and include the following command in the body of the message: **file /ftp/internic.info/x500.org.request**.

Find People with the Finger Utility

Finger is a utility program that you can use to locate publicly available information about individual Internet users. There are a couple of ways to use Finger. You can access the World Wide Web site **http://alpha.acast.nova .edu/cgi-bin/finger**, which is run by Nova Southeastern University, Fort Lauderdale, Florida. This Web page brings up a query form where you can enter anyone's e-mail address. The program then searches its database and returns any available information about that person. Information may include a real name, address, and phone number.

If you have a dial-in Internet account where you get an on-screen UNIX prompt, such as > or $, you can enter the command **finger**. This will display a list of all the users who are currently logged on to your Internet provider's system. The command can also provide a list of individuals who have accounts on computers at remote sites (**finger@remote-hostname**) or detailed information about a specific individual (**finger username@hostname**).

Here are a few examples that show how this works. I first connect to my Internet account using the Terminal program in Microsoft Windows. Then when I get the UNIX $ prompt, I type **finger**. The computer quickly returns a display of other people who use the same service provider and are currently logged on to the system. This is a quick way to find out who's using the system. Here is the display (you'll note that my name also appears on-screen):

```
$ finger

Login       Name         TTY       Idle   When     Where
root        Superuser    pts/13    17 Sat 17:39   tech.rmii.com
dand        Dan Duncan   pts/3        Sat 17:45   pm5.rockymtn.net
eager       Bill Eager   pts/10       Sat 18:06   pm2.rockymtn.net
awade       Allen Wade   pts/17    3:09 Sat 14:49   slip159.rmii.com
lacey       lacey        pts/7        Sat 14:58   pm8.rockymtn.net
bmuth       Bernie Muth  pts/5        Sat 18:13   pm1.rockymtn.net
camden      A.C. Schulte pts/8        Sat 17:10   pm5.rockymtn.net
halfro      Craig Allen  pts/21       Sat 17:57   pm2.rockymtn.net
gpoole      Gregory Poole pts/15      Sat 17:04   pm1.rockymtn.net
rtaylor     Roy Taylor   pts/14       Sat 17:18   pm1.rockymtn.net
```

If you want to find specific information about one individual, use **finger <their name>**. Following, you see the results when I type **finger eager**. The system presents information that includes my real name and areas of interest. I have keyed in this information previously and anyone who types in **finger eager** sees this:

```
$ finger eager
Login name: eager                    In real life: Bill Eager
Directory: /u/e/eager                Shell: /bin/sh
On since Jun  3 18:06:00 on pts/10 from pm2.rockymtn.net
Unread mail since Fri Jun  2 19:41:09 1995
Project: Internet and World Wide Web Books
Plan:
Helping people and companies use the practical applications of the
Internet.
$
```

Finally, you may want to find out about a person who uses a different service provider or has an Internet account on a computer that is in a different state or country. I know that my father has an account at Bucknell University, so I type in a finger request using the format finger name@remote host, as seen here:

```
$ finger eager@bucknell.edu
[bucknell.edu]
Searching phonebook from coral.bucknell.edu for "eager"...
MailName                Name and Department/Class Year
eager@bucknell.edu      Eager Gerald                    Art Dept
-- 1 record found --
$
```

This is not an extensive record, but it does tell me which department my father works in. Finger works best when you know someone's last name and the name of the computer he uses to connect to the Internet.

Access Electronic Phone Books with Gopher

There are a number of Gopher sites that offer searchable electronic phone directories, also known as **name servers**. Much more than simple directories, these name servers offer comprehensive search fields where you can search for and locate information about a person's name, title, department, phone or fax number, e-mail address, home or work address, birthday, and even high school. A common name server system is known as CSO—which comes from the Computer Services Organization at the University of Illinois, where the software was created.

Often, name servers are site specific. For example, you can connect to the server for NASA, Hewlett-Packard, or The University of California and search for information about the employees, faculty, or students who participate in that specific organization, company, or college.

University of Notre Dame List of Institutions

Gopher address: **gopher.nd.edu**

Path: **1/Non-Notre Dame Information Sources/Phone Books—Other Institutions**

One site that's worth knowing about is The University of Notre Dame Gopher site. Here you'll find a menu-based list of name servers from around the world. From this one site you have access to thousands of institutions that use the CSO name servers. The list is maintained by Joel Cooper and any updates to the list should be sent to **cooper@utopia.cc.nd.edu**.

Tip
You'll come across name servers at numerous Gopher sites. They are easily recognized as Gopher menus and are usually labeled as either phone directory or phone books.

III

People Resources

Begin by selecting (from a series of menu options) an area of the world. Choices include:

1. Africa

2. Asia

3. Europe

4. Middle East

5. North America

6. South America

There are also selections that let you access the X.500 and WHOIS name searching systems, described earlier in this chapter. Once you select an area of the world, you get a list of the institutions that currently run name servers and let the general public access their data. Figure 11.14 shows both the main menu and a sub-menu of institutions in North America. Notice the little telephone icons next to the names—these are open name servers. The magnifying glass icons let you search for documents at the institutions.

Fig. 11.14
The University of Notre Dame maintains a Gopher site that offers an extensive list of electronic telephone directories.

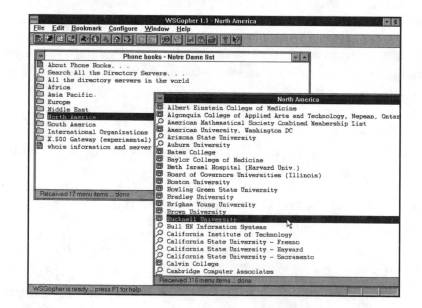

You can scroll down this alphabetical listing and click the specific phone directory that you want to search. A large percentage of the phone directories on this list are colleges and universities in the United States. If you have a friend or son or daughter who is going to college, you stand a good chance of finding that person's address via this system. There are also many government directories and a few corporate directories.

How might these directories be useful? My father is a professor at Bucknell University in Lewisburg, Pennsylvania. Let's say that I win the million dollar lottery (which hasn't happened yet) and I can't wait to share the news. Unfortunately, I don't have my dad's work phone number. I find Bucknell University on this list, enter a search using the last name **eager**, and instantly receive the information I need. Figure 11.15 shows the search entry box and a few of the search fields and figure 11.16 shows the results from a name server search. In summary, there are three steps to this process from the Notre Dame main phone directory menu.

1. Select a specific region of the world from the Gopher menu.

2. Select a specific institution that you want to search.

3. Select the search field that you want to look for and enter your search criteria.

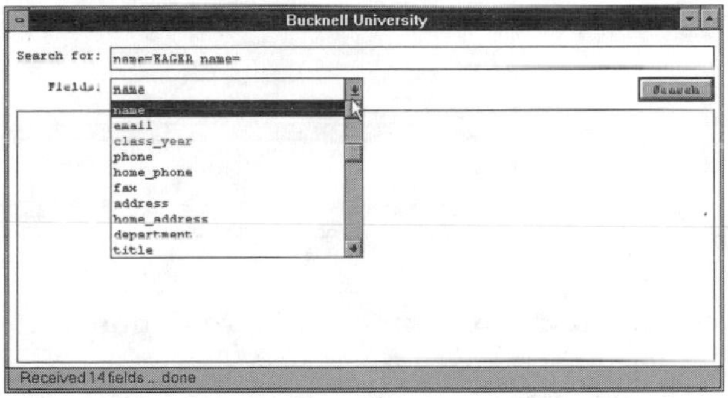

Tip

For searches using CSO name servers, you can broaden your search by using an asterisk (*) as a wildcard. For example, use Apple* to locate Applegate, Appleman, Appleton, and so on.

Fig. 11.15
After you select a specific institution's name server, you are prompted to enter search terms, such as a last name or a department.

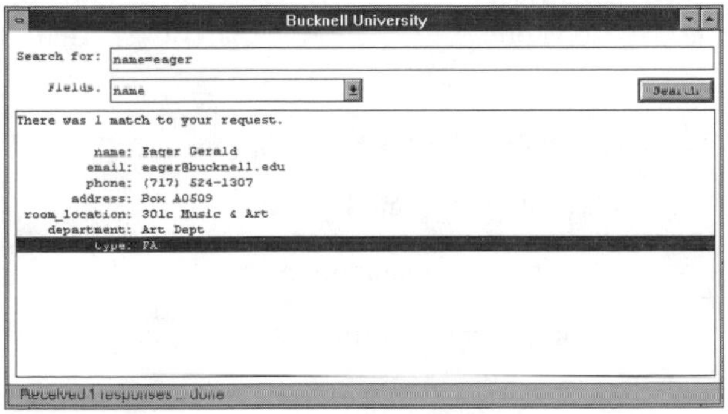

Fig. 11.16
Here a CSO name server search provides details about the person's e-mail address, phone number, department, and mailing address.

III

People Resources

SpIcE of Life Gopher Server
Gopher address: **gopher.cs.ttu.edu**

Located at the Department of Computer Science, Texas Tech University in Lubbock, Texas, this Gopher server not only has an intriguing nickname, it also contains a tremendous amount of useful information about people and places around the world. Figure 11.17 shows both the main Gopher menu and the submenu that appears when you select Phone Books.

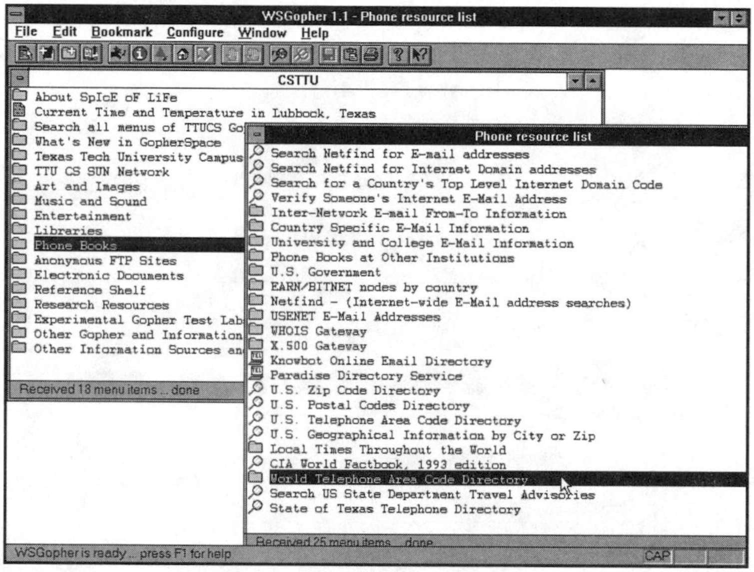

Fig. 11.17
Nicknamed the SpIcE of Life, the Gopher server for the Department of Computer Science at Texas Tech University contains an invaluable list of phone books and name searching systems.

Remember you can access Gopher sites using a Web browser. Figure 11.18 shows the same site using the Netscape browser. To access the site using a Web browser, the URL address is **gopher://gopher.cs.ttu.edu**.

SpIcE is a particularly useful site because the Phone Books menu has many selections that open up various Internet name searching systems (see fig. 11.19). You can:

- Search Netfind for e-mail addresses

- Search Netfind for Internet domain addresses

- Verify someone's Internet e-mail address

- Access phone books at other institutions

- Access phone books from the U.S. government

- Search through UseNet e-mail addresses

- Access the WHOIS name directory

- Access the X.500 Directory systems

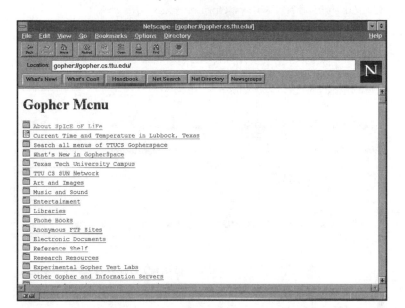

Fig. 11.18
This is a view of the SpIcE of Life site using Netscape

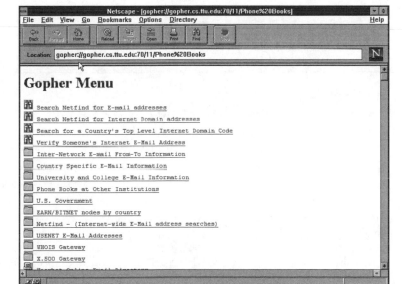

Fig. 11.19
The Phone Book menu at the SpIcE of Life site.

SpIcE World Country and Telephone Area Codes

Don't have a clue how to direct dial Borgosesia, Italy? Don't call operator assistance! The World Telephone Area Code Directory is exactly what it sounds like, a comprehensive directory of country, regional, state, and city area codes. As figure 11.20 shows, Gopher makes this easy to use.

1. Select a menu of a global region, like Europe.

2. Select a specific country, such as Italy.

3. View and scroll down through a list of area codes.

Fig. 11.20

Click Gopher menus to navigate through the World Telephone Area Code Directory.

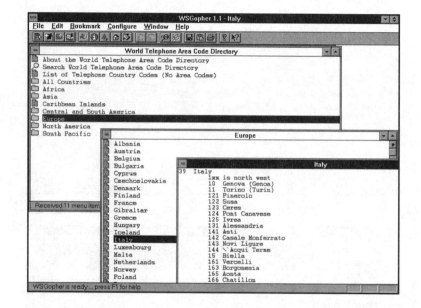

SpIcE U.S. Geographical Information by City or ZIP

What's the ZIP code for Spokane, Washington? Or, for that matter, the population, elevation, longitude, and latitude? You may not need this type of detailed information on a daily basis, but it's nice to know that it's there. From the SpIcE main menu, select Phone Books, and then choose U.S. Geographical Information by City or ZIP. When the search field appears, enter the name of the city or town for which you're looking, press Enter, and you'll get a full report.

Figure 11.21 shows how this process works in a search for Indianapolis, Indiana. Notice that the keyword Indianapolis locates towns in Iowa and Oklahoma with the same name. If you want to narrow the search, add the state abbreviation after the town, as in Indianapolis, IN.

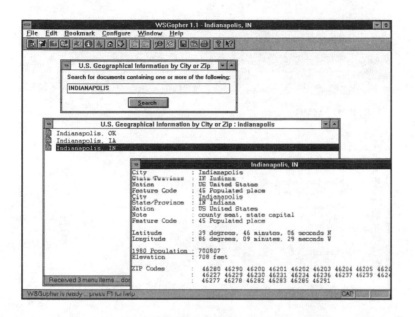

Fig. 11.21
Search to locate detailed information about any town in the United States.

Use WAIS To Find People with Similar Interests

You can use the searching capabilities of WAIS to locate files that contain records of people who may share your interests. This takes a little digging, but the results may prove valuable. First you need to locate a WAIS search system. Here's how you navigate to one using the menu selections of the SpIcE Gopher.

1. SpIcE main menu

2. Other Gopher and Information Servers

3. WAIS Based Information

4. Search Directory of All WAIS Servers

Menu selections 2, 3, and 4 may be found on numerous Gopher sites. When you select item number 4, you'll get a search box. To begin, enter the keyword **addresses.src**. The .src ending tells WAIS to locate only searchable entries. You could also try other keywords with the .src ending, such as mail.src or gardening.src. Figure 11.22 shows the variety of results that this type of search generates. Many of the directories offer information on people who have specific professional or recreational interests.

III

People Resources

Fig. 11.22
A search of WAIS for **addresses.src** retrieves a list of searchable directories related to the keyword addresses.

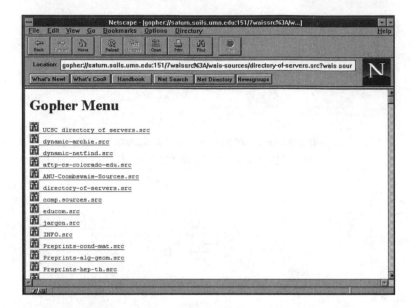

International Pen-Pal E-mail List

You don't have to be 12 years old to enjoy sending and receiving messages from people around the world who share your interests. But how do you find them? Bruce Nault II has created a list of people who participate in an international pen-pal system using e-mail. There is no cost to post your name on the list or to receive it. The following are two addresses where you can send a message to obtain a copy of the application form and a copy of the list itself.

bnault@marios.com

bruce.nault.ii%f216.n132.z1.@e-tech.havr.ma.us

In response to an inquiry about the list, Bruce writes (via e-mail, of course):

"The list has been very successful so far. I've gotten replies from all over the world. The list doesn't consist of a majority of people from one particular country; there are more submissions from Germany and England than there are from the U.S.! Also, the list includes one word about every person on it. I've seen just about every imaginable hobby and tons of different professions. So, if someone's looking to write to someone with a particular interest, he will probably find someone with that interest on this list."

Summary

With its global connectivity and millions of users, the Internet offers one-stop shopping for information about people and companies. Applications range from locating the address of long-lost friends, to getting the phone number of a company you want to do business with, or accessing the area code for a foreign country. These applications will become commonplace as the Internet continues to develop new directories and phone books and more people and companies place their records on the Internet.

Part IV

Search Commercial and Educational Services

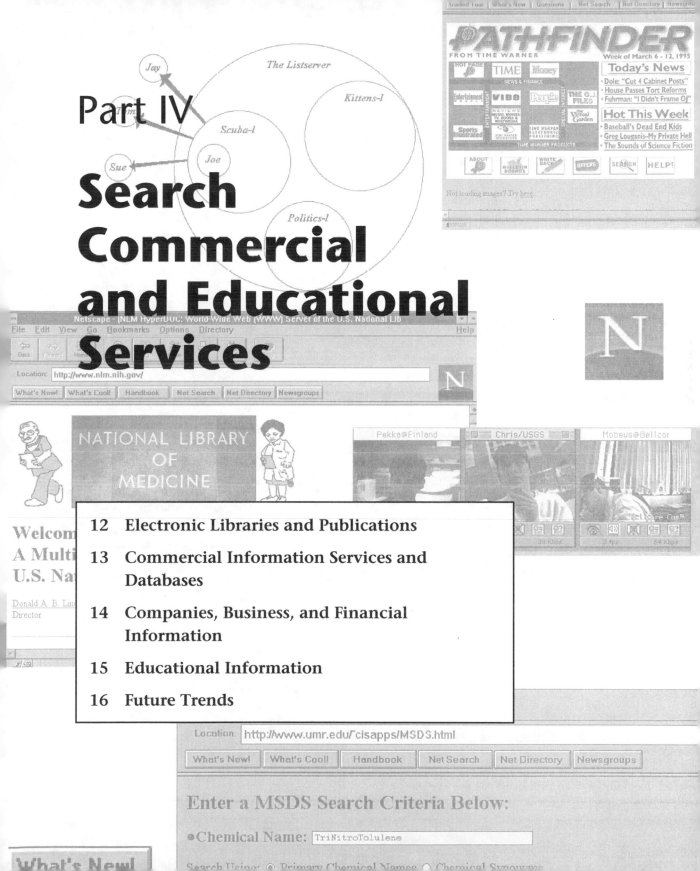

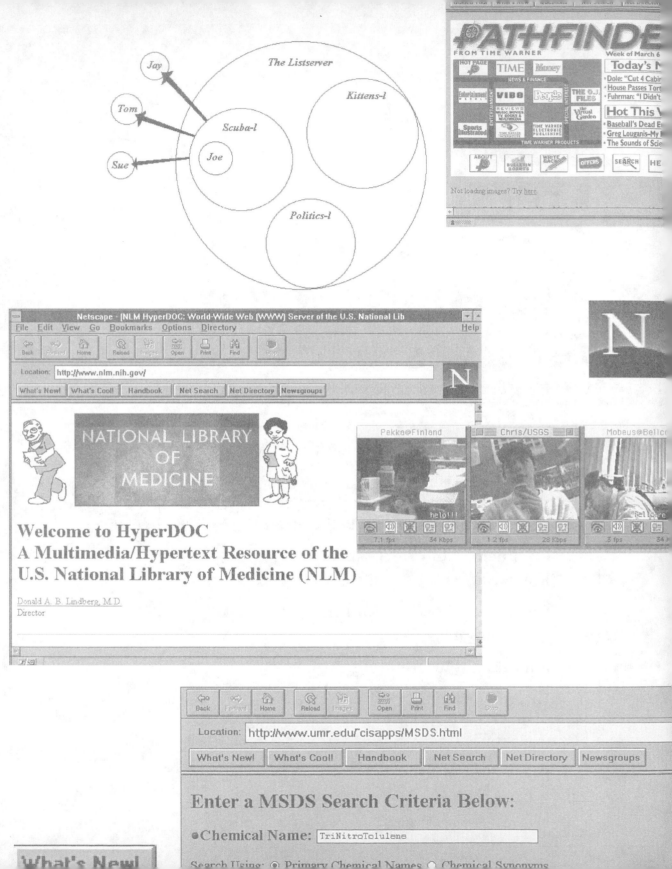

Chapter 12

Electronic Libraries and Publications

When you are looking for information, where is a better place to go than a library? Well, the Internet has some incredible electronic libraries online and ready for you. Additionally, electronic publications are springing up all over the place. All you need are the tools to find particular libraries and publications.

Whether your ultimate destination is an electronic library, publication, or specific piece of information, the Internet can help you if you know where to start. This chapter will not only help you get started, it will highlight some of the best services on the Internet.

In this chapter, you will learn:

- What some of the hottest gopher sites for libraries and publications are

- What some of the hottest Web sites for electronic publications are

- Where some of the best electronic libraries are located

- How to find electronic libraries and publications on the Internet

The U.S. Library of Congress: Searching For and Retrieving Publications

The U.S. Library of Congress, or LOC, is perhaps one of the more famous and useful library resources on the Internet today. Because of the U.S. Government's attempt to reduce the cost of government operations, it has spent enormous sums placing its material in electronic form (sort of counter-intuitive). Thankfully, the Internet is becoming a popular publishing ground for government and commercial information systems.

Before you rush onto the Internet to pull up the latest work of your favorite author, you need to be aware of a couple of facts. First, for the past thousand years, mankind has not had the benefit of electronic information. Therefore, a considerable amount of information remains in print form, not electronic form. Second, it costs money to convert from printed to electronic form. This means you will rarely find large collections of free electronic information. If someone goes through the effort of converting a work of literature into electronic form, you can bet he will want to charge you for it. The exception seems to be government and educational institutions. Collections at such institutions, however, are not too large and seem to grow at a rather slow pace.

Third, the Internet is not about to remove copyright claims on recent works. This adds to the incentive for electronic publishers to charge you for access to electronic publications: Electronic publishers, themselves, pay or collect royalties and are therefore not too eager to provide free access to some works.

The LOC is bound by these facts, and therefore doesn't have the entire LOC collection of works available online. It is, however, working toward converting special collections to electronic form on the Internet, but its main attraction is the powerful LOC Information System, which provides catalog access to all its volumes. You can use this information to order a work through inter-library loans.

One of the more popular U.S. Library of Congress services is LOCIS, the Library of Congress Information System. It provides access to the library's card catalog, as well as selected topics such as copyright, legislative, and foreign law. You can reach LOCIS via Telnet at **telnet://locis.loc.gov**.

Figure 12.1 shows the opening screen to the LOCIS system. It is available for public access, although it is very limited in electronic access to specific volumes, because it is a bibliographic and information retrieval system only. It does have basic and advanced search techniques for a variety of records (catalog records for LOC's collections, records citing federal legislation, records for copyright registrations, and so on). There are a few full-text federal laws on LOCIS, but these are rare.

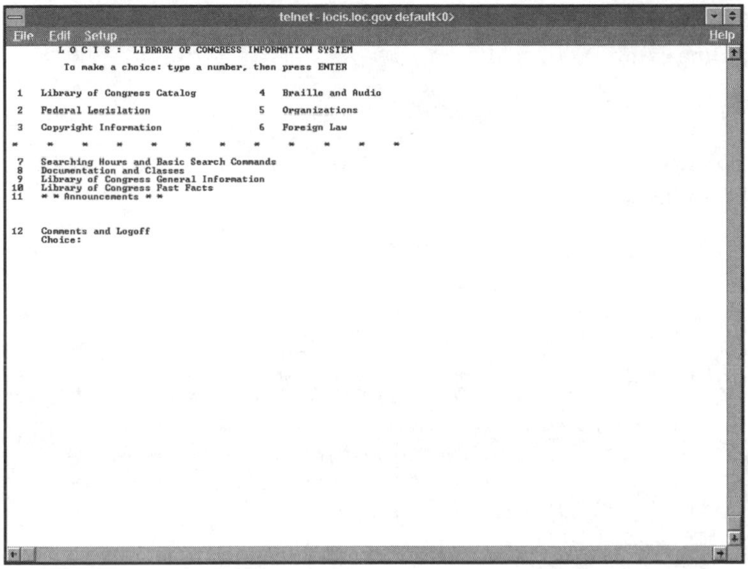

Fig. 12.1
U.S. Library of
Congress' LOCIS
System is only
available via
Telnet.

To obtain information found with LOCIS, the Library of Congress lends material from its collections to U.S. libraries through standard inter-library loan, or ILL, procedures. Consult your local library's ILL office. The Library of Congress' Photo Duplication Service provides a range of duplication services. For more information, call (202) 707-5640 or fax (202) 707-1771.

You can also obtain more information about LOCIS from the Library of Congress' MARVEL system. This system is Gopher-based and provides access information about LOCIS, LOC collections, and other information about the library. It is located at **gopher://marvel.loc.gov/11/locis/**.

If you are interested in seeing what collections are available online, I suggest you warm up your Web browser and check out the LOC's Web home page. The LOC has done a tremendous job on their Web server, and has provided several important collections for Web browsing.

Figure 12.2 shows the Web home page for the LOC. This Web home page is located at **http://www.loc.gov/**.

The LOC is using the Web to present information about the library as well as slowly introduce materials from certain special collections over the Internet. Some of the current LOC Web offerings include:

■ Historical collections from American Memory

■ Descriptions of some of the Library's American Special Collections

- Several Library of Congress exhibits (including the Gettysburg Address online exhibit)

- Thomas Legislation on the Internet

- Country Studies and the POW/MIA Database from the Federal Research Division

- Access to LOC MARVEL and LOCIS

Fig. 12.2

The U.S. Library of Congress looks great from the World Wide Web.

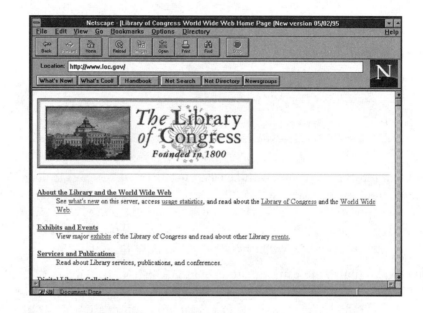

In addition, the library is developing a Global Electronic Library, which links to Web meta indexes and search tools, government information, Internet resources, newspaper and current periodical lists, and eventually other Web resources categorized by subject.

Figures 12.3 through 12.5 show the initial pages for some of the special electronic collections offered by the LOC. Figure 12.3 shows Historical Collections, which represents the initial effort by the LOC to establish the National Digital Library. Figure 12.4 shows the initial Web page to Thomas, the online database U.S. Legislative information. This information includes the Congressional Record, copies of various bills, and other legislative information.

Fig. 12.3
The American Memory, Historical Collections for the National Digital Library, by the U.S. Library of Congress, is located at **http:// rs6.loc.gov/ amhome.html**.

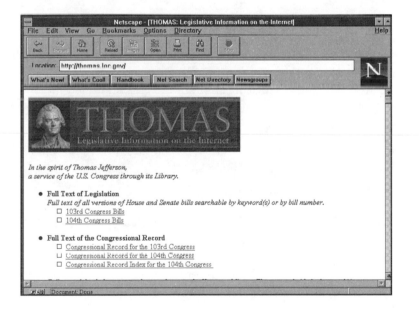

Fig. 12.4
The U.S. Library of Congress also sponsors Thomas, online access to U.S. Legislative information, located at **http:// thomas.loc.gov/**.

Figure 12.5 shows the entry to the Vietnam Era Prisoner of War/Missing in Action Database. This database is searchable with pointers to various texts concerning the Vietnam War, and is located at **http://lcweb2.loc.gov/ pow/powhome.html**.

Fig. 12.5

Vietnam Era Prisoner of War/ Missing in Action Database is available online from the U.S. Library of Congress.

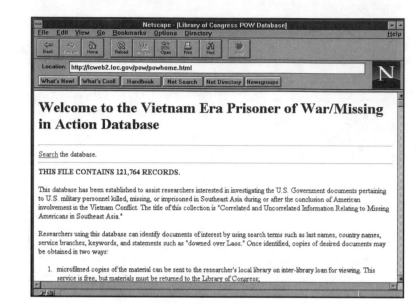

Library Consortiums

There appears to be a number of library consortiums who work to consolidate library information and tie various libraries information systems together. This means you can access the collective knowledge of hundreds of libraries by simply stopping at one of the library consortiums.

This chapter does not describe the relationships of various library consortiums. Instead, it presents what's available and how they seem to relate on the Internet. There is much overlap and it appears relationships between the various libraries change rather frequently.

CARL: The Colorado Alliance of Regional Libraries

CARL, Colorado Alliance of Regional Libraries, is a corporation that markets a turnkey library management system to large networked libraries nationwide. In addition, they offer various products and services, including UnCover (discussed in the next section), to libraries and information providers.

Over 450 libraries are currently supported on the CARL System, which is comprised of 32 interconnected CPU locations that link over 14,000 dedicated terminals. Such libraries include the Atlanta/Fulton Public Library, the Baltimore County Public Library, the Boulder Public Library, the Chicago Public Library, the Denver Public Library, the University of Idaho Library, and the University of Maryland System. Access to this system is available by Telnet. To connect via the Web, use the URL **telnet://database.carl.org**.

As you can see from figure 12.6, accessing CARL at this location gives you access to a number of services and products. Many are fee-based and require you to obtain a subscription. For more information about CARL, such as product and services subscription information, access their Web home page, shown in figure 12.7, at **http://www.carl.org/carl.html**.

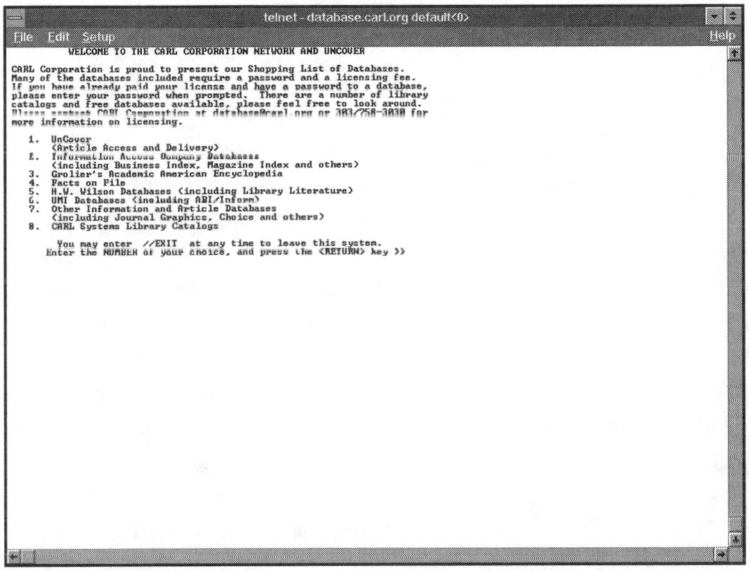

Fig. 12.6
The initial screen for CARL, which is only available via Telnet.

Fig. 12.7
The Web home page for CARL, Colorado Alliance of Regional Libraries. This home page provides access to other CARL services.

You can also use Gopher to check out the latest from CARL at **gopher://pac.carl.org/**.

I recommend using Gopher or the Web to look over the information concerning CARL. They boast a powerful variety of products and services that will make online access to electronic information fast and easy.

UnCover: The Periodical Searching Tool with Faxback Option

The folks at CARL have a very powerful and useful service: UnCover is a periodical searching tool with the ability to fax documents back for a fee. UnCover is an online table of contents index and article delivery service for approximately 17,000 magazines and journals. It boasts the ability to order and search citations of approximately 6 million articles through a simple online order system, and the system adds 5,000 citations daily. Table of contents information is entered into the database as the journals are received from the publishers, so issues are indexed online at about the same time that they arrive in libraries or on the newsstand. This makes UnCover one of the most up-to-date magazine resources available. Finally, almost every article cited in UnCover can be ordered online and delivered to your fax machine within an average of 24 hours, for a modest fee. To access UnCover, you can Telnet to the same system that you would if you were telnetting to CARL at **telnet://database.carl.org**.

Searching the UnCover database is free, but you must pay for any articles you order. Articles cost $8.50 U.S., plus any copyright royalty fees. For people located outside the U.S. and Canada, a fax surcharge may apply. Before you can use UnCover to send articles to your fax machine, you can purchase an UnCover access password for $900 U.S./year to receive a $2.00 U.S. discount on every article you order.

Libraries and other institutions may purchase gateway access and receive article discounts, dedicated ports, customized screens, and local periodical holdings display. Gateway access ranges from $5,000 U.S. to $10,000+ U.S. per year.

Figure 12.8 shows you what UnCover's Web home page looks like. You can use it to learn more about UnCover and access its system through a Telnet session at **http://www.carl.org/uncover/unchome.html**.

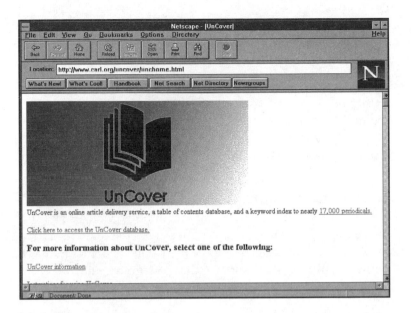

Fig. 12.8
The Web home
page for UnCover.

If you want to do more than search for citations in the UnCover database,
you will have to obtain a subscription. To contact the folks at UnCover for
more information, you can contact UnCover in North America at:

Brenda Bailey
Marketing and Client Liaison
The UnCover Company
3801 E. Florida Ave. #200
Denver, CO 80210
(303) 758-3030
bbailey@carl.org

Letty Alvarez
UnCover Product Manager
Readmore
22 Cortlandt Street
New York, NY 10007-31994
(800) 221-3306
alvarez@readmore.com

Or outside North America at:

Jane Beddall
UnCover Product Manager
BH Blackwell
Hythe Bridge Street
Oxford OX1 2ET
+44 865 261 362
uncover@blackwell.co.uk

OCLC: The Online Computer Library Center

OCLC, or Online Computer Library Center, is another good example of library consortiums. OCLC is a nonprofit computer service and research organization whose participants include more than 19,000 libraries in the U.S. and 61 other countries and territories. OCLC systems help libraries locate, acquire, catalog, and lend library materials.

OCLC represents the world's largest library information network, and offers products and services that help libraries further access information and reduce information costs. Figure 12.9 shows the Web home page for OCLC located at **http://www.oclc.org/**.

Fig. 12.9
The OCLC home page gives you access to text-based or graphic-based libraries and journals.

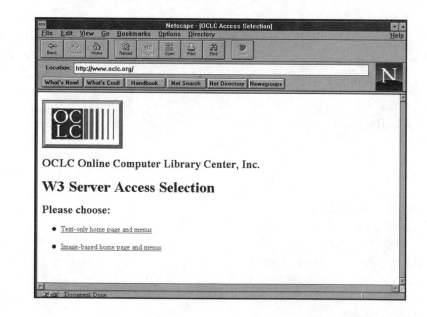

OCLC contains several fee-based services available to subscribers, including:

- **OCLC Online Union Catalog (OLUC).** The world's largest and most comprehensive bibliographic database. Libraries use the OLUC and OCLC's computerized telecommunications network to process materials and share information.

- **EPIC service.** Geared toward the "information professional," providing access to over 43 databases with easy access through the Internet at **telnet://epic.oclc.org/**.

- **FirstSearch service.** Provides online access to more than 40 databases, including ArticleFirst, BusinessNews, ContentsFirst, INSPEC, MEDLINE, WorldCat (the OCLC Online Union Catalog), and WorldScope GLOBAL. It offers a FastDoc service: full-text document ordering and delivery, per-search or subscription pricing, access to documentation files through the Internet, and WAIS full-text searching compatibility. Subscribers to FirstSearch may reach the service at **telnet://fscat.oclc.org/**.

- **OCLC Electronic Journals Online service.** Online access to full text of journal articles. This service is accessed through the Web at **http://www.ref.oclc.org:2000/**.

Contact Regional Support Centers for OCLC Service and Support

If you are interested in learning more about OCLC, click your Web browser to **http://www.oclc.org/**. Use the following list of OCLC-affiliates as a contact to learn more.

In North America, these affiliates represent library consortiums that make up OCLC.

AMIGOS Bibliographic Council, Inc.
Suite 500
12200 Park Central Drive
Dallas, TX 75251
(214)-851-8000
(800) 843-8482 (National)

Bibliographical Center for Research (BCR)
14394 East Evans Avenue
Aurora, CO 80014-1478
(303) 751-6277
(800) 397-1552 (National)

(continues)

IV

Commercial & Educational

(continued)

BCR Ames Office
295 Parks Library
Iowa State University
Ames, IA 50011
(515) 292-1118
(800) 383-1218 (National)

CAPCON Library Network
Suite 400
1320 19th Street, N.W.
Washington, DC 20036
(202) 331-5771
(800) 543-4599 (MD and VA only)

Federal Library and Information Center Committee (FEDLINK)
Library of Congress
Washington, DC 20540
(202) 707-4800

ILLINET/OCLC Services
Illinois State Library
300 South Second Street
Springfield, IL 62701-1796
(217) 785-1532

Indiana Cooperative Library Services Authority (INCOLSA)
5929 Lakeside Boulevard
Indianapolis, IN 46278-1996
(317) 298-6570
(800) 733-1899 (IN only)

Michigan Library Consortium (MLC)
Suite 8
6810 South Cedar Street
Lansing, MI 48911
(517) 694-4242
(800) 530-9019 (National)

MINITEX Library Information Network
S-33 Wilson Library
University of Minnesota
309 19th Avenue South
Minneapolis, MN 55455-0414
(612) 624-4002
(800) 462-5348 (National)

Missouri Library Network Corporation (MLNC)
10332 Old Olive Street Road
St. Louis, MO 63141
(314) 567-3799
(800) 969-6562 (National)

Nebraska Library Commission (NEBASE)
The Atrium
Suite 120
1200 N Street
Lincoln, NE 68508-2023
(402) 471-2045
(800) 307-2665 (NE only)

NELINET, Inc.
Two Newton Executive Park
Newton, MA 02162
(617) 969-0400
(800) NELINET (New England only)

OHIONET
1500 West Lane Avenue
Columbus, OH 43221-3975
(614) 486-2966
(800) 686-8975 (OH only)

PALINET
Suite 262
3401 Market Street
Philadelphia, PA 19104
(215) 382-7031
(800) 233-3401 (National)

Pittsburgh Regional Library Center (PRLC)
103 Yost Boulevard
Pittsburgh, PA 15221
(412) 825-0600
(800) 242-3790 (PA, WV, and MD only)

Southeastern Library Network, Inc. (SOLINET)
Suite 200
1438 West Peachtree Street, N.W.
Atlanta, GA 30309-2955
(404) 892-0943
(800) 999-8558 (National)

(continues)

(continued)

State University of New York (SUNY)
SUNY/OCLC Network
State University Plaza
Albany, NY 12246
(518) 443-5444
(800) 342-3353 (NY only)

Wisconsin InterLibrary Services (WILS)
Room 464
728 State Street
Madison, WI 53706
(608) 263-5051

Therefore, the OCLC represents a rather powerful means to reach a very large collection of library information. As mentioned earlier, you do have to pay for the good information sources, and OCLC is no exception.

Interestingly, several of the OCLC affiliate members also have connections to the Internet and you can obtain free access to many of their services. The following are a few of the affiliates that are available.

ILLINET

ILLINET is an OCLC-affiliate that represents the collection of libraries in the state of Illinois. As you can see in figure 12.10, if you Telnet to **telnet://illinet.aiss.uiuc.edu** you will reach a gateway that provides access to Illinois libraries and other services, such as CARL and UnCover (discussed in the previous sections).

Once connected with ILLINET, you can choose any of the options listed. Unless you have accounts with IBIS or CARL, you aren't going far with those options. You can, however, access the services listed for ILLINET Online or the UIC Library Catalogs. Figure 12.11 shows you the ILLINET Online Public Access Gateway, which shares resources with approximately 50 ILCSO libraries (shown in figure 12.12), as well as some 800 Illinois libraries.

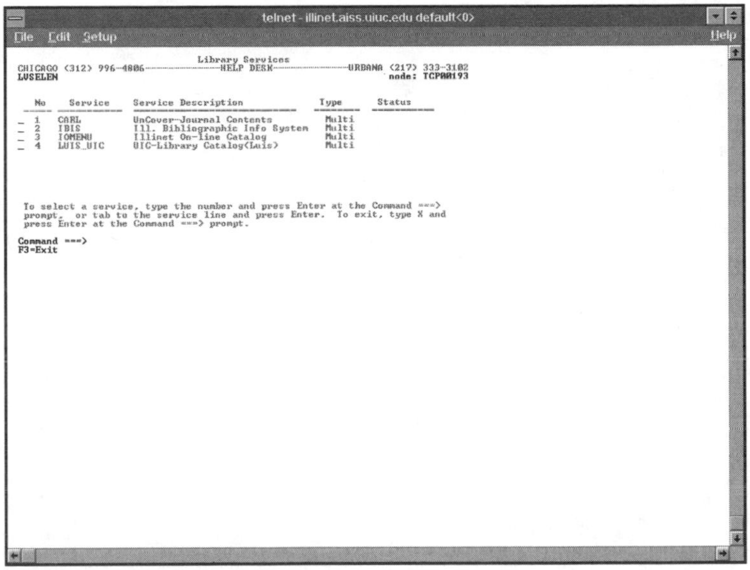

Fig. 12.10
ILLINET provides access to a rather large collection of library information systems in Illinois.

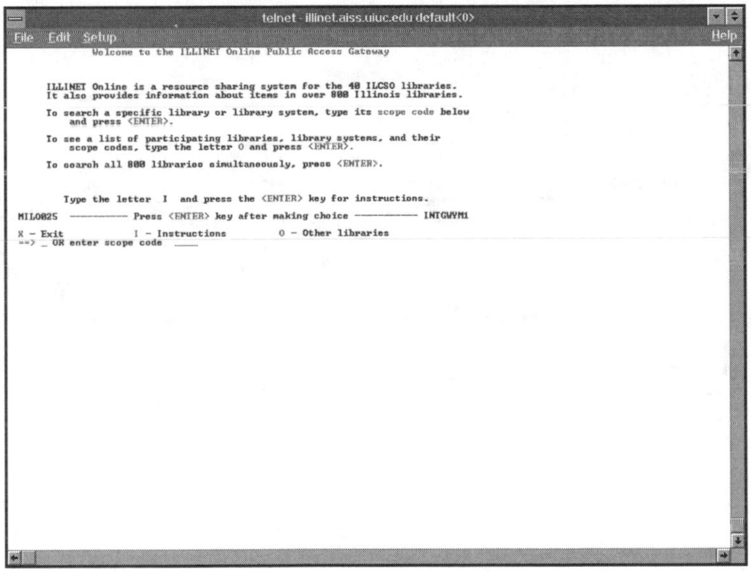

Fig. 12.11
The ILLINET Online Public Access Gateway provides access to some 800 Illinois library systems.

ILLINET allows you to search the available online library systems by subject, title, and author. What you have access to is a rather large collection of card catalog systems that helps you zero in on important or interesting publications. This system will also tell you what libraries have specific volumes. Consider it your online card catalog system without having to go to the library.

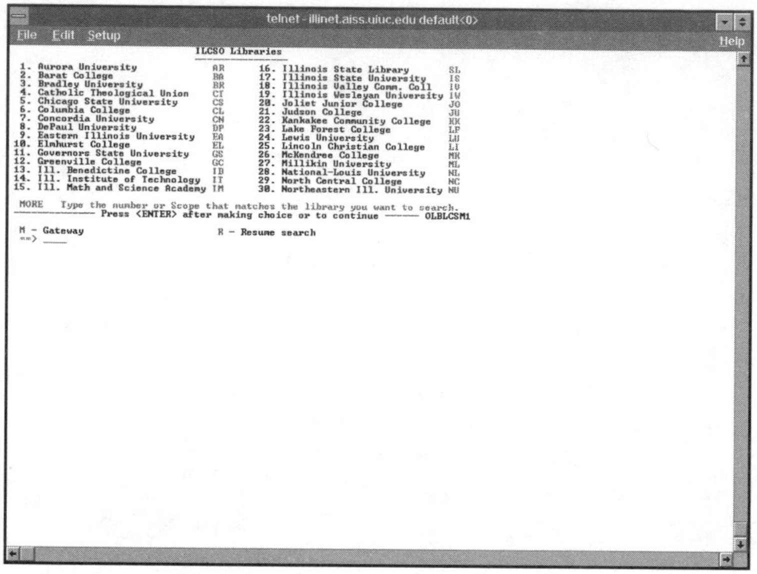

Fig. 12.12
An example of some of the ILCSO member libraries, part of ILLINET.

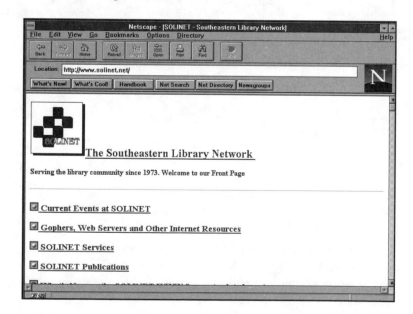

SOLINET: The Southeastern Library Network

SOLINET is the Southeastern Library Network, and represents another OCLC-affiliate. You can access its Web home page at **http://www.solinet.net/** which is depicted in figure 12.13.

Fig. 12.13
SOLINET represents the Southeastern Library Network, another regional center for library information and access.

SOLINET provides access to its regional libraries, but on a subscription basis. The Web home page shown in figure 12.13 is worth a glance over, however, because some of its regional libraries have Web home pages of their own. There is a wealth of information here, if you are willing to look. Don't expect to find too much information, unless you are a subscriber to OCLC.

SUNY Libraries

SUNY libraries are another example of OCLC affiliates. SUNY is available at the Gopher address **gopher://slscva.ca.sunycentral.edu/**.

SUNY provides quite a bit of information, and is intermixed with SUNY college information.

Project Gutenberg Electronic Texts: Download a Novel

Project Gutenberg was established to distribute 10,000 public domain **etext files** by December 31, 2001. An etext file is an electronic text readable by both humans and computers. Generally, Project Gutenberg has fictional and informational texts. Typically, the etexts are classic novels, stories, or poems, and one doesn't have the ability to search the etexts.

The Web URL for the FTP archives for Project Gutenberg is **ftp:// mrcnext.cso.uiuc.edu/etext/**. Texts are arranged by years, then title. For example, recent 1995 additions to the archive are located in **ftp:// mrcnext.cso.uiuc.edu/etext/1995/**.

The Web home page for Project Gutenberg is shown in figure 12.14 and provides a wealth of information about the project. You can learn how to volunteer your services, about the mission of the project, or what the latest and greatest etext volumes are. To reach the Web home page for Project Gutenberg, click your Web browser to **http://jg.cso.uiuc.edu/pg/ pg_home.html**.

Additionally, be sure to check out the subject listing of informational texts, located at **http://jg.cso.uiuc.edu/pg/lists/subject.html**.

Fig. 12.14
Project Gutenberg
has hundreds, if
not thousands, of
electronic texts
and books.

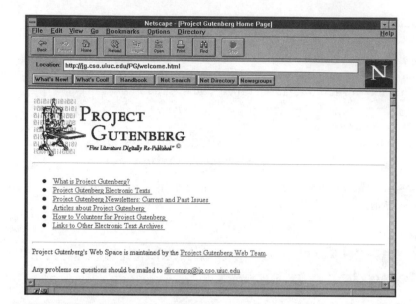

A Sample Listing of Project Gutenberg's Etexts

Project Gutenberg exists on the work of hundreds of volunteers who are working to convert old, classic texts to etexts. These documents have had their copyrights long expire, and to have them available in etext form means you can download an entire novel to your computer. The following is a small example of the etexts available:

Aesop's Fables

The Adventures of Tom Saywer by Mark Twain (Samuel Langhorne Clemens)

Caesar's Commentaries in Latin (Books I thru IV) by Julius Caesar

Clotelle; or *The Colored Heroine* by William Wells Brown

Discourse on the Method of Rightly Conducting the Reason, and Seeking Truth in the Sciences by Rene Descartes

The Europeans by Henry James

Flower Fables by Louisa May Alcott

From the Earth to the Moon and a Trip Around It by Jules Verne

The Hunting of the Snark by Lewis Carroll

The Insidious Dr. Fu Manchu by Sax Rohmer

The Jungle Book by Rudard Kipling

The Legend of Sleepy Hollow by Washington Irving

The Mayor of Casterbridge by Thomas Hardy

Narrative of the Life of Frederick Douglass, an American Slave by Frederick Douglass

Peter Pan by J. M. Barrie

The Republic by Plato

The Return of Sherlock Holmes by Sir Arthur Conan Doyle

The Scarlet Pimpernel by Baroness Orczy

The Wonderful Wizard of Oz by L. Frank Baum

CMU's Books Online, Listed by Title

Carnegie Mellon University maintains a rather comprehensive list of online books and etexts. Unlike Project Gutenberg, CMU's list references material at other Internet locations, which can be a variety of formats, including HTML and other formats. The URL at **http://www.cs.cmu.edu:8001/Web/ booktitles.html** has links to several hundred hypertext books listed by title.

Electronic Newsstands

Electronic magazines are becoming quite popular on the Internet. Maybe this is because magazines are something people like to glance through, and the Internet provides a great way to search for and find material that interests you most.

Whatever the reason, there are some resources you just have to know about. This includes commercial electronic newsstands, as well as references to free **e-zines**, or electronic magazines.

The Electronic Newsstand

The premier electronic newsstand on the Internet is The Electronic Newsstand, as shown in figure 12.15. The Electronic Newsstand is located at **http://www.enews.com/** or **gopher://gopher.enews.com/**.

The Electronic Newsstand is a fee-based service, which allows full access and searching capabilities to many of the most popular magazines and reference material. As you can see from figure 12.15, it presents a very nice Web interface into the material. For more information, connect to the Electronic Newsstand's Web or Gopher server.

Tip

Most of the etexts within Project Gutenberg's archive represent very large files (between 500 Kb to 2 Mb. Therefore, it is in your best interest to download the compressed version of these texts if you have a slow connection to the Internet.

Tip

If you are looking for an online book to read, check out CMU's Books Online—a reference to online material.

Fig. 12.15
The Electronic
Newsstand
provides online
access to many of
the most popular
magazines.

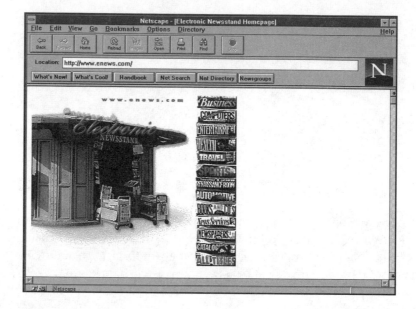

The E-Zines-List

E-Zines are the latest craze on the Internet. If you're interested in seeing what's available for online perusal, I highly recommend one of the most comprehensive e-zine lists on the Internet. This list is none other than the E-Zines-List, published by John Labovitz.

Figure 12.16 shows the initial Web home page for the E-Zines-List, which provides a detailed explanation of many e-zines and whether it comes from a fee-based service or not. You can use this list as a springboard to the e-zines themselves.

If you are interested in e-zines, I recommend you click your Web browser to John's E-Zines-List at **http://www.ora.com:8080/johnl/e-zine-list/**.

The E-Text Archive

The E-Text Archive Web home page maintains an impressive collection of electronic texts. This is a Gopher server that provides access to its archives through a rather extensive topical index.

Take a look at figure 12.17 to see the Web home page of the E-Text Archive, located at **http://www.etext.org/**.

Or the Gopher server can be reached at **gopher://gopher.etext.org/**.

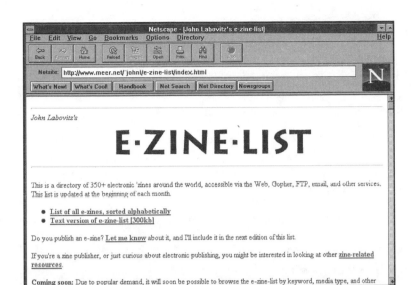

Fig. 12.16
John Labovitz's
E-Zines-List is
one of the most
comprehensive
lists of e-zines on
the Internet.

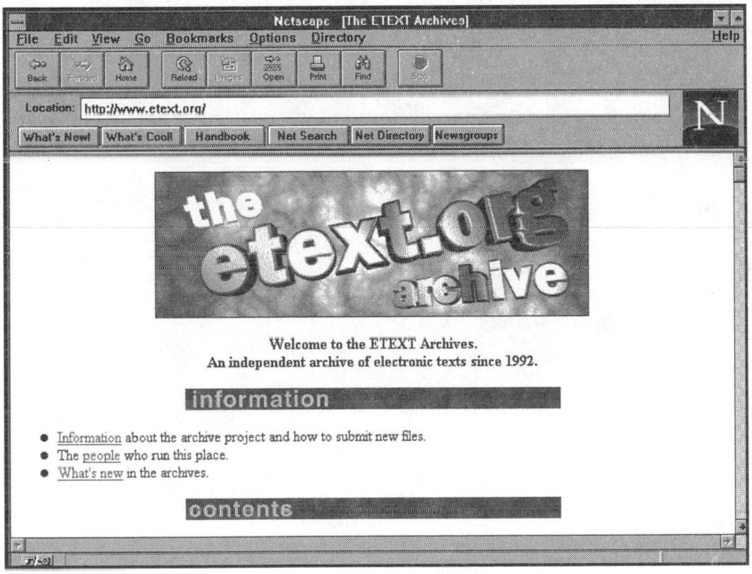

Fig. 12.17
The E-Text Archive
is a good starting
place for many
online electronic
texts, journals, and
magazines.

Commercial Information Providers

For years, several commercial information providers have used proprietary systems for access to their databases. Today, however, the Internet provides open access to very powerful databases. For a fee, you can use the Internet to reach some of the best information sources available.

In chapter 13 you will learn about some of the popular commercial electronic database providers. Many of those databases are available through the Internet for a fee. In addition to those commercial providers listed in chapter 13, there are two additional commercial databases worth noting.

- **Questel/Orbit.** Questel/Orbit markets an online information service geared toward those interested in intellectual property, scientific, chemical, technical, and business information. Its databases represent some of the most technical journals and references in the world, including extensive patent and trademark databases. For more information, see **http://www.questel.orbit.com/patents/oqovw.html** or call:

(800) 456-7248	North America
(1800) 226 474	Australia
(0800) 446 106	New Zealand
(0800) 289512	UK
01 30 81 14 06	Germany
06 02 27 38 6	Netherlands
02 07 93 11 5	Sweden
16 78 72 083	Italy
+33 (1) 4614 55 55	France

Tip
WESTLAW provides comprehensive legal information, as well as access to DIALOG.

- **WESTLAW.** WESTLAW is the product of West Publishing Company, and represents extensive legal and business related information. As a competitor of LEXIS-NEXIS, WESTLAW offers the same type of information, but has the benefit of West's 115 years of legal publishing experience. You can learn more about WESTLAW by contacting West's Web server at **http://www.westpub.com/** or you can call:

(800) 336-6365	North America

Gopher Specific Resources

While this chapter has already covered quite a bit of the ground work, I have generally concentrated on Web access and home pages for information. There is, however, quite a bit of information available in Gopher form. This means, of course, Web users have access to the information, as well as Gopher users. But, it means that Gopher users can make use of such information without having to Telnet to an anonymous Web account to access it.

For more information about anonymous Web accounts, I highly recommend Que's *Using the World Wide Web* or Que's *Using Internet E-Mail, Special Edition*. Both books will tell you more than you will ever need about Internet e-mail and the World Wide Web. They will also explain how to find anonymous Web accounts, so you do not have to miss out on information exclusively available on the Web.

The following sections point to some of the better Gopher resources on the Internet today.

Barron's Guide to Online Bibliographic Databases

For a comprehensive listing of online bibliographic databases, *Barron's Guide to Online Bibliographic Databases* is for you. This guide is located at **gopher:// vixen.cso.uiuc.edu:70/11/Libraries/Barron**.

Be forewarned, however, because this guide is huge. There are quite a few bibliographic databases and this list seems to cover them all: Fee-based and free. Once you download the list, you can use the information to access these databases using Gopher, the Web, or Telnet.

Internet Library Catalog from Yale

Yale maintains an extensive collection of links to Internet Library Catalog systems. It is geared very much like the *Gophers of the World* at the University of Minnesota's Gopher Server.

You select the catalog reference of interest by navigating through a series of menus from continent to nation, to region, to state, to city, to the actual library. This makes it easy to focus on those libraries closest to you.

The Internet Library Catalog Reference at Yale is located at **gopher:// libgopher.yale.edu:70/11/**.

Michigan Library Consortium

The Michigan Library Consortium is another OCLC-affiliate organization of libraries. They have placed themselves in Gopherspace at **gopher:// mlc.lib.mi.us:7042/11/.mlc**.

You will find loads of information about the various members of the Michigan Library Consortium, as well as some references to online information and services. It's a good stop if you are located in this region of the world.

Noonan Guide to Internet Libraries

One of the most comprehensive guides to online library catalog systems is the *Noonan Guide to Internet Libraries*, which lists over 250 public libraries around the world and how to reach them. It is more complete than Yale's Internet Library Catalog, but doesn't have the benefit of simply using the menu to select the library you wish to go to. This list is located at **gopher:// gopher.uiuc.edu:70/11/Libraries/Noonan**.

Texas State Electronic Library

The Texas State Electronic Library is an amazing resource. It has directions to contact a variety of sources, with most information directly searchable. It is located at **gopher://link.tsl.texas.gov:70/1**.

World Wide Web Specific Resources

Tip

When looking for Web resources, spending a few extra minutes to *surf* known resources will usually yield valuable unknown resources.

You have already learned that the Web is a very powerful research tool. So powerful, in fact, that if you have access to the Web, you don't need access to Gopher because the Web is just as capable of using Gopher servers as Gophers themselves. In other words, if you have access to the Web, you have access to Gopher.

National Library of Medicine

The National Library of Medicine, pictured in figure 12.18, is maintained by the U.S. National Institutes of Health. It boasts an incredible array of medical information, including texts, journals, pictures, and animation sequences. Much of the information is only available through billed accounts with the National Library of Medicine, however. It is located at **http:// www.nlm.nih.gov/**.

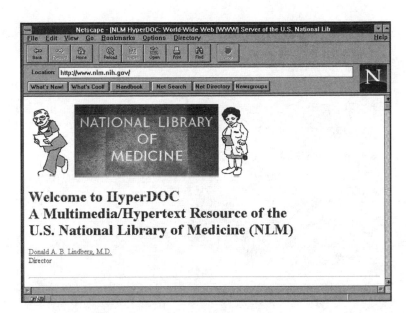

Fig. 12.18
The U.S. National Institutes of Health maintains the National Library of Medicine, a wealth of medical information on the Internet.

Use the National Library of Medicine to put you in touch with many medical resources on the Internet, as well as the Library's own medical databases. The Library's Web server has information on how to become a subscriber and Internet user of their databases.

For more information about the National Library of Medicine and the information available via the Internet, see the Web page for NLM or contact:

> MEDLARS Management Section
> National Library of Medicine
> 8600 Rockville Pike
> Bethesda, MD 20894
> Fax: (301) 496-0822

The Internet Public Library

The Internet Public Library, located at **http://ipl.sils.umich.edu/**, is a very good place to begin a search for online books and publications, shown in figure 12.19. It maintains a rather extensive collection of book and etext references. That is, you can use this Web server as a springboard to reference lists that will put you in contact with the book or publication that interests you most.

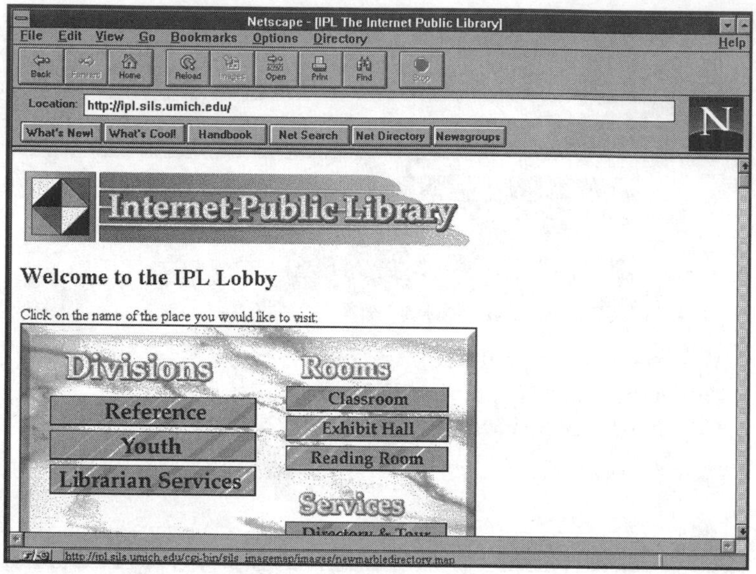

Fig. 12.19
The Internet
Public Library is
a great place to
begin your search
for online books
and publications.

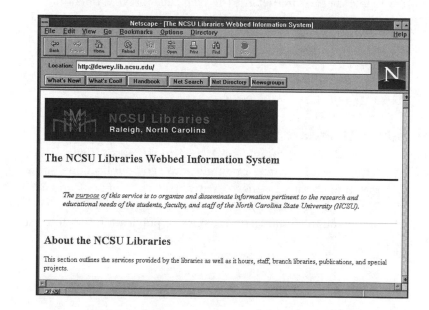

North Carolina Webbed Library

Like many other online libraries, the North Carolina Webbed Library maintains extensive online resources, but the best services are fee-based.

In figure 12.20, the home page for NCSU Library's Webbed Information System is located at **http://dewey.lib.ncsu.edu/**.

Fig. 12.20
NCSU Library's
Webbed Informa-
tion System is
available on the
Web.

University of Georgia Libraries

Figure 12.21 shows the home page to the University of Georgia Libraries, which contains information on how to access its two publicly accessible citations databases: GALIN and LIBRA. The URL to this home page is **http://scarlet.libs.uga.edu/**.

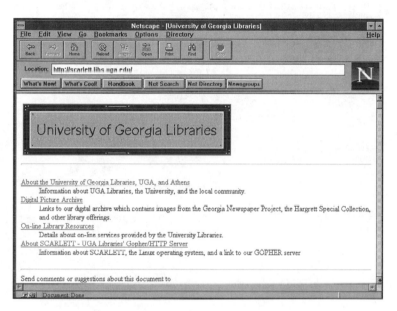

Fig. 12.21
The University of Georgia Libraries is a good starting point for online citation systems.

One warning, however: GALIN and LIBRA are not generally available on the Internet. They are available to other libraries with the use of special equipment.

Summary

The Internet comprises the sum-total of mankind's knowledge because it is connected to the world's greatest databases and information servers. Unfortunately, the best information comes with a price. But, the Internet is still becoming a great place for free information, as more and more people become members of the Information Superhighway.

You now know where the world's libraries are located on the Internet. You can use them to find many of the resources or references you seek. Additionally, many people on the Internet are working hard to provide free, publicly accessible books, journals, and texts. You can use many of the resource guides listed in this chapter to help you identify these sources of information.

Finally, you should have noticed the heavy bias toward the Web. The Web makes the Internet a very friendly place to conduct online research and investigation, since you can merely click on a hypertext link within a Web document to reach a new document. This just isn't possible with Gopher, where you must write down any resource pointers in the documents you read, or hope a menu item points in the direction you are trying to go.

Chapter 13

Commercial Information Services and Databases

Do you think a journal article, a case study, or a file could be worth $1,000? In many instances information can be worth much more. Consider a lawyer who is able to locate a legal precedent that wins a $300,000 settlement; a chemist who discovers a formula that helps create a drug worth millions in the pharmaceutical marketplace; an investment broker who finds information about a company that has the potential to triple sales in one year; or a surgeon who uncovers a clinical study that helps save a patient's life. Information does have value, and companies known as *information providers* recognize the value in creating, organizing, and selling information.

Many times information providers are companies that are already in the information business—such as publishers and direct mail companies. These companies already have a vast amount of electronic information and they can easily turn it into a product. Dow Jones News Retrieval, for example, is a service by the same company that publishes *The Wall Street Journal.* On other occasions companies that have databases will contract with another firm to sell their information. As an example, Reed Reference Publishing sells their *Marquis Who's Who* database that has biographies of 82,000 individuals through the online service Dialog.

Traditionally these companies have sold their information databases directly to subscribers, much in the same way that America Online sells its service to subscribers. They now recognize that the Internet represents a tremendous source for new business opportunities. In response, they are simultaneously using the Internet (primarily the World Wide Web) to provide information about their services as well as allowing people to connect to and access their databases.

In this chapter you'll learn about three of the world's largest information providers and the specific services and information databases they offer.

- Dow Jones Information Services: News, periodicals, and financial information.

- LEXIS-NEXIS: News, business, and legal resources.

- Dialog: Databases on every topic you can think of.

The Internet: Gateway to Networks and Databases

Question: *Why should you pay to access a commercial database to find information when the Internet offers so much?*

Answer: *That's a good question.*

Since you already have access to the Internet and know about the various search tools at your disposal, you may want to start your search on the Internet. It's clearly the least expensive way to locate information. However, the commercial databases do offer some unique advantages and information sources that you won't find on the Internet. These include:

- One-stop shopping to search and locate information from numerous databases. It's easy to jump from a database on one subject to a database on another subject.

- Extensive and current information with millions of new records and articles added each week.

- Detailed information for professionals that is not available anywhere else, such as reports on public and private companies, legal case studies, and global news databases.

- Delivery of full text on articles either on-screen, via e-mail, or by fax.

- Can be configured to maintain your search terms for future searches.

- Can remember your areas of interest and continue to search through information when you are off-line.

You can use the Internet's World Wide Web to visit the home pages of all of the following information providers without paying a fee. These Web sites offer terrific information about the information that's available on the different databases. In fact, the Dialog Web site lets you do a free Web search for any subject, then it tells you what files and databases contain relevant information—all before you connect.

However, if you want to search the databases and view articles you have to sign up. Fees range from $1.50 to retrieve one article to as much as $240 per hour. Clearly, time is money when you use a commercial database. Speed becomes an important element in locating information. If you can locate the perfect file in 1 minute as opposed to 30 minutes, you save a lot of money.

Business Information: Dow Jones Information Services

Web URL address: **http://dowvision.wais.net/**

Telnet: **djnr.dowjones.com**

(At the What service please prompt, type **DJNR**, press Enter, and type your password.)

In the world of finance, knowledge about industry trends, stock market activities, interest rates, corporate mergers, and new products can be a valuable commodity. The fastest way to receive this information is with an electronic network like the Internet.

With more than a century of experience in the information business, Dow Jones has taken the lead in developing online services for the financial world In fact, almost half of the company's revenues now come from the sale and delivery of electronic information and electronic publishing. The Dow Jones Information Services Group offers two distinct services that you can access through the Internet. One is DowVision, which lets you search for articles and information using the World Wide Web (and a Web browser). Dow Jones News/Retrieval is a separate service that provides comprehensive corporate information, business and financial news from more than 67 databases. Don't be put off if you think you can only use these services to find information about stock prices because you can search for, and usually find, articles about any subject.

The DowVision Web Site

DowVision is a Web-based information service. The effort is a collaboration between Dow Jones and WAIS Incorporated—the company that develops WAIS search engines. The service lets you search for information and receive

Tip
These services all have keyboard commands that make it easy to perform searches and quickly jump from one database to another. For example, with LEXIS-NEXIS the command *.nd* means next document and on Dialog *Begin 436* opens the UPI news database. Clearly it's advisable to learn these commands before you waste a lot of online time. The Web sites provide great overviews of navigation and search commands.

full-text articles from *The Wall Street Journal,* Dow Jones News Service, Dow Jones International News Services, Japan Economic Newswire, Canada Newswire, Business Wire, PR Newswire, *Investext Abstracts*, and *Professional Investor Report.*

Although at some point in time this will be a commercial service, it has been free during its initial testing period. The home page address for DowVision is **http://dowvision.wais.net/**. To register for the service (during its free or even non-free stage) visit **http://dowvision.wais.net/ registration.html**.

Figure 13.1 shows the DowVision home page. Here you can begin your search by entering keywords or a search term and selecting the databases that you want to search. Let's see what happens with the term "tax rates." Figure 13.2 shows the results. You get a nice display that has the headlines of relevant articles, the number of words, and a score that indicates how closely articles match your search criteria. Headlines are hyperlinks to the full-text stories. Figure 13.3 shows the display of one of the articles. This service makes it easy to locate articles about any subject for research or business applications.

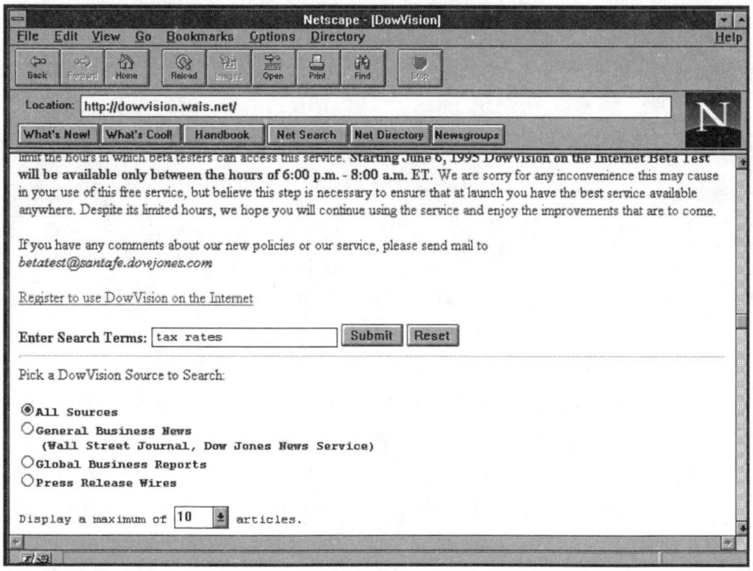

Fig. 13.1

Start your search for business and news articles at the DowVision home page.

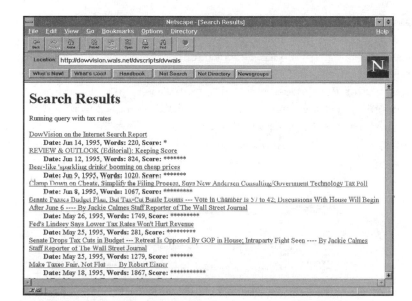

Fig. 13.2
The result of a DowVision search displays article headlines with information about the date and size of each article.

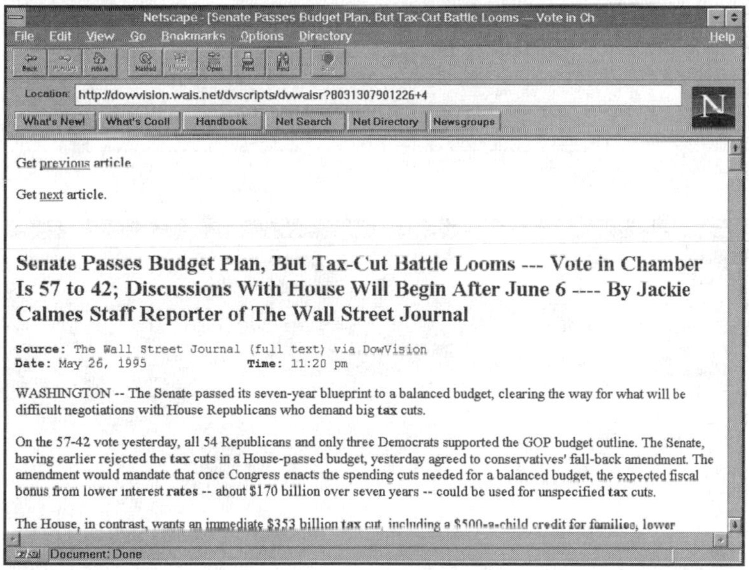

Fig. 13.3
Click on a headline of interest and the full-text appears on-screen.

Dow Jones News/Retrieval

If you need detailed financial information you can turn to the Dow Jones News/Retrieval (DJNR) service. DJNR can either be accessed via the Internet using Telnet or with proprietary software designed for the service. The Telnet address is **djnr.dowjones.com**. At the What service please prompt, type **DJNR**, press Enter, and then type your password (you need to be a registered user with a password to access DJNR). Figure 13.4 shows the main menu for DJNR during a Telnet session, and figure 13.5 shows the Dow Jones software (TestSearch Plus) that helps you formulate and conduct Boolean searches of the databases.

Fig. 13.4

This is the main menu for Dow Jones News Retrieval using a Telnet session.

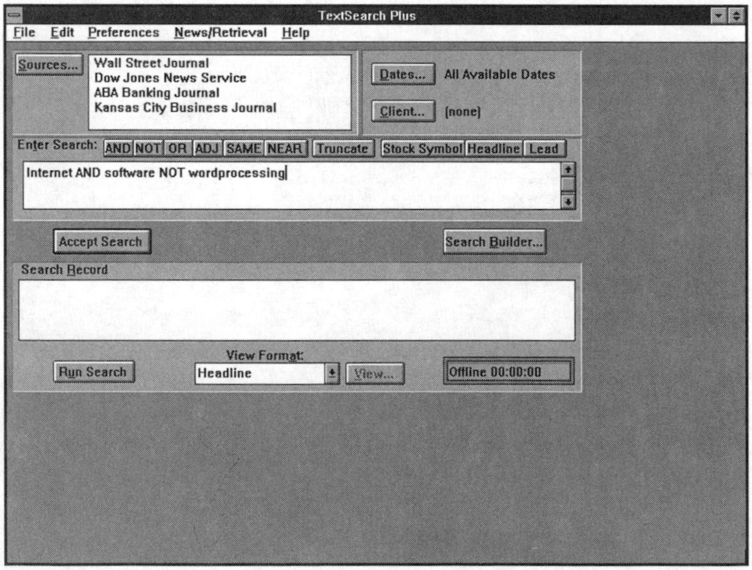

Fig. 13.5

This is the Windows-based software that Dow Jones provides to help you search through the database of 35 million articles.

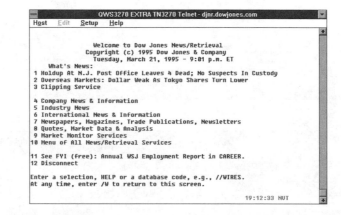

The text library of this service contains some 35 million articles, and 20,000 new articles are added each day. In all, the service provides access to 1,800 different publications. One of the nice features is a personalized electronic "clipping" service. You enter keywords or search terms that you have an on-going interest in (maybe "Internet software") and select specific publications. Then, the service will scan articles that appear each day and either save the articles for you on DJNR, or send them to your Internet electronic mailbox.

The company and stock-based information is extensive. In addition to real-time stock quotes you can locate information about corporate performance and management profiles, quarterly revenues, profit margins, return on total assets, the number of shares traded in one week, P/E ratios and analysis of the potential earnings through the year.

Table 13.1 shows a summary of a few of the information sources on DJNR.

Table 13.1 Publications Available on Dow Jones News/Retrieval	
The Wall Street Journal	Full Text Back to January 1984.
The New York Times	Same day full text.
Chicago Tribune	Full text back to January 1989.
Other publications	More than 1,250 general business and industry trade magazines.
Press Releases	
PR Newswire, Businesswire	Press releases from companies, government agencies, and so on.
Canada Newswire	Releases from 5,000 Canadian sources.
Company Information	
Dun's Financial Records	Financial reports on 1.8 million companies.
Zacks Corporate Earnings Estimator	Earning-per-share estimates for 4,800 companies.
Standard & Poor's Online	Profiles of 4,700 companies.
Market Data and Stock Information	
Dow Jones Real-Time Quotes	Real-time stock quotes form several stock exchanges.
Tradeline	20 years of historical information on stocks, bonds, mutual funds.
Wall Street Week Online	Transcripts from the PBS program.

How Much Does It Cost?

Dow Jones uses information-based pricing for DJNR. You pay for the information, not the time online. The cost runs $1.50 per 1,000 characters that you print, display, or download.

For more information contact:

Dow Jones News/Retrieval
P.O. Box 300
Princeton, NJ 08543
(800) 522-3567

Legal Information and News: The LEXIS-NEXIS Connection

There are several ways to access LEXIS-NEXIS through the Internet. You can visit their Web or FTP site or use Telnet.

Access By	Address
Web URL address	http://www.lexis-nexis.com/
FTP (anonymous login)	ftp.meaddata.com
Telnet	nex.meaddata.com

The LEXIS-NEXIS information databases are your passport to extensive information and articles that feature legal, news, and business information. LEXIS-NEXIS is a division of London-based Reed Elsevier—one of the world's largest publishing and information companies. If you wonder how anyone can make money selling information consider that LEXIS-NEXIS has more than 700,000 subscribers and annual revenues now exceed $500 million.

What attracts people to LEXIS-NEXIS? To begin with you have access to 5,620 distinct databases. If that sounds like a lot then certainly you'll be even more impressed to learn that the service maintains approximately 417 million documents online and adds another 1.8 million new documents each week. You'd have to be a really good speed reader to keep up with this information flow.

There are two distinct information services here. Begun in 1973, LEXIS is designed to be an extensive research tool for legal professionals. LEXIS contains archives of federal and state case law, statutes from all 50 states, state and federal regulations, and public records. LEXIS maintains 45 distinct libraries that cover all fields of legal practice including tax, securities, banking, medical, environmental, energy, and international.

In the area of case law, attorneys and legal researchers use LEXIS to search for precedents for cases, to examine a judge's ruling on a case or even to review the testimony of a witness in a case. It's also possible to locate specific state and federal codes and regulations relating to most industries. In the area of patent law, you can search documents that chronicle 20 years of U.S. patents. And, if you just need a quick legal reference there are several online resources such as the Martindale-Hubbell Law Directory, which lists attorneys by both state and specialty.

If you don't live in the U.S. or are researching legal issues in other countries, LEXIS contains libraries of English, French, and Canadian law as well as legal materials from Australia, New Zealand, Ireland, and Scotland.

NEXIS is a separate service that provides full-text news and business information. Subscribers to LEXIS automatically get access to NEXIS. The NEWS Library offers current and archived news and information from more than 2,400 sources. For example, NEXIS is the only online service to offer the complete text of *The New York Times* with stories that date back to 1980. NEXIS also carries other news publications including:

- *Business Week*

- *The Economist*

- *Fortune*

- *Los Angeles Times*

- *The Washington Post*

NEXIS also has online transcripts of national network and regional television broadcasts and news and features from Cable News Network and National Public Radio. Other international news services and newswires from China to Mexico provide daily reports and articles. And if you're more of a magazine person, there are hundreds of articles from mainstream and esoteric magazines and journals.

Where To Begin with LEXIS-NEXIS

The very best starting point for LEXIS-NEXIS is the Web site (**http://www. lexis-nexis.com/**), which is well organized and contains a tremendous amount of information about the service, the databases that are available, and the commands and searching techniques for the services. You can go through the Web site to connect with and start a Telnet session, which is how you access the databases. There is one catch. If you aren't a registered user, you can't access their databases because you need a login name and password once the Telnet session begins.

What's at the LEXIS-NEXIS Web Site?

Figure 13.6 shows the home page for LEXIS-NEXIS. It's easy to navigate through this site as you click on clearly labeled buttons.

Fig. 13.6
The LEXIS-NEXIS Web site offers a tremendous amount of useful information about the information and search techniques that the service offers.

Tip
There is one advantage of using a browser to first connect to the Web site, then Telnet to the database. Using your mouse and Windows-based programs you can jump between the Web site and the Telnet session. So, if you forget a command or the name of a database, it may be faster to jump back to the Web site, locate the information you need, and then continue with the Telnet session.

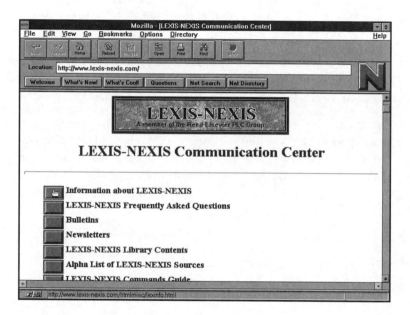

Here's a brief summary of the information that the home page links will open:

■ Information about LEXIS-NEXIS

Background about the company and general overview of the services.

■ Frequently Asked Questions

Two FAQ lists are available. One contains general questions about connectivity such as, "What is the fastest speed I can access the LEXIS databases?" The answer is 9600 bps. The second list offers practical advice for searching the databases. For example: "How do I find biographical or background information on a certain individual?" The answer is to look in the PEOPLE library, check the file ALLBIO and enter a name, such as Bill Clinton.

- Bulletins

  A variety of press releases and service announcements.

- Newsletters

  Several online newsletters that provide information about different services. These include:

  - Information professionals update

  - In-house newsletters

  - Insight

  - Media Insight

- LEXIS-NEXIS library contents

  This is a hypertext A to Z listing of all the different libraries that are available. For example, you can get a quick overview of the information and files that are available in the American Bar Association (ABA) Library. You'll find that there are several publications on many aspects of legal proceedings including the ABA Journal; information on membership in the ABA and the organization's constitution and bylaws.

- Alpha List of LEXIS-NEXIS sources

  Another A to Z listing, but this one covers the many sources of information that contribute to the different libraries. You also are told which library and even which file contains the source information. Here's an example:

Source	Library	File
Alaska tax cases	FEDTAX	ALAS
American Economist	NEWS	AASAPII
Archives of Ophthalmology	GENMED	AROP

- LEXIS-NEXIS command guide

  This is a detailed listing of the different commands that you use to navigate through the information on LEXIS-NEXIS. If you want to save a lot of time (and money), you should refer to this before you use the service. When you Telnet into LEXIS-NEXIS you'll be using your keyboard to enter commands for navigation and searching. For example, when you get a list of relevant articles and want to move forward one document you either need to type in **next doc** or **.nd**. You are no longer in the point-and-click world of the Web.

■ Educational customers

Information for educational organizations that use LEXIS-NEXIS.

■ E-mail contacts

E-mail addresses for several LEXIS-NEXIS departments.

How To Use LEXIS-NEXIS

Assuming that you're so enthralled with the idea of having instant access to more than 400 million documents that you've signed up to try LEXIS-NEXIS, here are a few pointers for using the service. With LEXIS-NEXIS you move through layers of information, starting at a top level and weaving your way toward specific information and articles. You start with a specific library and then search specific files in the library. The first screen offers a list of library options as seen in figure 13.7.

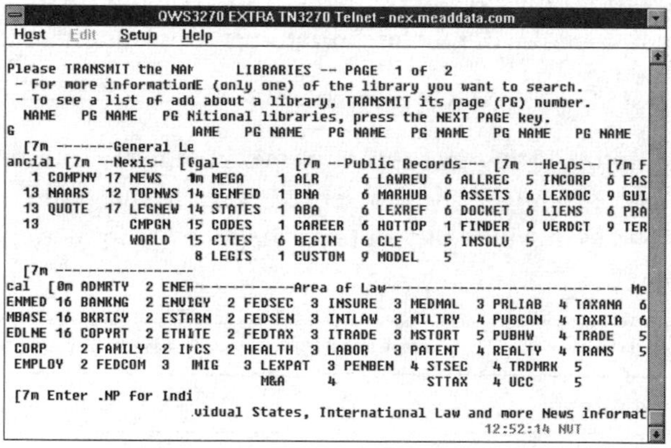

Fig. 13.7
The LEXIS-NEXIS main screen invites you to select a specific library to begin your search of the databases.

Once you select a specific library you're ready for a search. LEXIS-NEXIS allows for three different methods to search for information including FREESTYLE™, Boolean, and Easy Search™. FREESTYLE lets you phrase "plain English" searches such as "recent articles about gun control." Boolean searching allows you to use the Boolean search parameters to narrow a search. Here are two examples.

```
Need:  Recent articles in the news about gun control.
Library:  NEWS
File:    CURNWS
Search phrase: (gun control) AND date is 1995

Need: A list of law firms in Kansas City that have more than 30
employees.
Library:  MARHUB
File:    ARDIR
Search phrase:   city(kansas city) and firm-size(>30)
```

The Easy Search option uses online menus and screen prompts to assist with the formulation of search requests. It then selects the correct areas of a specific database to begin a search. Once you perform a search on a specific library or file, LEXIS-NEXIS keeps the search term in memory and you can quickly jump to a different library to search it using the same term.

How comprehensive are the databases? Very. As an example, I wanted to locate articles and information about the rehabilitation process involved after surgery on the anterior cruciate ligament—a ligament in the back of your kneecap. First I select the National Library of Medicine MEDLINE Database as a good starting point. I use the search term "anterior cruciate ligament" thinking this is pretty specific. The database locates more than 1,000 references. I try again with "anterior cruciate ligament rehabilitation." Now a manageable 6 references to medical articles come up including:

```
TITLE: The biomechanics of anterior cruciate ligament rehabilita-
tion and reconstruction.

AUTHOR: Arms SW; Pope MH; Johnson RJ; Fischer RA; Arvidsson I;
Eriksson E

CITE: Am J Sports Med 1984 Jan-Feb; 12 (1): 8-18

TITLE: Modern trends in anterior cruciate ligament rehabilitation:
nonoperative and postoperative management. 51 REFS

AUTHOR: Irrgang JJ

CITE: Clin Sports Med 1993 Oct; 12 (4): 797-813
```

How Much Does It Cost?

There are two options. The LEXIS-NEXIS basic fee structure charges you for each search with searches ranging from $6 to $40 or more depending upon the number and selection of databases you choose. An alternative plan does not charge per search, but instead has a higher charge for connecting to the service. You should discuss your information needs with a LEXIS-NEXIS customer service agent to get the best deal.

For more information contact:

LEXIS-NEXIS
9443 Springboro Pike
P.O. Box 933
Dayton, Ohio 45401
(800) 227-4908

Science and More: Knight-Ridder Information Resources

Owned by Knight-Ridder Information, Dialog is one of the largest online information research services. Since 1972, Dialog has provided librarians and researchers with electronic access to articles, conference proceedings, news, and statistical information. Today the service offers more than 450 databases which encompass some 330 million articles, abstracts, and citations.

Access By	Address
Web URL address	http://www.dialog.com
Telnet	dialog.com

The databases cover all subject areas, from accounting and aerospace to family resources, federal documents, financial and stock market information, college databases, and employee benefit plans. What's more, each database can lead to an enormous amount of information on one subject. For example, the Academic Index database provides an index of some 1,450 scholarly publications and the full-text of 250 journals. Perfect for that overdue term paper. And if reading is more than a hobby, you can access the complete text of 60 U.S. and international newspapers.

Business information searchers will enjoy several finance-related databases including Predicast, Moody's, Standard and Poor's TRW, and Dun and Bradstreet. These databases offer detailed information about specific industries, companies (including annual reports), products, and even profiles of senior executives. In fact, there are financial profiles on more than 12 million U.S. firms and 1 million international companies. So you can easily perform research on a company because you are interested in purchasing stock or because you need a little competitive intelligence for your business plan.

Where To Begin with Dialog

Dialog maintains a Web site with the URL address **http://www.dialog.com**. You can also ask questions or send comments about the service to **info@www.dialog.com**. And, there's a Dialog mailing list that you can join via the Web site that'll send you news updates about the service.

Figure 13.8 shows the Dialog home page. You can click on four areas for information:

- **Frequently asked questions:** This brings you a page where you can choose question and answer format for information about business, science, general, or technical information.

- **Databases:** From this page you can use the Web forms interface to enter a keyword search that locates relevant Dialog databases.

- **Publications:** Again, a page that lets you enter a search to locate periodicals that have articles that meet your needs.

- **Commands, features, and services:** A comprehensive list of the Dialog commands.

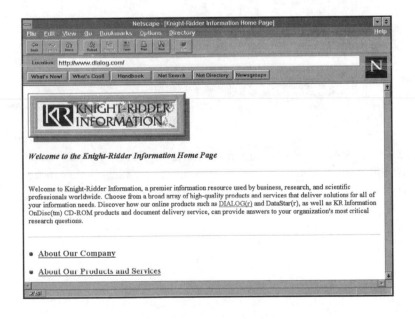

Fig. 13.8
The Dialog World Wide Web home page provides access to information and sample searches.

Getting on Dialog and Searching for Information

You can either directly Telnet to Dialog (dialog.com), or start with the Web site and click on the link that opens a Telnet session. Once the Telnet connects you'll have to enter a Logon ID and password to use the service.

There are several ways to navigate and search Dialog. Figure 13.9 shows the main screen. Option #3—Help in Choosing Databases For Your Topic—provides a subject listing of the databases that makes it easy to locate an appropriate database for your search. If you've already done your homework and chosen a specific database—either by using the Web site search tools or reviewing a hardcopy database catalog—you can immediately jump to a specific database. Option 6—DIALOG Menus—provides a menu-based navigation system that is very similar to the Gopher system—one menu leads to another.

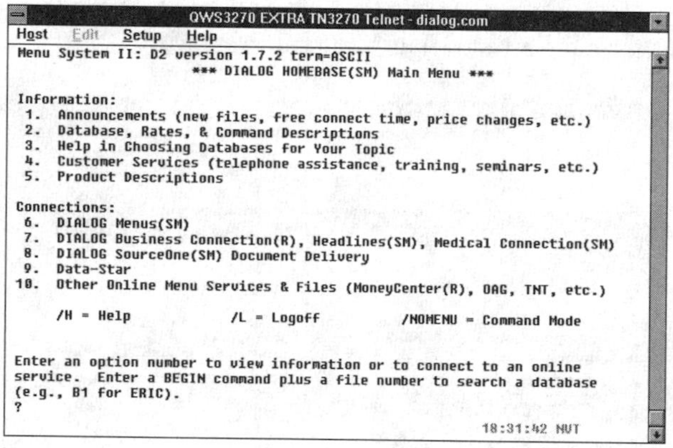

Fig. 13.9
The Dialog main menu screen.

Let's take a look at a search using this option. Say you want to locate information and articles about the topic of "computer privacy." You can navigate your way to this information by selecting various menu choices (see fig. 13.10 through 13.13).

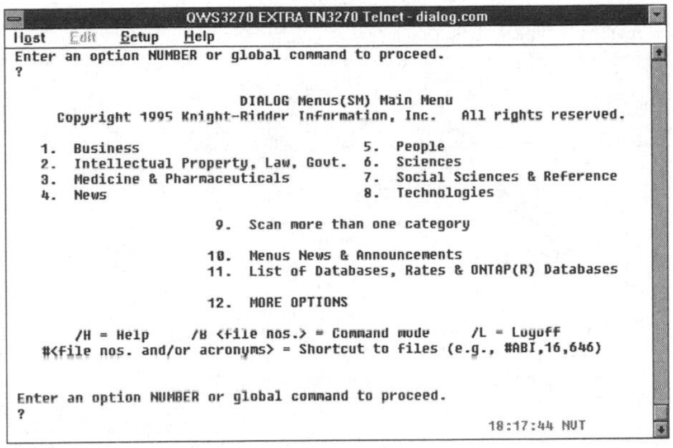

Fig. 13.10
Intellectual Property, Law, and Government is the first choice in using menu navigation to locate articles about computer privacy.

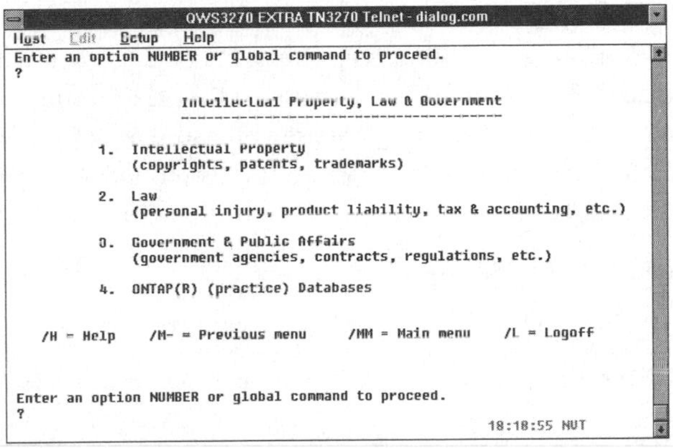

Fig. 13.11
The search continues now selecting Government and Public Affairs.

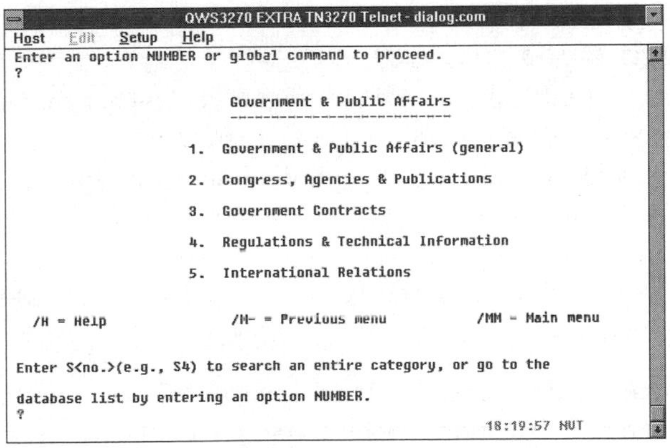

Fig. 13.12
Third stop select Government and Public Affairs (general).

Fig. 13.13
Finally, locate and search the Legal Resource Index database.

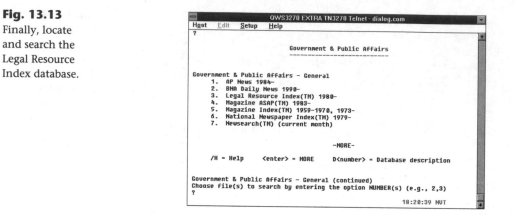

```
┌─────────────────────────────────────────────────────────────────────┐
│                    QWS3270 EXTRA TN3270 Telnet - dialog.com        ▼ │
│  Host    Edit    Setup    Help                                       │
│  ?                                                                 ▲ │
│                              Government & Public Affairs              │
│                              -------------------------               │
│                                                                      │
│   Government & Public Affairs - General                              │
│       1.  AP News 1984-                                              │
│       2.  BNA Daily News 1990-                                       │
│       3.  Legal Resource Index(TM) 1980-                             │
│       4.  Magazine ASAP(TM) 1983-                                    │
│       5.  Magazine Index(TM) 1959-1970, 1973-                        │
│       6.  National Newspaper Index(TM) 1979-                         │
│       7.  Newsearch(TM) (current month)                              │
│                                                                      │
│                                                                      │
│                                  -MORE-                              │
│                                                                      │
│       /H = Help      <enter> = MORE      D<number> = Database description │
│                                                                      │
│   Government & Public Affairs - General (continued)                  │
│   Choose file(s) to search by entering the option NUMBER(s) (e.g., 2,3) │
│   ?                                                                  │
│                                                 18:20:39 NUT         │
└─────────────────────────────────────────────────────────────────────┘
```

Tip

One of the advantages of using the Dialog Menus to weave your way toward a database is that, like Gopher, you come across other paths and prospective databases that may prove useful.

The Legal Resource Index contains articles and indexes from more than 750 law journals. You can get to this screen much faster if you know that you want this database by entering the database code and jumping to it directly from the first screen. Once at this database you can search by subject, title, author and date. Using the subject option, the search term "computer and privacy" locates 113 articles which include articles with titles that include:

```
ECPA and online computer privacy

Pointers for American legislation on computer privacy

Computer privacy, not secrecy (from The New York Times)

Has the computer changed the law?

Access to electronic records
```

How Much Does It Cost?

Each database in Dialog has it's own fee structure. You get charged by the hour for searching as well as a one-time fee each time you print or download an article or reference. On the high end of the spectrum there are databases like the CHEMNAME database which runs $240.00 per hour or the CLAIMS U.S. Patents Abstracts from 1950 to the present which cost $120.00 per hour. For $30.00 per hour you can access Peterson's College Database or Standard & Poor's Daily News.

You must complete an application form to get a new account. To receive an application form, information brochure, and price list contact the sales department at (800) 334-2564.

For more information contact:

Knight-Ridder Information
2440 El Camino Real
Mountain View, California 94040
(800) 3-Dialog

Summary

The commercial services reviewed in this chapter play an important role in the management and delivery of electronic information. In many cases the thousands of databases and millions of articles and files these services offer cannot be found on any other Internet site or system. What's great is that you now can go *through* the Internet to access and use these services.

The best way to learn whether one of these services may be beneficial for your specific information needs is to connect with their Web page and explore the information there. If you still have questions, call the companies (they all have toll-free numbers) and ask them to send you brochures that describe the content of the databases. If you like what you see, sign up.

Chapter 14

Companies, Business, and Financial Information

"Nothing is so dear and precious as time." This maxim, written in the 1500s by French humorist Francois Rabelais, remains as true today as it was almost 500 years ago. Time is definitely a valuable commodity when it comes to the world of business and finance. And you can use the Internet to search for and locate a tremendous amount of business-related information.

For example, you can search for a specific business or company—one that can supply and deliver furniture for your new office next week or one that wholesales the gear you need for a camping trip. You can even locate toll-free phone numbers for companies. The Internet is also an invaluable source of business and financial information. Check out the current price of a specific stock that you want to add to your portfolio, or view the historical price performance of a mutual fund. You can download press releases, view patent and SEC filings, and locate trading partners around the world. These are a few examples of the practical applications of searching for business-related information on the Internet.

In this chapter, you learn:

- How to find and search Internet sites that maintain databases of information about or by companies

- Where to go if you need a quick financial report on a company

- How to find late-breaking financial and business news

- Where you can get stock market information and current stock prices

How To Locate Businesses and Companies

There are several Web sites that offer searchable databases that'll help you locate business—both in cyberspace and in the real world. And, if you're tired of reading information on-screen, submit Web forms to receive one of 10,000 hard copy brochures and catalogs.

AT&T Toll-Free Numbers

URL address: **http://att.net/dir800**

Who can resist a toll-free telephone number? Well, if you're looking for toll-free numbers for travel reservations, catalogs, or anything else, you can now turn to the Web instead of a switchboard operator (see fig. 14.1). The AT&T 800 Web directory has more than 150,000 listings from AT&T's business and consumer yellow-page 800 directories.

Fig. 14.1
The AT&T toll-free Web site helps you quickly find toll-free phone numbers for products and companies.

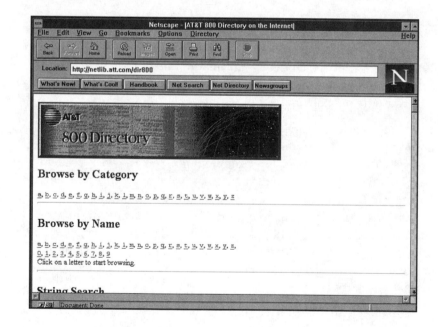

The home page tells us: "It's designed to help you shop for the things you need and want without leaving the comfort of your home or office. You can use this directory to buy almost anything from anywhere in the United States—from gifts and flowers to things for the home and unique and hard-to-find items."

You can search through the database in the following four different ways:

1. Choose an A to Z category. For example, the letter E hyperlinks to eggs, engines, exports, and so on.

2. Choose by an alphabetical listing of companies. Again, select the letter E and you get a list of companies that includes Ebony, Eaton, and Exxon.

3. Enter a search term into an on-screen Search String entry box. For example, enter the keyword **piano**, submit it, and within seconds you'll have a list of all of the companies with toll-free numbers that sell, rent, tune, or otherwise deal with pianos (see figure 14.2).

4. Enter a phone number into a Phone Number Search to find matching phone numbers and companies. This might be helpful if you're looking for a company, or want to see whether someone already has an 800 number that you really want.

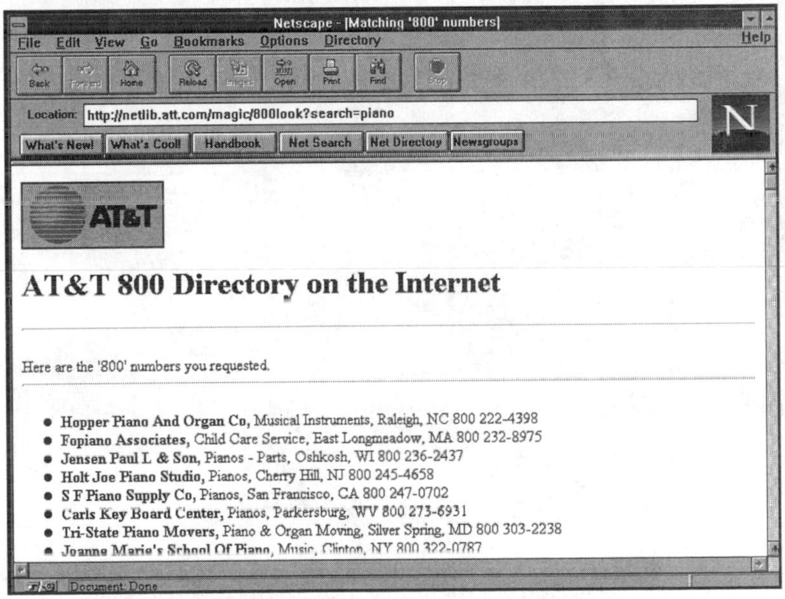

Fig. 14.2
A search of the AT&T 800 number directory delivers a long, alphabetical listing of companies that sell products or services related to your keyword—this one was for "piano."

Open Market's Web Commercial Site Index
URL address: **http://www.directory.net/**

As you can see in figure 14.3, this is a fantastic site if you are looking for Web sites that represent commercial businesses. You'll find everything from Web-based flower stores to sites that focus on real estate. There are more than

4,000 listings (Web sites) in this database. Here's a break down of sites by category that will give you a sense of the records that are available. By the time you read this, the number of sites will be much greater.

Category of Sites in Database	Number of Sites
Other Indexes	44
States, Cities, and Towns	38
Business and Commercial	3669
Government	52
Organizations and Non-Profits	154
Other	58

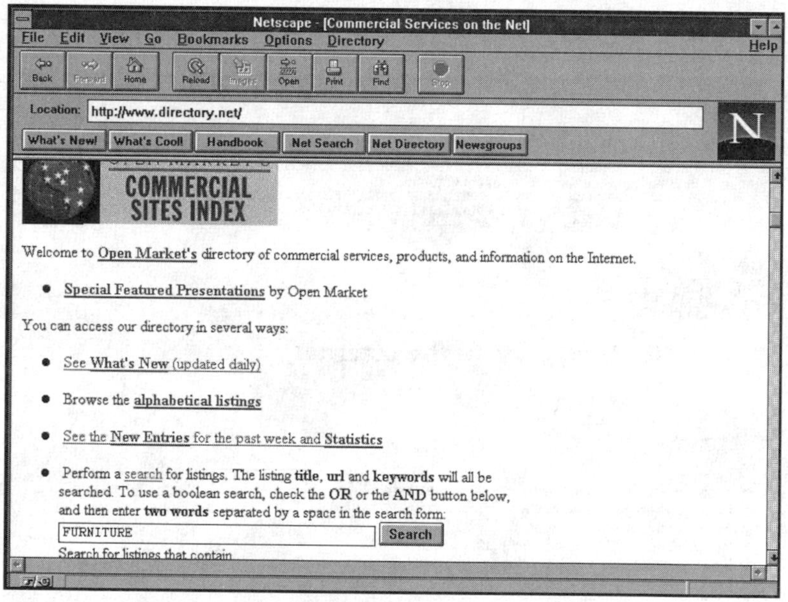

Fig. 14.3

The Open Market Web site lets you search for companies and businesses that have Web sites that relate to your needs. Once you get a listing of relevant companies, you can jump directly to their home pages.

You can begin your search from the home page. Enter a short description of the type of product or service you're looking for—perhaps "Internet Training"—and you'll receive a hypertext list of sites that fit the bill. The Web sites are indexed not by name, but rather by keywords, which the site authors submit to Open Market. This means that a search for "auto" is just as likely to find the Dealernet Web site as it is the AutoNetwork site. You can jump directly from this list to any of the sites. A daily What's New feature provides short descriptions of new sites. If your company has a Web site, you can add it to this valuable database.

Catalog Mart (10,000 Business Catalogs Online)

URL address: **http://catalog.savvy.com/**

Gopher address: **catalog.savvy.com/**

This site combines the convenience of online searching with the convenience of leisurely looking through product catalogs and shopping at home. You can select one (or several) of 800 different topic areas that encompass some 10,000 catalogs, ranging from bowling equipment to drafting supplies to hot tubs. Enter your name and real (home or office) address and you'll receive free catalogs that relate to your interests and needs.

Questions and comments can be sent via e-mail to **cats@savvy.com**.

Finding Financial Information on the Internet

How much is IBM stock selling for? What is the five-year historical trend for earnings per share for Motorola? Who is the CEO of Sears, Roebuck & Co.? Use the Internet to search for and locate the answers to these and other questions.

A good place to start your search is by using one of the World Wide Web searchers. Either start with a broad keyword or search term, such as "stocks" or "real estate," or look for information about a specific company by entering its name, such as "American Express."

Investment Newsletters

From timely tips to reports about corporate acquisitions, business and financial newsletters have always been a rich source of information for both part-time and professional investors. Whereas subscriptions to these publications can run thousands of dollars per year, the Web now boasts several free financial newsletters. Use the Yahoo search engine (**http://www.yahoo.com/**) and perform a keyword search for "newsletters" to get a current index of Web-based investment newsletters. Here's a brief overview of a few that are available:

Market Beat by Tom Petruno

URL address: **http://www.quote.com/newsletters/petruno/**

A column of advice and information for investors, Market Beat is published three times a week and made available by the Los Angeles Times. To get this via e-mail, send a message to **petruno@netcom.com**, put the word **subscribe** in the subject field, and leave the body of the message blank.

NASDAQ Financial Executive Journal

URL address: **http://www.law.cornell.edu/nasdaq/nasdtoc.html**

The Financial Executive Journal is a shared project of the Legal Information Institute at Cornell Law School and The NASDAQ (SM) Stock Market. The server provides back issues of the journal for your review.

The Capitalist by Net Worth

URL address: **http://networth.galt.com/www/home/capital**

This is a rather extensive investment-based Web site that offers a variety of online newsletters, information on mutual fund performance, prospectuses on companies, and promotional literature.

Wall Street News

URL address: **http://Wall-Street-News.com/forecasts/**

The home page states "Our news comes directly from financial newsletters published by Wall Street's leading forecasters. WSTN goes beyond just reporting the news, we forecast tomorrow's news today." If this sounds enticing, you can subscribe to receive WSTN's Wall-Street-News Hotline broadcasts via e-mail (no charge involved). Send a message to the mailing list **listserv@netcom.com**. Leave the subject blank. The body of your message should be **subscribe wall-street-news**.

Quote.Com

URL address: **http://www.quote.com**
FTP address: **ftp.quote.com**

Quote.Com offers both free and subscription-based Web, FTP, and e-mail services. As you might guess from the name, the site does include up-to-the-minute stock information (see fig. 14.4). There's also information on exchanges outside the U.S., commodity futures, mutual funds, treasury securities, balance sheet data, company profiles, market analysis by Standard & Poor's analysts, and yes, even weather forecasts for commodity futures traders. Tap into Hoover's company database, which provides profiles of more than 1,000 public companies with historical overviews, sales and revenue information, and names of executives. Both BusinessWire and PR Newswire continuously post the latest press releases from small and large companies.

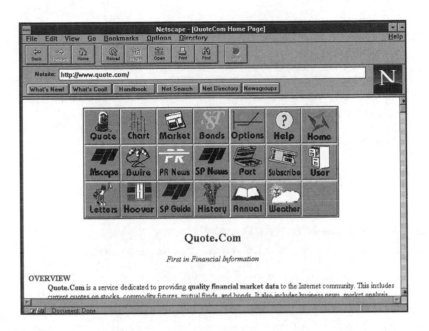

Fig. 14.4
The Quote.Com home page offers buttons that link to a variety of business and financial information including stock quotes, news wire press releases, and corporate financial reports.

IV

Commercial & Educational

Many of the Quote.Com services involve searching. For example, if you want a stock quote or a financial report on a company, you have to enter the stock symbol to receive the quote. There's no charge to get five free quotes per day. For a basic service fee of $9.95 per month, you can get as many as 100 quotes per day and access to full coverage of press releases that are put out continuously by both BusinessWire and PR Newswire. These are the world's largest electronic press release services and most companies use one or both of these services when they release news.

If you're a basic subscriber, you can use Quote.Com to find historical price and volume for any stock symbol on a single day in history. To use this feature:

1. Either click the History button on the home page or load **http://www.quote.com/sub/history.html**.

2. Enter the symbol and a specific date.

3. Submit the form to receive the price quote.

> **Note**
>
> You can also retrieve news headlines for specific stocks via e-mail. Send a message to **services@quote.com.** The subject of your message should be in the format:
>
> > Subject: news aaa bbb ccc
>
> where aaa, bbb, and ccc represent the ticker symbols of specific stocks in which you're interested. You will receive a message by e-mail that includes a list of headlines from Quote.Com and instructions to retrieve the entire text. You need a basic subscription with Quote.Com to use this feature.

Experimental Mutual Fund Charts

URL address: **http://www.ai.mit.edu/stocks/mf.html**

The site is maintained by the Artificial Intelligence Lab at MIT. This experiment is a raging success. It may provide insight into how computers may someday eliminate certain human jobs—like displaying the historical value of mutual funds (see fig. 14.5). The data is supplied at no charge by InterTrade, a company that sells subscriptions for you to receive computer disks of historical data.

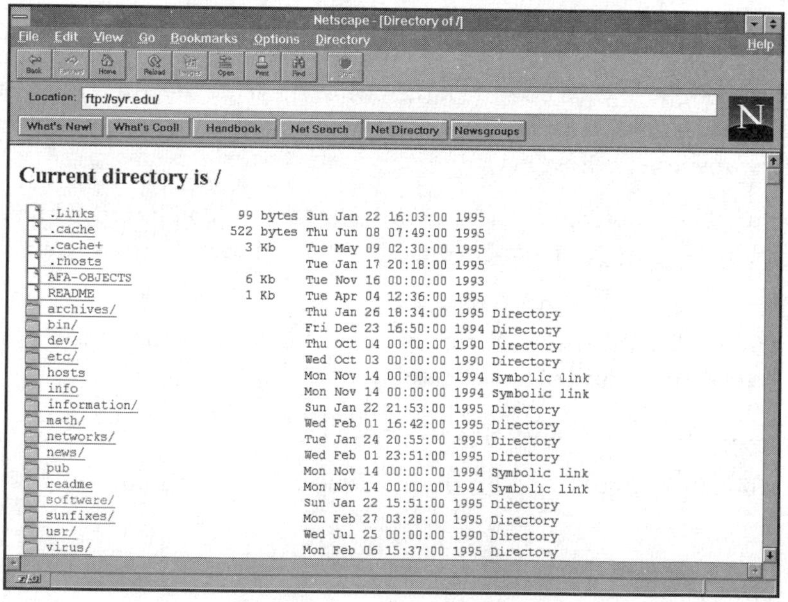

Fig. 14.5
Pick a fund, any fund. This screen displays the historical price performance for the Phoenix High Yield Fund. You can locate hundreds of different mutual funds and retrieve similar performance charts.

The home page has an A to Z hypertext index. Click a letter of the alphabet and jump to funds that begin with that letter. There are hundreds of funds in the database. Click the name for a specific fund and a chart of its recent price performance appears on-screen. The charts are generated on demand the first time they are requested and you may need to wait a few seconds for a specific chart to appear. You should note that these charts haven't been adjusted for share distributions and there may be dips (usually in December) that reflect these distributions.

J.P. Morgan & Company
URL address: **http://www.jpmorgan.com**

The banking and financial company J.P. Morgan has jumped headfirst into the Internet and Web. To position itself in the world of finance, the company began a risk measurement service called RiskMetrics™. This service uses mathematical formulas to help investors (primarily institutional) evaluate risks of investments. Daily, these risk data sets are posted to the Web. In addition, there is information about the government bond index, mortgage refinance index, and mortgage purchase index on the Web.

Tap into Searchable Government Databases and Reports

The U.S. government maintains archives of documents and databases of information that literally fill buildings and warehouses all across the country. In an effort to simplify the amount of man-hours that it takes to deal with this volume of paperwork (not to mention print and mail it), a lot of publicly accessible information is being put online and onto the Internet. Here are some excellent starting places that offer search tools.

Town Hall
URL address: **http://www.town.hall.org/**
FTP address: **ftp.town.hall.org.** (anonymous login)
Gopher address: **gopher.town.hall.org**

Maintained by the Internet Multicasting Service, this Web site offers access to several useful searchable databases. From the home page, select "Government Databases." You then get several new options including:

U.S. Patent Database

This area opens the data archives of the U.S. Patent and Trademark Office APS/full-text feed. The archives contain records for all patents currently

Tip
If you know the five letter symbol of a mutual fund, you can speed things up a bit. Choose Open URL on your browser and enter **http://www.ai.mit.edu/stocks/mfgraph?FUNDNAMEX**. FUNDNAMEX is the symbol of the fund you want to chart—this symbol always ends with X.

issued in 1994 and 1995. If you're thinking about patenting a new product, invention, or process, you should check here first. You enter a keyword query in the search dialog box to look for specific records on patents (see fig. 14.6). You can also use compound searches such as musical AND instruments.

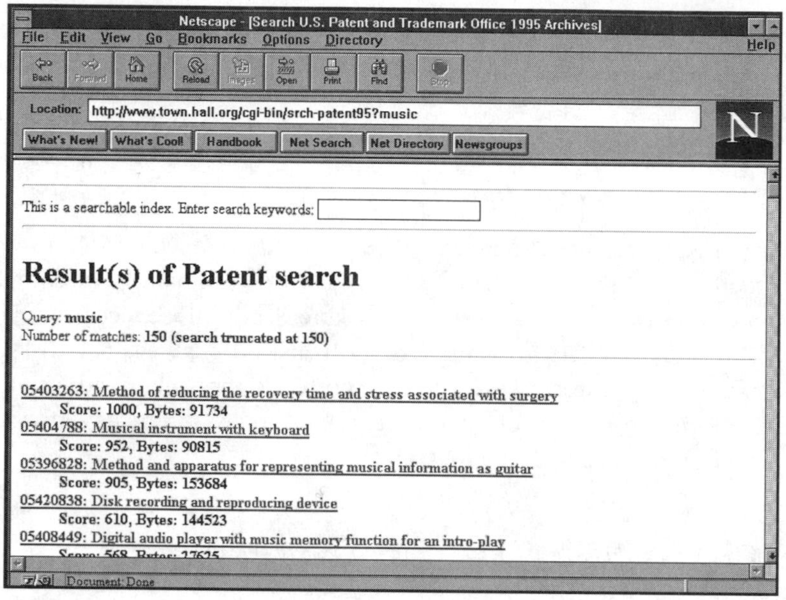

Fig. 14.6
A search for patents that relate to music retrieves more than 200 entries.

Securities and Exchange Commission

When you choose this database, you access the EDGAR Dissemination project. This research project is funded by a grant from the National Science Foundation to New York University's Stern School of Business.

The database consists of electronic filings that are submitted by corporations to the Securities and Exchange Commission (SEC). Although not every company and corporation files electronically, those that do participate in this system. You can receive information and documents on any 1994 and 1995 filings to the SEC that are available to the public. Non-electronic filings, filings that aren't open to the public, and information prior to 1994 are not available.

Using the EDGAR search engine, you can enter the name of any company or corporation. As with other search engines, you'll find that very general names, like Johnson, will find records on many different companies. So, the more specific you can be with your search term, the more likely you are to get useful listings (see fig. 14.7). For example, a search for US WEST Inc. locates several documents that the Regional Bell Operating Company filed with the SEC. When you search for these documents, be as precise as you can when entering the name of the company for which you are searching.

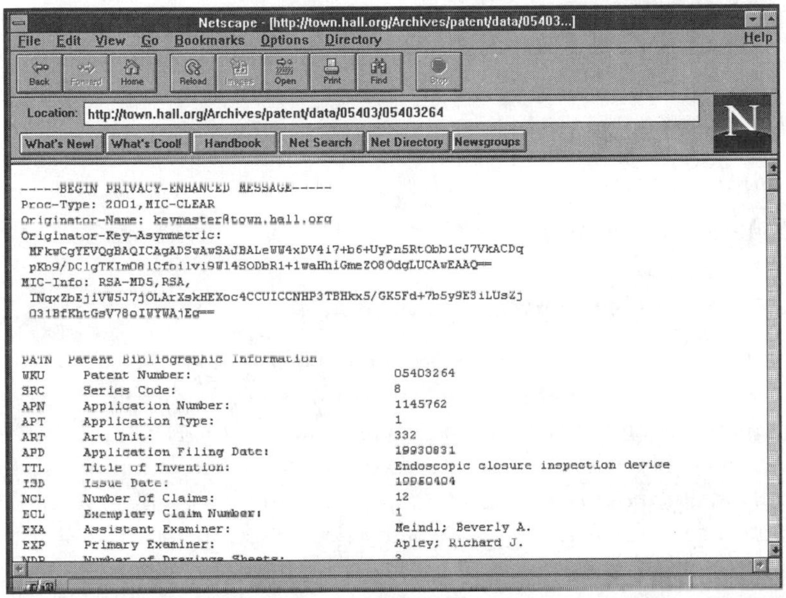

Fig. 14.7
Here is a registration statement that US WEST, the telephone company, filed with the SEC that is available for public review on the EDGAR system.

> **Note**
>
> If you want more information on this project, send an e-mail to **mail@town.hall.org** with **send edgar/general.txt** in the text of the body.

FedWorld

URL address: **http://www.fedworld.gov**

Have you ever read a newspaper article or listened to a radio report that sited a government study or report? This Web site is the place to go if you want to see that report for yourself. The National Technical Information Service maintains this home page to help people deal with the challenge of accessing the vast amount of U.S. government information. How vast? NTIS provides users access to over two million documents, studies, and databases, and adds about 1,300 titles each week. This Web server is extremely popular and has been accessed more than a half a million times.

From the home page, you have three main choices. First, you can go to the FedWorld FTP site that includes information on business, health, the environment, and the White House and National Performance Review. Second, you can link to the FedWorld Telnet site that has information about 50 different agencies—you can order publications and learn about federal job opportunities. Third, you can click an alphabetical index that can help you locate and then access specific federal WWW sites. Rather than displaying a long list of servers, the alphabetical section has subject categories, such as Environmental Resources. When you click a category, it opens a menu of servers that focus on that topic. This is a good starting point to jump into the U.S. Government.

SURAnet Network InfoCenter (FDIC banking information)
Web URL address: **gopher://fdic.sura.net:71/**

This Internet Gopher site provides Federal Deposit Insurance Corporation (FDIC) information. Here you'll find everything you want to know, but were afraid to ask, about the FDIC. Most people know that the FDIC is the government agency that insures our bank accounts for $100,000. But there is a lot more. Find out about FDIC assets for sale, read a survey of real estate trends, examine a quarterly banking profile, and discover statistics on the banking industry.

Congressional Legislation—THOMAS
URL address: **http://thomas.loc.gov**

At this site, you find full text of the House and Senate bills—search by keyword or bill number—and Gopher access to the House directory. Read interesting articles, such as "How Our Laws Are Made," which describes the process by which legislative proposals become law. Soon there will be a link to the full text of the Congressional record! There's also a form for sending mail to the U.S. Congress. C-SPAN, the cable network devoted to U.S. Government activities, has a link on this page with details about the program schedule.

University of Michigan Economic Bulletin Board
URL address: **gopher://una.hh.lib.umich.edu/11/ebb**
Telnet address: **ebb.stat-usa.gov** (log in as guest)

Bulletin board is an understatement. This site should be called a business and financial treasure chest (see fig. 14.8). You can, for example, find out about trade leads with companies in Armenia (a republic of the former Soviet Union) or check out the daily treasury report, which details the current cash and debt status of the U.S. Treasury (just so you know, the numbers are rounded off in millions).

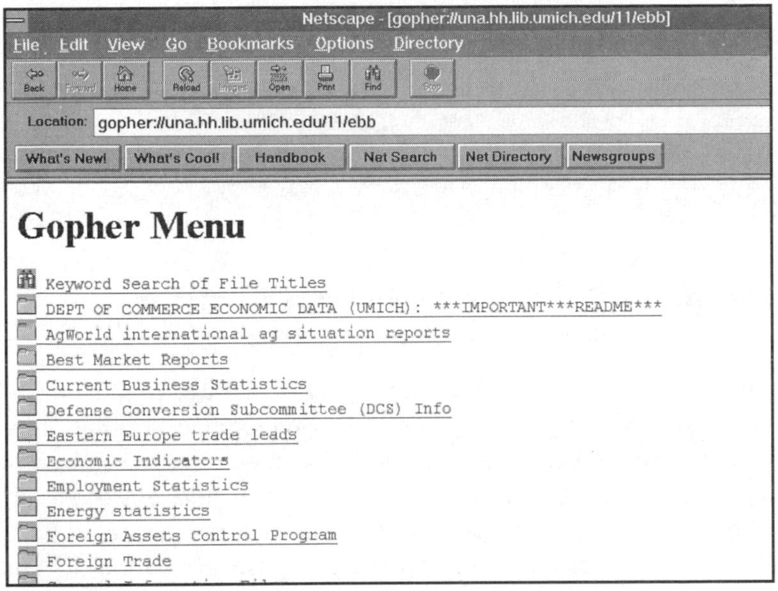

Fig. 14.8
The University of Michigan Economic Bulletin Board Gopher provides a wealth of information about economic trends in the U.S., as well as reports on foreign companies seeking trading partners.

The directories and file areas contain current economic and trade information, such as U.S. state-by-state export reports, regional economic and employment statistics, international agriculture and energy reports, and foreign trade information.

The site also provides access to U.S. Commerce Department's Economic Bulletin Board, which encompasses a set of more than 700 data files covering 19 areas related to the U.S. economy. The people managing this site update the information and data every day. There are economic indicators (such as the Gross Domestic Product and Consumer Price Index), fiscal and monetary data (like Treasury bill rates), and interest and foreign exchange rates.

If you don't see a Gopher menu selection that suits your needs, start with the first selection, labeled "Keyword Search of File Titles." This brings up a search screen in which you can enter keywords or search terms. General terms, such as "Japan," will fill the screen with titles (and files) while more specific terms, such as "Georgia economy," will find one or two documents.

Tip
If you want to jump straight to reports about the economic condition in U.S. states, try the address **gopher:// una.hh.lib. umich.edu/11/ ebb/employment**. Here you'll find information on the civilian labor force, unemployment statistics by state, nonagricultural payrolls by state, and household employment.

Note

Some of these files are *big*, and to accommodate their size they're stored in compressed format. Files labeled with extensions of EXE are either compressed versions of one very large file or multiple files that are combined. These compressed files are expanded into their original format by typing the name of the file (with or without

(continues)

(continued)

the EXE extension) at the MS-DOS prompt or double-clicking the file name in File Manager. For a list of files in the University of Michigan Department of Commerce Economic Data area that are available in compressed format, do a keyword search and enter **.exe** to retrieve a menu of these files.

Counterpoint Publishing's Federal Register

Gopher address: **gopher.counterpoint.com:2002**

Every business in the United States is directly affected by government regulations. And, every working day of the year, the Government Printing Office (GPO) publishes the Federal Register, a huge document that provides both industry and the general public with a set of current regulations and legal notices that are issued by federal agencies. Companies use information in the Federal Register to examine and comment on proposed regulations that may affect their company or industry. In one year, the Federal Register may encompass a quarter of a million pages. That's a lot of information, even for professional researchers, to sort through.

This site has both a "free" and a "subscription" side to it. If you subscribe to Counterpoint's Daily Federal Register, you get access to copy that is identical to that found in the printed version. You can search through the text and documents using a variety of Internet search tools and systems, including Gopher, WAIS, and Telnet. You can search both by search term and by agency.

There is no charge to access the entire Table of Contents of the daily Federal Register, an alphabetical listing of articles, the text from portions of the notices, and articles. Here is one citation that gives you a sense of the detail that's in this publication.

```
Citation: 60 FR 17662 (PROPOSED RULE)
Department: DEPARTMENT OF ENERGY
Agency: FEDERAL ENERGY REGULATORY COMMISSION
Title: Real-Time Information Networks; Notice of Technical Confer-
ence and Request for Comments
```

The Global Village: International Business on the Net

You know the Internet is a global communications system. It only makes sense that there are sites that offer searchable databases of business and financial information relating to countries around the world. Following are reviews of some of the most useful sites.

The World Bank
URL address: **http://www.worldbank.org**

If you need to find out what is going on in international finance or trends in the economies of specific countries, this is the Web server for you! The World Bank Group consists of the following:

- The International Bank for Reconstruction and Development (IBRD), the primary lending arm of the World Bank

- The International Development Association (IDA), the World Bank affiliate that lends funds on concessional terms to poor countries

- The International Finance Corporation (IFC), which finances private sector projects and advises businesses and governments on investment issues

- The Multilateral Investment Guarantee Agency (MIGA), which promotes foreign direct investment through guarantees, policy advice, and promotional services

You can jump from the home page to two areas that contain a wealth of information on the financial status, economic development projects, and social and environmental conditions in countries around the world. Some of the available information is found in books, articles, and documents (many of which are for sale) in the World Bank Publications section. A second area, the World Bank Public Information Center (PIC), maintains a variety of economic reports and environmental data sheets. You can view these reports online or download and print one copy.

Hong Kong Web Server
URL address: **http://www.hk.super.net/~rlowe/bizhk/
bhhome.html**

This server offers a wealth of information about doing business in Hong Kong, which, as many businesspeople know, is a leading manufacturing and financial center and a gateway to doing business with China. A link to BizHK provides a trade contacts service (see fig. 14.9). This home page matches Hong Kong businesses with potential trading partners worldwide. More information is available by sending e-mail to **rlowe@hk.super.net**.

Through this server, you can access a database of more than 1,000 companies in Hong Kong. You can click alphabetically through the database and find company contacts, financial data, product information, addresses, and phone numbers. Special sections focus on two major areas for business opportunities: the Hotel, Tourism, and Travel industry and Textiles, Fabrics, and Clothing. The home page also has links to economic statistics that relate to Hong Kong and press releases about business trade, such as an overview of the imports and exports between Hong Kong and the United Kingdom.

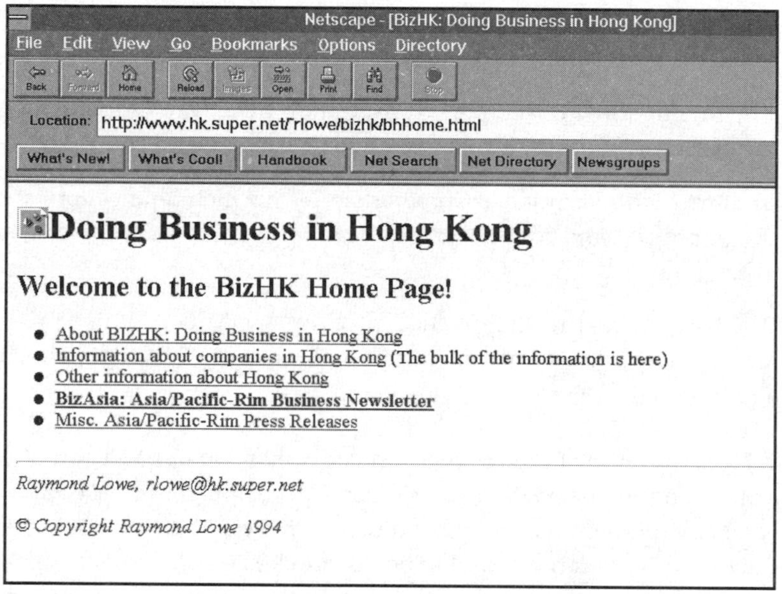

Fig. 14.9
The BizHK Web site focuses on business in Hong Kong and offers a database of hundreds of companies, including contact names, addresses, and phone and fax numbers.

European Commission Host Organization (European Databases)

URL address: **http://www.uni-frankfurt.de/~felix/echo.html**
Telnet: **echo.lu**

ECHO (the European Commission Host Organization) is a non-commercial organization established in 1980 to encourage the development of information services and online databases in the European Community (EC). So, if you want to tap into information that has a European slant, this is the place. The previously listed Web site address has information about ECHO. If you want to access the service, you need to Telnet.

ECHO is partially a demonstration site that highlights the benefits of electronic information services for business by making databases available in a variety of EC languages. In fact, from the main menu (Telnet), you can select from English, German, French, Italian, Portuguese, and a few other languages.

ECHO databases cover four areas: user guidance, community research and development, market and business opportunities, and the languages. You can, for example, access the I'M-GUIDE, which is a directory of electronic information services available in Europe. Another database, the Information Market Forum, provides a directory of people and companies that have expertise in information services. ECHO also provides a gateway for contact with individuals involved in exhibitions, conferences, and seminars.

Newsgroups Offer Business Insight and Information

Newsgroups can be a terrific source for timely business information. Because people from all over the globe participate in these electronic chain letters, you'll find interesting advice, opinions, and news about companies and financial dealings that occur everywhere. You can also read late-breaking news and wire service stories.

Get the News from ClariNet

You'll never have to worry about missing the morning paper once you try these newsgroups. ClariNet (see fig. 14.10) is a commercial firm that acquires news stories (known as news feeds) from international news sources like Reuters and the Associated Press wire services—the same services that provide news information to newspapers. ClariNet then sorts and converts these stories into a variety of newsgroup categories (which are amazingly similar to the sections in the daily newspaper) and sends them out as newsgroup articles.

You can read these stories, which often present late-breaking news faster than you can get from television or radio, by subscribing to one of the ClariNet newsgroups (assuming your service provider offers these). For the top news stories of the day, you should check out **clari.news.urgent**, **clari.world. top**, and **clari.news.briefs**. Here's a brief overview of a few more clari newsgroups that focus on business topics:

clari.nb.business

This newsgroup offers international business news stories, with headlines such as "Dell UK Splits Into Two Divisions" and "Germany—Siemens' 4-Pronged Business Plan."

clari.world.americas.canada.business

This newsgroup has lots of stories and information about business events in Canada.

clari.apbl.stocks

This newsgroup contains stock news related to the Dow Jones and Wall Street. You'll find out whether the Dow average rose, whether advancing issues edged out decliners, how many shares have traded at any given hour, and information on several stock market indexes.

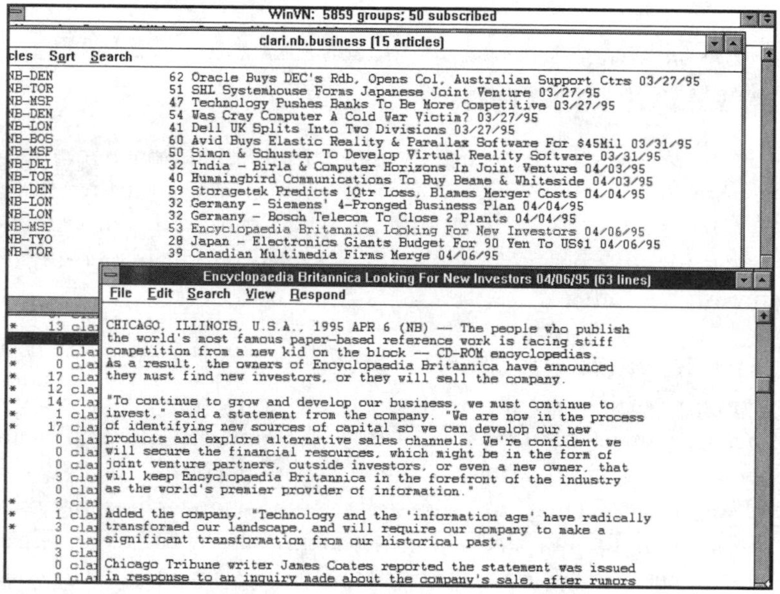

Fig. 14.10
There are several newsgroups that offer timely business and financial information. The ClariNet groups have stories that come directly from wire services.

Other Business Newsgroups

There are several alt.business newsgroups including **alt.business.import-export**, **alt.business.internal-audit**, and **alt.business.misc**. These are mostly person-to-person comments and thoughts related to various aspects of business. There are also several miscellaneous newsgroups that relate to business, such as **misc.invest.stocks**, that include postings on what the stock market is doing and notes on individual stocks.

Mailing Lists That Focus on Business

In addition to the newsgroups, there are mailing lists that concentrate on business information. Here are a few that offer messages related to your financial portfolio. They might even open doors to international trade.

Futures Market

Contact address: **sub.futures@stoicbbs.com**

This is a mailing list for discussion of futures and commodity trading.

To subscribe: Send e-mail to **sub.futures@stoicbbs.com** and use **Subscribe Futures <your e-mail address> <your full name>** as the body of your message. You'll receive acknowledgment of subscription and information about how to participate.

International Trade

Contact address: **info--request@tradent.wimsey.bc.ca**

Business is a global topic. This mailing list posts messages that discuss international trade, overviews of global companies, and tips on successful investing.

Stock Market

Contact address: **sm--request@world.std.com**

This is a daily mail message that provides a review of activity on the Stock Market. Also, the moderators answer questions on topics related to financial investment.

Summary

You don't have to be a Wall Street stockbroker to take advantage of the Internet resources in this chapter. Indeed, one of the great aspects of the Internet is that it levels the playing field for business and financial information. Now, using your PC, modem, and Internet connection, you can access the same information, business reports, real-time stock quotes, financial newsletters, and press releases that a few years ago had been available only to company executives and financial analysts. So whether you require a toll-free number for a company that sells portable computers, want to know if the stock in your IRA is going in the right direction, or need to find a trading partner overseas, you can use the Internet to search for and locate relevant information.

Chapter 15

Educational Information

Some of the earliest applications of the Internet were for education. In fact, universities were connected to the Internet almost from its inception. Today, the Internet links together thousands of universities, K-12 schools, and laboratories, as well as millions of faculty, instructors, and students. Educators and students from all parts of the globe use the Internet to share and search for information. With a little help, it's possible to obtain information about any conceivable topic and increase and enrich the learning experience for both the teacher and student.

In this chapter, you will learn:

- ■ Where to find applications, services, and resources for teachers

- ■ Where to find applications, services, and resources for students

- ■ How to locate educational resources and where to go for more information

Applications for Educational Information

So, what is the Internet anyway and how can it affect or enhance the learning environment in the classroom? How might a large computer network help kids and students learn? How can students be encouraged to use computers?

These types of questions are often on the forefront of the educators' minds when confronted with the possibilities of the Internet in education or the classroom. When confronted with these types of questions, it's important to understand what the Internet offers and how it helps the education process. Let's review some of the benefits to Internet access in the classroom.

First and foremost, Internet resources help to increase classroom resources. Because the Internet is connected to thousands of organizations, schools, libraries, laboratories, and facilities, you can use the Internet to make use of these resources remotely without leaving the classroom. These shared Internet resources significantly increase the amount of information available for all students with Internet access.

Second, more information, data, images, and software is available through the Internet than any other educational resource. Original source materials from government agencies, libraries, and research centers are available for the asking. These materials can help with classroom projects, collaborative efforts, curriculum materials, and idea sharing that would not be possible otherwise.

Third, Internet access significantly increases outside contact with experts, scientists, educators, and other students. Students can use others located on the Internet to enhance the learning environment of the classroom, just as your students will enhance the learning environment for others. Just consider your students contributing their ideas in NASA experiments. The NASA scientists are rewarded with new approaches, questions, and ideas from your students, while your students learn from communicating with the scientists.

Fourth, the Internet can help to break down educator isolation. By having access to similar educators and experts from around the world, you have an opportunity to discuss and obtain feedback from others. For example, a school librarian could discuss the benefits of CD-ROM libraries with other librarians on the Internet.

Fifth, because the Internet is truly worldwide, students are encouraged to improve their geography skills as they attempt to discover where new friends and resources are located. People from all 50 U.S. states, over 60 nations, and all continents are represented on the Internet. From Israel, Russia, England, Canada, Brazil, Japan, India, and more, students will be encouraged to learn more about the lands they touch through the Internet.

Sixth, using the Internet improves computer skills. This environment provides an excellent way for students and educators alike to become familiar and proficient in computer use for research, education, and recreation.

Finally, because there are so many different nationalities represented on the Internet, using the Internet to communicate with others will improve language and communication skills. People in different regions use words differently to describe themselves and their environments. Opening the doors for students to communicate with new people improves the way students communicate and express themselves. Unlike passively watching television, the Internet requires the student to interactively communicate with others. Such interaction with others helps students to improve their own communication skills as they learn from others.

Teacher Information (Curriculum, Resources, and Other Contacts)

As mentioned in the previous section, the Internet's tremendous resources can help you improve the educational experience of your classroom by breaking down isolation barriers. You can use the Internet to tap into the ideas and advice of other educators and experts to help you with curriculum and resource management. Additionally, the Internet provides the mechanisms to reach other contacts and establish a peer network.

World Wide Web Services for Educators

There are quite a few services on the Internet that help educators teach students by providing information, lessons, and services to enhance education. Some of the resources indicated in this section help you, as the educator, use the Internet as a teaching aid or make a case for Internet access at your institution.

MathMagic
URL address: **http://forum.swarthmore.edu/mathmagic/**

MathMagic is a telecommunications project designed to motivate students to improve their math skills while using the computer to enhance their problem-solving strategies and communications skills. This program is divided into four K-12 student categories. Students form teams and pair up with another team to engage in problem-solving dialog.

All that is needed to participate in this program is e-mail, because it operates through a mailing discussion list. They have a great Web site, as shown in figure 15.1, that explains all the details of this program. You can call (915) 533-2902 or send e-mail to **alanh@laguna.epcc.edu**.

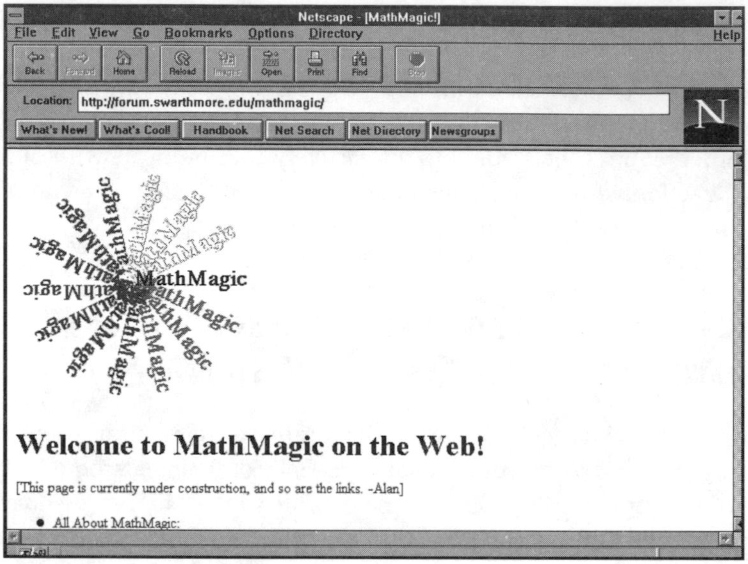

Fig. 15.1
MathMagic is a great example of how to use the Internet as a device to improve the quality of education. Math, computer, and communications skills are all used in this educational exercise.

Getting Internet into the School—A FAQ
URL address: **http://chs.cusd.claremont.edu/www/people/rmuir/rfc1578.html**

This FAQ, or Frequently Asked Questions, provides answers to commonly asked "Primary and Secondary School Internet User" questions. It is geared toward the educator considering enhancing the educational experience by incorporating the Internet in the classroom experience.

This FAQ addresses everything including what the Internet is, how educators can incorporate this resource into their busy schedules, and where schools get the money for connecting to the Internet. Without a doubt, this is a must-read for educators.

The NASA K-12 Internet Initiative
URL address: **http://quest.arc.nasa.gov/index.html**

The NASA K-12 Internet Initiative is devoted to providing support and services for students and teachers to fully utilize the Internet. They have provided information for educational grants (currently under review as the Republicans have their way in Congress) as well as programs that put students in touch with NASA scientists, engineers, and researchers. In particular, they have a very interesting Online Interactive Projects program.

Figure 15.2 shows the initial Web home page for the NASA K-12 Internet Initiative.

Fig. 15.2
The NASA K-12
Internet Initiative
helps students and
teachers fully
utilize the Internet
with special
support and
educational
programs.

IV

Commercial & Educational

The U.S. Department of Education

URL address: **http://www.ed.gov/**
Gopher address: **gopher://gopher.ed.gov/**

The U.S. Department of Education provides quite a bit of resource and information on the Internet through their Gopher and Web sites. In particular,
you can find department-wide initiatives, educational research, statistics,
press releases, announcements, bulletins, and even educational software.

In figure 15.3, you can see the initial home page of their Web server. The
U.S. Department of Education has two guides of interest to educators: the
Teacher's Guide to the U.S. Department of Education and the Researcher's
Guide to the U.S. Department of Education. These guides compile and cen-
tralize important departmental information for researchers and teachers to
improve their access to programs, services, and publications.

The Teacher's Guide to the U.S. Department of Education is located at **http:
//www.ed.gov/pubs/TeachersGuide/index.html**. The Researcher's
Guide to the U.S. Department of Education is located at **http://
www.ed.gov/pubs/ResearchersGuide/index.html**.

Fig. 15.3
The U.S. Department of Education Web Server provides separate department resource guides for students and educators.

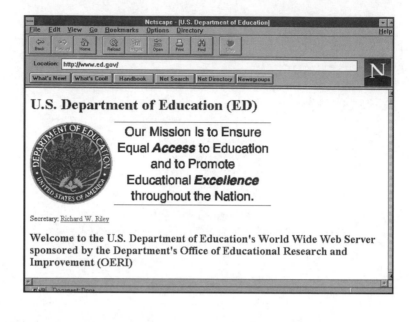

Explorer
URL address: **http://unite2.tisl.ukans.edu/**

The Explorer database was jointly created by the Great Lakes Collaborative and the University of Kansas UNITE group to engage educators and students in creating and using multimedia resources for active learning and "on time" delivery.

This site is devoted to mathematics and natural science curriculums, using multimedia as a learning and presentation platform. Software, documentation, and course outlines for pre-K to adult level education are available. The mathematics and natural science folders, in particular, contain an impressive number of unique lessons. Figure 15.4 shows what the opening screen for Explorer looks like.

EdWeb
URL address: **http://k12.cnidr.org:90/**

EdWeb is advertised as a hyperbook that is addressed to educators interested in educational computing and networking, as shown in figure 15.5. This site maintains articles, resource indexes, and discussions about the trends in education reform and the Internet.

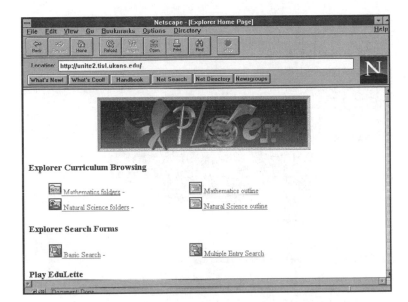

Fig. 15.4
Explorer provides access to an impressive collection of curriculum ideas, lessons, and outlines for mathematics and natural science.

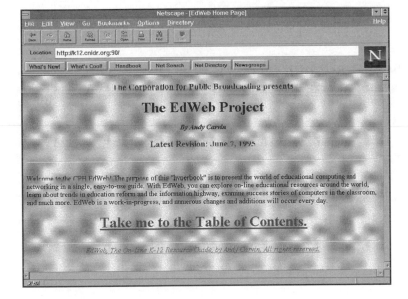

Fig. 15.5
EdWeb is a great reference for educators looking for online educational references, trends in educational reform, and examples of online projects.

Cisco Educational Archive and Resources Catalog
URL address: **http://sunsite.unc.edu/cisco/**

Figure 15.6 shows the Cisco Educational Archive, which is meant to be a one-stop location for educators, with a resource searching capability that can bring you instantly to hundreds of educational sites. Furthermore, it provides access to the Virtual Schoolhouse, which provides reference pointers to schools, libraries, museums, exhibits, teaching resources, and more.

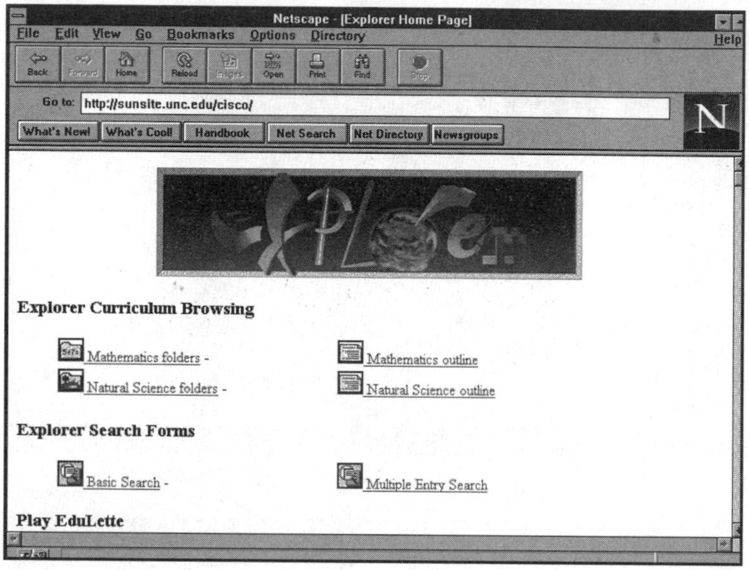

Fig. 15.6
The Cisco Educational Archive's CEARCH engine provides a very fast way to search for educational materials, information, and services on the Internet.

Educator Mailing and Discussion Lists

Tip
When using CEARCH to look for educational information, remember to broaden your search if you don't find what you are looking for.

As mentioned in the Educator's Guide Series section that follows, the Internet provides access to your peers through mailing and discussion lists. These lists give you the ability to communicate with others, like yourself, who are concerned with educating groups of students. You can use these lists as focal points to discuss ideas and obtain advice or comments about the learning process.

Interestingly, there are an overwhelming number of educator discussion lists on the Internet. Only a few are discussed here to give you a feel for what's available.

American Sign Language

ASLING-L is the American Sign Language Discussion List. A great list for educators of deaf students, deaf students, or others interested in learning more about sign language. To subscribe, send the message **subscribe ASLING-L Your Name** to **listserv@yalevm.bitnet**.

Once you have subscribed, you can participate by sending messages to **ASLING-L@yalevm.bitnet**.

BEHAVIOR

The BEHAVIOR Discussion List was created to discuss behavioral and emotional disorders in children. To subscribe, send the message **subscribe behavior Your Name** to **listserv@asuacad.bitnet**.

Once you have subscribed, you may participate by sending messages to **behavior@asuacad.bitnet**.

Consortium for School Networking

The Consortium for School Networking Discussion List (COSNDISC) was created to help educators discuss and learn about methods for networking educational institutions. To subscribe, send the message **subscribe cosndisc Your Name** to **listproc@yukon.cren.org**.

You can post to COSNDISC by sending your messages to **cosndisc@yukon. cren.org** after you have subscribed.

EDNET

The EDNET Discussion List is devoted to K-12 to university educators exploring the Internet. To subscribe, send the message **subscribe ednet Your Name** to **listserv@nic.umass.edu**.

You can post to EDNET, after you have subscribed, by sending your message to **<ednet@nic.umass.edu>**.

Intercultural E-Mail Classroom Connections

The Intercultural E-Mail Classroom Connections Discussion List (IECC) was created to help educators find partner classrooms for international and cross-cultural e-mail exchange. Rather than a discussion list seeking pen pals, it is devoted to seeking classroom partners. You can subscribe by sending the message **subscribe** to **iecc-request@stolaf.edu**.

Once subscribed, you can send your messages to **iecc@stolaf.edu** to participate in discussions.

> ### Note
>
> If you are interested in Intercultural E-Mail Classroom Connections, you should make an effort to take a look at their Web home page. This home page has information and supplemental references to the IECC discussion list, as well as a suite of other discussion lists. Additionally, you can browse archives of many of the IECC discussion lists.
>
> The IECC Web homepage is shown in figure 15.7, and located at **http://www.stolaf.edu/network/iecc/**.

Fig. 15.7
The Intercultural E-Mail Classroom Connections Web home page provides a resource for educators to find educational partners to enhance cultural exchange among their students.

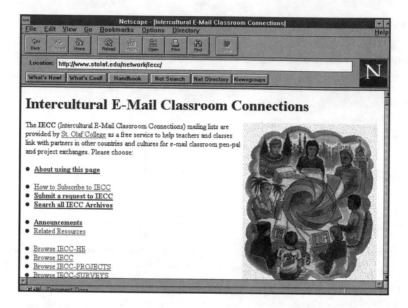

K12ADMIN

K12ADMIN is a discussion list for K-12 educators interested in educational administration. To subscribe, send the message **subscribe k12admin Your Name** to **listserv@suvm.syr.edu**.

You can participate, after you have subscribed, by sending your messages to **k12admin@suvm.syr.edu**.

Library & Media NET

LM_NET is a discussion list for school library and media specialists around the world. To subscribe, send the message **subscribe LM_NET Your Name** to **listserv@suvm.syr.edu**.

After you have subscribed, you may participate in the discussions by sending your messages to **LM_NET@suvm.syr.edu**.

NEWEDU-L

NEWEDU-L is a discussion list exploring the way educators and society educates. To subscribe, send the message **subscribe NEWEDU-L Your Name** to **listserv@uscvm.bitnet**.

After you have subscribed, you can participate by sending your messages to **NEWEDU-L@uscvm.bitnet**.

PENPALS-L

The PENPALS-L Discussion List is designed to help people seek and find e-mail pen pals. You can subscribe by sending the message **subscribe penpal-l Your Name** to **listserv@unccvm.bitnet**.

You post to PENPALS-L by sending messages to **penpals-l@unccvm.bitnet** after you have subscribed.

While I have only covered a few of nearly one thousand mailing lists, I believe you have an idea of the possibilities. Keep in mind that I have only provided a few grains of sand from a very sandy beach. There is much more out there.

Note

Have you noticed a pattern in how to use mailing lists? Almost all mailing lists are controlled by a "listserv," "listproc," or "something-request" address. You have to subscribe to a list before you can participate. Then, once you have subscribed, you send e-mail to the name of the list, not the "listserv," "listproc," or "something-request" address.

That is, every mailing list has two important addresses: the listserver address and the mailing list address. The listserver address is used for commands such as *subscribe*, *unsubscribe*, and *index*. The mailing address is used to send e-mail to other subscribers of the mailing list.

Student Information (Help with Projects, Peer Networking)

There is quite a bit of effort on the Internet to facilitate the classroom experience by providing students with the tools necessary to communicate with other students, enhance the classroom experience, and enjoy information not easily made available in the classroom, local libraries, or museums. The Internet provides a wonderful experience for students who are interested in many educational topics, such as science, politics, literature, and foreign lands.

The resources listed here can help students on their journey of discovery.

Kids Web

URL address: **http://www.npac.syr.edu:80/textbook/kidsweb/**

Kids Web is a World Wide Web digital library for school kids. It is intended to be a one-stop shop for school children using the worldwide resources of the Internet. This site groups topics into several main categories, including the Arts, Sciences, Social Studies, and Miscellaneous (which includes Fun and Games, Reference Material, and Sports). Figure 15.8 shows the Web home page for Kids Web.

Fig. 15.8
Kids Web is a digital reference library for schoolkids. It is geared toward young school children just beginning their discovery of the Internet.

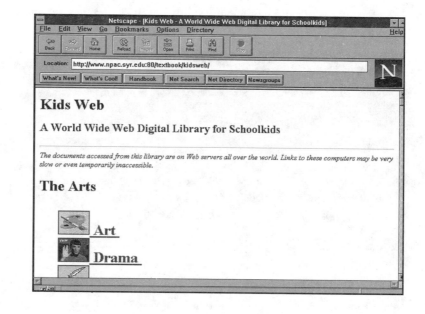

DeweyWeb—School of Education

URL address: **http://ics.soe.umich.edu/**

Figure 15.9 shows the DeweyWeb Web Server, an experiment using the Web as a means to provide educational materials to students, as well as facilitate communication between students from all over the world. That is, DeweyWeb serves students information, as well as provides an opportunity to contribute their own observations and findings.

For example, The Journey North is an interesting project accessible from DeweyWeb. The Journey North serves as a great example of how the Internet can be used by students to contribute to each other's learning experience.

This project is made up of different themes such as the environment, wildlife migration, different cultures, and more. The project incorporates maps of various scientific expeditions where students can click to learn more about specific regions and contribute to the project by sending what they know of certain regions. While students share observations on wildlife migration with each other, they also receive reports from actual explorers on their training trips.

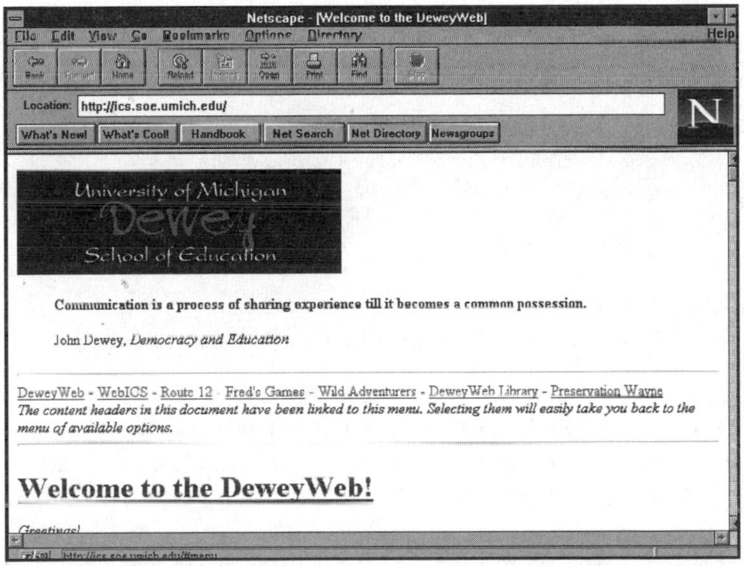

Fig. 15.9
The DeweyWeb School of Education provides a forum for students to learn, as well as contribute, based on their own experiences, findings, and observations.

The DeweyWeb Library
URL address: **http://www.umich.edu/~jmillr/WWW-libraries.html**

This is a list of many access points for Web access around the world, compiled with an eye toward addressing various classroom goals. It is a springboard to some very interesting resources, including more meta indexes for more educational information.

> ## Note
>
> Many Internet resources may contain information related to what you are looking for, but may not necessarily have exactly what you need. To help you find exactly what you are looking for, you might want to use a **meta index**.
>
> A meta index is a large collection of particular resources. For instance, the DeweyWeb Library is devoted to educational resources and material. They may not have, however, specific information concerning nuclear engineering. You could use a meta index located at the DeweyWeb Library to help you find something on nuclear engineering either by a specific reference or reference to another meta index specializing in education or engineering.
>
> In this way, meta indexes can help students or educators reach very particular sources of information. When someone talks of surfing the Internet for a specific resource, meta indexes help make surfing quicker, easier, and more successful.

The HotList of K-12 Internet School Sites—USA
URL address: **http://toons.cc.ndsu.nodak.edu/~sackmann/k12.html**

This list provides a simple but effective way to travel to K-12 schools in the United States. As shown in figure 15.10, this makes it easy for students to travel to other regions of the United States to access elementary, middle/junior, and high schools.

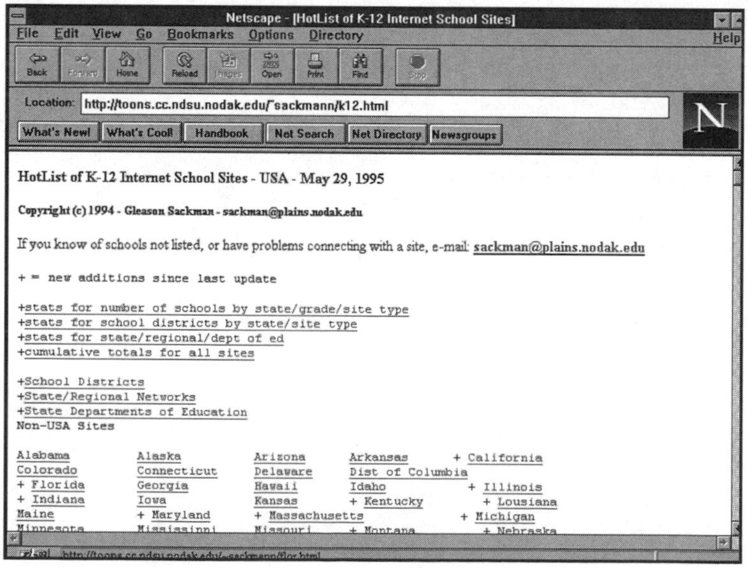

Fig. 15.10
The HotList of K-12 Internet School Sites presents a simple Web interface to help students reach other schools on the Internet. Consider this HotList a meta index to other K-12 schools.

Current Weather Maps & Movies
URL address: **http://rs560.cl.msu.edu/weather/**

Current Weather Maps & Movies, shown in figure 15.11, is sponsored by the UNIX Computing Group at Michigan State University. It serves as an excellent example of the wide range of resources available on the Internet that are not available to students elsewhere.

For instance, this resource contains up-to-date weather maps of the United States, Europe, Africa, Antarctica, and the entire world. Additionally, it boasts an Interactive Weather Browser, where you can point-and-click on a map of the United States to obtain the current weather for any particular region of the country.

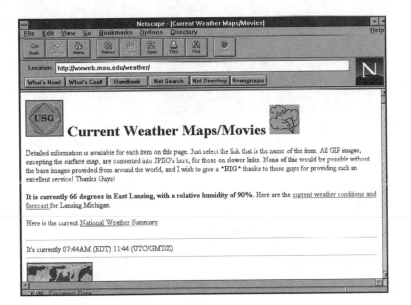

Fig. 15.11
Current Weather Maps & Movies contains some fascinating and up-to-date weather information for the United States and abroad.

This location can be used for schoolchildren and students of all ages to learn more about world and local weather. This site contains maps and movies of weather patterns and predictions from around the world.

The JASON Project
URL address: **http://seawifs.gsfc.nasa.gov/scripts/JASON.html**

The JASON Project was founded by Dr. Robert D. Ballard in 1989, after receiving thousands of letters from children wanting to know how he discovered the RMS Titanic. Each year, a two-week scientific journey is mounted in some remote part of the world, where a real-time broadcast occurs to a network of educational, research, and cultural institutions around the world.

This Web site, as shown in figure 15.12, has information about the project, as well as online interactive lessons and tours for children. For example, 1995's expedition was entitled JASON VI: Island Earth, which took students on a voyage to Hawaii's volcanoes, observatories, and unique environments. On their Web site, students can tour some of this landscape as well as learn about volcanoes on Io and other scientific information and facts that are related to the project's expeditions.

Fig. 15.12
The JASON Project is an excellent opportunity for students to explore remote regions of the world from the comfort of their classrooms.

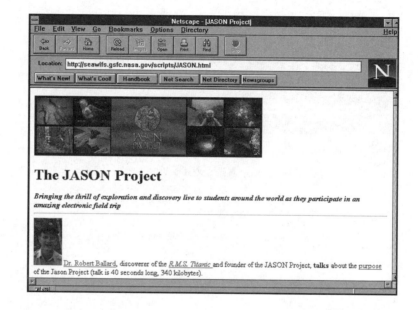

The Exploratorium
URL address: **http://www.exploratorium.edu/**

The Exploratorium is located at the Palace of Fine Arts in San Francisco, California. This site is a fine example of how the Internet allows students to tour a museum without ever leaving the classroom. It is a museum of science, art, and human perception with over 650 interactive "hands-on" exhibits, and has placed some interesting material on the Internet available for your access. Figure 15.13 shows the initial Web home page for the Exploratorium.

For example, the Exploratorium sponsors The Learning Studio, where special exhibits are available from the Web. This exhibit displays perceptual experiments, optical illusions, and communications training. Many of the exhibits consist of not only graphic pictures of the experiment, but descriptions of the principle behind the experiment.

Fig. 15.13
The Exploratorium by the Palace of Fine Arts in San Francisco offers over 650 interactive hands-on exhibits.

Specific Educational Sites and Services

In addition to the resources we've reviewed, there are a few specific ones that you should be aware of. The following educational resources are making significant headway to education reform by using Internet technology to enhance the learning environment.

AskERIC
URL address: **http://ericir.syr.edu/Main.html**
Gopher address: **gopher://ericir.syr.edu/**

AskERIC, or Educational Resource Information Clearinghouse, is the premiere starting place for educators, providing an extensive collection of K-12 education-related material. This resource contains resource guides, curriculum information, lesson plans, educational bibliographic databases, and educational mailing list archives. Their Web server is depicted in figure 15.14.

In addition to the wealth of information available at AskERIC, it is an "Internet-based question-answering service for teachers, library media specialists, administrators, and others involved in education. The hallmark of AskERIC is the human intermediary, who interacts with the information seeker and personally selects and delivers information resources within 48 working hours." This means you can contact educators on the Internet who will help you find the resources you seek on AskERIC or other resources located on the Internet.

Fig. 15.14
AskERIC contains a wealth of information for educators, including online lesson plans and resource guides.

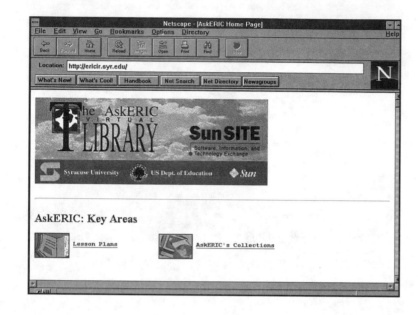

Anyone involved with education can send an e-mail inquiry (via the Internet) to AskERIC. Simply address your message to **askeric@ ericir.syr.edu**.

Academy One

URL address: **http://www.nptn.org/cyber.serv/AOneP/**
E-mail address: **info@nptn.org**

Academy One is a K-12 educational resource for students, educators, and parents. It is a great starting place for informational and educational Internet resources, as well as a host to some very good programs, including the National Education Simulations Project Using Telecommunications (NESPUT), an international activity in which real-life activities are simulated via telecommunications for educational purposes.

Figure 15.15 shows the Web home page for Academy One. While this site has many resources available for anyone on the Internet, some of the resources cannot be accessed by non-affiliate organizations, such as access to online databases. You must send e-mail to the e-mail address to inquire how to make your organization an Academy One affiliate, so your users may access some of the material located here. You may also call (216) 247-5800 for more information.

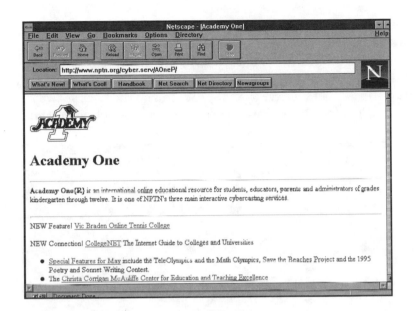

IV

Commercial & Educational

Fig. 15.15
Academy One highlights interactive services and resources for K-12 educators and students alike. It is a great springboard to other educational materials and references on the Internet.

Web 66: A K12 World Wide Web Project
URL address: **http://web66.coled.umn.edu/**

Figure 15.16 shows Web 66, which is based on the tradition of Route 66. This is a K-12 World Wide Web project that aims to help K-12 educators learn how to set up their own Internet servers, link K-12 Web servers and the educators and students at those schools, and to help K-12 educators find and use K-12 appropriate resources on the Web.

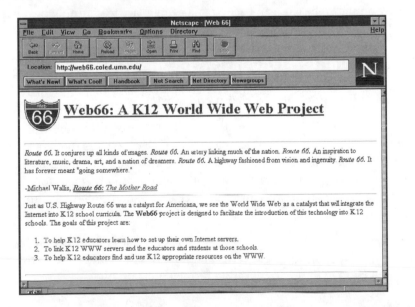

Fig. 15.16
Web 66, or Route 66, is attempting to map out the Internet for educators and their students, as well as provide technical expertise and support to bring your institution online.

With these aims in mind, you can find quite a bit of information that explains how to set up educational institutions on the Internet, Web pages you can borrow to configure your own Web server, Internet resources of interest to K-12 educators and students, and other information. While you are there, be sure to check out the Registry of K-12 Schools on the Web, shown in figure 15.17 and located at **http://web66.coled.umn.edu/schools.html**.

Fig. 15.17
The Registry of K-12 Schools on the Web contains a very comprehensive list of K-12 schools from around the world. It has a map-drive interface that kids can use to go to Web sites at locations that interest them.

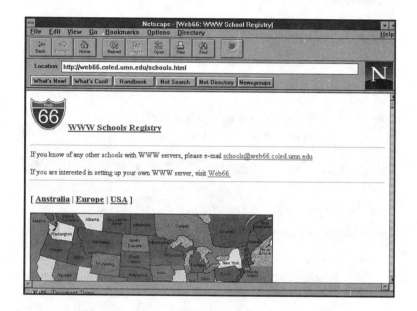

Use this Web Registry of K-12 Schools as a springboard to other K-12 schools already on the Web. This can be a great starting place for forming peer networks for students to send e-mail to other students.

Consortium for School Networking (CoSN)

URL address: **http://www.cosn.org/**
Gopher address: **gopher://digitial.cosn.org**

The Consortium for School Networking, or CoSN, advocates educational institution access to the Internet, and has a range of services that are aimed at improving education through networking technologies. In particular, CoSN provides lobbying services, networking information, mailing lists for educators and educational networking specialists, and resource references to other educational material.

CoSN can be reached at (202) 466-6269 or send e-mail to **membership@cosn.org** to learn more about CoSN and how you can contribute to their lobbying effort to improve education through networking.

NASA: Using The Web As An Educational Tool

URL address: **http://mosaic.larc.nasa.gov/nasaonline/
nasaonline.html**

NASA plays a rather large role in educational use of the Internet. Unlike the
prior two references to NASA sites within this chapter, this particular site is
devoted to making the most of the Internet in the classroom. Once an educational institution is linked, this resource can be used as a tool for students to
learn more about space, science, and engineering. The folks at NASA have
worked hard at making a resource children would find interesting and full of
amazing wonders; and NASA's efforts have seem to have paid off.

Many educators, in addition to using the Internet as a peer network for themselves and their students, see the Internet as an educational tool for their
students. For example, without even leaving the classrooms, students can
discover wonders that will excite and stimulate their minds. Figure 15.18 is
an example of the wonders that await students on the Internet. This figure
was obtained from the Web URL **http://stardust.jpl.nasa.gov/planets/**,
at NASA's Jet Propulsion Laboratory:

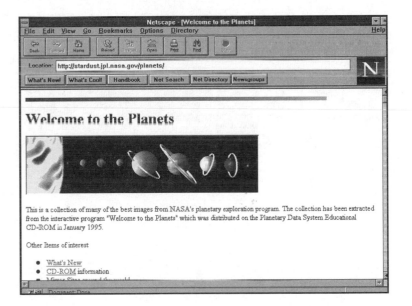

Fig. 15.18
The Planets home
page by NASA's
Jet Propulsion
Laboratory has a
wealth of informa-
tion about the
planets of our solar
system and the
unmanned space
probes.

NASA has a wealth of information that students can access to learn more
about the U.S. Space Program, the Solar System, and science in general.
Without having to participate in a lengthy and costly field trip, students can
access quite a bit of government, science, health, medicine, and literature
information on the Internet. NASA happens to have some of the most

spectacular information available on the Internet, including Hubble Telescope and Space Shuttle pictures.

Meta Educational Resources

While these resources are not necessarily produced or maintained by educators, they are great places to reach information or resources of interest to teachers, students, and parents. In particular, they will help you reach other educators' resources not listed in this chapter, as well as help you reach the latest and greatest information.

These guides also make a great starting point for just about any search, aside from education.

The Web Virtual Library for Education
URL address: **http://www.csu.edu.au/education/library.html**

The World Wide Web Virtual Library contains many topical indexes to help people reach Web resources on the Internet. One of those topical indexes is devoted to education, shown in figure 15.19. This list breaks down resources into various categories, such as books, journals, software, education clearinghouses, regional educational authorities, and institutions.

Fig. 15.19
The World Wide Web Virtual Library has a special index for educational resources. While not as comprehensive as some of the other educational meta indexes, this list is sure to help you reach your destination.

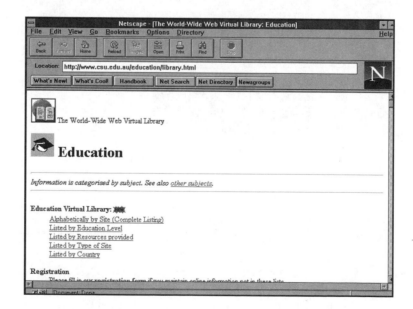

The Educator's Guide Series

The Educator's Guides were created by Prescott Smith, Univ. of Mass. at Amherst, and are two comprehensive guides for UseNet and mailing list discussion areas. They can help you identify certain discussion areas that are key to your area of interest or education level.

The Educator's Guide to Mailing Lists can be found at **ftp://nic.umass.edu /pub/ednet/educatrs.lst**. The Educator's Guide to UseNet Groups can be found at **ftp://nic.umass.edu/pub/ednet/edusenet.gde**.

Sites of Interest to Educators

Judi Harris, University of Nebraska at Omaha, and a team of 24 eastern Nebraska teachers and 41 teachers and trainers from Texas who were enrolled in graduate Internet-based telecomputing courses during the spring 1992, spring 1993, and summer 1993 semesters at the University of Nebraska at Omaha and the University of Texas at Austin, built a rather impressive list of resources of interest to educators.

This resource is listed as The Internet Resource Directory and split into four pieces: LISTSERVs, Telnets, ftp, and an infusion of ideas with Internet technology and applications.

- Part 1: LISTSERV Discussion Groups of Interest to Educators

  URL address: **gopher://una.hh.lib.umich.edu:70/00/ inetdirsstacks/education%3Aharris1**

  This part contains hundreds of mailing lists of interest to educators, with information on each list and how to subscribe.

- Part 2: Telnet Sites of Interest to Educators

  URL address: **gopher://una.hh.lib.umich.edu:70/00/ inetdirsstacks/education%3Aharris2**

  This part contains Telnet and Gopher references with explicit instructions on how to reach particular areas of interest.

- Part 3: File Archives (FTP Sites) of Interest to Educators

  URL address: **gopher://una.hh.lib.umich.edu:70/00/ inetdirsstacks/education%3Aharris3**

  This part will put you in touch with the enormous archives available on the Internet. Everything from programs of interest to educators to mailing list archives are discussed.

■ Part 4: Educational Telecomputing Application/Infusion Ideas

URL address: **gopher://una.hh.lib.umich.edu:70/00/ inetdirsstacks/education%3Aharris4**

This final part discusses some of the possibilities and potential with using the Internet as an educators tool. There are links and references to various education projects, current activities, and examples. It makes a great reference for the educator trying to convince a school board to fund Internet access into the school.

Online Educational Resources

URL address: **http://www.nas.nasa.gov/HPCC/K12/edures.html**

Online Educational Resources has produced a wonderful reference to online information for educators and students. There is something for everyone here, such as information for K-12 schools, undergraduate- and graduate-level education, online libraries and other reference materials. Figure 15.20 shows the initial Web home page for this resource.

Fig. 15.20
The Online Educational Resources represents yet another reference to many resources for educators and students alike.

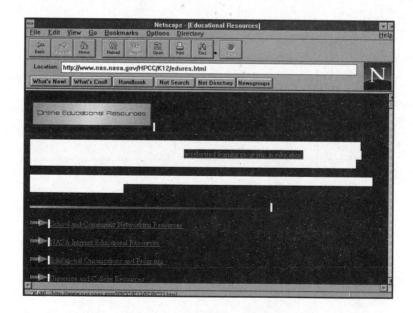

Summary

In this chapter, you have learned about some of the more important educational aspects of the Internet. In particular, you should have a good grasp of where and how to find teacher- and student-level applications, services, and resources. Additionally, you should know where to go for more information about educational topics and resources.

Finally and most importantly, you should have a broader understanding of informational services available on the Internet and how to coordinate these services to enrich the educational experience.

Chapter 16

Future Trends

This book details a wide range of techniques and facilities designed to help you locate and obtain information. Some of the changes we're seeing today are indications of the rapid evolution of the population, capacity, and capability of the myriad of networks that make up what we currently know as the Internet. While most of the material this book covers relates to searching for text or file descriptions, the next wave of resources on the Internet will be a massive amount of interactive multimedia and searching for resources will become much more challenging. The challenge will ultimately be answered by the introduction of more powerful hardware and communications in conjunction with more dynamic search tools, but for the time being we will have to rely on enhancements to the existing text searching facilities.

Currently, the total rate of growth of information available in only a few days on the Internet is more than any one individual could absorb in an entire year. The increased use of high-speed fiber backbones and rapid connections to individual users on the net will dramatically increase the use of high resolution graphics, sound, and multimedia in general. This means that the demand for more sophisticated search tools, specialized data filters, and intelligent information gathering agents will be of paramount importance.

Consider searching a graphical database using the pattern of an object in a picture such as a vase, a building, or someone's face. How about asking your computer to search voice and speech libraries looking for a specific phrase that you input by talking into a microphone. These may sound a little bit like science fiction, but for a price, the technology already exists to do this and it is only a matter of time before the cost of that technology is driven down enough so that the average consumer can afford it.

More immediately, we will see growth in the area of sophisticated search engines such as Verity's Topic Architecture search agents, Oracle Corporation's ConText or Fulcrum's Surfboard. Also of significance are rudimentary video conferencing tools via Cornell University's CU-SeeMe utility, which uses the Internet's Multimedia Backbone protocol or MBone.

Searching Software and Digital Agents

The science of **artificial intelligence**, AI for short, focuses on creating software and hardware that provides computers with human-like reasoning and thinking capabilities. Speech recognition technology that today allows simple commands to be understood will, within a decade, allow us to talk to personal computers, bank machines, and automobiles. Advanced imaging technologies combine video input devices with computers to create computer vision, which companies use to evaluate product defects in the manufacturing process. **Expert systems**, a branch of artificial intelligence, stores the knowledge of human experts in computer programs that analyze and solve problems. An expert system could, for example, guide a person through a series of questions and answers to evaluate simple medical problems.

The benefits of artificial intelligence have profound implications when applied to communication networks. Much in the way that computer viruses maliciously weave their way through systems, "good" application programs can search through global networks. These programs are the electronic butlers of the 1990s, variously called digital agents (DA), knowbots (knowledge robots), or softbots. Their function is to help people accomplish daily errands and cope with the ever increasing volume of information. They sort electronic mail, leave reminders about appointments, make travel arrangements, deposit electronic funds, and search for information.

If, for example, you need to write a research paper about Supreme Court rulings on the issue of privacy, send a DA to look through all the public and commercial databases and deliver an indexed listing of the search results. For shopping, tell the digital agent you want to purchase a 35mm camera with autofocus and built-in strobe for under $300, and it searches retail databases and presents its findings.

The companies creating the first generation of digital assistants are dealing with issues that include how the DA gets permission to access information repositories, how companies charge for information, what language best suits communication with DAs, and what mechanism will prevent millions of wandering DAs from straining network resources.

The potential tasks of a digital agent are quite varied; some may be based on traditional search engines, where an agent will "learn" by watching the kind of information you typically review. You activate an agent in learn mode while you browse and it begins to compile a profile of your activity, frequently visited sites, commonly asked questions, topics of interest, and so on. The longer the learning process continues, the stronger your agent's profile will be on your mode of operation. When you feel comfortable, you can turn the agent loose and let it go search for items while you get back to your normal lifestyle. Periodically, you can review what information the agent has returned and make some minor corrections to its search profile. The activities and functions performed by an agent are steeped in artificial intelligence. This has a feature called heuristics, which essentially means the system can modify itself by learning.

Other agents may use pre-defined criteria and could be employed to fulfill other tasks such as to automatically handle incoming electronic mail, news reports, and bulletins. The agent could alert you to special events by cellular phone, electronic mail, or digital voice or alpha-numeric pager.

There are many developments in the sophisticated search engine/agent categories, some of which are discussed in this chapter.

Verity's Topic
Web URL address: **http://www.verity.com**

Verity Inc has launched an agent type product that will search a variety of media data types and databases including, disks, CD ROMs, LAN drives, and the Internet. The product called Topic uses a combination of topic filtering and a natural language type of query. One of the agent's functions is to construct an HTML-based Web page that presents you with the result of its activity. In a press release Verity describes the application of Topic as follows:

"Verity's technology is designed to make it easier for individuals, workgroups, departments and enterprises to filter, search, retrieve, analyze and navigate a wide variety of data sources to get the informatin they need. Powerful agents search across vast amounts of data, delivering only the most relevant information directly to the desktop."

Fig. 16.1
Verity Topic
search showing
drill-down
hierarchy.

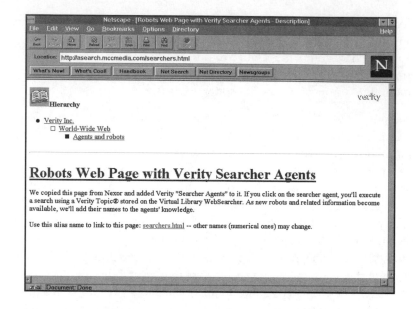

Topic lets you use natural language search expressions, which overcome many of the limitations of search engines that require carefully constructed queries using keywords to get the right kind of response. Instead of a search engine request that looks like like "WWW+Search+Agents" this could look more like "Show me agents that search the World Wide Web." Of course the first instance is shorter but not really that clear, the second instance might pull in more hits because it should be able to equate WWW with World Wide Web. In the first instance, only hits with "WWW" would be found, not ones that had it fully spelled out or just had "Web." Another example of a question that you could ask by using Topic would be "How is Bob Dole doing in the presidential race?" The result would be a list of articles and press releases that relate to this topic.

There is Topic agent software for Windows, Windows NT, OS/2, Macintosh, and several other computer platforms. The price range is between $95 and $495. Check out the Web site for additional details.

Fulcrum® Surfboard™

Web URL address: **http://www.fultech.com/**

Fulcrum is looking at Surfboard as a full-featured paperless information delivery service. The claim is that delivering corporate information using traditional paper-based methods or CD-ROM can be expensive and difficult to manage. Fulcrum Surfboard offers a publication alternative giving users the ability to browse and easily retrieve published documents.

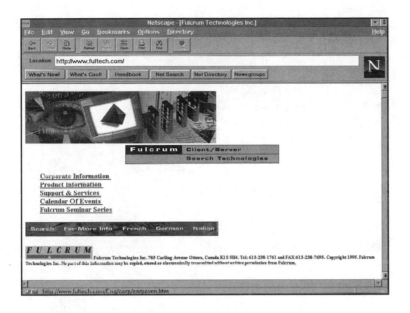

Fig. 16.2
Fulcrum Web site
home page.

Fulcrum takes a slightly different approach than Verity using a search methodology called **intuitive searching**. This methodology allows users to highlight one or more documents, or simply part of a document and then search out other documents that are similar in content. From a WWW standpoint, this could prove invaluable; it would be like saying "OK, that's pretty close but not quite right—please use what you displayed and look for another 20 documents that are similar."

One added benefit is that intuitive searching is interactive. As a user browses through any retrieved material, they can elect to guide the system by highlighting any relevant material of particular interest. Using this input, the system then retrieves additional documents that match the users' newly defined and focused interests. This search and refine technique can rapidly zero in on precisely what the user is looking for.

Context-sensitivity is also featured in intuitive searching; if you have some very "flowery" wording in a document, only the key word components will be primarily used in the search. Intuitive searching focuses only on the terms that are most useful in discriminating between relevant and irrelevant documents.

> **Note**
>
> Context-sensitivity has been available for some time as an assistant in word process-
> ing software, thesaurus, and grammatic support utilities. An example would be
> where you are searching for a phrase like: *A final decision will be made in a timely
> manner.* The search engine isolates the key components "decision" and "time" and is
> sensitive to their placement and a myriad of alternative meanings. A sophisticated
> context-sensitive engine would cause the discovery of similar phrases like: *The final
> decision will be made after due consideration and in the fullness of time* and *A conclusion
> to the resolution of this matter will be acted upon forthwith.* As you can see, these
> phrases are quite different but have the same key components in the right places.

Oracle's ConText

Web URL address: **http://www.oracle.com/**

Oracle Corporation provides a text interpretation system called ConText. This
type of technology is yet another indicator as to what we can expect to be
developed as tools to help us successfully retrieve accurate information from
virtually any source, including the Internet, in a precise fashion based on our
needs.

One of ConText's main features is its ability to rapidly extract themes and
trends from volumes of text. To achieve this, ConText uses advanced linguistic analysis and content extraction from the text base. The linguistic analysis
is essentially a huge table of information about the countless number of ways
to say the same thing. This allows ConText to take into account colloquial-
isms and other specific language peculiarities. After applying this analysis, the
essential content of the document is established. Consider the following
"colorful" examples:

> Yonder heavenly canopy is a wonderful shade of blue.
>
> Och aye, it's a braw blue sky we have here.
>
> Yo dude, check out the crazy weather and cool blue sky.

The essential content of these sentences could be reduced to "The sky is
blue."

With the massive amount of information available, it is frequently impossible
for an individual to rapidly grasp and understand the information presented
to them following a search. ConText can be applied as a speed-reading filter
to take a huge amount of text and highlight relevant parts based on the level
of information required by the reader. The rate or style of speed-reading are

defined as "full," "read," "skim," "review," "glance," or some more customized definition of how the reader would like to read. The net result of the speed reading filter on retrieved documents would be the addition of highlights over selected key words. For example, a "glance" filter, when applied to a number of documents relating to geographical data, might only highlight the actual place names. A "skim" filter might higlight only the place names and accompanying sentence. A "review" filter might simply highlight the opening and closing paragraphs in each section.

Oracle ConText has an internal lexicon that contains over 600,000 words and phrases with up to 1000 pieces of linguistic knowledge about each individual word. ConText also uses a built-in thesaurus to classify words by theme or concept. As you can imagine, today, all this activity requires more horsepower than an average desktop machine, so a fairly powerful server is required to run ConText.

Open Text Web Indexing System

Web URL address: **http://www.opentext.com**

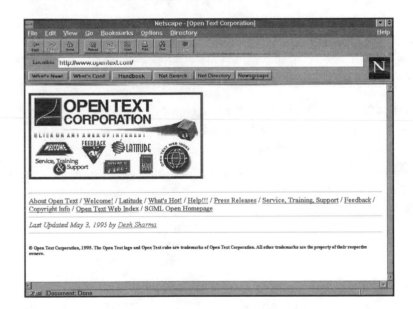

Fig. 16.3
Open Text Web site home page.

Open Text Corporation is a vendor of text retrieval technology originally aimed at the Document Management arena. Open Text has announced the availability of a search site managed by UUNet and is using a form of Web crawler to amass its data. The Open Text site offers two types of search: a Quick Search and a Compound Search. The quick search is similar to most of the other phrase/keyword searches described throughout this book. The compound type of search goes beyond the normal key word search and does not require the user to learn any kind of special Boolean commands. Instead, the compound search uses a form approach where the user selects the operators and can limit the search to specific parts of the document or in links.

> **Note**
>
> UUNET Technologies Inc., located in Falls Church, Va., is the original commercial Internet service provider, offering a complete suite of Internet services. AlterNet®, UUNET's publicly available network, comprises points of presence throughout the United States, and maintains direct links to Canada, India, Japan, Russia, South Africa, Sweden, and Thailand.

The Open Text page features a forms-based Web Index that currently contains over one million home pages, 10 million links, and one billion words to search among. The Open Text indexing and retrieval system will be included alongside Oracle's ConText technology as a part of Oracle's Book product.

Currently, the Open Text site is free to use and hopefully will stay that way. This is a valuable way for Open Text to illustrate its technology, which can effectively be used in many other applications such as Document Management.

California Software—InterAp
Web URL address: **http://www.calsoft.com**

InterAp is a Windows-based suite of agent-based applications aimed at providing anyone with a comprehensive Internet interface for home and office use. InterAp is delivered as a series of user-friendly modules, including E-mail, Web Browser, Scheduler, and Scripting. These application modules all operate together using a familiar drag-and-drop method. InterAp also features common menus, commands, and toolbars. InterAp is designed to be sophisticated, powerful, full featured, and, most importantly, simple to use.

For the more sophisticated user, InterAp provides a powerful scripting language and scheduler. This will allow you to set your system up to periodically gather online material of particular interest. If you have the need to gather a large number of resources, you can use the scheduler to activate these search-and-retrieval missions during periods when Internet performance is optimum.

For those of you who like to program, the NetScripts API (Application Programming Interface) is a powerful tool that fully integrates with the InterAp modules. Using Visual Basic, Visual C++, or any other programming languages, you can easily create custom programs or online agents to perform extensive search/retrieval missions and other time-consuming tasks. Included with the InterAp package is a set of predefined intelligent agent type scripts that were created using the NetScripts API. The Scheduler module allows you to control the timing and use of any intelligent agents you have created.

Multimedia and Video Conferencing

The Internet is full of sights and sounds. In fact, one major contributor to the explosive growth of the Internet will be brought about by the widespread use of real-time multimedia, including video conferencing, "telephone" conversations, cooperative workflow products, and interactive gaming.

MBONE

The MBONE, which stands for Multi-Media BackBone, came about from an experimental simultaneous audio and video internet broadcast meeting of the main Internet governing body (the closest thing to Internet government) called the Internet Engineering Task Force (IETF). The main theme was to provide a mechanism in the form of a testbed to carry the IETF transmissions and support continued experimentation between real-time videoconferenced meetings. Of course, as with much Internet development, these foundations will undoubtedly spawn more widespread usage and production of supporting tools.

The MBONE itself is best described as a "virtual network," or a series of slices through the existing Internet network. MBONE is piggy-backed on the existing Internet Protocol, because the concept of multicast routing is not familiar to many of the current production routers. Within the Internet itself, there are a number of special routers that can successfully perform multicast routing. Between each of these routers are special virtual short-circuit fast-path connections called IP "tunnels" that allow information to be passed directly between multicast routers. This method effectively speeds up the communication rate that is neccessary for effective multi-point real-time motion video and audio.

The MBONE virtual network will be implemented worldwide and with the widespread use of fiber backbones, the potential transmission bandwidth will increase several orders of magnitude before the year 2000.

Internet Talk Radio

Web URL address: **http://www.town.hall.org/**

Daily, the non-profit Internet Multicasting Service produces and distributes a radio talk show, Internet Talk Radio (ITR). The 30 to 90 minute program has a format similar to National Public Radio, and it carries two NPR shows—TechNation: Americans and Technology and SOUNDPRINT. Topics of discussion include book reviews, industry events, and analysis of new technical proposals. There are also some general interest program features such as "Taking Care of Planet Earth" and "Technology and Health Care."

Shows are recorded and produced digitally with an 8,000 per second sampling rate, and saved as audio files that vary in size between 15 and 45 megabytes. Programming is distributed to FTP sites across the U.S. and can be downloaded and played on your computer (providing you have a soundboard and speakers). The e-mail address for basic information is **info@radio.com**.

CU-SeeMe

Web URL address: **http://magneto.csc.ncsu.edu/Multimedia/Classes/ Spring94/projects/proj6/cu-seeme.html**

A programming team from Cornell University developed CU-SeeMe, an application that enables multiple Internet users to communicate with video-, audio-, and text-based information. The program can either be used for video conferences between two people, or can connect multiple users at multiple sites. Compatible with both IBM and Macintosh computers, the program establishes a series of on-screen windows, one for each user. Windows can be individually sized, and transmit black and white video, audio, and text. For reception, a minimum 14.4 kbps modem is necessary, and to send video, users need a video capture board, video camera, and 56 kbps or even a T-1 transmission line.

Much of the initial work on the Macintosh came about because of the ease of integration with the additional video conferencing components such as cameras and microphones. The Macintosh also offered a much richer set of multimedia support tools at that time. Recently, much of those multimedia resources and control tools have become readily available on Microsoft Windows, (Win 3.1, Win NT 3.5, and Win 95) platforms. CU-SeeMe has been ported to those environments. CU-SeeMe displays 4-bit grayscale windows at either 320x240 or half that diameter, 160x120. CU-SeeMe provides a one-one connection to another videoconferencee.

Using what is described as a **reflector**, many can participate in a single conference. A reflector is similar to a teleconference bridge in that participants sign into it and are collectively reflected out as a group to all that are signed in. A multicast conference could have a small group of video-conferencees in two-way mode and a larger group (or virtual audience) logged in as view only. Each CU-SeeMe participant can select a send, receive or two-way mode for his or her individual session. Figure 16.4 illustrates a 3-way videoconference. The Global Schoolhouse Project uses CU-SeeMe as part of an educational project that enables students, grades 4 through 12, in schools in California, Tennessee, and Virginia to collaborate on research projects.

Note

You can download a Macintosh or Windows-based version of CU-SeeMe from the FTP site at Cornell University.

> FTP site: **gated.cornell.edu**

> Directory: **/pub/video/**

> Web URL address: **ftp://gated.cornell.edu:/pub/video/**

Various filenames for different versions include:

MAC

Mac.CU-SeeMe0.60b1

Mac.CU-SeeMe0.70b15

Mac.CU-SeeMe0.80b1

Mac.CU-SeeMe0.80b2

MacTCP

PC

PC.CU-SeeMeW0.34b4

PC.CU-SeeMeW0.34b5

Fig. 16.4
CU-SeeMe 3-way
conference.

Associations, User Groups, and Electronic Commerce

There will be many more companies, cooperatives, associations, user groups, and information brokers appearing on the Net over the next few years. One of the more immediately noteworthy directions is the advent of digital cash using some sort of Internet currency or commercial transaction privacy to allow the safe use of credit card numbers online. Two main components are critical to the success of this environment; one is the indelible digital signature, and the other is guaranteed transaction privacy.

Digital signatures are a way to uniquely identify and authenticate individuals to ensure they are who they say they are. One way to achieve this is to issue them as unique uncopiable codes—amazingly enough the most likely place you will get these in the future is at your local Post Office! Why the Post Office you may ask? Well, they are considered to be the most likely nationwide organization that has international connections in place that could deliver such a service effectively. In reality, they are also the most likely organization to suffer a loss of existing traffic as electronic communications and commerce booms.

Electronic Media—Magazines, Newspapers, and Advertising

Several publications have made definitive statements that there will be online versions of their magazines available in 1995. Some have gone as far as to say that they will no longer be making paper versions in the near future and will completely switch away from that medium to use the Internet instead. To give you a flavor of what is available online, an illustration of the Web Page for the San Jose Mercury News—an online daily newspaper is seen in figure 16.5. Figure 16.6 shows another online periodical, this time it's an online version of *Wired* magazine called *HotWired*. There are a growing number of additional magazines on the Web from *Omni* to *Playboy*.

In order to offer more than can be obtained from the traditional paper copy alone, most of the online versions of publications provide keyword and full-text search facilities for both current and past issues. Additional features can include such features as an online information subscription service where relevant articles of interest are e-mailed to the subscriber.

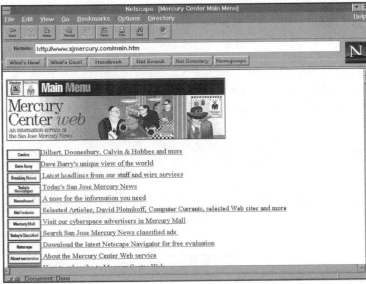

Fig. 16.5
You would expect the San Jose Mercury News, a premier Silicon Valley newspaper, to be one of the first online! Web URL address: **http://www. sjmercury.com**.

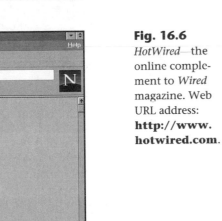

Fig. 16.6
HotWired—the online complement to *Wired* magazine. Web URL address: **http://www. hotwired.com**.

Information Associations

There are many associations already present on the Internet. Some of the most useful today are in the medical, pharmaceutical, and safety environments. I have only illustrated a small handful as samples of the vast number of associations and information bases available on the Internet.

One area of particular global concern is that of chemicals—how to handle them, what to do if you come into bodily contact them, and how to dispose of them. A worldwide charter has been drawn up to address these potential hazards by implementing a global standard of labeling and identification. The actual handling, disposal, and safety aspects of chemicals are contained in Material Safety Data Sheets or MSDS. I found many locations that carried huge collections of MSDS as figure 16.7 illustrates.

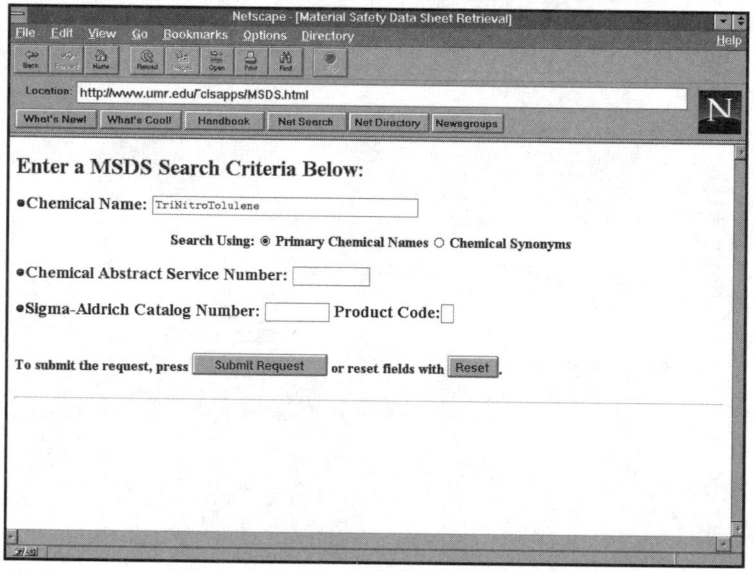

Fig. 16.7
Online material specification data sheet.

One company in particular, the Pharmaceutical Information Associates, has a vast series of Web pages showing valuable and often critical information on drug treatment and interactions. I have included some of the URL locations so you can locate these on the Web.

- Web URL address: **http://pharminfo.com/pialtd/piahp2.html**

- Web URL address: **http://oncolink.upenn.edu/**

- ■ Web URL address: **http://oncolink.upenn.edu:80/pia/**

- ■ Web URL address: **http://pharminfo.com/pubs/transgen/ tg_hp.html**

Summary

The incredible growth of the Internet shows no signs of slowing down. Not only is there growth in the number of people who are connecting to and using the Internet, but also in the volume of information that's available on Internet servers in all corners of the world. More information is a "good news/bad news" situation. The good news is that it will be increasingly likely that whatever you need to know or learn will be available in cyberspace. The bad news is that as the pile grows it becomes increasingly difficult to locate that needle in the electronic haystack. The new generation of searching software programs is designed to help with this critical task—even to the point where the programs continue to search for your "information request" while you're out playing a round of golf or conducting a business meeting. And the skills, techniques, and knowledge that you've gained by reading this book will help make your next Net search a big success.

Index

PLUG YOURSELF INTO...

THE MACMILLAN INFORMATION SUPERLIBRARY™

Free information and vast computer resources from the world's leading computer book publisher—online!

FIND THE BOOKS THAT ARE RIGHT FOR YOU!

A complete online catalog, plus sample chapters and tables of contents give you an in-depth look at *all* of our books, including hard-to-find titles. It's the best way to find the books you need!

- ● STAY INFORMED with the latest computer industry news through our online newsletter, press releases, and customized Information SuperLibrary Reports.

- ● GET FAST ANSWERS to your questions about MCP books and software.

- ● VISIT our online bookstore for the latest information and editions!

- ● COMMUNICATE with our expert authors through e-mail and conferences.

- ● DOWNLOAD SOFTWARE from the immense MCP library:
  - Source code and files from MCP books
  - The best shareware, freeware, and demos

- ● DISCOVER HOT SPOTS on other parts of the Internet.

- ● WIN BOOKS in ongoing contests and giveaways!

TO PLUG INTO MCP: →   WORLD WIDE WEB: **http://www.mcp.com**

GOPHER: gopher.mcp.com

FTP: ftp.mcp.com

| Home Page | What's New | Bookstore | Reference Desk | Software Library | Macmillan Overview | Talk to Us |

Complete and Return this Card
for a *FREE* Computer Book Catalog

Thank you for purchasing this book! You have purchased a superior computer book written expressly for your needs. To continue to provide the kind of up-to-date, pertinent coverage you've come to expect from us, we need to hear from you. Please take a minute to complete and return this self-addressed, postage-paid form. In return, we'll send you a free catalog of all our computer books on topics ranging from word processing to programming and the internet.

Mr. ☐ Mrs. ☐ Ms. ☐ Dr. ☐

Name (first) [ ] (M.I.) ☐ (last) [ ]

Address [ ]

City [ ] State [ ] Zip [ ]

Phone [ ] Fax [ ]

Company Name [ ]

E-mail address [ ]

1. Please check at least (3) influencing factors for purchasing this book.

Front or back cover information on book .... ☐
Special approach to the content .... ☐
Completeness of content .... ☐
Author's reputation .... ☐
Publisher's reputation .... ☐
Book cover design or layout .... ☐
Index or table of contents of book .... ☐
Price of book .... ☐
Special effects, graphics, illustrations .... ☐
Other (Please specify): _____ ☐

2. How did you first learn about this book?

Saw in Macmillan Computer Publishing catalog .... ☐
Recommended by store personnel .... ☐
Saw the book on bookshelf at store .... ☐
Recommended by a friend .... ☐
Received advertisement in the mail .... ☐
Saw an advertisement in: _____ ☐
Read book review in: _____ ☐
Other (Please specify): _____ ☐

3. How many computer books have you purchased in the last six months?

This book only .... ☐   3 to 5 books .... ☐
2 books .... ☐   More than 5 .... ☐

4. Where did you purchase this book?

Bookstore .... ☐
Computer Store .... ☐
Consumer Electronics Store .... ☐
Department Store .... ☐
Office Club .... ☐
Warehouse Club .... ☐
Mail Order .... ☐
Direct from Publisher .... ☐
Internet site .... ☐
Other (Please specify): _____ ☐

5. How long have you been using a computer?

☐ Less than 6 months   ☐ 6 months to a year
☐ 1 to 3 years   ☐ More than 3 years

6. What is your level of experience with personal computers and with the subject of this book?

	With PCs	With subject of book
New	☐	☐
Casual	☐	☐
Accomplished	☐	☐
Expert	☐	☐

Source Code ISBN: 0-7897-0242-8

7. Which of the following best describes your job title?

Administrative Assistant .... ☐
Coordinator .... ☐
Manager/Supervisor .... ☐
Director .... ☐
Vice President .... ☐
President/CEO/COO .... ☐
Lawyer/Doctor/Medical Professional .... ☐
Teacher/Educator/Trainer .... ☐
Engineer/Technician .... ☐
Consultant .... ☐
Not employed/Student/Retired .... ☐
Other (Please specify): _____ ☐

8. Which of the following best describes the area of the company your job title falls under?

Accounting .... ☐
Engineering .... ☐
Manufacturing .... ☐
Operations .... ☐
Marketing .... ☐
Sales .... ☐
Other (Please specify): _____ ☐

Comments: _____
_____
_____

9. What is your age?

Under 20 .... ☐
21-29 .... ☐
30-39 .... ☐
40-49 .... ☐
50-59 .... ☐
60-over .... ☐

10. Are you:

Male .... ☐
Female .... ☐

11. Which computer publications do you read regularly? (Please list)

_____
_____
_____
_____
_____
_____
_____
_____
_____

Fold here and scotch-tape to mail.